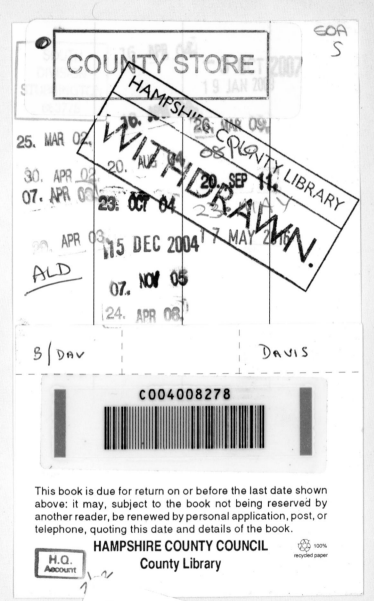

SAMMY

WITH MATERIAL NEWLY REVISED

FROM *YES I CAN* AND *WHY ME?*

———

FARRAR, STRAUS AND GIROUX

NEW YORK

SAMMY

AN AUTOBIOGRAPHY

—

SAMMY DAVIS JR.

AND JANE AND BURT BOYAR

Farrar, Straus and Giroux
19 Union Square West, New York 10003

Copyright © 2000 by Burt Boyar Investments LLC
All rights reserved
Distributed in Canada by Douglas & McIntyre Ltd.
Printed in the United States of America
Designed by Jonathan D. Lippincott
First edition, 2000

Library of Congress Cataloging-in-Publication Data
Davis, Sammy.
   Sammy : an autobiography : with material newly revised from Yes I
can and Why me / Sammy Davis, Jr., and Jane and Burt Boyar.
     p. cm.
  ISBN 0-374-29355-4 (alk. paper)
    1. Davis, Sammy.   2. Entertainers—United States—Biography.
I. Boyar, Jane.   II. Boyar, Burt.   III. Title.
PN2287.D322 A3 2000
792.7'028'092—dc21
[B]   00-027742

Portions of this book have been previously published in *Yes I Can* (Farrar, Straus and Giroux, 1965) and *Why Me?* (Farrar, Straus and Giroux, 1989).

Photo Acknowledgments: Will, Sammy, and Sam Sr. in *Mr. Wonderful* and *Las Vegas, 1967*: photographs by Milton Greene. Sammy and May Britt on Broadway, 1965: photograph reprinted from *The Saturday Evening Post*, 1965.

We ain't what we oughta be,
we ain't what we wanta be,
we ain't what we gonna be,
but thank God we ain't what we was.
—MARTIN LUTHER KING, JR., 1960

PROLOGUE

We never discussed why we were attracted to each other. For me it started with Sammy's performing talent. He was the quintessential entertainer: he danced brilliantly, more easily than most people walk, and if that didn't get you he sang, and if that didn't get you he did impressions and one-liners, and played the drums, the xylophone, did amazing quick-draw stunts with Colt .45s. He did everything that could be done on a stage and did it better than anyone had ever done it before him. And probably ever will.

One Sunday evening, when Sammy was headlining a benefit at the Waldorf-Astoria, his music had not arrived and the show was starting. Backstage, Jane and I were panicking. A singer-dancer without music? Sammy calmed us. "If I can't walk on and entertain them with only a pocket comb and tissue paper then I'm not the entertainer I'm supposed to be."

On other turf he was not so sure of his footing. During the run of *Golden Boy*, just after *Yes I Can* was published, the New York *Herald Tribune* invited Sammy to be the principal speaker at their "Book and Author Luncheon." I accepted for him. He protested, "They'll look down their noses at me. What am I gonna say to all them librarians?" (He spoke perfect English but affected bad grammar at moments like this.) Jane and I assured him they were just normal people who liked books. This man who had played before the President of the United States and the Queen of England was uneasy about that lunch for weeks. On the night before the luncheon Sammy staged "an accident" in the rumble scene in *Golden Boy* and played the rest of the show with his neck slightly out of kilter—except when he had a big song. He spent the night at Mount Sinai Hospital "under observation." Sammy loved hospitals. They were total protection. You could avoid any phone call, break any contract by being hospitalized. When we arrived there in the morning he was hiding from us in his bed, wearing a Styrofoam neck brace. "You canceled the luncheon, right?"

"Impossible. They've been promoting it in the paper every day. A thousand women are on their way to the Waldorf at this minute."

We took our places on the dais and Sammy was introduced. The neck brace alone got an ovation. Then, without a song, without a dance, starting simply by saying, "I feel so diminutive . . ." he masterfully ad-libbed forty minutes. Never before or since have I heard a speech receive shouts of "Encore." In the limousine en route to his house on 92nd Street, he gave Jane and me a look and removed the neck brace.

. . . Sammy Davis, Jr., is another of the hole-in-the-heads who carries a gun . . .

. . . Sammy Davis, Jr., is Chita Rivera's Mr. Wonderful offstage, too . . .

. . . Jack Carter is demanding two more songs in *Mr. Wonderful* . . .
                            —"Burt Boyar's Broadway," 1954

Sammy was, at the time I wrote those items, in Philadelphia, where *Mr. Wonderful* was trying out—a 1950s expression for today's "workshopping." I had never met him. I was in New

York City, writing a daily Broadway column for the *Morning Telegraph* that appeared in the Newhouse newspapers and Walter Annenberg's Triangle Publications. In Walter Winchell's words, Jane and I had "ringside seats to the greatest show on earth."

Due to Sammy's presence in Philadelphia, my column was being featured prominently in the *Inquirer*. If Sammy didn't catch it there, Sam Davis, Sr., would show it to him in the *Morning Telegraph*—left-hand column, front page—where a horseplayer like Sammy's father saw it every day. Without intending it, I was a daily frustration to Sammy. "Who the fuck *is* this guy?" "How does he fucking *know* this stuff?"

I knew all that stuff because the William Morris Agency held weekly meetings of every department at which the agents discussed details of their clients' business and personal lives. This was mimeographed and circulated so that all agents were current on what was happening with all the agency's clients. They didn't know there was a Deep Throat in their midst, selling me the minutes of the meetings every week. Having published those secrets embarrasses me now, but in that day and at that age, twenty-eight, it was how I made a living and I thought it was important.

It was my custom to call every celebrity arriving in New York and wheedle at least a few words for the column. In Sammy's case I waited until *Mr. Wonderful* had opened on Broadway. The show was unanimously stoned by the critics— and with good reason. It was a dog. With fleas. But they *raved* about the last forty minutes, in which Sammy did his normal Las Vegas–Copacabana–Miami Beach nightclub act. In fact, a knowing theatergoer would wisely have eschewed the first act of *Mr. Wonderful*, enjoyed a leisurely dinner, and arrived in time for the finale. It kept the show running for the year that Sammy had committed to stay on Broadway.

Despite my wise-guy column, or because of it, Sammy took my call and said, "What do you say we have dinner together? At Danny's."

When we'd walked into the restaurant, it had been "Good

evening, Mr. and Mrs. Boyar. So very nice to meet you." An hour later, as we left Danny's Hideaway together, Sammy was alongside Jane doing her "model's walk" with his hips ahead of his shoulders. Tapping his finger on her large fur cossack hat, he called inside, "And who lives in *here*, Janie?"

He apologized for leaving early, but he had to do a show. "How about us having dinner together . . . say . . . five nights a week?"

As it turned out, we were together seven nights a week, except those few weekends Jane and I spent on Long Island with her father. After a while, Sammy openly resented even these separations. "So, you're off to the country without me, eh? That's okay . . . fine . . . have fun . . . just leave me here . . . alone . . . with all of my friends."

For Sammy, I think our relationship started off as "neutralizing the enemy." Then he saw us as useful: a wholesome married couple to blunt the scandal magazines. *Confidential* had bounced him around, accurately, with Ava Gardner and Marilyn Monroe. Although *Confidential* was driven out of business, the *National Enquirer* (it was just starting up) and other scandal sheets reported obsessively, and with hostility, on his marriage to the blond Swedish movie star May Britt and his affairs with Kim Novak and Jean Seberg. ("The haters got so bad at times that I used to think: I'm gonna get me the blondest, whitest chick there is and shove her in their faces and say, 'Yeah! And how do you like what I'm gonna be doing to her?' ")

Also, we were bodyguards of a sort: white and Jewish New Yorkers (we later adopted Catholicism) who were known, attractive, and well dressed. With us riding shotgun it was easier for Sammy to get past the snobbish doormen at some of the Fifth Avenue and Park Avenue buildings to which he was invited as a guest of honor, a great catch. More than once he had been told, "Use the service entrance."

I guess that Jane and I fell, platonically, in love with Sammy. We were inseparable from that first day. Nightly, after dinner, Jane and I went off to cover what was happening at the Copa, the Latin Quarter, the Stork Club, and El Morocco, or a movie premiere or Broadway play opening that evening. Then we met Sammy after *Mr. Wonderful* and accompanied him to the benefits he did every night, sometimes two. The charities sent limousines to bring him to their events in Westchester, on Long Island, or in Brooklyn. While Sammy restored himself, sleeping en route, Jane and I would look at each other and wonder what we were doing there.

When he had collected that evening's plaques and gold wristwatches we usually went to the Harwyn, on East 52nd Street, the only first-line supper club to which Sammy was welcomed by its owner, Ed Wynne. Social arbiters such as Sherman Billingsley (the Stork Club) and John Perona (El Morocco) would bar a Broadway star because of his skin color, but welcome pimps, pornographers, and call girls as long as they were white.

Usually the "family" was waiting for us at Sammy's table: the show's dance captain and Sammy's girlfriend, Chita Rivera; George Gilbert, who co-produced *Mr. Wonderful*; and Michael Wettach, its assistant stage manager. Sometimes we were joined by Sammy's close friends Amy and Milton Greene. We closed every evening at his apartment atop the Gorham Hotel on West 55th Street. This was his "safe house," where he controlled the elements, where there could be no hard stares or deliberately slow service.

I referred to us as "family," and we really were, at that point, the closest thing to a family in Sammy's life. Sam Sr. had an apartment in the Gorham too, but he had his own social life. Sammy supported his mother, Elvera, all of his life, but he had never lived with her or known her well. She was brought in for photo ops when Sammy required a mother. Occasionally he would invite her for a week in Las Vegas or Miami Beach, but they never grew close. In New York he had us. On the road, playing clubs, he knew someone in every town—Chicago, Boston, Buffalo—who considered himself Sammy's best friend and waited all year for him to return to play another engagement. Those locals provided his "best friend in Chicago," ". . . in Boston," ". . . in Buffalo," and though they and Sammy were thick for the length of his engagement, he would soon be off to New Haven, Philadelphia, and Minneapolis–St. Paul, where other best friends awaited him. The truth is, Sammy loved us all and we all served and belonged in various corners of his life, but his one lasting best friend was the audience.

At the Gorham we played Monopoly every night (with 14-karat gold charms from Jane's bracelet as tokens). We listened to records, we acted out *Hamlet* and *Othello* from books Sammy provided, and we talked. We talked a lot. Sammy was effortlessly an original. I asked him, "What do you do that you learned from other people?"

"Nothing. What I've learned from other people is everything that I do *not* want to be."

And what made him work so hard? "Success has a million friends, but when you die you die alone."

Sammy had two portions of every day, the good news and the bad news. The good news was when he was playing to, and being loved by, an audience. When they were telling him how special he was. The bad news was when he had to step offstage and into the reality of being black—a star, but a black star in a white world. If he kept moving fast enough through Cartier and Dunhill, clowning with friends, he did not notice the bad news. But dawn rose inexorably, and as he saw yawns of fatigue he'd snap at Chita, "You've got to get up early and practice, right?" Of course, he let her go. He invented excuses to keep everyone with him for as long as possible, but eventually we all had to go to bed. Jane and I always waited until he was asleep on the sofa bed, when we removed his shoes, covered him with a blanket, and tiptoed out. One night as we reached the door we heard, "I'm not sleeping yet."

"Sam, we've got to get home and write the column."

"Then, tomorrow night why don't you do it here?"

To my own amazement we dropped off our typewriter and paper early the next evening and at 5 a.m. while Sammy was sleeping we wrote a not-so-hot column. We took the typewriter home the next day and explained that his idea had not been a winner. No argument. Work was sacred.

Starring on Broadway was career-building and artistically valuable to Sammy but financially crippling, as he shared his $6,000 a week with his "uncle" Will Mastin and Sam Sr., instead of the $15,000 to $25,000 he was accustomed to earning in nightclubs and Las Vegas. After agent's commissions Sammy's $1,800 didn't have a minute to live. But he didn't change his "star" lifestyle, he just did it on credit instead of cash and was broke during that whole year.

We spoke on the phone every day. "I've got to hang up," I would say, "the bank is going to close." "Okay. Get some for me too." If it was a good week I had fifty dollars in the bank, so I'd withdraw thirty and give Sammy fifteen for getting-around money. Sometimes, after the Harwyn, at three in the morning we would do *Babes in Arms* and literally dance our way along the streets to the Gorham, Fred Astaire-ing up and down the stoops of brownstones. In bad weather we'd ride those few blocks in a cab. I'd take out a five to pay the driver the $1.25 fare, plus a generous tip, a total of two dollars. Sammy would nudge me. "Give him the five, baby, I'm a star." We never kept track of who owed what. And through two successful book publications, after once agreeing how we'd split the proceeds there was never a single discussion about money.

Sammy hated to personalize autographs because he feared misspelling even the simplest name. But he read everything. It was 1955. Unidentified Flying Objects fascinated him. We went to the Doubleday bookstore, which was then on the northeast corner of Fifth Avenue and 53rd Street, and he bought every book they had on UFOs, a dozen of them, and he read every word. When he was back on the road playing nightclubs he paid his own musicians and did a show for the troops at an Air

Force base so that he would be invited to tour the UFO research facilities.

I cannot describe the pain of seeing a friend receive standing ovations, in those days when they had to be earned, then leave the theater and be called "nigger." After an especially hurtful racist outrage, staring out of his penthouse window at Manhattan's streetlights going off, avenue by avenue, imagining the people waking up from sleep, Sammy murmured, "We really should let them know. We really should tell them."

We talked about how, and it evolved into a book, which, after we had a thousand-page first draft, was rejected by most New York publishers, scorned by some (Harcourt, Brace refused to read it), and became *Yes I Can.*

Jane and I had never written a book; we had no idea how to do it, only the passion. We took a one-year leave of absence from the newspaper column and lived with Sammy on the road on and off for the next four years, tape-recording every night, if we could force him to. He hated to look back, even more so to talk about the past. Recalling many of his life's experiences, even to us, embarrassed him. So we got what we could from him, filled in with more from Sam Sr., Will Mastin, his grandmother, his buddies, and the roadies, and then we went back to him to confirm, embellish, deny. He rarely denied. If it had happened, he would let us tell it, but the permanent ground rule was: "Make *me* the heavy."

In 1963 we were working on the final draft of the manuscript with Sammy, staying with him and May at their home in the Hollywood Hills during the ninth month of her pregnancy with their daughter Tracey. Because of the picketing by neo-Nazis and the public outcry against their marriage Sammy kept May safely at home in a mink-lined prison. He gave formal dinner parties for which he hired a party chef for just the four of us. We all had to dress up. To the nines. Even pregnant, May was tall and stunningly elegant. Jane bought a new dress each time and she was second to nobody. We spent two hours getting ready and we made killer entrances. Then the three of us sat around feeling gorgeous, waiting for Mr. Wonderful to appear.

When he made his entrance, always last, he stood posed at the raised end of the living room, immaculately tailored, not a wrinkle, and he wiped us all out.

Sammy never wore a piece of clothing twice without having it washed or dry-cleaned. If he merely tried on a suit or a shirt and decided against it, it went to the cleaner before returning to his closet. He took pleasure in shining his own shoes. It relaxed him, and "nobody does it as well as I do."

Sammy was the consummate gentleman and was protective of friends. Though he never used a smutty word onstage, offstage the expletives were as abundant as anyone else's. We were with him and a few of his roadies when he said something like "Who the fuck cares?" then quickly, "Excuse me, Jane." When the others had left she said, "Sam. I appreciate it but we're buddies, I've heard that word, you don't have to excuse yourself to *me*."

"I know that. And if we'd been alone I wouldn't have mentioned it, but Murphy and Morty were here and I don't want them, or anyone, to think they can speak that way in front of you."

During this period he did occasional club dates "to keep body and soul together." I watched every show I could, never tiring of them, because they were never the same. He was the only nightclub entertainer I have ever seen who did not have a set act. Before each performance he would tell his conductor, George Rhodes, "I'll open with . . . and . . ." and then it was up for grabs. By the time he had finished those few musical numbers he knew what the audience wanted—jokes, dancing, more songs, impressions. You could watch him perform for a week and never see the same show twice. He was always spontaneous, always inventing things, because "if I have to sing 'The Candy Man' two shows a night—and, God save us, I can't avoid it—if I don't find new ways to do it I'll go out of my mind."

Finally the manuscript was complete and we delivered it to Roger Straus and Robert Giroux (almost the only major publisher who would have us). Roger said, "We'll hire an outside editor to cut it down about thirty percent." Mr. Giroux assured us, "Interlineally. You'll never miss a word." Exhausted, we were delighted to leave it in their hands. Roger said, "It's a plumbing job. Go to Florida. Swim around a little."

We went to California and stayed with Sammy and May on Evanview Drive in the Hollywood Hills, in a house that they had not been able even to *rent*, much less buy, until Frank Sinatra flexed some muscle.

Soon, we received the first few chapters, edited by a man who had written a book about Las Vegas. He had rewritten Sammy's narrative in the third person and invented cutesy chapter headings like "Up from Show Biz." We sent Roger a telegram: "You were right. He *is* a plumber. But let him work on a toilet."

We rushed back to New York on the *Super Chief*. The next editor "corrected" Sammy's English until he sounded like a schoolteacher. The next, a writer for *The New Yorker*, slash-cut thirty-seven consecutive pages. When we gingerly pointed out that a dozen different threads no longer connected, she attempted suicide (on her own time she was in the throes of a tragic love affair). The next editor thought he *was* Sammy, rewriting the fights because "he's got to hit back sooner."

Roger sighed. "I haven't edited a book since *The Lost Weekend* but I'll do it myself." From then on it was easy. He would point to a line or a paragraph he had marked and say, "Icky." We always agreed. Out it went. To make Roger's life easier and save him pencils, we had a stationery store make a rubber stamp that said "Horseshit pie," a Roger Strausism, with a hand that pointed at what he didn't like.

Publication date for *Yes I Can* was set for September 15, 1965.

On September 1 Roger called. "Kids, you won't believe this but sit down and enjoy it. We've got the front cover of the *Trib*'s Sunday book review section. And it's a rave."

Through our mutual euphoria, in my blissful ignorance I asked, "What about the *Times*?"

"Kids . . . kids . . . be glad if we get mentioned. If you were James Joyce or Hemingway it would be a miracle to hit both covers on the same Sunday. The editors hate for that to happen."

Roger Straus is cool. Not today's "cool," I mean yesteryear's: calm, in control, like Cary Grant and John Wayne. A man who goes through life unruffled.

A few days later Roger learned ruffled. His voice was vibrating: "Don't leave the apartment. Keep the phones open. There's a rumor . . . just a rumor, of course . . . but they say that we also got the front cover of the *Times*. It's probably horseshit. On the same Sunday. I've got someone bringing me an advance copy . . . in an hour . . . stay where you are . . ."

It really happened. "The Hat Trick." Printed. For distribution in both of New York's big Sunday papers on September 19.

Clay Felker was the editor of *New York*, which was then the *Herald Tribune*'s Sunday magazine. We had been roommates before Jane and I married. He was excited. "You've got a great review coming up in two weeks. How about if I send Dick Schaap to write a piece on you and Jane and Sammy for the magazine?"

Then he called again. "The promotion director says that as Sammy is all over the paper on the nineteenth, if he'll go to WPIX-TV and tape a few thirty-second spots we'll call it 'Sammy's Sunday' and promote the hell out of it on television, in the daily paper, on the sides of the trucks . . ."

On September 16 the seven New York dailies struck and "Sammy's Sunday" never happened. Our two front covers were never distributed. Some two million of them. Weeks later, we would see them every night at our newsstand, used as "wrappers" to prevent the baling wire from cutting the bundles of daily newspapers.

On Thursday night at the Majestic Theater, Sammy smashed every glass and bottle in his dressing room, closed down *Golden Boy*, and fled to Hawaii for a rest.

On Monday, comedian Corbett Monica flew from Canada to New York and read a copy of *Yes I Can* that he had bought in the Toronto airport. On the *Tonight* show he spontaneously told Johnny Carson, "I just read the most wonderful book I have ever read about being a performer. I laughed, I cried, I learned . . ." Carson, a friend of Sammy's, let Corbett run with it for the full segment. Then he himself brought it up when they came back from the break.

On CBS radio, Garry Moore, whom we didn't know, was moved to go on the network and plug the book every day for a week. Meanwhile the rest of the newspapers throughout this big country did not go on strike, and they spread the news, and *Yes I Can* spent twenty-eight weeks on the best-seller list.

In 1970 Jane and I moved to Marbella, Spain (where we lived until Jane's death in 1997), but we never lost contact with Sammy. We touched noses with him in Paris, London, and Monaco, and when we went back to work with him on *Why Me?* we lived with him and Altovise at their house in Beverly Hills.

Ladies and gentlemen, the world's greatest entertainer, Mr. Sammy Davis, Jr.

Burt Boyar

SAMMY

1

They liked me.

The audience was leaning in to me, nodding, approving, and as I finished big with "Birth of the Blues" their applause was a kiss on the lips.

It was November 1954, we were playing the New Frontier in Las Vegas, and after twenty-six years we were starting to make our move. People were hearing about the Will Mastin Trio and "the kid in the middle." We were contenders and they were rooting us in.

The glow from the casino was lighting up the desert, and as the doors swung open and people came out, the sound of money, laughs, and music poured past them as if there was just too much hilarity inside to stay bottled up. It was out of my way but I felt like walking through there for the sheer joy of knowing I could.

"Swingin' show, Sam." . . . "Here, make room for Sammy."

"Thanks, not tonight. Gotta run into L.A. Catch ya tomorrow."

The crowds opened up for me and I circled the room twice, getting loaded on the atmosphere they'd kept us away from the other times we'd played Vegas, when there'd been a law against me, when it had been "Sorry, but you're not allowed in the casino—you understand." While the other acts had laughs and gambled, we went back to the colored side of town and we "understood." But now we didn't have to understand.

Two of the chorus chicks at the roulette table made room for me. I had no desire to gamble, but people were gathering around. I dropped five one-hundred-dollar bills on the table. "On the red, please." I heard "Sammydavis . . . Sammydavis . . ." The chicks were digging the big-time move. The dealer spun the wheel. I shook my fist at him. "If you yell 'black' there's gonna be a race riot." It got a laugh. The ball clicked into the red six. I split my winnings, slid one pile to each of the girls, and playing it "Cary Grant on the French Riviera," I turned and rode away on their gasps.

Walking to my suite, I enjoyed the bittersweet of contrast, remembering, "You people can't stay here. You'll have to find a boardinghouse in the—uh, on the other side of town." Now they wanted us enough so that we were bigger than Jim Crow. They were paying us $7,500 a week, the best money we'd ever made, but that was the least of the payoff. A genie had materialized out of show business and said, "You're going to be a star, now you're as good as anybody," and he'd handed us a solid-gold key to every door that had ever been slammed in our faces.

I called room service for a hamburger. There was a knock at the door. One of the chorus kids was standing there wearing skintight blue jeans. I laughed. "They've got crazy room service here." She didn't understand the joke but she laughed anyway. When you're making it you get laughs with "Good morning."

I told Charley, my dresser, "You drive the first half while I catch a few hours' sleep in back." As the car rolled down the Strip toward the highway, I saw the big neon sign flashing my name across the desert. I could smell the brand-new leather as I rested my face against it and I kissed that expensive seat with all the love I had for everything it represented.

I was glad to take over the driving. Nobody's invented booze that'll give you a kick like the first few times you drive your first Cadillac convertible. The sun was coming up over the mountains and I saw the day growing bigger, brighter every minute. It seemed as though nothing bad had ever happened. I was actively aware that the edge of the window was exactly the right height for my left elbow. My fingers fit perfectly into the ridges around the steering wheel, and the clear desert air streaming in through the window was wrapping itself around my face like some gorgeous, swinging chick giving me a facial.

I turned on the radio and I heard my own voice singing "Hey, There." Oh, God! What are the odds against turning on the radio to the exact station at the exact moment when a disc jockey is playing your first hit? For a second I was afraid that life was getting so good that something would have to happen to take it all away. But the car, the suite in Vegas, the hit record, were the start of a new life. It had all come from show business and as long as God let me keep my talent it would keep on coming. We were building, and any day now we'd really break wide open and I'd be a star. A real goddam *star!* And nobody could ever again tell me, "Here, this is your corner of the world. Stay there." And that would be it, that would be goddam *it!*

We were on a double-lane highway. A green car passed me, the first car I'd seen in ten minutes. I was on my way to record my first movie sound track. I visualized myself driving through the gate at Universal in my own Cadillac convertible. The guard was tipping his hat. "Good morning, Mr. Davis. They're waiting for you on sound stage Number One."

The green car was slowing down but it wasn't pulling over to the right; they were pulling over to the left. I knew a woman was driving because I'd noticed her hat. I moved into the right lane but as I did she started moving into it, too, but not all the way, she was straddling the two lanes. Now what the hell is she trying to do? Oh, she's not going to make a U-turn on the parkway! Or is she? Why else would she be slowing down? She must have missed her turnoff. I got way over to the right to give her room but still she stayed in the middle . . . then a little left

. . . a little right . . . now it looked like she wanted to stop. Make up your mind, lady. She cut sharp to the left, hooking out to make a wide U-turn, then stopped, stretched out across both lanes like a roadblock. I had to use the oncoming lane to swing around her. But suddenly several cars were coming toward me. I was boxed in. I hit my brakes. Only a second ago she had seemed to be a mile away. I was jamming on the brake with all my strength and pulling back on the wheel as though hoping I could pull the car to a stop with my two hands. I knew I was going to hit her. I cut the wheel as hard as I could toward her rear fender, trying at least not to make it broadside where the driver was sitting. . . . I saw the impact spin her car completely around and hurl it out of sight, then my forehead slammed into my steering wheel.

Then I heard Charley moaning in the back. Thank God, he was alive too. I felt blood running down my face and into my eyes.

I was afraid to see what had happened to Charley. When I turned around he was trying to get up off the floor. "Charley? You okay?" I opened my door and got out to help him. I reached into the back seat and took hold of his arm. When he stood up I could see his jaw hanging loose and blood coming out of his mouth. "Oh, God! I'm sorry, Charley."

Someone said, "It's Sammy Davis." I started up the road to see what had happened to the woman, but a soldier stopped me. "They're all right over there. We better get you to a hospital."

I pulled the soldier over to Charley. He had both hands in front of his mouth and the blood was pouring through his fingers. I put my arm around him. He looked up at me and made a horrible choking sound, trying to speak. He pointed to my face, closed his eyes, and moaned. As I ran my hand over my cheek I felt my eye hanging there by a string. Frantically I tried to stuff it back in, like if I could do that it would stay there and nobody would know, it would be as though nothing had happened. The ground went out from under me and I was on my knees. "Don't let me go blind. Please, God, don't take it all away. . . ."

I heard a siren, and I knew I was in an ambulance. Can it really happen this way? Twenty-six years of working, and taking it, and reaching—was all that for nothing? Can you finally get it and blow it so fast? Was that little touch all there was for me? For my whole life? I'm never going to be a star?

They're going to hate me again.

2

The fear of losing success begins when you become entrenched with it. In my case it became an obsession. When I came out of the Army, desperate to become a star, if the devil had been waiting for me I think I would have made the deal.

It didn't happen that way. There was no devil involved, at least not the one with the pitchfork and the tail, but the manic pursuit of success cost me everything I could love: my wife, my three children, some friends I would have liked to grow old with. And it cost me two or three fortunes which I might still have if during those desperate years I hadn't been so single-sighted that a million dollars was just three words.

Yet there was never a reasonable alternative. I've heard people say, "When you finally reach the top you find that everything you wanted was there at the bottom." That is not how it was for me.

I was born in Harlem on December 8, 1925. My father was the lead dancer in Will Mastin's *Holiday in Dixieland*, a vaudeville troupe in which my mother, Elvera "Baby" Sanchez, was a top chorus girl. She remained in the line until two weeks before I was born. Then she boarded me with friends in Brooklyn, and continued on the road with my father and the show.

My grandmother, Rosa B. Davis, came out from Harlem to see me and wrote to my father, "I never saw a dirtier child in my life. They leave Sammy alone all day so I've taken him with me. I'm going to make a home for that child."

"Mama" was housekeeper for one family for twenty years, cooking, cleaning, ironing, and raising their children and me at the same time.

One day she returned to my nursery school. The nurse was surprised. "We thought you were on your job, Mrs. Davis."

"Something told me get off the streetcar and see what you're doing with my Sammy. Now I find you put these two other children in his carriage with him and you got Sammy all scrooched up in a corner of his own carriage. I bought that carriage for Sammy. Paid cash for it. Now you got him so he can't stretch out in his own carriage. Get those kids out of Sammy's carriage."

She began taking me to work with her. On her days off she took me to the park and put me on the swings. Nobody else could push or touch me. Her friends snickered, "Here comes Rosa Davis and her Jesus." Mama's reply was: "He's a Jesus to me."

When I was two my parents had a daughter, Ramona, whom they sent to live with my mother's family. Six months later they separated. My mother joined another traveling show, *Connors' Hot Chocolate*, and my father came home to get me.

"Sam, this child's too young to go on the road."

"Hell, Mama, I'm his father and I say he goes on the road. I ain't leaving him here so's Elvera can come take him away. 'Sides, I want my son with me."

When the train moved into the tunnel and I couldn't see Mama anymore I stopped waving and settled back in my seat. My father started taking off my coat, my leggings, and my hat. "Where we goin', Daddy?"

He put his arm around me. "We're goin' into show business, son."

———

Our first stop was the Pitheon Theater in Pittsburgh. I was backstage with my father all day, but at night he left me at the rooming house with a chair propped against the bed and often I didn't see him again until the next afternoon. Will Mastin came in every morning, bathed me in the sink, and made my breakfast, Horlick's malted milk, which he mixed with hot water from the tap. He spent hours making funny faces at me and I loved making the same faces right back at him. One afternoon I was in the dressing room playing with the makeup, trying to use the powder puffs and tubes and pencils on my face the way I always saw my father and Will doing it. Will was watching me. "Here, let me show you how to do that." I sat on his chair while he put blackface on me. Then he took a tube of clown white, gave me the big white lips, and winked, "Now you look like Al Jolson." I winked back. He sent for our prima donna, who sang "Sonny Boy." "Next show," he told her, "take Sammy onstage, hold him in your lap, and keep singing no matter what happens."

As she sang, I looked over her shoulder and saw Will in the wings playing our game, rolling his eyes and shaking his head at me, so I rolled my eyes and shook my head right back at him. The prima donna hit a high note and Will held his nose. I held my nose too. But Will's faces weren't half as funny as the prima donna's, so I began copying hers: when her lips trembled, my lips trembled, and I followed her all the way from a heaving bosom to a quivering jaw. The people out front were laughing. When we got off, Will knelt to my height. "Listen to that applause, Sammy, some of it's for you." My father was crouched beside me too, smiling, pleased with me. "You're a born mugger, son, a born mugger." He and Will both had their arms around me.

When we arrived at our next town Will began giving out meal tickets to the troupe. Once an act had its name up on a theater, there were restaurants in show towns that would give food on credit. They'd issue a meal ticket good for a week's food and we'd settle with them on payday. "Here you are,

Mose Gastin. You got a meal ticket coming to you same as any-one else in the troupe."

"Okay, Massey." I couldn't say Mastin. Why he called me Mose Gastin or where he got that name I don't know.

Will built up a new show called *Struttin' Hannah from Savannah*. Curvy, sexy Hannah was struttin' from Savannah to New York. On the way, she'd pass a house with a picket fence, see me playing in the yard with a pail and shovel, and do a slinky Mae West kind of walk over to me. "Hi, Buster. Any place around here where a lady can get a room?" She'd turn to me and roll her eyes, but the audience could only see me wildly rolling my eyes back at her. "Hey, are you a little kid or a midget?" Then she'd wink, also without the audience seeing it, and I'd wink back hard and long.

Between shows I'd stand in the wings watching Moss and Fry, Butterbeans and Susie, the Eight Black Dots, and Pot, Pan & Skillet. It never occurred to me to play with the pail and shovel, they were my props, part of the act, and I didn't think of them as toys. At mealtime, I'd sit with my father, Will, and the other performers, listening to them talk about the big vaudeville acts that played the Keith "time." Keith was far over our heads. Shows like ours, *Connors' Hot Chocolate*, and *McKinney's Cotton Pickers* played small time like TOBA and Butterfield but there was no end of stories to be heard about the great acts who worked the big time.

We always rented the cheapest room we could find, and my father and I shared the bed. He'd turn out the light and say, "Well, good night, Poppa." Then I'd hear a scratching sound. I'd sit up, fast. "What's that, Daddy?"

"I didn't hear nothin'."

The scratching would start again. I'd be suspicious. "Lemme see your hands."

"Fine thing when a kid don't trust his own daddy." He'd hold both hands in the air and I'd lie down, watching them. The scratching would start again.

"Whatsat, Daddy? Whatsat? Lemme see your feet too."

He put his feet in the air along with his hands. "Now how d'you expect a man to sleep like this, Poppa?" The game was over then and I'd snuggle in close to him where it was safe.

We were playing the Standard Theater in Philadelphia when he said, "Good news, Poppa. There's a amateur dance contest day after we close. Course, there's sixteen other kids'd be against you. And all of 'em older'n you. You suppose you c'd beat 'em?"

"Yes." I was only three but I'd spent hundreds of hours watching Will and my father work, and imitating their kind of dancing. They were doing a flash act—twelve dancers with fifteen minutes to make an impression or starve.

The other kids in the contest were dancing in fox-trot time but when I came on, all the audience could see was a blur—just two small legs flying! I got a silver cup and ten dollars. My father took me straight over to A. S. Beck's shoe store and bought me a pair of black pumps with taps.

We hung around Philadelphia hoping to get booked, but our money ran out and my father had to call Mama for a loan. She told him, "That's no life for Sammy if you gotta call me for money. I'm sending you fare to bring him home."

He told Will, "Trouble is, I can't bring myself to leave him there and travel around without him now. I'll just have to get me a job around home doin' somethin' else." I saw tears in my father's eyes. "I'll always wanta be in show business, Will. It's my life. So anytime you need me . . ."

Massey picked me up, "Be a good boy, Mose Gastin. And don't worry. We'll be working together again someday."

Mama was waiting up for us when we got home. I put on my shoes and ran into the front room to show them to her. Mama turned on her player piano and I did my routine. She smiled. "My, oh my! You're a real dancer now." She shook her head at my father. "You buy him shoes when you don't have money for food. I always knew you was smart."

After a week my father was still without a job. "I couldn't bring myself to look for nothin' outside of show business, Mama. I'll do it tomorrow. I really will."

He was spending his time backstage with the dancers at the Odeon Theater. When he came home he'd just stare out the window, shaking his head. "I can dance circles around them guys. I'm over them like the sky is over the world, and they're making a hundred fifty a week."

Before I was born he'd driven cabs in New York, shined shoes, cooked, pulled fires on the Erie Railroad, and run an elevator at Roseland Dance Hall. Then he'd won some Charleston contests, met Will, and from then on there was only one way of life for him.

One night he saw Mama and me dancing. That was the first thing that brightened him up. "Mama, just whut'n hell do you call what you're doin' with him?"

"We're doin' the time step."

He laughed. "Hell, that ain't no time step."

I couldn't stand the way he was laughing at me. I tried harder to do it the way he'd shown me but he kept shaking his head. "Damnedest thing how he can do some tough ones and can't do the easiest of all. Here, lemme show you again." He did a time step. "Now you do it." I tried. "Hell, you ain't doin' nothin'." I kept trying, harder and harder, but I couldn't get it right. "Here, looka this." He showed me his airplane step and some of the really hard steps I'd seen him and Will do in the act. Then he went back to the window.

I heard Mama laughing excitedly. "Look at your son flyin' across the room."

I was doing a trick of his with one hand on the floor, the other in the air, and my two feet kicking out in front of me. He snapped out of his melancholy. The harder he laughed, the harder I kicked. He bent down and put his face right in front of mine. "Betcha I can make you laugh, Poppa." He made a very serious face and stared at me. I bit my lips and tried desperately to keep a straight face, but that always made me die laughing.

He went back to the window, staring at the street, leafing through an old copy of *Variety*. Suddenly he smacked the arm of the chair. "Mama, I'm wiring Will to send me a ticket. I'm in the wrong business here."

She snapped, "You ain't in *no* business here."

"Maybe so, but it's better to go hungry when you're happy than to eat regular when you're dead. And I'm good as dead out of show business."

A few days later a letter arrived Special Delivery from Will. My father pulled his suitcase out from under the bed. I ran to the closet for my shoes and put them in the suitcase alongside his. He took them out and I held my breath as he stared at them, balancing them in one hand. Then he put them in the suitcase. "Okay, Poppa, you're comin' too."

Holding hands, we half walked, half danced toward Penn Station.

"Where we goin', Daddy?"

"We're goin' back into show business, Poppa!"

3

We rarely remained in one place more than a week, yet there was never a feeling of impermanence. Packing suitcases and riding on trains and buses were as natural to me as a stroll in a carriage might be to another child. Although I had traveled ten states and played over fifty cities by the time I was four, I never felt I was without a home. We carried our roots with us: our same boxes of makeup in front of the mirrors, our same clothes hanging on iron pipe racks with our same shoes under them. Only the details changed, like the face on the man sitting inside the stage door, or which floor our dressing room was on. But there was always an audience, other performers to watch, always the show talk, all as dependably present as the walls of a nursery.

We arrived in Asheville, North Carolina, on a Sunday, and Will gave everybody the day off. We were doing the three-a-day, from town to town, so most of our troupe spent the time catching up on sleep, which was also the cheapest thing they could do. I wasn't tired, so I wandered into the parlor of our rooming house. Rastus Airship, one of our dancers, was reading a paper, and Obie Smith, our pianist, was rehearsing on an upright. I started doing the parts of the show along with him. Rastus left the room and came back with Will and my father and I did the whole hour-and-twenty-minute show for them, doing everybody's dances, singing everybody's songs, and telling all the jokes. People were coming in from other rooms, and from the way they were watching me I knew I was doing good. When I finished our closing number, Will said, "From now on you're going to dance and sing in the act." My father picked me up, said "Damned if he ain't," and carried me around the room introducing me to everybody we'd been living with for the past year. "This is my son. Meet my son, Sammy Davis, Jr."

She was much prettier than any of the girls in our show. I started to shake hands with her but she knelt down and hugged me and when she kissed me her eyes were wet.

"You cryin'?"

"I'm happy to see my little boy, that's all."

"I can dance."

"No kidding. Let's see."

I did one of my father's routines but she started crying again. "Don't you like the way I dance?"

"Darlin', I love everything you do. I know that dance and you did it as good as your daddy."

That was more like it. I did half our show for her. Then we went outside and she held my hand while we walked.

"You like show business, Sammy?"

"Yes."

"You happy?"

"Yes." From the moment we'd left the theater all I could think of was my father and Will would be doing the show without me.

She asked, "How'd you like a nice ice cream soda?"

"No, thank you."

We came to a toy store. "Let's go in and buy you a present." I didn't want a present. I just wanted to get back to the theater, but she bought me a ball. Outside, she said, "Let's see you catch it, darlin'." I'd never done it before and I put my hands up too late and it hit me on the cheek. It didn't hurt but it scared me. I just watched it rolling away.

"Get it, Sammy."

"I don't want it." I was sorry as soon as I'd said it.

We walked a few more blocks. "Is there anything you'd like to do?" I didn't tell her, but she understood.

I ran ahead of her into the dressing room. My father was putting on his makeup. "You do the show yet, Daddy?"

"Nope. You're just in time."

I ran for my costume. My mother started to leave but I grabbed her skirt. "Don't go."

As I danced I saw her watching me from the wings, and smiling. She liked me and I hadn't even done my tricks yet. When I went into them I could only see her out of the corner of my eye, but she wasn't smiling anymore. I wasn't able to turn around again and when I got off she was gone.

My father picked me up. He was hugging me very tight, patting my back, as he walked toward the dressing room. "Your mother had to leave, Poppa. She said to tell you she loves you."

Mama told the truant officer, "Yes, sir, I'll bring him over tomorrow." But when he'd gone she told me, "You're five years old and they want you at the school but you'll meet all classes of children and I don't want you playing with nobody's children."

From then on she watched at the window for truant officers. The first time she spotted one she told me, "Sammy, now we're gonna play a game called Fool the School. There'll be a knock on this door but just sit in your chair and don't make a sound. We can wait long as he can knock."

That night, she told my father, "You gotta get him a tutor when you're on the road 'cause the bulls are going to lock me up sure if they catch me!"

Whenever they could, Will and my father found someone around the theater to tutor me in how to read and write.

We moved from New England into the Midwest, covering most of Michigan in theaters, burlesque houses, and carnivals, changing the size of the act to as many as forty people, depending on what the bookers needed. We were in Lansing doing a "Four and a Half"—Will, my father, two other dancers, and me as the half—when a woman came storming backstage with the theater manager. "There he is. It's shameful." She knelt down, put her arms around me, and, glaring at Will and my father, "You Fagins! You should be in jail for what you're doing to this poor, suffering child."

I had no idea what a Fagin was, but I knew that I wasn't suffering. My dancing was getting better, the audiences liked me, and I was always with my father and Massey—I had everything.

The manager paid Will off that night. "Sorry, but I can't fight her. She's too big. If she says the kid's too young to be on the stage then he's too young even if he was fifty."

"How about if Sammy don't work?"

He shook his head. "With the kid you're a novelty, but I'm up to my ears in straight dance acts."

Weeks passed as we hung around the parlor of our rooming house hoping for some booker to call, but my benefactor was powerful enough to have closed off all of Michigan to us and all we heard was the landlord telling us, "You owe me twenty-eight dollars now."

We went to dinner at our usual restaurant and Will looked at the menu hanging on the tile wall.

"The special is beef stew."

"That's what I want," I said.

My father went to the steam table and brought back a special. I'd half finished it when I noticed that they weren't eating. "Our stomachs are a little upset, Poppa. But you clean your plate. You needs food to stick to your ribs in this kind of weather."

They watched me eating my stew and the roll that came with it. My father snapped his fingers. "Hey, Will, maybe a cup of soup'd do our stomachs some good." He finished his soup and crackers. Then he wet his finger, ran it inside the cracker paper, and licked off the crumbs that stuck to it. He took a small piece of my roll. "Maybe I'll just mop up a little of your gravy, Poppa. To see if it's fresh-cooked."

The next night I had chicken and rice but they only had coffee.

The landlord sprang out of the parlor. "No point goin' to y'r rooms. You're locked out! I'm holding your things till you pay up."

Will was stunned. "In all my years in show business nobody ever had to hold my clothes to get paid. . . ."

"Well, I'm holding 'em now. I'm sick of you show business deadbeats. Maybe you wanta go through life without doing a day's work t'get a day's pay, but I mean t'be paid for my room. If you're not here with my money in a week I'll sell your things for junk. Now get out before I have y'locked up."

The temperature had dropped below freezing. Will said, "We'll go over to the railroad station. It'll be warm there."

While I slept on a bench wrapped in my father's overcoat they took turns walking around the waiting room pretending to use the telephone and asking the station patrolman questions like "You mean there's no train out of here till morning?" so we wouldn't be arrested for vagrancy.

My father was gently shaking me. "Wake up, Poppa. They're lockin' up for the night. We'll go over to the bus station." When that closed at midnight we started walking, looking for any place that would be warm and open, stopping in doorways every few minutes for a break from the fierce wind. Finally we ran to the front of a small hotel.

My father sauntered over to the room clerk. "Good evening. I'd like to rent two of your best suites for the night."

The clerk didn't look up. "We don't have rooms for you people."

"Look, I have a six-year-old boy—can we at least stay in the lobby?"

"You can't stay here."

"How 'bout if we just leave the boy for a few hours? It's freezing cold outside."

My father patted my head. "They don't like show people here, Poppa. How'd you like a free ride?" He unbuttoned his overcoat and closed it around the two of us.

Outside, a woman came running up to us. "Excuse me, my name is Helen Bannister. I was in the lobby. I'm on my way home and you're welcome to come with me, if you like."

She cooked bacon and eggs, and as we all sat around the table Will explained. She said, "I have an extra room you can use until you get on your feet."

Two days later Will burst into the house. "We're booked in Atlanta, Georgia, and I've got an advance." He tried to pay Miss Bannister at least for our food, but she wouldn't accept anything. "What happened to you the other night was inexcusable. I'm happy that I was able to help you."

As we left, my father said, "Once a year we oughta say the name of Helen Bannister. That lady saved our lives."

We were playing a roadhouse in Hartford, Connecticut. My father said, "We got the day off, whaddya say we take in a movie?"

Halfway through the picture he leaned over and whispered, "You stay here and watch the picture, son. I'll just be next door at the bar gettin' me a few skull-busters. Be back for you like always."

The picture was going on for the third time when I felt his hand on my arm. "You ready to go now, Poppa?"

After dinner he took me back to the hotel. "See you later, Poppa."

I knew he was going out drinking. The next day, in the dressing room, I asked Will why. "Your daddy's lonely, Sammy. There's no one he cares about and it makes him feel bad. The whiskey makes him feel better."

"Don't he care about me?"

"He cares the whole world about you, Sammy. But he needs a woman to love too. You'll understand someday. . . ." He took hold of my hand and made me stand up. "Take off your clothes and hang them up. Never sit around in what you wear on the stage. We've always had the name of the best-dressed colored act in the business and we're gonna keep that name."

One is about all we ever had of anything but you'd never see wrinkles in our pants or makeup on our shirts and we shined our shoes every time we came off.

As I started my big number my father slipped out into the audience and on cue a half-dollar flew toward me and clanged noisily onto the stage. I danced to it, picked it up, flipped it in the air, caught it, put it in my pocket, and nodded "Thank you" without losing a beat, and it started raining money.

My pockets were so heavy with coins that I could hardly dance in our closing. When we got to the dressing room I dumped the money onto a table. "Hey, Poppa, this looks like our best night yet." He stacked the nickels, dimes, and quarters. "Twelve eighty-five! You realize this is as much as we get in salary for a whole night's shows?" He swung me in the air. "You're the breadwinner, Poppa. Damned if you ain't. You, I, and Will are gonna put on our best clothes, go over to the Lobster Restaurant, and have us some real full-course dinners."

Our party was going full blast when my father was suddenly very drunk. I tried not to let him see I'd noticed, but he snapped, "Why're you lookin' away from me?" His eyes narrowed. "You're holdin' out money!" He slapped me and I fell off the chair. "I'll teach you to cheat your own father. . . ." I lay on the floor waiting for something to happen. I opened my eyes and looked up. He was standing over me, crying, his arms hanging loose at his sides, shaking his head like he couldn't believe what he'd done. He knelt down, picked me up, and, carrying me in his arms, walked out of the restaurant hugging and kissing me. "Oh God, I'm sorry, Poppa. I didn't mean it. Honest I didn't mean it."

"I didn't hold out money, Daddy."

"I know, Poppa, I know."

In the middle of my big number the next night I saw him watching me. He looked sadder than I'd ever seen him. I kept trying to let him see me smiling at him so he'd know it was okay.

When we got off, Will took me aside. "You didn't have your flash tonight. And you weren't dancing, neither. Now, I know you're troubling and you're worried about Big Sam, but you can't take any thoughts onstage with you except the show you're doing. Always be thinking when you're out there or the audience'll start to outthink you and then you'll lose them."

"I'm sorry I lost 'em, Massey."

He put his arm around me. "We all have troubles sometimes, Mose Gastin, but those people out front don't want to know 'em. No matter how bad you're hurting, leave your troubles here in the wings, and come on smiling."

I was seven and we were in New York when Will started taking me with him to the booking offices. "Listen carefully to everything that's said, Sammy. There's two words in show business, 'show' and 'business.' The dancing and knowing how to please the audience is the 'show' and getting the dates and the money is the 'business.' I know you like to dance and sing and be on the stage in front of the people, but if you don't get money for it, then you ain't doing nothing but having a good time for yourself."

The man behind the desk looked at Will. "I've got a great spot for you with Minsky in the Liberty Theater here on Forty-second Street, but I didn't realize Sammy was still so small. He's going to be a problem. The Geary Society's got that law that no kid under sixteen can sing or dance on the stage."

My father laughed slyly. "Don't give no thought to that. We been workin' Sammy under the cork. We blacks him up, he's got a Jolson suit, we bills him as 'Silent Sam the Dancing

Midget,' and the way he dances there's no chance of anyone catching wise."

Two women and three cops climbed onstage, over the footlights. My father yelled, "It's the Geary Society. Go to Mama." I slipped between the cops and was halfway home before I stopped running. As soon as I was with Mama, surrounded by the safety of our apartment, I burst into tears.

Mama looked me in the eyes. "What's wrong, Sammy? Somebody hit you?" I shook my head and sat down. "Then why you crying?" I didn't say anything. "Well, wash up for dinner. If there's nothing wrong, then there's no need to be crying." I walked toward the bathroom. "Sammy, where's your father?"

I couldn't keep it from her any longer. "I don't know, Mama. We were doin' the act when some cops came . . ."

Will walked in and Mama turned on him. "Mastin, is Sam in jail?"

"Well—uh, yes, Mrs. Davis."

"What'd he do?"

"Well, it's a long story. . . ."

"I think it's a short story. I told him don't take Sammy downtown on that stage. That's a burlesque theater you're in and he's right in the center of attraction with people packed in on both sides waitin' to see those naked girls. . . ."

An hour later, my father came in smiling, but one look at Mama and he sat down and stared at the floor.

"So you finally got yourself locked up, Sam. That's fine things to show a little child. That's really good bringin' up."

"Come on, Will, we better get outta here." He turned to me. "Start gettin' your stuff together."

I stood up. Mama snapped, "Don't you do it, Sammy." I sat down again, fast. "Sam, where do you think you're going?"

"Hell, Mama, they wants me in front of a judge tomorrow, so I'm gettin' outta New York. And I'm takin' my son with me."

"You ain't takin' Sammy nowhere, or I'll have the Thirty-second Precinct bulls on you. You got no booking, you got no money. You think I'm gonna let you take this child running from the bulls, wandering to beg food with no place to sleep? Not while I'm able to work."

"Mama, you got no say. Sammy's my son and I say he comes with me."

Mama was adamant. She took me to court and won custody.

Back at the apartment Mama laid down the law to Will and my father. "You heard with your own ears. The judge said his own father and mother ain't capable of raising him and he gave Sammy to me. Legal!"

Will cleared his throat. "Uh—Mrs. Davis, I just got us a fine booking up in Boston next week. Naturally it's your say if we can take Sammy along with us."

I wanted desperately to go with them. After a while she said, "All right, Sammy. I know you want to sing and dance and be in show business more than anything, so you can go. Mastin, you and Sam sit there and listen to me tell you how you'll take care of this child. You won't let him eat no hot dogs, and no hamburgers neither. Give him chicken and be sure and give the leg, not the breast, it's too dry. And don't let him eat close to the bone. And when he says he's had enough don't you tell him 'There's food on the plate.' Let him leave it. He'll eat as much as he wants and that's enough. And don't give him no pork chops. You and Sam can eat all the pork you want and all the pig tails but don't you give none to Sammy. If you can't get him chicken legs, then give him a piece of beef. Don't you upset his stomach. If he gets sick on the road, you won't have the money to call a doctor and you'll kill my child."

"All right, Mama, we'll do just like you say."

She handed him a bottle of Scott's Emulsion. "Always keep a bottle of this and give it to him three times a day till he's sixteen. There'll be times you don't have heat in the room and this'll keep him from catching cold. . . ."

I tugged at my father's arm as he, Massey, and I approached Grand Central Station. "Where we goin', Daddy?"

"We're goin' to the railroad station."

"But where else we goin'?"

He winked at Will. "Well, let's see . . . from there we're catchin' the smokey to Boston."

"I *know* that, but where *else*?"

He hoisted me onto his shoulders, laughing, "We're goin' back into show business, Poppa. Back into show business."

4

My father came into the dressing room. "Timmy French give up the ghost. Let everybody go and he's runnin' a elevator at some hotel."

Will sat down and slowly turned his hat on the tip of his finger. It slipped and fell to the floor but he didn't reach down to pick it up. He spoke, but to neither of us. "Timmy had a good show."

Vaudeville was dying. Wherever we went, for meals, or between shows in the greenroom, backstage, there was none of the usual atmosphere of clowning around. Everybody seemed afraid and they spoke only of acts that had been forced to quit the business.

A performer from the next dressing room looked in and saw me brushing our high silk hats. "Not much point in that," he said, "there's hardly anyone out front to see 'em. They're all across the street at the goddam talkies."

I put down the hat, half finished. Will turned to me. "Sammy, brush that hat till it gleams." He was speaking with controlled anger. "And remember this like it's your Bible. If there's one person or one thousand sitting out there, you gotta look as good and work as hard for that one man as you would for the one thousand. Never sluff off an audience. They paid their money and you owe them the best you got in you."

My father and Will burst into Mama's in the middle of the afternoon. "C'mon, Mose Gastin, you're gonna be in the talkies." My father took my suit out of the closet. "Ethel Waters is doin' a two-reeler called *Rufus Jones for President* and you've gotta audition 'cause they're looking for a seven-year-old who c'n sing and dance to play Rufus. And that's gonna be you."

We filmed it at the Warner studios in Brooklyn. The idea of the picture was that Rufus Jones falls asleep on his mother's lap and dreams he's elected President. When Rufus Jones attended a cabinet meeting, there were signs saying "Check Yo' Razors at the Door." He appointed a "Secretary in Charge of Crap Shooting" and a Secretary of Agriculture to "make sure the watermelons come in good and the chickens is ready fo' fryin'."

We'd used some of the movie money to buy a Victrola, and I spent hours every day winding the machine and listening to the big names—Cab Calloway, Chick Webb, the Dorseys, Duke Ellington, and Jimmie Lunceford. I played a Chick Webb record for Mama and told her I wanted a set of traps like he played, but she didn't understand and she bought me a toy drum. With that as a start I built a set of traps with bottles, tin pans, glasses of water, and anything that would make the sounds I wanted, and sat in the front room playing along with Chick Webb, trying to capture all his licks.

My father came roaring in. "Hell, Mama, *damn!* He don't never stop playin'. He's drummin' and the neighbors are goin' knock knock knock—he's gotta cut it out!"

"You don't like it? Move out. Sammy's got to practice."

"Practice for *what*? To be in a show business there ain't gonna be?" He slammed his door. Mama turned to me and smiled. "Sammy, you just keep practicin'."

At last, Will arrived at the apartment with the news we'd been waiting for. Mama rushed in from the kitchen, a bunch of greens in her hand. "What's all this ruckus about?"

Will took off his hat. "We're booked, Mrs. Davis. Six weeks firm and maybe more after that." We all sat around him while he explained. "I've been trying to fight the talkies, trying to sell the bookers on how much show business we can put on a stage with our big shows, but I had to face up to the fact of the talkie being the attraction today. What the theaters need is small acts that can do the vaudeville half, then go back out and give 'em another eight or ten minutes while the stagehands are setting up the sound horns for the talkie. It's gotta be a simple act with no props and scenery, but fast and flashy enough to hold the audience even with the work going on. And that's us. I've cut down to just the three of us." Then the excitement left his face and he turned away. "There's no more *Holiday in Dixieland*, no more *Shake Your Feet* or *Hannah from Savannah* . . . I'll miss our big shows . . . those were really shows." He looked at me. "How come nothing's ever what it was till it's gone?" I knew I wasn't expected to understand or answer. He smacked his knee. "Well, that's all past now. The business has changed, so we're changing with it."

5

This was the first time I'd ever seen my name on the front of a theater. "Will Mastin's Gang, Featuring Little Sammy." I asked, "What's 'featuring' mean?" My father said, "That means you're something worth seeing. Ain't many eight-year-old kids got their name out front like this."

Will said, "From now on it's just the three of us. We're a trio and we'll split our money three ways. You're an equal partner now, Sammy. Your daddy and me will open strong to form the impression. Then you've got to go out there and keep 'em going. Start strong to get them, then pace yourself so you hold them, but save yourself for your big finish. There's only two things to remember in show business: making an impression and leaving them with it." He put his arm around my shoulder. "Do your best, Mose Gastin, but don't ever worry, 'cause whatever you do your daddy and me'll come on and it'll be okay."

I was in the middle of my big number when a drunk began heckling me. I kept dancing but I lost all my flash and only went through the motions until my number was over. I closed the dressing-room door against the mild applause and burst into tears. I didn't know what the drunk had been saying, but I knew I'd done a bad show because of him and the audience hadn't liked me enough. I couldn't face my father or Will.

When they came in, I stuck my head into my lap and kept crying. My father patted my shoulder. "No need to cry, Poppa. Not over one fool drunk."

"They didn't like me."

"Well, that just shows they don't know nothin'." He picked me up in his arms and wiped my face with his handkerchief.

Will said, "Sammy, something good happened tonight. You gave a bad performance, but you'll never let yourself get thrown that way again. One thing you can't ever forget: if anybody out there gets to you, ignore him and wait till you can make a clean exit."

My father rubbed his chin thoughtfully. "I'd say I'm kinda in the mood for the glen plaid with the pearl-gray shirts." He'd chosen our best clothes for our first look around Joplin, Missouri. Will and I nodded and we started getting dressed. My clothes were exact miniatures of theirs, with breast-pocket handkerchief, vest, gold watch and chain, spats, and a cane. My father set the pearl stickpin into my necktie and we went downstairs to the bulletin board, where there was always a card with the name of a nearby restaurant that had good food.

Vern and Kissel, a good act, and friends of ours, were coming up the stairs from the greenroom. They were on their way to eat too, so we all went together. "How you been makin' out against the talkies?" . . . "Great. We just played some time for Dudley in Detroit." . . . "Hey, you guys look like ready money. . . ." We walked down the street, happy to be working, talking show talk, laughing all the way to the restaurant. It was a big square room with a completely round counter. "Sammy's a full partner now. Wait'll you see him doin' my African Zulu Charleston Prance . . ."

The counterman smiled. "Evening, folks. You niggers'll have to sit on the other side."

The countertop was painted white halfway around and brown on the other half. He was pointing to the brown section.

Vern said, "But we're together . . ."

"Sorry, bub, you ain't together in here. Black 'n white don't sit together in here even if you're brothers." He grinned. "Although 'tain't likely."

Vern was on his feet. "Let's get out of here."

The muscle in Will's cheek was moving up and down. He looked at his watch. "No point in spoiling your meal. If we leave here you won't have time to find someplace else."

The counterman shrugged. "Fact is, it's no different elsewhere in these parts, so you might as well make do."

My father took my hand, and we moved over to the brown side. Vern and Kissel moved to the seats next to us on the white side where the line ended. Nobody said much anymore.

Back at the theater, Vern and Kissel were talking to the stage manager. They were angry, pointing down the street, but I couldn't hear what they were saying. My father and Will stood with me on the stairs waiting for them. The stage manager was listening and shaking his head. Then he hit the palm of his hand with his fist, strode over to the bulletin board, tore the restaurant's sign down, and came over to us. "I'm damned sorry about this, Mr. Mastin, Mr. Davis. . . ."

My father said, "I'd as soon not discuss it now." He glanced toward me. They walked away and all of them stood near the door talking low. I inched up closer, but Will saw me and took my hand. "C'mon, Sammy, we'll go upstairs and get ready for the show."

Will didn't say a word as we got undressed.

"Massey?"

"Yes, Sammy?"

"What's goin' on?"

Again the muscles of his face tightened and started moving. "Nothing for you to be worrying yourself over."

"I'm not worryin'. I'm just wonderin' what happened. We were havin' fun and then everybody got mad and now downstairs they're talkin' about it. . . ."

"Talk-*ing*, Sammy. Say the word the way it's supposed to be said. Don't be lazy."

"What's a nigger?"

Will walked over to his makeup chair and sat down. "That's just a nasty word some people use about us."

"About show people?"

"No. It's a word some white people use about colored people. People like us whose skin is brown."

"What's it mean, Massey?"

"It don't mean nothing except to say they don't like us."

"But Vern and Kissel like us, don't they?"

"Yes. But show people are different. Most of 'em don't care about anything except how good is your act. It's others I'm talking about. Someday you'll understand. . . ."

My father walked in. "Don't you think about it, Poppa. That guy was jealous 'cause we're in show business and he's gotta be pushin' beans all his damned life. Don't you even give it a thought."

I was all the more confused. Vern and Kissel were in show business and he hadn't called them niggers. The way Will and my father were so angry and hurt I knew the word must have meant just us and it must have been terrible. The closest I could come is that somehow it meant we were different from other people in a way that was bad. But that didn't make any sense at all. I wasn't any different from anybody else.

"Betcha I can make you laugh, Poppa."

My father was crouched in front of me making his poker face. I fought it, as I always did, but in a minute I was rolling on the floor.

My father handed me a package. "Play this on your machine, Poppa, and see how a *headliner* sounds." It was Louis Armstrong's new record: "I'll Be Glad When You're Dead, You Rascal You." I played it a dozen times and then tried to sing it making his sound. My father was lying on the bed reading a newspaper. He jumped up and got Massey from the next room. I did it again, thrilled by how much they liked it.

"Don't that hurt your throat, Poppa?"

"Feels fine."

Will said, "Then that goes into the act." He smiled. "I'll introduce you as Satchmo himself, and you'll come running on carrying the brass trumpet and big white handkerchief like he does."

Bill Robinson was playing at the Plymouth Theater while we were in Boston. He and Will were the best of friends since a poker game years before when somebody pulled a gun on him and Will saved his life. Between our shows Will brought me to the Plymouth so I could stand in the wings and watch. I'd heard about "Bojangles" all my life but I'd never seen him work and it was shocking to see how different his dancing was from ours or any I'd ever seen. We'd exhaust ourselves, arms and legs flying six ways to the moon, and come off limp and wet. But Mr. Robinson had his hands in his pockets and he was going up and down a flight of stairs and around the stage like he was taking a stroll set to music. He wasn't even trying to get the audience, yet I'd never seen anyone go over so big. As he came off and passed by me, I knew I'd just seen the biggest dance act in the business, but his face wasn't even damp.

He brought us back to his dressing room, handed his jacket to his valet, and put on a beautiful robe with his initials on it. His valet opened a curtain in front of a clothes rack. I had never seen so many shoes in one place in my life.

"Whose are those?"

Mr. Robinson was eating a pint of ice cream. "Mine, kid."

I counted twenty-five pairs of shoes. I couldn't take my eyes off him. "Lemme see you dance, kid." Will nodded that it was okay and I did my whole routine.

"That's good. But make it so the people can understand it. Make it look easy."

As we walked back to the rooming house, Will said, "Mose Gastin, you just met the biggest in the business." He stopped walking. "When Bill Robinson plays the Palace he gets *thirty-five hundred dollars a week*. That's as big as anyone can get."

Bill Robinson was his own style, but we had to fight for our lives every time the lights went up. We were booked on the strength of our reputation as a clean act that could be depended on for fast and furious flash dancing. Probably fifty percent of our flash came from our dread of the word "canceled." There were no unions and at the whim of a theater manager any show could be our last. We played theaters where if an act wasn't going over, someone out front would yell, "The hook! Get the hook!" and a giant hook would swoop out from the wings and drag the performer off the stage. As he went off, the audience splattered him with fruit and rotten eggs. Sometimes it was a hundred-pound sandbag that swung down and knocked the performer off his feet in the middle of his act. Hook or sandbag, what made this man get up off the floor and try again at another theater is one of the unanswerables about show people, but they dragged better performers off those stages than many who are stars today.

In 1941 we were booked into the Michigan Theater in Detroit with Tommy Dorsey, to pinch-hit for his regular opening act, Tip, Tap & Toe. I was fifteen.

A fellow in his twenties, standing near the bulletin board backstage, held out his hand, "Hi ya. Frank. I sing with Dorsey."

Frank Sinatra was the vocalist on most of my Tommy Dorsey records. I stood in the wings at each performance, eating up Dorsey's music. The audiences loved Frank. He had a different style from other band vocalists. Easy and simple, and he sang the words so that they weren't just an excuse for him to be singing the melody.

He and I went out for sandwiches a few times between shows, or we sat on the dressing-room stairs talking show business. After three days Tip, Tap & Toe got to town and we moved on.

We had a ninety-dollar La Salle, in which we'd been traveling, and often sleeping, and with no bookings we headed toward New York.

Mama was watching us from her window one flight up, shaking her head, calling out, "Here come the gypsies!" I ran up the stairs two at a time and threw my arms around her. She kissed me quickly. "We can have our hellos in a minute. First go down and tell your father to park that junk away from in front of my house."

I stood in line at the box office of the Paramount Theater watching expensively dressed men paying for tickets as though it meant nothing to them. Then it was my turn. I asked to see the manager, and when he came out I smiled, "Do you recognize performers?" He passed me by the ticket taker, but as always, I felt like a moocher for bumming my way in.

After the show I walked up Broadway. A crowd of fans were gathered outside the stage door of the Loew's State. I could feel the anxiety in the air, like nothing mattered to them except getting a look at the person who was going to walk out of that door. Then the door opened and Bob Hope stepped out and was swallowed up by the crowd until I couldn't see his beautiful clothes anymore or the smile on his face like all this was coming to him and he expected it. I watched him get into a beautiful new car and drive away and I pictured the kind of place he must be going to, with elevator men and everybody calling him "sir" and bringing him letters and flowers and anything he wanted.

I hardly felt like I was in the same business. I took the subway uptown and I ran the few blocks from the station, eager to get home and ask my father, "Do you think we'll ever make the big time?"

I was leaning across the kitchen table, looking straight at him. He shook his head slowly. "I don't know, Poppa. If it's meant for us to make it, then I guess we'll make it."

I kept looking at him, needing more, wishing he'd said,

"Yes, we'll make it," or even "No. Not a chance." Anything would have been better than an answer that told me nothing.

Our fortunes had hit such a low that we'd been home for five months without getting even a one-nighter. The people Mama worked for had moved out of town and she couldn't find another job. For the first time in our lives we were on relief, waiting helplessly for the checks to arrive, hoping every day that Will would come running up the stairs and say, "We're booked."

The handwriting on the wall was saying, "You're out of the business." Months passed and we went nowhere but to the pawnshop until everything we owned was there except our radio, the last link between us and show business.

My father and I killed our evenings sitting in the kitchen near the stove, listening to the radio and playing pinochle, with him still trying to cheat me as though we were playing for $100,000 a hand. I looked forward all day to Jack Eigen's celebrity interview program from the lounge of the Copacabana. I never tired of listening to the celebrities. When they talked show business they weren't dreaming as we were. These people were making movies, hit records, doing radio, and starring on Broadway. Eigen's catchphrase was "I'm at the Copa, where are you?" And almost every time he said it I threw down my cards and shouted back, "I'm in my goddamned hole in Harlem, that's where I am."

With vaudeville dead and even the Palace running movies, variety acts like ours were moving into nightclubs, and *the* top-drawer club was the Copacabana. Everything else was either the way up or the way down.

I lost interest in the pinochle and listened to Jimmy Durante describing his new home in Hollywood, then George Raft talking about the picture he'd just made . . . and the sound of people laughing and clinking glasses in the background . . . Joe E. Lewis was just passing through New York and he'd dropped in for a drink and to say hello. . . .

We listened to them talking about "the glamorous Copa" and the fabulous homes stars had just bought or were building, with swimming pools and golf courses. I looked around our railroad flat with the windows closed in the back room to keep out the smell of the garbage that people threw out of their windows. I snapped off the radio. "Come on, Dad." He knew where I wanted to go. We did it all the time. We only had fare for one way, so we whistled as we walked. It took us a while to get there but we had nothing but time.

It was a freezing night, but we stood in the doorway of a building at 15 East 60th Street, directly across from the Copa, watching the people going inside, the doorman helping them out of their limousines and cabs, tipping his hat, holding the door for them until they disappeared inside, laughing. Why shouldn't they laugh? They had everything, importance, clothes and jewelry like I'd never seen anywhere but in movies. God, they were beautiful.

We waited to see them again when they came out. I clenched my fists. "Someday I'll play that place, so help me God. I'm gonna have Mama there and when we go home, there won't be a goddamned empty icebox. And I won't have to wait till Easter to buy a new suit. I'll buy them whenever I want them, ten at a time . . . I'm gonna be a star."

Then, all the way home on the A train, I wondered—will I ever be a star?

The music stopped abruptly: "We interrupt this program for an urgent news bulletin: The Japanese have just bombed Pearl Harbor. President Roosevelt is expected to issue a declaration of war . . . The United States is at war with Japan . . ." I put down the piece of birthday cake I was holding and looked from face to face around the room at my Uncle Bubba's place, where we were celebrating my sixteenth birthday on Sunday, a day early. "We repeat, the Japanese have just bombed Pearl Harbor . . ."

My father whistled down a cab and we headed for the Army

recruiting office in Times Square. The cab fare was unimportant. Money had no meaning anymore. For the first time in my life and probably my father's, something was more important than show business. We were gripped by patriotism and there was nothing else to do but join the Army. I loved my country not so much for anything it had given me, but for the most fundamental reason: it was mine. And maybe I took extra pride in it because being an American was the only big-time thing I had going for me.

"What about Massey, Dad? You think he'll join up too?"

My father roared, "Will? Hell, he was too old for World War *One*."

I sat back in the cab totally involved in being "the young man about to leave his loved ones," and the ride to Times Square was a montage of movie scenes: I was marching with thousands of men singing "You're a Grand Old Flag." Pat O'Brien was my captain and Spencer Tracy was the chaplain in our outfit. Between 125th and 42nd streets I won my wings in the Army Air Corps, and I saw myself zooming off on dangerous missions, bombing enemy ships and dogfighting with Zeros. As we stood outside the recruiting office at the end of a long line, I pictured myself coming home on leave to show Mama my Army Air Corps uniform with the peaked cap, the glamorous one that everyone knew was worn only by flyers, because it had soft edges for earphones to be worn over it. . . .

The master sergeant said, "You're too young. Come back in two years." He told my father, "Overage. Sorry. Next man. . . ."

We were playing the Fortune Club in Reno when I was ordered to report to the Presidio of Monterey, the induction center for the San Francisco area. I showed the notice to my father. He sat down on the bed and didn't even try to smile. "Well, Poppa, I guess this is it." Will was shaking his head, as though unable to believe it was really happening. "We're splitting up the act."

All in all, it had been sixteen happy years of sometime-eating but always thinking and working together as a unit. Certainly show business had not chosen us or held out its arms and rewarded our love, but even the hard times had been good times, at least in retrospect, and there was never a moment when one of us regretted that we chose to stick it out.

The rent didn't get paid but Will and my father spent $150 on a gold wristwatch for me, with a stopwatch built into it, a chronograph, the kind the Air Corps was using. I'd been dying to own one for a year and they must have borrowed the money to buy it. Will said, "We always had the name of the best-dressed colored act in show business. Can't let 'em think different about us in the Army."

At six o'clock Saturday morning the three of us were standing outside the induction center making our awkwardly manly goodbyes. My father said, "Now, Poppa, you're goin' in a boy but you'll come out a man. You'll meet all kinds of people but just do your job like you're supposed to and nobody can bother you. That's all I got to say 'cept I know you'll do good and we'll be waitin' for you when you come back."

A whistle sounded. "Okay, Mose Gastin, you're on. Just treat it like show business. Give 'em the best you got."

It was like I had two fathers. I hugged and kissed Will and turned to my dad. I grabbed him with all my strength and kissed him goodbye. "So long, Poppa. I'm proud of my boy." Reluctant to go, yet for lack of knowing what else to say that might keep me there a few more minutes, I checked the time on my wristwatch, which I'd polished almost every hour in the last few days. The dial was a blur. I kept telling myself I'm a man going into the Army and I'm going to fly a plane.

6

A PFC was sitting on the steps of a barracks, sewing an emblem onto a shirt. I walked over to him. "Excuse me, buddy. I'm a little lost. Can you tell me where 202 is?"

"Two buildings down. And I'm not your buddy, you black bastard!"

The corporal standing outside 202 checked my name against a list. "Yeah—well, wait over there till we figure out what to do with you."

I was at the infantry's Basic Training Center at Fort Francis E. Warren in Cheyenne, Wyoming.

I sat on the steps where he'd pointed. Other guys were showing up and he checked them off. "Inside. Take the first bunk you see." Then I heard, "Sit over there with Davis."

A tall, powerfully built guy dropped his gear alongside mine. "My name's Edward Robbins." We shook hands and he sat down next to me. One by one, men were arriving and being sent inside. They kept on coming but no one else was told to wait with us. Then, finally, there was no point in hoping against the obvious. It was clear that we were the only ones being held outside while all the white guys were going right in.

The corporal went inside. We were sitting in front of a screen door, so even though he lowered his voice I could hear every word. ". . . Look, those niggers out there are assigned to this company. I'm gonna stick 'em down there. You two guys move your gear so I can give 'em those last two bunks."

"Hey, that's right nexta me. I ain't sleepin' near no dinge."

"Look, soldier, let's get something straight right off. I'm in charge of this barracks and . . ."

"I ain't arguin'. I'm only sayin' I didn't join no nigger army."

Edward and I looked straight ahead.

"What about the can? Y'mean we gotta use the same toilets as them?"

"That's right, soldier. Now look, we got no fuckin' choice. They used t'keep 'em all together, but now for some fuckin' reason they sent 'em here and we gotta put up with 'em."

It was impossible to believe they were talking about me.

"Yeah, but I still ain't sleepin' nexta no nigger."

"What the hell's the Army need 'em for? They'll steal ya blind while ya sleep and they're all yeller bellies . . ."

"Awright, knock it off. I don't want 'em any more'n you do but we're stuck with 'em. That's orders."

They weren't even trying to keep their voices down anymore.

There was the sound of iron cots sliding across the wooden floor. The corporal beckoned from the doorway. "Okay, I'll assign your bunks. Let's go," he snapped, "on the double." I felt like a disease he was bringing in.

There were rows of cots on both sides with an aisle down the center. The guys had stopped talking. I could feel them staring as we followed the corporal down the aisle. He pointed to the last two cots on one side. "Those are yours. Now, we don't want no trouble with you. Keep your noses clean, do as you're told, and we'll get along." He walked away.

The bed nearest to ours was empty. All the cots were about two feet apart from each other except ours, which were separated from the rest by about six feet—like we were on an island.

A few of the men sort of smiled and half waved hello. Some wouldn't look over at us. The nearest, a tall, husky guy who must have been a laborer or an athlete, kept his back turned.

A sergeant came in and from the center of the barracks announced, "I'm Sergeant Williams. I . . ." His glance fell on the space between the beds. He turned to the corporal. "What is *that*?"

The corporal whispered how he'd handled things. Sergeant Williams spoke sharply: "There is only one way we do things here: the Army way! There will be exactly three feet of space, to the inch, between every bunk in this barracks. You have sixty seconds to replace the beds as you found them. *Move!*"

He came over to me. "What's your name, soldier?"

"Sammy Davis, Jr."

"Of all the men here did you arrive first or last or what?"

"About in the middle."

"Did you choose this bunk?"

By this time the barracks had been rearranged. "All right, Davis. Move your gear one bunk over." He turned to Edward. "You do the same."

He addressed us all. "No man here is better than the next man unless he's got the rank to prove it."

I sat on the end of my bunk, the shock gone, immense anger growing within me until my legs were shaking and it was impossible for me to keep them still. I couldn't give them the satisfaction of seeing how they'd gotten to me. I saw one of the other guys polishing his boots. That was a good idea. The boots were a brand-new, almost yellow leather and we'd been told to darken them with polish. I took off my watch and laid it carefully on the bed. I opened my shoeshine kit, took out the polish and brush, and began rubbing the polish into the leather, doing the same spot over and over, concentrating on it, working so hard that I could blank out everything else from my mind. Suddenly another pair of boots landed at my feet. "Here, boy, you can do mine too."

It was the guy who had the bed next to me, and he'd already turned away. I grabbed for the boots, to throw them at his head—but I didn't want to make trouble. I put them down beside his bed.

"Hey, boy, don't get me wrong, I expected t'give you a tip. Maybe two bits for a good job."

"I'm no bootblack. And I'm no boy, either."

"Whoa now, don't get so uppity, boy." He shrugged and walked over to Edward. "Here y'are, boy. You can do 'em."

"Yes, suh! Glad t'do 'em, suh."

"Well, that's more like it. Glad somebody around here knows his place. And you don't have to call me sir. Just call me Mr. Jennings. Y'see, in the Army you only call the officers sir."

"Yes, suh, Mr. Jennings, and my name is Edward. Anything you needs . . ."

I was alone in that barracks.

Jennings was talking to a couple of the other guys. "This may work out okay. One of 'em's not a half-bad nigger." He came by Edward's bunk with three more pairs of boots. Edward's face fell for a second but he brightened up right away. "Yes, suh, you just leave 'em here and I'll take care of 'em."

"You oughta thank me for settin' up this little business for you."

"I *do* thank you." He smiled broadly. "Oh, yes, suh. I thanks you kindly."

Edward was avoiding my eyes. Eventually he looked up and moved his head just the slightest bit. For a split second he opened up to me and I saw the humiliation he was enduring because his fear of trouble was stronger than his need for dignity. I hoped he'd look up again so I could let him know I was sorry I'd judged him and forced him to let me look inside him.

Perhaps this was how he had to live, but I wasn't going to take it from anybody. I wasn't going to let anybody goad me into fights and get myself in trouble, either. I was going to mind my own business and have a clean record.

Jennings flopped onto his bunk. He sat up, reached over, and took my watch off my bed. "Say, this ain't a half-bad watch." He looked at me suspiciously.

"Put it back."

"My, but you're an uppity one. Hey, Philips . . . catch!" He tossed the watch across the barracks. I ran to get it back but Philips lobbed it over my head to another guy, who threw it back to Jennings. I ran after it, knowing how ridiculous I looked getting there just as Jennings threw it over my head again, that I shouldn't chase after it, that I was only encouraging them, but I was afraid they'd drop it and I couldn't stop myself.

"Atten*shun!!!*" Sergeant Williams walked straight to Jennings. "What've you got there?"

Jennings opened his hand and showed him my watch.

"Whose is it?"

Jennings shrugged.

"It's mine."

Sergeant Williams brought it to me. Jennings grinned. "Hell, Sarge, we were just kiddin' around . . ."

"You're a wise guy, Jennings. In the Army we respect another man's property. You just drew KP for a week." He left the barracks.

Jennings glared at me. "I'll fix you for this, black boy."

Hours after lights-out I lay awake trying to understand. How many white people had felt like this about me? I couldn't remember any. Not one. Had I been too stupid to see it? I thought of the people we'd known—agents, managers, the acts we'd worked with—those people had all been friends. I know they were. There were so many things I had to remember: the dressing rooms—had we been stuck at the end of corridors off by ourselves? Or with the other colored acts? Ridiculous. Dressing rooms were always assigned according to our spot on the bill. And the places we stayed? They *were* almost always colored hotels and rooming houses, but I'd never thought of them like that. They were just *our* rooming houses. But did we *have* to go to them? Wasn't it because they knew us and because they were the cheapest? Sure, there were people who hadn't liked us, but it had always been "Don't pay attention, Poppa, he's just jealous 'cause we got a better act." Or: "They don't like us 'cause we're in show business." And I'd never questioned it. In the last few years I'd known there was prejudice and hate in the world. I remembered several times Will telling me, "Someday you'll understand."

Most of the men in our barracks gave me no problems, either because they didn't care or because after a day of Basic they were too tired to worry what the hell I was. But there were about a dozen I had to look out for. They clustered around Jennings and their unity alone was enough to intimidate anybody who might have wanted to show friendliness toward me. When that group wasn't around, the others would be pleasant, but as soon as one of them showed up, nobody knew me. The sneers, the loud whispers, the hate-filled looks were bad enough, but I didn't want it to get worse. I tried to keep peace with Jennings without Tom-ing him. I hoped that if I was good at my job he'd respect me, but when I was good on the rifle range he hated me all the more. If I was bad he laughed at me. I found myself casually but deliberately standing on a different chow line, always finding a place at one of the tables far away from him in the mess hall.

I was fastening the strap on my watch before evening mess and it slipped off my wrist and fell to the floor next to Jennings' bed. Before I could reach it he stood up and ground it into the floor with the heel of his boot. I heard the crack. He lifted his foot, smiling coyly. "Oh! What *have* I gone and done? Sure was foolish t'leave your watch on the floor. Tough luck, boy."

The glass was crushed and the gold was twisted. The winding stem and the hands were broken off and mangled. I put the pieces on the bed and looked at them.

"Awww, don't carry on, boy. You can always steal another one."

I looked at him. "What've you got against me?"

"Hell, I ain't got nothin' against you, boy. I like you fine."

I knew I should swing at him or something, but I was

so weakened from the hurt of it that I couldn't get up the anger.

I wrapped the pieces in some paper and put it in my pocket. Maybe it could be fixed.

Overnight the world looked different. It wasn't one color anymore. I could see the protection I'd gotten all my life from my father and Will. I appreciated their loving hope that I'd never need to know about prejudice and hate, but they were wrong. It was as if I'd walked through a swinging door for eighteen years, a door which they had always secretly held open. But they weren't there to hold it open now, and when it finally hit me it was worse than if I'd learned about it gradually and knew how to move with it.

Sergeant Williams walked out of the mess hall with me. "I was looking over the service records and I see that you were in show business. We have shows at the service club every Friday. If you'd care to help out I'm sure it would be appreciated."

After the show, I was standing backstage with one of the musicians and I suggested we go out front and have a Coke.

He said, "Maybe we better go over to the colored service club. You don't want trouble, do you?"

"Trouble? I just entertained them for an hour. They cheered me. Hey, look, God knows I don't want trouble but there's gotta be a point where you draw the line. Now, I don't know about you, but I'm thirsty and I'm goin' in for a Coke."

A few of the guys who'd seen the show pulled chairs up to their tables for us. Jennings was at a table with four of his buddies. I sat with a group from our barracks and it was the happiest hour I'd spent in the Army. I luxuriated in it. I had earned their respect; they were offering their friendship and I was grabbing for it.

After an hour or so I said good night and headed for the door. As I passed Jennings' table he stood up. "Hey, Davis, c'mon over here and let's get acquainted." He was holding out his hand. It would have been satisfying to brush him off, but if he was trying to be friendly it seemed better to accept it and keep peace.

He pulled out a chair for me. "Man, where'd you learn t'dance like that? I swear I never saw a man's feet move so fast. By the way, you notice I ain't callin' you 'boy.' "

"Have a beer, Davis." One of the guys pushed a bottle toward me. "Here y'are," Jennings said, "here's one nobody touched."

"If you don't mind I'd rather have a Coke."

"Hey, old buddy, you're in the Army. It's time you got over that kid stuff. Learn to drink like a man. You're gonna like it."

The others were watching me. One of them grinned. "Yeah, you oughta learn to drink if you're gonna be a soldier."

Jennings said, "Listen, you're gonna insult me in a minute. Any man who won't drink with me . . ."

"Okay, I'll try it."

"That's better. Now, I'll tell you how to drink beer. It can't be sipped like whiskey or a Coke. To really get the taste of beer you've gotta take a good long slug."

The others raised their bottles. Jennings said, "Here's to you." I picked up my bottle to return their toast. I had it halfway to my mouth when I realized it wasn't cold. It was warm. As it came close to my nose I got a good whiff of it. It wasn't beer.

"Hell, don't smell it, man! Drink it!"

I took another smell and all at once I understood the smiles, the handshakes, the friendliness from Jennings. Somebody had taken the bottle empty into the men's room and come back with it filled.

Jennings was saying, "Come on, drink up, boy . . ."

I put the bottle on the table. The faces in front of me zoomed in like a movie close-up and I could see every bead of perspiration, every blink of their eyes. The noise in the room was growing loud then low, loud then low.

"Drink it yourself, you dirty louse."

Jennings roared with laughter. "Hell, he even curses like a Coke drinker, don't he?"

I tried to stand up, but my chair wouldn't move. Jennings had his foot behind it, trapping me. The old hate was back in his face. "You wanta live with us and you wanta eat with us and now you came in here and you wanta drink with us. I kinda thought you loved us so much you'd wanta . . ."

I felt a warm wetness creeping over the side of my shirt and pants. While he'd been talking he had turned the bottle upside down and let it run out on me. I stared at the dark stain spreading over the khaki cloth, cringing from it, trying to lean away from my wet shirt and wet pants. My pocket was so soaked I couldn't put my hand in for my handkerchief.

Jennings jumped up, pointing to me, jeering loudly, "Silly niggers can't even control themselves. This little fella got so excited sittin' with white men—look what he did to himself."

I was out of the chair and on top of him. I had my hands on his throat with every intention of killing him. I loved seeing the sneer fall from his face, replaced by dumb shock as I squeezed tighter and tighter, my thumbs against his windpipe. He was gasping for breath. In a desperate effort he swung around fast, lifting me off the floor. My own weight dragged me off him and I flew through the air and crashed into one of the tables. Within seconds the area was cleared as though we were in a ring together.

Until this moment it hadn't been a fight, it had been an attack by 115 pounds of rage propelled by blind impulse. I hadn't known it was going to happen any more than Jennings had. The weeks of taking it, the time of looking for peace, of avoiding trouble, had simply passed, and it just happened, like a pitcher overflows when you put too much into it.

But we both knew it was going to be different now: he was a foot taller than me and half again my weight, or more, and without the advantage of surprise I was like a toy to him. He was taking his time, grinning to his friends, caressing the knuckles of his hands. He raised his fists and began circling, licking his lips, anticipating the pleasure he was going to take out of me.

I flew into him with every bit of strength I had. His fist smashed into my face. Then I just stood there watching his other fist come at me, helpless to make myself move out of the way. I felt my nose crumble as if he'd hit an apple with a sledgehammer. The blood spurted out and I smelled a dry horrible dusty smell.

"Get up, you yellow-livered black bastard, you stinking coon nigger . . ." I hadn't realized I was on the floor. I got to my feet and stumbled toward him. He hit me in the stomach and I collapsed. I was gasping for breath but no air was coming in and I was suffocating. Then suddenly I could taste air, and the figures in front of my eyes straightened out and became people again. I got up and went for him. He was methodically hitting me over and over again, landing four to every one of my punches, but they weren't hurting me anymore, they were just dull thuds against my body. Then his fist was beating down on the top of my head like a club. Someone shouted, "Don't hit 'im on the head, Jen. Y'can't hurt a nigger 'cept below the forehead." He kept pounding me and I felt myself slipping to the floor again. I grabbed his shirt with one hand to keep myself from falling so I could hit him in the face with my other hand. I had to stay on my feet and keep hitting him, nothing else mattered, and I was glad to trade being hit ten times by him for the joy of feeling my fist smash into his face just once. I hung on and kept hitting him and hitting and hitting . . .

A guy named O'Brien, from my barracks, was holding a wet cloth against my face. "You'll be okay. The bleeding's stopped."

I was propped up against the side of the PX. It was very quiet. Another guy was there. Miller. They were part of the group that always avoided trouble with Jennings. He smiled. "You might feel better to know that you got in your licks. I think you closed one of his eyes and you definitely broke his nose. He's wearing it around his left ear." I started to laugh but a shock of pain seared my lips. My head was pounding like it was still being hit. I opened my mouth carefully to ask how long I'd been out.

O'Brien said, "Take it easy." He grinned and showed me the cloth he was wiping my face with. "You ripped his shirt when you fell and you had part of it in your hand. You had a death grip on it even after you went out."

They walked me back to the barracks. Sergeant Williams was waiting in the doorway. "Very smart! Well, get over to the infirmary with Jennings."

I had sent Jennings to the infirmary. What beautiful news. Gorgeous! Miller and O'Brien were waiting to take me there. I shook my head and thanked them. I wasn't going to give Jennings the satisfaction of seeing me in the infirmary, not if my nose fell off entirely.

Lights were out but on the way to my bunk some of the guys stopped me and told me that when I'd fallen off Jennings he was starting to stomp me but Miller and O'Brien had stepped in and pulled him away. I realized that I'd broken the barracks into two groups: the haters and the guys in the middle who didn't care enough to take sides or who didn't want to get involved. It had never occurred to me that some might swing over to my side. But when Miller and O'Brien saw that I was down and Jennings was *still* kicking me they had to get involved, and say, "Hey, wait a minute. Nobody's *that* bad."

I got into bed and tried to turn over on my stomach but the bruises were murder. Still, as much as I hurt, the worst pain wasn't so bad that I wouldn't do it again for the dignity I got from hitting back.

Jennings had beaten me unconscious and hurt me more than I'd hurt him, but I had won. He was saying, "God made me better than you," but he lost the argument the minute he had to use his fists to prove it. All he'd proven was that he was physically stronger, but that's not what we were fighting over.

I'd never been so tired in my life, but I couldn't sleep. I hated myself for those weeks of tiptoeing around trying to avoid trouble. I'd been insane to imagine there was anything I could do to make a Jennings like me. I hadn't begun to understand the scope of their hatred. I was haunted by that voice yelling, "Y'can't hurt 'im 'cept below the forehead." My God, if they can believe that then they don't even know what I am. The difference they see is so much more than color. I'm a whole other brand of being to them.

How long would I have gone on not knowing the world was made up of haters, guys in the middle, Uncle Toms? I couldn't believe I was going to spend the rest of my life fighting with people who hate me when they don't even know me. But I kept hearing that voice and I knew I'd hear it again, out of another mouth, from another face, but spouting the same ignorance. I tried to stay awake to think it out, but my head was throbbing and the room began tilting to the left, then the right. . . .

"Come on, Davis. Out of the sack." Sergeant Williams was leaning over me, tilting the bed. "I told you to go to the infirmary last night. You're a damned fool. I'm putting you on sick call this morning and you will report there immediately after mess. That's an order." Everybody else was outside for morning muster. I'd slept right through reveille.

I looked across the mess hall. Jennings had a strip of tape across his nose and his left eye was so swollen that he wouldn't be opening it for a week. The guys were buzzing and pointing at us and I made three trips back to the food counter for things I didn't want, just so that he could see me with no tape on my face, practically dancing there, as though I'd been to a health farm all month.

We were loaded with Southerners and Southwesterners who got their kicks out of needling me, and Jennings and his guys never let up. I must have had a knock-down-drag-out fight every two days and I was getting pretty good with my fists. I had scabs on my knuckles for the first three months in the Army. My nose was broken again and getting flatter all the time. I fought clean, dirty, any way I could win. They were the ones who started the fights and I didn't owe them any Queensberry rules. It always started the same way: a wise-guy look, a sneer—once they knew how I'd react, they were constantly maneuvering me into more fights. To them it was sport, entertainment, but for me the satisfaction which I had first derived diminished each time, until it was just a tiresome chore I had to perform. Somebody would say something and my reaction would be: Oh, hell, here we go again. But I had to answer them. Invariably, I'd walk away angrier than when the fight had started. Why should I have to keep getting my face smashed? Why should I have to fight to break even? Why did I always have to prove what no white man had to prove?

I kept in touch with my father and Will by phone. They'd tried doing a double, but all their material was geared to three people, so eventually they put a girl in the act. Then for a while they had a roller skater named Joe Smythe working with them. "We're makin' ends meet, Poppa. They ain't what you'd call huggin' and kissin' but we're gettin' by killin' time till the day you come home. So do your job in the Army and then get back as fast as you can." I never bothered to tell them what my job in the Army was exactly.

The guy in front of me finished with the washbasin, and as I moved forward, a big redneck grabbed me by the T-shirt and yanked me back so hard that I stumbled clear across the room, hit the wall, and fell down.

"What's *that* for?"

He drawled, "Where I come from, niggers stand in the back of the line."

I got up, gripped my bag of toilet articles, and with all the strength I had, hit him in the mouth with it. The force and shock knocked him down. I stood over him, fists ready. Blood was trickling out of his mouth. He wiped it away with his towel, then looked up at me. "But you're still a nigger."

Sergeant Williams motioned for me to follow him to his room. "Sit down, Davis." He offered me a cigarette. "That's not the way to do it, son. You can't beat people into liking you!"

The moment I'd heard "But you're still a nigger," I'd known that this was not the way to fight.

"Okay, you've punched your way across the camp. What've you proven? After you beat him up did Harcourt respect you any more? You've got to fight a different way, a way that you can win something lasting. You can't hope to change a man's ideas except with a better idea. You've got to fight with your brain, Sammy, not your fists."

It seemed as though I passed Harcourt a hundred times each day, and I was haunted by that mocking voice telling me, "But you're still a nigger." He never said another word to me, but his eyes were saying it in the way they passed over me—as though I wasn't there.

I was on latrine duty and I passed Sergeant Williams' room. The door was open and I saw him stretched out on his bed, reading. He must have had a hundred books in there. "Are these yours, Sergeant? I mean, do you own them all?"

"Yes. Would you like to read one?"

I wanted to but I'd never read a book and I was afraid of picking something ridiculous and making a fool of myself.

Sergeant Williams sat up. "You'll get a lot more out of them than you do from those comic books you read."

He chose a book. "Start with this one. You may not enjoy it right away but stick with it."

It was *The Picture of Dorian Gray* by Oscar Wilde. I began reading it early that evening. After taps, I went into the latrine, where the lights stayed on, and sat on the floor reading until after midnight. When I got off duty the next day I bought a

pocket dictionary at the PX and started the book from the beginning again, doing my reading in isolated places so people
wouldn't see me looking up words.

When I'd finished it I gave it back to Sergeant Williams and
we discussed it. He handed me three more and told me in what
order to read them and we had long discussions about each one
as I finished it. He took a book from his shelves, *The Complete
Works of Shakespeare.* I laughed. "You have to be kidding with
that. I mean, I never spent a day in school . . ."

His voice had an edge to it. "I never said you should be
ashamed of no schooling. But it's not something to be proud of,
either."

He gave me Carl Sandburg's books about Lincoln, books by
Dickens, Poe, Mark Twain, and a history of the United States. I
read *Cyrano de Bergerac,* entranced by the flair of the man; by
the majesty of speeches I read aloud in a whisper, playing the
role, dueling in dance steps around the latrine; imagining myself that homely, sensitive man, richly costumed in knee
breeches, plumed hat, a handkerchief tucked into my sleeve, a
sword in my hand. I feasted on the glory of the moment when,
making good his threat, he drove the actor from the stage, and,
as the audience shouted for their money back, tossed them his
last bag of gold and admitted to Le Bret, "Foolish? Of course.
But such a magnificent gesture." And it was. Glorious! I put my
hand in my pocket, and, clutching a fistful of silver, I slipped
out into the night, sword in hand, to drive the actor from the
stage. Then, as fops and peasants alike shouted for their money
back I hurled my handful of coins into the air. They landed,
clanging against the side of the barracks. A light went on. A
voice yelled, "Corporal of the guard." I ran like hell.

The more education Sergeant Williams gave me, through his
books and our discussions, the greater hunger I developed for
it. When I ran out of his books I found others at the post library and then reread the ones he had.

7

As I got offstage at the service club, a fellow came over to me. "That was one hell of a show you just did. Will you come out front and have a drink with me?" He offered his hand. "My name is George M. Cohan, Jr."

We sat down together and he said, "You've heard about the big show every camp's going to be doing for the intercamp competition? Well, with all the stuff you know and with my dad's special material, which I know backwards, I'll bet we could get that assignment. All the guys trying for it will just be using stuff out of the Special Services books. But with us writing our own, something fresh, we couldn't miss."

"Well, naturally, I'd love to do it."

"Great. The general has the say. As long as I know you want to try for it with me, I'll make an appointment to see him about it."

He told me, a few days later, that the general would let us do an audition at the officers' club. Using a few pros we found around camp and a few semipros, we put together a small-scale version of what we had in mind. I did an impression of Frank Sinatra that night, with the bow tie and the corny business of him being so weak and skinny that he had to hold on to the microphone. The general sent for us as soon as we'd finished and told us to be in his office the next afternoon. He wanted to hear the rest of our ideas.

A WAC captain, his adjutant, sat in on the meeting and as we described our show she found enough stumbling blocks to build a wall around the camp. She said she'd let us know.

Outside, George said, "We've got to butter her up, or she'll kill it entirely."

We dreamed up excuses to go to her office and always brought along bunches of flowers that we'd picked. The captain was getting to like us and it seemed as if she was swinging over to our side.

I stopped off to leave a bundle of new material we'd worked out. She said, "Tell me something about yourself, Davis. You were a professional performer?"

"Yes, Captain. Since I was three."

"Where did you perform?"

As I spoke she leaned back in her chair, listening, waving away the clerks who occasionally tried to speak to her. Her interest triggered a stream of show talk and "the old days" poured out of me, until I began to feel like an old vaudevillian.

She smiled. "When I heard your ideas in the general's office they seemed so professional that frankly I doubted you'd be able to execute them. But now that I understand your background, and from what I know of George, I'm convinced you and he are up to the job. I'd like you to work out a budget for scenery, props, and costumes and drop it off here as soon as you can." She walked me to the door, shook hands, and smiled. "I probably shouldn't say this but you boys have quite an edge over the others. We'll have official word for you by Friday."

Leaving, I felt like doing a Fred Astaire number, tap-dancing across the tops of the long row of desks leading to the front door. Show business had given me something to offer the Army.

By Thursday afternoon when George and I left the captain's office after dropping off a two-pound box of candy, our final and most glorious effort, he, the captain, and I were almost buddies, and as the door closed behind us George sighed, "All we can do now is keep our fingers crossed."

As I started toward my barracks, a couple of headquarters clerks called out to me. A PFC with a heavy Southern drawl smiled. "The captain told us to take you to meet her over at Building 2134."

"Her wish is my command." I walked with them, wondering why she hadn't just told them to bring me back to the office. Maybe she wanted me to look at a warehouse of props and scenery they'd used in other shows. We'd gone about half a mile, to a semideserted part of the camp, to barracks that weren't in use. I followed the PFC into 2134. One of the men closed the barracks door behind us. They shoved me into the latrine. Four others were in there, obviously waiting for us.

"Sorry, nigger, but your lady love won't be here."

"What is this?"

"This ain't nothin' but a little powwow some of us in the office thought we oughta have with you." The PFC spit in my face. I tried to reach up to wipe it away but they were holding my arms. "Oh, I'm sorry. Here, I'll wipe it for you." He slapped me across the face, then backhanded me.

The seven of them crowded around me. The PFC was breathing heavily and a vein in his forehead was pulsing. "We've been watching you makin' eyes at the captain and we decided we oughta have a little talk with you."

"Making eyes? Wait a minute . . ."

He hit me again. "Niggers don't talk 'less they're spoke to." He punched me in the stomach and I collapsed, hanging by the arms from the two guys who were holding me. "Now, like I was sayin', we get so sick to our stomachs seein' you playin' up to her, and tryin' to make time, that we thought you'd appreciate us explaining a few things. Not to say the captain would give an ape-face like you the time of day, but we figured we should smarten you up some so you stop makin' such a fool of yourself.

"Now, what you gotta learn is that black is black and it don't matter how white it looks or feels, it's still black, and we're gonna show you a little experiment to prove it so's you won't think we're trying to fool you none."

One of the others was stirring a can of white paint. Two of them tore my shirt open and off my back. The PFC had a small artist's paintbrush, which he dipped into the paint can. They held me in front of a mirror. He wrote "I'm a nigger!" across my chest. Then he wrote something on my back. When he was finished with that he took a larger brush and began to cover my arms and hands with white paint. I watched the brush going back and forth over the hair on my arms until every strand was covered and plastered down.

"Now," he said, "we're gonna let this paint dry so we can finish our experiment proper. So while we're waiting, you c'n give us a little dance."

They let go of my arms. My legs felt like cardboard buckling under me. The door out of the latrine was completely blocked. Two of them were in front of it and the other five were surrounding me.

"Come on, Sambo, give us a little dance!"

I just stood there, dazed, looking at them. My mouth was bone-dry. My throat was closed. I tried to talk but no words would come out. The PFC said, "Guess he don't understand English." They held me again while he picked up the brush and wrote on my forehead, grinning, taking pleasure in his work, doing it slowly, carefully. When he finished they dragged me back to the mirror. He'd written "Coon" in white paint that was dripping into my eyebrows.

"Now listen," he said, "you gotta understand me. When I tell you we wanta see you dance for us then you gotta believe we wanta see you dance. We're trying to be gentlemen about this. We figured you don't teach a hound nothin' by whipping him, so we're trying to be humane and psychological with you, but if we're takin' all this trouble on your education then you gotta show a little appreciation and keep us entertained durin' all this time we're givin' up for you. So, come on, Sambo, you be a good little coon and give us a dance."

They let go of my arms again. I couldn't move a muscle. The PFC punched me in the stomach. "Dance, Sambo." When I got

my wind back I started moving my feet and tapping, staring incredulous and numbed.

"That's better, Sambo. Keep it going. And a little faster. . . ."

I danced faster, stumbling over my own legs.

"Faster, Sambo, faster. . . ."

I moved as fast as I could. As I got near the PFC, he hit me
in the stomach again. "Didn't you hear me say faster, Sambo?"
They made me keep dancing for at least half an hour, until I
couldn't raise my feet off the ground.

"Okay, that's enough of that. You're not that good." He
turned to the others. "I really thought we were gonna have us a
treat, didn't you?" They all acted disappointed. "Well, guess we
can't be mad 'cause you don't dance good. Anyway we gotta
get back to your education."

I could feel the paint tightening on my skin.

"Now, we figure you've got the idea you're the same as
white 'cause you're in a uniform like us and 'cause you dance at
the shows and you go in and sit down with white men and because you think you got manners like a white man with your
flowers and candy you give our women. So we gotta explain to
you how you're not white and you ain't never gonna be white
no matter how hard you try. No matter what you do or think,
you can't change what you are, and what you are is black and
you better get it outta your head to mess around with white
women.

"Now lookit your arm. Looks white, don't it? Well, it ain't.
Watch and see." He poured turpentine on a rag and began wiping my arm in one spot. When my skin showed through the
paint he grinned. "There. Y'see? Just as black 'n ugly as ever!"

He rubbed some turpentine on his own arm. "See the difference? No matter how hard I keep rubbin', it's still white. So,
like I said, white is white and black is black." He poured the
rest of the turpentine down the drain.

"Okay, you ugly little nigger bastard. We're lettin' you off
easy this time. I mean we coulda been nasty and painted all the
rest of you, but we figured you're a smart nigger and you'll get

the idea fast, so because we're peace-lovin' fellas we don't wanta hurt you none, so we didn't do that. Now we're gonna be leaving you here but remember that we did you this big favor, see? And if you should decide to tell anybody anything 'bout our little lesson, well first of all we'd just have to admit we caught you makin' passes at the captain, and that sure wouldn't do neither of you no good, and then besides that we'd have to find you again and give you another lesson 'cept we'd have to try harder to make you understand, like maybe open up your skin a trifle and show you it's black under there too. So just take our little lesson in the spirit we meant and we're willin' to let bygones be bygones and you'll stay away from the captain. Right?"

Then I was alone. I looked at myself in one of the mirrors. I wanted to die. I sat on the floor and cried.

I stayed there for an hour, maybe two hours, I don't know, I lost track of time, trying to understand it. Why would they want to do this to me? I thought of a hundred questions—but no answers. I'd have given my life to hear my father say, "Hell, Poppa, they're just jealous of our act." I wanted to believe anything but that people could hate me this much.

The more the paint hardened, the more it drew on my skin. It was starting to pull the hairs on my arms and it itched terribly. I couldn't think of anyplace where I could find some turpentine. I tried to wipe some of the paint off with toilet paper but it tore and stuck to the paint and only made it worse. I hated going back to the barracks. Some of the guys would laugh and some would feel sorry for me and one would be as bad as the other. But I wanted Sergeant Williams to see me. I wanted to hear him tell me again, "You've got to fight with your brain."

I'd missed evening formation. Most of the camp was in the mess halls, so it was easy to sneak behind buildings back to the barracks. It was empty. I got my towel and aftershave lotion and went into the latrine. I poured half a bottle on the towel and rubbed until it hurt but it didn't help at all. There were voices outside, Sergeant Williams and some of the guys. I hid in the shower. When I heard the other guys' steps going toward their bunks I ducked into Sergeant Williams' room.

He closed the door. "Who did it?"

I shook my head.

"Don't be a fool. They'll be court-martialed and sent to the stockade for years. Nobody can get away with this."

I wasn't afraid. I just wanted it to be over. I'd get no satisfaction out of putting them in jail. If they were arrested there'd be a trial and everybody in camp would know about it. I just wanted to forget that it ever happened.

There was no pity in his face—just sadness. Not only for me but for the depth of what he with his wisdom could read into what had happened.

He left the room, cautiously, and sent someone to the motor pool for turpentine. Then he locked the door, soaked his towel, and began wiping the paint off my skin. For the next hour and a half he didn't say one word. I sat there naked to the waist until he was finished. Then he gave me soap and a brush and sent me to the shower room.

Bits of paint clung to my pores. I stood under the hot water brushing them out, rubbing until rashes of blood trickled to the surface, brushing, harder and harder, until I'd scraped the last speck of white out of my skin.

It wasn't lights-out yet but I got into bed. The guys were talking on all sides of me. I pulled the blanket over my head, trying to hear nothing. All I could think was, nobody, nobody in this world is ever going to do this to me again.

George made room for me to peek through the curtain. The general was sitting in the first row. The house was packed.

For the first time in eighteen years of performing I didn't want to go on. I scanned the faces waiting to be entertained. The redneck from my barracks was in the third row. How can you run out and smile at people who despise you? How can you entertain people who don't like you?

George was holding out his hand. I put mine in his and he

smiled, "Buddy, after they see our show I'm worried they're going to want us around for ten years." The music was two bars away from my cue. I took a deep breath and rushed on. I did my opening number, forcing myself to concentrate on the one thing I was out there to do: entertain the audience.

As I was taking my bow, enjoying the applause, absorbing the payoff for a month of night-and-day work, I glanced over to where the redneck was sitting. He wasn't applauding. Our eyes met and I caught something in his face that I'd never seen there before. It wasn't warmth—he was trying to show no recognition at all. At that moment, I knew that because of what I could do on a stage he could never again think "But you're still a nigger." I'd gotten to him. He'd found something of me in six minutes of my performance which he hadn't seen in the barracks in all those months.

My talent was the weapon, the power, the way for me to fight. It was the one way I might hope to affect a man's thinking.

I was bowing to the audience and smiling, by reflex, but my awareness of any outside happening was overwhelmed by the birth of potency surging through my being.

We played the show for a week and it was as though the spotlight erased all color. I could feel it in the way they looked at me, not in anything new that appeared in their faces, but in something old that was suddenly missing. Sometimes offstage I passed a guy I didn't know and he said, "Good show last night." My talent was giving me a pass which excluded me from their prejudice. I didn't hope for camaraderie. All I wanted was to walk into a room without hearing conversation slow down, and it was happening. I was developing an identity around camp and it was buying me a little chunk of peace.

The manager of the Chetwood, a small hotel in Los Angeles, seemed to be taking an hour to get them to the phone. Finally:

"Poppa? That you?"

"I'm out of the Army, Dad. I'm taking the next train."

". . . cut it out, Will. How c'n I hear what he said with you askin' what he said?"

"Hello, Massey. Get my clothes cleaned and pressed, I'm coming back into the act."

I left the PX and walked around the camp, remembering my first day in Cheyenne, waiting outside the barracks. I had a detached feeling about it now, almost as though it had happened to someone else. But it was me all right, and I wasn't about to forget it.

Prejudice had been crammed down my throat. I'd gone into the Army like a kid going to a birthday party, and they'd taught me well all that my father and Will, with the help of show business, had so lovingly kept from me.

I knew that above all things in the world I had to become so big, so strong, so important, that those people and their hatred could never touch me. My talent was the only thing that made me a little different from everybody else, and it was all that I could hope would shield me *because* I was different.

I'd weighed it all: What have I got? No looks, no money, no education. Just talent. What do I want? To be treated well. I want people to like me, and be decent to me. How do I get there? Only one way with what I have to work with. I've got to be a star! I have to be a star like another man has to breathe.

They were waiting for me in the Los Angeles station. They'd had no way of knowing what train I was on, so they'd met them all until I arrived. Their clothes were wrinkled from sitting around the station and they were dead tired, but they looked great to me.

At the Chetwood, I got out of my uniform and changed into one of my old suits. It fit perfectly. My father was sitting on the bed. He was looking at my wrist. "Where's your gold watch, Poppa?"

I still had it wrapped in paper. When he saw the smashed,

twisted parts, he looked at me, hurt, heartbroken. "How'd that happen?" He was staring at the watch he and Will had gone into hock to buy. "Gee, Poppa, you shoulda looked after a watch like this. It's valuable."

"I'm sorry, Dad. It got smashed on maneuvers."

I was silent for a few minutes, lost in thoughts of Jennings and the others like him, loathing them, yet grimly grateful to them for wising me up. My father was studying me, his eyes shadowed, questioning. His voice was quiet. "It wasn't no fun, huh, son?"

I shrugged a denial—"It was the Army"—and I turned away.

"Hey, Poppa?"

I looked around.

"Betcha I c'n make you laugh."

He put on his poker face and stared at me solemnly. I was suddenly terribly depressed, remembering how that had never failed to send me into hysterics and obscure any problems we had. All my life we'd just laughed and looked away from trouble.

The poker face grew even more solemn.

I forced a smile, then a laugh. There was a terrible, frustrated look in his eyes as he too realized that it couldn't work anymore.

Will came in and my father smiled as though he'd been waiting for him. "Poppa, here's your homecomin' surprise. We're set to go back to work as a trio. At four hundred a week."

Will nodded. "The way it come about is that we bumped into an old pal of ours, Arthur Silber. You won't remember, but we worked the same bills together till vaudeville went under. Today he's the biggest independent agent in the West. Soon as we hung up from your call we went over and saw him and he signed us for a big show he's putting together for the Japanese-American troops in Hawaii. We leave for Honolulu in ten days."

We shook hands three ways and went out for dinner. They

asked me about the Army and I told them the kind of stories they wanted to hear. They got a thrill out of hearing that I knew George M. Cohan, Jr., and I described the show we'd done. As I talked, I had to work half from memory, half from imagination. It was all yesterday, and all I could concentrate on was tomorrow.

8

Being in front of audiences, each of which was going to lift us closer and closer to the top, was a joy. We left Hawaii with almost a thousand dollars saved. I wanted to savor every indication of progress, so in the cab from the airport to Los Angeles I asked my father, "How about us moving into a better hotel?"

He looked at me like, yeah, let's live, and told the driver, "Make that the Morris over on Fifth Street."

We ran up the stairs, hardly feeling the weight of our bags, and stopped at my room. I pulled the string on the lightbulb hanging from the ceiling. It was the first room of my own I ever had. It was freshly painted and it had a private bathroom with a toilet and sink. My father glanced around happily. "Makes our old places look like San Quentin." He started down the hall to his own room and called back to me, "Here's the showers."

Toward the end of the week Mr. Silber said, "I'm sorry things aren't working out as fast as I'd expected. I hate to suggest it but I can put you into the Cricket Club here in L.A."

Will asked, "What's the money like?"

"Massey, that's the least of it. Who's gonna see us at the Cricket Club? My God, we played better places than that before I went into the Army."

Mr. Silber nodded sympathetically. "I know you did. And it's only two hundred fifty a week, but at least it'll pay the rent till things get rolling."

The door to my room was opening. The hotel manager's head appeared, then he pushed the door the rest of the way and stepped in, holding a passkey hanging by a chain from a wooden block. My father was behind him in pajamas and bathrobe. The manager left, shaking his head.

I took off my earphones and turned off the Woody Herman record I'd been listening to.

"Poppa, what in hell's goin' on here? The guy at the desk come by my room and says he's been knockin' at your door for ten minutes and he was gonna open your room to quiet you down." He looked at the drums I was holding between my knees. "When'd you start playin' bongos?"

"I picked 'em up this afternoon."

"What for?"

"I don't know, I figured I oughta know how to play 'em, maybe they'll work into the act somewhere. I'm sorry they got you out of bed. I was using the earphones so nobody'd hear the record, and I thought I was tapping the drums quietly."

He sat on the bed. "You feel like a little pinochle? Unless you're tired?"

"How the hell can I be tired?" I lit a cigarette and paced the room. "I don't get it, Dad. It's two weeks since we closed the Cricket and still not a word from Mr. Silber."

"He talked to Will today and it ain't a case of him not tryin'. The fact is clubs ain't fallin' all over themselves fightin' t'book us."

"You go back to bed, Dad. I don't feel much like playing cards."

He stood up. "It's almost five, Poppa. I wouldn't mess with the drums no more tonight."

I turned on the radio and lay there absorbing what sounded

like a hundred pieces playing the Axel Stordahl arrangement, swelling, softening, opening a path for Frank Sinatra's voice to come through singing "I'm going to buy a paper doll that I can call my own . . ." I appreciated his professionalism, the way all that music served as no more than a frame for his voice. He sang free, unencumbered, as easy as if he were in a shower, yet all the elements came together in a big-time sound that gave me chills.

He was "Frankie," "The Voice," and the "Bow Tie," he was "loved and idolized by millions." I read every word I could find about his records, his pictures, his long-term deals, his personal appearances, his homes, friends, the big openings he made bigger just by appearing. Everyone he knew, everything he did was lavish and spectacular. He personified the word "star."

The announcer was signing off the air. "Your Hit Parade has been broadcast from the NBC studios in Hollywood." I turned it off. "I'm going down there to see him next week."

"Hell, he ain't about to remember you and you ain't gonna get nowheres near him, anyway."

"I know, but I want to watch him work."

My best chance for a ticket was in the servicemen's line, so I got my Army uniform out of a box, ironed it, and went down to NBC three hours early to be sure I'd get in.

After the show I hurried to the stage door. There must have been five hundred kids ahead of me, waiting for a look at him. When he appeared, the crowd surged forward like one massive body ready to go through the side of the building if necessary. They were screaming, fainting, pushing, waving pencils and papers in the air. I stood on tiptoe trying to see him. God, he looked like a star. He wasn't much older than a lot of us but he was so calm, like we were all silly kids and he was a man, sure of himself, completely in control. He acted as if he didn't know there were hundreds of papers being waved at him. He concentrated on one at a time, signing it, smiling, and going to the next. He took my paper and looked at me. "Don't I know you?"

"Well, we were on the bill with you in Detroit five years ago."

"What's your name?"

"Sammy Davis, Jr."

"Didn't you work with your old man and another guy?"

"That's us. Remember?" Oh, God! Obviously he remembered.

"Yeah, sure. I hate 'Sammy.' I'll call you Sam. Why don't you come back next week and see the show. I'll leave a ticket for you." The kids were pressing toward him, shoving papers in his face for autographs. He touched me on the arm. "See y'next week, Sam."

I was looking for a box office when an NBC guard walked over to me. "Hey, you! The end of the line."

"But Frank Sinatra left a ticket for me." Even I was struck by how ridiculous it sounded.

The guard was giving me a "Yeah, sure" look, but he took me over to the Guest Relations desk. They went through a stack of envelopes. There was nothing for me. I was almost out the door when a uniformed page came running up to me and asked my name. He looked at an envelope. "Then this must be for you." It had one word on it. "Sam."

He ushered me through a private door to a seat in the front row of the reserved section. And after the show he removed me from the line that was inching up the aisle. "Mr. Sinatra would like you to come to his dressing room."

It was at least five times the size of my room at the Morris, with a bed, easy chair, couch, icebox, bar, and phonograph. I could see into the tiled bathroom. It had a stall shower and a bathtub, and the rich, thick towels were initialed FS. Someone gave me a Coke. Important-looking people were coming in.

"Beautiful show, Francis . . ."

". . . that last song, Frank."

"You were in great voice, baby, great!"

They were sponsors and NBC executives and they introduced themselves to me as if I must be Somebody because I was in there too.

He had the aura of a king about him and that's how people were treating him. Anything he said made them laugh. And me too. Half the talk was inside jokes about the business, jokes I didn't begin to understand, but just being there was so exciting that everything he said seemed wonderful and funny. I kept thinking, "I can speak to Frank Sinatra and he'll hear me." But I couldn't think of anything clever enough to say, so I just watched him, smiling and laughing at his every word.

He didn't say anything directly to me and I was beginning to wonder if he remembered who I was and that he'd sent for me, but as he was leaving he turned to me. "Hey, Sam. Maybe next week you'll come and watch rehearsal." He put his arm around my shoulder and we walked out the stage door together and into the mob of screaming kids. He was reaching for his pen to sign autographs. He smiled at me and said over the uproar around us, "So long, Sam. Keep in touch."

When I got back to my room, Will was waiting for me. He said, "Glad you're back, Sammy. I was just telling Big Sam there's no sense just sitting here not even making expenses, so I called Joe Daniels and he's set us for a tour of the North at two hundred fifty a week."

"But, Massey, it's the same dead end—we'll be *buried* there. Who'll see us? We need . . ." I stopped, knowing that I'd hurt him, that he'd expected me to be glad just to be working. "I'm sorry, Massey, you're right."

My father came into the dressing room and flopped onto a chair. "Well, I covered every street downtown. Nothin'! Tomorrow I'll go back over to Mrs. Clark's and see if she's expectin' anything to open up. Meantime, we'll have to sleep in here."

Will asked, "You mean there's nothing in the whole city of Spokane?"

"Ain't that many colored rooming houses to start with."

"What about a hotel?"

"Ain't a single colored hotel around."

Colored side of town? Colored rooming house, colored ho-tels? Colored, colored, colored! And the way they were accept-ing it, so matter-of-factly. "Whaddya mean *colored* rooming house? Why must it always be colored rooming houses and col-ored hotels . . . ?"

"Now, Poppa, you know better'n this."

"I do like hell! Why do we have to live *colored* lives?" I was out of my chair, pacing our dressing room. "Y'mean we have to let people say, 'You're colored, so you gotta sleep in your dress-ing room'? Where, Dad? Where do we sleep? On the god-damned floor?"

"Now, Poppa, that's how it is, and no use fightin' it. That's how people are."

"Nobody has to tell me about people. I found out how they are. And it ain't 'cause they're jealous we're in show business." As I was saying it I was sorry, but the heat was pouring out of my body. "I'll get us a room. In the whitest goddamned hotel in town."

As I spun through the revolving door, I glanced at the clean lobby, the uniformed bellboys, and the elevators. Yeah! I saun-tered up to the front desk and practically yawned. "I'd like three single rooms for the next ten days. We're appearing in the show downtown . . ."

"I'm terribly sorry, sir, but we're filled. There isn't a va-cancy. The manager had to turn his own personal suite over to a guest, a steady guest who arrived unexpectedly . . ."

I'd known it would happen, yet I hadn't really *believed* it would.

". . . swamped. Truly swamped. Busiest we've seen it in . . ."

My air of showbiz and world traveler gone, I stood there staring at him. A moment before, it had been impersonal, I was a nuisance to be handled as he'd handled others before me, but I wasn't taking the gentle way out, playing the game, smiling:

"Well, thank you," like I'd tried and lost; and now he began perspiring around his forehead, doing "nervous hotel clerk" bits, coughing, looking around for the assistant manager and pretending to check the list of rooms. I guess this is what I'd wanted—to make it hard for him, to embarrass him. But there was no satisfaction.

The revolving door seemed so much heavier as I pushed my way to the outside.

". . . nervy nigger wanted a room. Some crust." A bellboy was telling the story to the doorman and he didn't care that I'd heard him. "Go on," he said, "get outta here. Go back where you belong." The face wasn't grinning or leering or mocking, it just looked at me with the contempt you have for something you dispose of with a DDT spray gun.

All the strength in the world was in my body as I hurtled toward that face and hit it.

I was sitting on the ground smelling that awful, dry, dusty smell like I had when Jennings broke my nose. The doorman helped me up and I walked back to the theater. I should have been embarrassed returning like this after all my big talk, but all I could think was that my nose was broken and I had to keep the blood from staining my shirt.

We made beds on the floor out of canvas tarpaulins, used our overcoats for blankets, and I made a pillow out of a rolled-up pair of pants. All I'd accomplished was to get my damned nose broken, so that for at least two weeks I'd be limited in what I could do onstage. I'd tried to hit an idea with my fists. I couldn't make that mistake again. Every drop of my physical and mental strength had to be concentrated on just one thing.

At breakfast I told Will, "I'd like to put in impressions of Jimmy Cagney and Durante and Edward G. Robinson."

He put down his coffee cup. "Sammy, what's wrong with you? Impressions of *white* people?"

"Why not?"

"You just can't." He was shaking his head. "They'll think you're making fun of them. No colored performer ever did white people in front of white people."

"But I did them in the Army and they went over great."

"That's a whole other story. Those soldiers are hungry for shows, plus the fact of getting 'em free, but this is show business and when the people put down their money they don't want to sit there wonderin' if you're trying to insult 'em. You just stick with Satchmo and B and Stepin Fetchit. Don't fool with those others, not for white audiences. You can't get away with something like that."

"Massey, I won't argue. You're the boss of the act. But all that should matter is if they're good or not."

"I don't mean t'say I told you so, but you also thought we wouldn't have t'sleep on the floor of our dressing room 'cause it wasn't right. Sammy, what's right and what's wrong don't always have say over what is."

In Seattle, after our fourth show, the musicians would sit in with a college band run by a kid named Quincy Jones. I went with them and we played, sang, and experimented until dawn.

There was a note under my door when I got home one morning. "Wake me whenever you come in. Everything's fine. Will."

I heard his bedsprings creak, then his slippers swooshing across the floor. He opened the door, smiling. "Go get Big Sam."

I looked from one to the other. "Okay, now we have a pajama party. What's it all about?"

Will said, "We're booked as the opening act at El Rancho Vegas in Las Vegas, Nevada. For five hundred dollars a week." He paused. "Mose Gastin, *now* tell me we're going to be buried."

The trade papers were bursting with news about Las Vegas. It was starting to become a show town. El Rancho and the Last Frontier were the first luxury hotels and there was talk about more being planned to go up near them.

My father was heating coffee on the hot plate. "The word is they're payin' acts twice as much as anywheres else. Free suites and food tabs." Will said, "They're out to make it the number one show town." I listened to them like I was watching a Ping-Pong game. ". . . flyin' customers in . . ." "*Variety* says . . ." "The whole business is watching what's happening in Vegas."

"Massey, I'm going to do those impressions."

The band was the biggest we'd ever worked with, the floor of the stage was springy and slick, the lighting was the most modern I'd ever seen. I was standing next to the stage manager. "Do I have it right about our rooms, that they're a part of our deal here?"

The manager came over to us as we finished rehearsing. "Sorry. We can't let you have rooms here. House rules. You'll have to find a place in the—uh, on the other side of town."

I picked up our suitcases. "Let's go, Dad, Will."

The hotels we'd passed in the town itself looked awful compared to El Rancho but even they were out of bounds to us. The cabdriver said, "There's a woman name of Cartwright over in Westside takes in you people."

It was Tobacco Road. A three- or four-year-old child, naked, was standing in front of a shack made of wooden crates and cardboard. The cab stopped in front of one of the few decent houses. A woman was standing in the doorway. "You boys with one of the shows? Well, I got three nice rooms for you."

When she told us the price Will almost choked. "But that's twice what it would cost at El Rancho Vegas."

"Then why don't you go live at El Rancho Vegas?"

"Pay her the money, Massey. It's not important."

Will counted out the first week's rent. My father smiled sardonically. "If the ofays don't get us, then our own will."

My father followed me into my room. "Not half bad." He sat down and I could feel him watching me. I threw a shirt into a drawer and slammed it closed. "Dad, I don't give a damn about their lousy rooms, I really don't. Right now, the only thing in this world that I want is their stage!"

As I danced, I did Satchmo. I shuffled across the stage like Stepin Fetchit. Then I spun around and came back doing the Jimmy Cagney walk to center stage and stood there, facing my father and Will, doing Cagney's legs-apart stance, the face, and then "All right . . . you dirty rats!" For a moment there was no sound from out front—then they roared.

In the wings Will said, "I'm glad I was wrong, Sammy." My father hugged me. "Poppa, you was *great!*" He put me down. "Whaddya say we get dressed after the next show and go look around the casino. I got fifty dollars that's bustin' t'grow into a hundred."

We went out the stage door and around the building. The desert all around us was dark but the casino was blazing with light. The door opened and as some people came out there was an outpour of sounds such as I'd never before heard: slot machines clanging, dealers droning, a woman shrieking with joy—and behind it all, a background of the liveliest, happiest music I'd ever heard. As I held the door open for my father, my head went in all directions to slot machines, dice tables, waiters rushing around with drinks, a man carrying a tray full of silver dollars.

I saw a hand on my father's shoulder. A deputy sheriff was holding him, shaking his head.

We rode to Mrs. Cartwright's in silence. I continued on downtown to a movie theater, where for a few hours I could lose myself in other people's lives.

I was waiting for the movie to begin when a hand gripped my arm like a circle of steel, yanking me out of my seat, half dragging me out to the lobby. "What're you, boy? A wise guy?" He was wearing a star badge and the big Western hat. His hand slapped across my face. "Speak up when I talk to you!"

"What'd I do?"

"Don't bull me, boy. You know the law."

When I explained I'd just gotten to town and had never been there before, he pointed to a sign. "Coloreds sit in the last three rows. You're in Nevada now, not New York. Mind our rules and you'll be treated square. Go on back and enjoy the movie, boy."

I had no choice but to go back in. A Mickey Rooney picture was on. After a while I glanced up to catch a song he was doing and I looked away, still steaming. Then I looked up again and I forgot the cop and the theater and the rules and I was dancing across the campus in a college musical. An hour later I was Danny Kaye git-gat-gattling my way through the Army. Then the lights went on and I was sitting in the last row of an almost empty movie theater, and I was a Negro in a Jim Crow town.

There was no bus or train out of Vegas until morning but I gladly paid fifty dollars to a musician for a lift into L.A. an hour after we closed. He dropped me a block from the Morris and I walked toward the hotel. Everywhere I looked were the dregs of Los Angeles, as if every pimp and dope peddler in town had moved onto Fifth Street. I reached the Morris but kept walking, almost running. I saw an empty cab and ran into the street to flag him down.

When we'd gone a few blocks, I began to feel the pressure easing.

"Made up your mind yet, buddy?"

"Yes. The Sunset Colonial, please." Lots of performers stayed there and I knew they'd take me. It was on Sunset Strip, in Hollywood, and it was more expensive but I knew that no matter what I had to do—or do without—I was never going back to Fifth Street.

I went over to the Frank Sinatra show and sent my name in. I was "the kid" to him and he let me watch rehearsals every week. I sat around the studio, inhaling the atmosphere of the Big Time like it was clean, delicious, fresh air. And I met people.

Through Jesse Price, a drummer, I made a connection at Capitol Records and got a contract for fifty dollars a side.

Will shrugged. "You didn't get much of a deal. The thing to

have is a royalty that'd come to a nickel apiece for every record they sell."

"Massey, when I'm Bing Crosby I'll ask for royalties. Right now what I want is this opening."

At the studio, I listened to the band running through the music: thirty-two bars of clichés, with all the musical riffs lifted from other people's hits. The conductor was swinging his baton with all the enthusiasm of a guy painting a house, and the band of staff musicians who ground out one session after another for no-names like me was playing like I was number 428. I knew I was lucky just to be getting the chance but I couldn't help hearing the contrast between this and the fresh, vital sound of the Hit Parade band.

It was 1946 and everybody else was rich and happy, tearing up their ration stamps and ordering their first new cars in five years. We, however, were bringing down the National Prosperity Average. We'd left L.A., plodding our way across the country, barely making expenses at the same old clubs, finally limping into New York and up to Harlem, where Mama was still on relief. We were a great big help, starving on occasional one-nighters and listening to Jack Eigen telling us he was at the goddamned Copa.

My father was tapping *Variety* with the back of his hand. "Accordin' to this, the Chicago clubs are usin' acts by the hundreds. The sayin' is 'You can burp and get booked.' "

"It's a long walk, Dad." I was skimming through *Metronome*, hoping maybe Capitol had taken an ad. Then I stood up and bowed. "*Metronome* has picked me, your son and heir, as 'The Most Outstanding New Personality of the Year.' Plus, 'The Way You Looked Tonight' has been chosen Record of the Year."

He read it and we screamed with laughter. He took an iron washer out of his pocket. It was the size of a quarter and we'd been using them to get cigarettes out of machines. He stood.

"Mr. Davis, I presents you with the first Iron Record ever given out in music. It's a honor which means: you sings good even if you sells bad."

I went downtown to *Metronome* to thank them, hoping they'd write more about me. I saw Barry Ulanov and George Simon, the editors, and sure enough they said they'd like to do a story on me, but they suggested I ask Billy Eckstine, who was playing the Paramount, to pose for a picture with me to give the story name value. He was a friend of the family and it was embarrassing to ask this kind of favor, but I called him.

He posed with me the next afternoon between shows and I started to leave. "Thanks a lot, B. I really appreciate it."

"Thanks for what? C'mon up and sit with me awhile." I followed him to the star dressing room. We had coffee and he asked how things were going for us. "You meeting the rent?"

"We're hungry, B."

He shook his head compassionately. "It's rough."

I thought about asking him for a loan. Pride is great but Mama and my father were at home with an empty icebox and not twenty cents between them, and I knew it would be like twelve times Christmas if I came back with a few dollars for food. "B, if you could lend me five dollars, I'd sure appreciate it."

He looked at his watch, a gold-and-diamond one that must have cost $500. "Come on downstairs and watch the show."

I stood in the wings waiting for him to go on. I shouldn't have asked him. Maybe he was broke, or maybe he just didn't want to lend me any money. It seemed that it would be nothing to him but you never know about people when it comes to money. He'd been great about taking the picture but that hadn't cost him anything. He was onstage and I could see the spotlight bouncing off a diamond ring he was wearing. We could eat on that for a year . . . he's got a helluva nerve keeping me on the string like this for a few lousy dollars, humiliating me, making me stand here like a moocher. It's a lesson I won't forget: keep your problems to yourself unless you know the guy you're telling them to is going to help you. I started to walk out, to show him I didn't need him. But I did need him.

I watched him work. He was everything I was not: tall and good-looking and sure of himself, and he had every right to be. He was a giant in the business, as hot as the news yet to come, and they were packing the place to see him. Everything he wore was made to order.

As he came off I said, "Great show, B. Thanks a lot for the picture. I've gotta cut and get uptown now."

"Here, wait a minute, you forgot this."

I left, hating myself for misjudging him, disgusted with myself for being so nowhere that I had to bum a few dollars from a man I didn't even know that well. When I was on the street I took it out of my pocket. It was a hundred-dollar bill. He'd known we were in trouble, but he had the sensitivity not to show it by offering me money. Instead he'd opened the subject so I could ask him if I chose to.

We hit Chicago laughing and scratching and ready to go. Will went out every day, from club to club, agent to agent, but we might as well have been out of town. People were standing in line for entertainment but after two months of stagnating at the old Ritz Hotel on Chicago's South Side we still hadn't been able to get on a stage.

The Ritz was a real theatrical hotel and the three of us sat around the lobby every day with other performers like in a scene from a corny M-G-M musical. Will pointed to a newspaper ad. "I see where Dick and Gene Wesson opened downtown. Damned fine billing, too." A pleasant nostalgia crossed his face. "Remember back in the thirties when we were workin' the *World's Fair Vanities* through Maine, Massachusetts, and Canada . . ."

I looked around the lobby at groups of performers clustered together having the same kind of talks. I couldn't stand the sight of all that failure lumped together. "I'm going upstairs."

My father stood up too, and spoke loudly, for effect. "Yeah, might as well go get washed up for dinner." We shared a Mr. Goodbar and a So-Grape.

I turned on the radio hoping that I'd hear one of my records. I listened to Frankie Laine's "That's My Desire" for about the tenth time that day. The same man who used to sing at Billy Berg's, the same talent, the same style, but from one month to the next he'd become a star, gone from $20 a Sunday to $5,000 a week. The disc jockey said, "That's it, folks, the biggest-selling piece of wax in America today. And here he is in person, *Frankie Laine*. Frankie, how does it feel to be sitting on top of the world?"

I snapped off the radio. "We've gotta get the hell out of this town. We can't just sit around mildewing in the damned lobby. If we've got any sense at all we'll go see the Wessons. Let's ask 'em outright if they'll lend us enough to get us out of town."

Into the pocket they went and gave us a hundred dollars. And that wasn't enough. The Wessons' manager, Sam Stefel, also managed Mickey Rooney, who'd just come out of the Army and was putting together a show to tour the RKO circuit. They called Stefel in Boston and got him to use us on the bill as the opening act.

9

Mickey Rooney walked into the Grand Ballroom of the Copley Plaza Hotel at twelve o'clock sharp. Will nudged me and pointed to his watch. "Now that's a pro for you." I got a light-headed feeling when I saw him come in with that go-go-go walk, just like he did in the movies. He faced the company and said, "Hi, my name is Mickey Rooney!" Then he started shaking hands, saying hello to us one by one.

I thought: it's nice of him not to take the attitude that he's a big star and everybody knows who he is; it was so warm for somebody that important and that famous to say, Hi, I'd like to meet you and this is my name. Yeah. When I make it, when I can walk into a room and everybody will know who I am just by looking at me, then I'll say, "Hi, my name is Sammy Davis, Jr. . . ."

He was standing in front of me, his hand out.

"Hi, my name is Sammy Davis, Jr." Oh, God! I tried to recover. "My name's Sammy, Mr. Rooney."

"The name is Mickey." He looked at me and shook his head. "Damn! I *never* find anybody who's shorter than me. *Everybody's* taller. Even you. And you're a midget!"

He ran through a single he was going to be doing, then the production numbers with the girls, songs from the M-G-M musicals he'd made with Judy Garland. After rehearsal he told Mr. Stefel, "I want Sam to work with me in the act." He turned to me. "What can you do besides the dancing?"

"I play drums, a little trumpet, I do some impressions. . . ."

"You're kidding! Who do you do?"

"Well, I've been doing Danny Kaye. The 'Melody in 4F' thing."

Sam Stefel cut in, "*You'll* do all the impressions, Mickey. They were hired to dance. We bought a dance act and we want a dance act. You'll do all the impressions and that's final."

On opening night, Mickey came to our dressing room and motioned for me to come out in the hall. "Look, Sam, about that Danny Kaye impression, at least sneak it in tonight till we can make it a regular thing. Do it over your dance for the first show when the critics are there so they'll get to see it." He ducked down the stairs before I could thank him.

The tempo of the first notes of our music was a fast and furious rat-a-tat machine-gun speed, and we never slowed down for the ten minutes we were on. And in the middle of it, I was doing Danny Kaye's git-gat-gattle better than I'd ever done it. We worked so desperately that it was like our feet never touched the ground until we were in the wings. We went back for our bow and were rushing off when Mickey walked on. He was the first man I ever saw walk onto a stage without being introduced. When the audience saw him, the applause doubled but he didn't acknowledge it, as though it were all for us. He called me back and I did a little step with him. He was pointing me up, showing his fans that he liked me so that automatically they'd like me too.

I was going to bed at four in the morning when the landlord pounded on my door. He was half asleep and burning mad. "There's a damned fool on the phone who keeps saying he's Mickey Rooney. I hung up on him twice but he keeps calling back. Now you get down there and tell him if he calls again . . ."

Mickey was tremendously excited. He had the reviews and he read them to me, not what they said about him, he read only what they'd written about us. "The best dance act to hit Boston in years." "Berry Brothers, Nicholas Brothers better forget it!" "The kid in the middle is funny!"

I stood in the wings watching every show Mickey did, soaking up his tremendous knowledge of the business. He was the multitalented guy who had to do everything: sing, dance, comedy, impressions, drums, trumpet, everything! And he did them all well. He'd do a vignette and make the people cry or laugh as he chose. Show after show I watched him devastate audiences with his talent and his energy. Mickey was the performer I admired more than any in the world.

As we left the theater one night he looked at the sign out front: "The Mickey Rooney Show" with pictures of him in different poses, and told Sam Stefel, "I want some of those pictures out. Instead of them, put 'The Will Mastin Trio, starring Sammy Davis, Jr.' "

He was taking space away from himself to make room for me. I tried to thank him but he cut me off: "Let's not get sickening about this."

A few weeks later Mickey told me, "We've got to close for a month. M-G-M wants me to do another Andy Hardy thing. But when that's finished I'm going to do a script called *Killer McCoy*. It's a remake of the old Robert Taylor picture *The Crowd Roars* and I want you as the fighter. I think you could play the hell out of it. I'll talk to them as soon as I get out there."

Our trio played two weeks in Reno. Mr. Silber and his son Arthur came out and I spent every spare minute with Art working out fake fights, stunt-man style, with grunts, groans, and falling over tables, all the things I'd have to know for the picture.

When we picked up the tour Mickey had no news on the picture yet. We were back in our routine of songwriting, playing gin between shows, and me standing in the wings at every performance. There were so many tangible things I could get from watching Mickey work: the use of a topical joke, using the people in the show for various effects, the little "class" touches that he had. But his greatest power was his ability to "touch" the audience. When Mickey was onstage, he might have been pulling levers labeled "Cry!" and "Laugh!" But it wasn't only because he was a fine actor, there was something more, and night after night I tried to understand it.

I asked my father, "How do you *touch* an audience?"

"Well, I been in this business all my life and you go out there and you do your show the best you can and if you're good you'll touch 'em and if you're bad they'll know it."

Will didn't understand either. They tried to give me answers but they were as much as saying, "A bird flies by flapping his wings." But how does he flap them that makes it different than when I flap my arms? How come I don't fly too? How did Mickey get inside of every person who watched him so that he wasn't just another performer to them? What was it about him that made them care so much?

We were at the Loew's State in New York, our last stop on the tour, and Mickey and I were playing gin in his dressing room. "Sam, about the picture. I heard from them last night. It's out." I kept shuffling the cards, trying not to react and make it tougher for him. He said, "I could give you a lot of crap about it, but honest-open M-G-M doesn't want to use you. They fought it tooth and nail. They don't know you and they don't know if you can act." He looked at me with sadness. "I don't think they want a colored fellow. They told me, 'Use a Mexican kid, it's less problems.' "

I walked uptown after our last show that night. Knowing Mickey, I could imagine how he'd fought for me with his position as he had with his fists, but still, someone who'd never met me, never seen me, could throw the whole dream down the drain by saying, "Use a Mexican kid. It's less problems." It wasn't "How good is he?" There was no "Let him do a screen test." Just plain, cold "No. He's a problem."

We were booked right into the Strand Theater on Broadway with Billie Holiday and Count Basie. Will came up to Mama's the day before the opening. "I just stopped by the theater and they said we gotta cut down to twelve minutes."

I slammed my fork onto the table. "The hell with that! Let someone else cut their act. We're doing twenty minutes."

"Now, Sammy, don't talk foolish. We're only the opening act. We can't get away with trying to run the whole show. . . ."

"Will's right, Poppa. We gotta go out there and give 'em twelve minutes like they want and not look for no trouble."

"Trouble? I just want to be seen."

"Who'll see us if we get canceled after the first show, Sammy?"

"Nobody'll cancel us if we're good enough."

We did twenty minutes. The audience was still applauding. Billie Holiday was waiting to follow us and I was embarrassed to face her, but she smiled and took my arm. "Come on, little man, you'd better carry me on or they'll never calm down."

One look at the house manager's face and I knew Will had been right, and now, as the ax was about to fall, I couldn't believe my own nerve.

"Where the hell do you guys get off disobeying my orders? What kind of a honky-tonk do you think this is?"

Will stepped forward. "We're sorry. We really are. We'll cut it right down to twelve minutes. . . ."

"Well, you're damned good'n lucky you went over so big. Keep the act as is and we'll cut eight minutes somewhere else."

I felt like a lion, fit and ready for the jungle, more powerful, more able to meet the world than I'd ever felt in my life. Will mopped his brow like "phew" and my father fell into a chair and sighed, "We got lucky that time." I was reeling drunk from the success of it. "That wasn't luck! This is how it's gonna be for us from now on. We're gonna take what we want. We can be the dirtiest bastards in the world as long as we've got what that audience wants."

"Wait a minute, Sammy . . ."

"Wait nothing. What we just saw is how life is. If you 'make it' you can have anything! But if you don't you can be the nicest guy in the world and they won't book you to play the men's room at intermission. Well, I'm gonna make it. And when I do what'll you bet they'll like me? They'll like me even if they hate my guts!"

Neither of them said another word. They were looking at me as though seeing me for the first time. I think I was seeing myself for the first time. And I liked it. I liked not "taking it" and I liked winning.

We left the Strand on an express train and rode it right into the yards. We wound up in Boston at a sailor haven called the Silver Dollar Bar for $110 a week. We floundered around New England, back to the world of two-dollar hotel rooms and deadly dull dates which I'd really believed we'd seen for the last time, as far away from "New York" as we'd ever been.

When you've never had a break you can say, "All we need is that one big break." But Mickey had been our break, he'd given us every opportunity, so there could be no saying, "Wait'll the big bookers get a load of our act." They'd seen us, the critics had seen us, and the people had seen us. And they'd all liked us. But as soon as we were off they forgot we'd ever happened.

We laid off at Mama's and every morning we'd go downtown to a booking office. When a call came in for an opening dance act, we were one of ten or twenty or a hundred who could fill the bill, so we'd sit there hoping it was we who had the strongest connection. And I was beginning to understand that's how it was going to be all our lives. We weren't an attraction that drew people to a theater, we were just a prop, a tool to open another man's show fast and lively, interchangeable with countless others just as fast and just as lively. We were one of a million like us in a world that was buying tickets to see one of a kind.

Lucky Millander's band was doing the stage show at the Strand. A colored comedy act was just going on as I sat down. They were pros, funny as hell, and I was laughing, but I wasn't enjoying myself. Something was bothering me. I listened to them saying, "Ladies and Gen'men, we's gwine git our laigs movin', heah." They were talking "colored" as Negro acts always did. I'd heard it a thousand times before, but for the first time it sounded wrong. They were labeling themselves. I watched them doing all the colored clichés, realizing that we were doing exactly the same thing. We'd always done them. They were an automatic part of our onstage personalities. It was the way people expected Negro acts to be, so that's the way we were. But now it was like I was seeing it for the first time and it offended me. Why don't they say "Gentlemen"? Why must it be "Gen'men"? If the joke is funny won't they still laugh if we call them "Gentlemen"? They don't expect every Jew to have a long nose, not every Irish performer has to do "Pat and Mike" jokes, so why must every Negro be an Uncle Tom?

Then I saw the trap of it: they were making no personal contact with the audiences. None! I saw that most Negro performers work in a cubicle. They'd run on, sing twelve songs, dance, and do jokes—but not to the people. The jokes weren't done like Milton Berle was doing them, to the audience, they were done between the men onstage, as if they didn't have the right to communicate with the people out front. It was totally the reverse of the way Mickey played, directly to the people, talking to them, kidding them, communicating with them.

By a lifetime of habit, by *tradition*, I too had been cementing myself inside a wall of anonymity. It didn't matter how many instruments I learned to play, how many impressions I learned to do, or how much I perfected them—we were still doing *Holiday in Dixieland*—still a flash act. That was how we set ourselves up, so that was how the audience would see us. I'd come offstage when I caught a look at myself in the dressing-room mirror. I looked again, staring at my zoot suit. It was horrible! I'd thought of it as a timely costume which got big laughs but I was doing exactly what I despised in other Negro performers—making people laugh *at* me. I was saying "Gen'men" with those clothes just as loud and clear as if I'd come shuffling on singing "Old Black Joe." I tore the suit off, unable to get out of it fast enough, and dropped it in the trash can.

I strode the floor of Will's room for hours, explaining everything I'd seen, everything I felt and wanted to do. He was gazing past me. "Okay, Sammy. The only thing is I've been doing an act one way all my life, the way I know, and making a living. Only a fool would throw away what he's lived on for forty years. But I won't stop you from trying new things if you believe in them. Maybe you're right that we've been sneaking in the impressions instead of framing them to get the most out of them. Take a straight eight minutes in the middle of the act and use it however you want. But your father and me'll do what we know and always did."

We were up North playing Portland when Will received a wire: "OPEN CAPITOL THEATER NEW YORK NEXT MONTH, FRANK SINATRA SHOW. THREE WEEKS, $1,250 PER. DETAILS FOLLOW. HARRY ROGERS." We passed that telegram back and forth like three drunks working out of the same bottle.

My father was gazing at it, "I ain't lookin' no gift horse in the mouth, but I'm damned if I can figure how come us."

Will shrugged. "Sinatra always has a colored act on the bill."

"Yeah, Will, but why *us*? I mean, with all the powerhouse acts around like Moke and Poke, Stump and Stumpy, the Nicholas Brothers, the Berry Brothers . . ."

"We're as powerhouse as the next and I guess Harry Rogers did a good job of agenting."

I stopped listening and counted the days on a calendar. We had three weeks to get ready. I could feel myself on the stage with our new act, smooth, organized, everything displayed to give it the best possible chance to go over—and at the Capitol Theater with Frank Sinatra where the *world* would have a chance to see us!

Alan Zee, the general manager of the Capitol, came over to us at rehearsal. "You ran sixteen minutes. Gotta cut it. Too long. Drop the jokes, drop the impressions, all we want is the flash dancing. Just give me six minutes. No more."

I ran after him. "Is there any chance of taking a little time out of Lorraine and Rognan?"

"Just cut your act. Don't worry about anybody else's."

"But, Mr. Zee . . ." He went through a door and closed it.

My father and Will walked over to me. "What the hell, Poppa. You'll get another chance." He put his arm around me. Will said, "I know how you feel, Sammy, but I hope you know that you can't get away with what you did at the Strand. Not here. Not for twelve hundred fifty a week."

The orchestra played the first bars of "Night and Day," the pit rose with Skitch Henderson conducting, the curtains opened, Frank Sinatra was onstage, and the kids began screaming hysterically and leaping up and down as though the seats were hot. He sang three numbers to get the show started. Then he said, "We've got three cats here who really swing and they're all too much but keep your eye on the little cat in the middle, because he's my boy! Here they are, 'The Will Mastin Trio and Sammy Davis, Jr.' "

Frank didn't just say, "Well, you're working and that's fine." He had our names up out front, he was wonderful to my family, and he had me to his dressing room between almost every show. At dinnertime he'd take me out to eat with him. Every time we stepped through the stage door there were hundreds of kids waiting for him. They even screamed at me, "Oh! You touched him. Let me touch you." Day after day they were in line for tickets at six in the morning, holding bags of sandwiches.

I stood in the wings at every performance watching him work. He'd walk to the microphone like he had nothing better to do, arriving there at exactly the moment his cue came up. As he rolled through a song I could see him almost smiling as he got to certain phrases, knowing the bobby-soxers were going to swoon as he sang them, and they did, as if he'd pressed a button. His effect on the audience was awesome: they held their breath during the quiet moments of a song as if they'd rather stop breathing than break the spell. Like Mickey, he was touching them, taking a mass of people and making them care.

"Pretty great, isn't he?"

Sidney Piermont, the head of all Loew's booking, was standing beside me. I whispered back, "He's unbelievable, Mr. Piermont."

We walked toward the dressing rooms together. "Your trio is doing a fine job."

"Thank you very much, sir, for booking us."

"Don't thank me." He smiled. "I fought against hiring you." He saw that I didn't understand. "You were booked strictly because Frank insisted on you. When I was lining up the show I asked him who he wanted. He said, 'Get Skitch to put the band together.' Then for the opening act I suggested the Berry Brothers and he said, 'Yeah, fine. No, wait a minute. There's a kid who comes to my radio show when he's in town, he works with his family, his name is Sam something. Use him.' Frank insisted, so I said, 'All right, Frank, if you want 'em you got 'em. How much do you want to give them?' 'Make it twelve hundred fifty.' Well, that was ridiculous. I argued, 'We can get the Nicholas Brothers for that kind of money and they've even got a movie going for them. They're hot.' He said, 'I don't want the Nicholas Brothers. I want Sam and his family. Twelve hundred fifty. That's it.' "

Frank had never even hinted at it. "Glad we're working together." Like it was a surprise to him too.

He invited the cast to a Thanksgiving dinner the day before closing. He had a basement rehearsal hall converted into a party room and his mother sent over pots and pots of delicious homemade Italian food. We were eating our heads off when somebody yelled, "Hey, Sammy, do the thing for Frank like you did for us." I'd been playing around with an impression of him. I hadn't done one since the Army but being with him all the time I was able to catch the physical things he does, his hands, his mouth, and his shoulders, as well as the voice.

He said, "Let's see it, Sam." He had no idea what it was and I was afraid he'd be offended. But he laughed. "Beautiful, beautiful. It's a scream. Listen, I want to talk to you tomorrow."

The next afternoon in his dressing room he asked, "Why don't you sing?"

"Well, I sing when I do impressions. As far as straight singing goes I made a few sides, but Capitol's melting 'em down for candles. I don't have a style of my own."

"Let me hear some of the impressions." I did a few and he began shaking his head. "You're ridiculous if you don't put those in the act. And you definitely should sing. Straight. You've got the voice, work on it, develop a style. And you should do as many of those impressions as you can. Do them all."

After the closing show, the members of the company came to his dressing room to say goodbye. I stood off to the side thinking how a star of Frank's stature had taken the time and thought to help me. We were so many miles apart in every way that it was hard to imagine why he would reach out for me as he had. When the last of them were gone I tried to let him know how grateful I was.

He gave me an "Are you kidding?" look and we shook hands. "So long, Sam." He looked me straight in the eye. "Anything I can ever do for you—you've got yourself a friend for life."

I nodded the best thank-you I could and went for the door. He called out, "Hey, Charley." I turned. "Take care of yourself, Charley. And remember—if anybody hits you, let me know."

10

I saw Buddy Rich standing on Broadway outside the Brill Building. He introduced me to the fellow he was with, Marty Mills, and nodded toward the second-floor windows of the Brill Building that said "Mills Music" in gold letters. "Marty's plugging songs for his old man. C'mon with us. We're going over to Mel's rehearsal." Perry Como had a fifteen-minute TV show every night on CBS and Mel Tormé and Peggy Lee were his summer replacements. I felt very "inside" going over there to drop in on a friend's rehearsal.

Later, Buddy, Marty, and I went to a movie at the Capitol and got out around two in the morning. Marty said, "Let's go over to Lindy's for a sandwich."

I copped out. "I don't have much money with me."

"We don't need money. I just sign my dad's name."

We were almost in front of the place, so I had to come right out with it. "I don't know how they feel about me in there."

"Are you kidding? I've been eating in there all my life."

The lights outside the restaurant were off. "Hey, it looks like they're closed."

"They're still open for the steady customers. The doorman'll let us in."

Through the glass door I caught sight of Milton Berle sitting at the head of a long table directly in front of the entrance. He had a big cigar in his hand and he was telling a story. He really looked like what he was: the idol of the hour, the King of Television holding court, with everybody laughing hysterically at every word he said. I nudged Marty. "Look."

"Berle's here every night. That's the Comics' Table. It's a regular thing for the comics and press agents and writers." He knocked on the door. The doorman appeared from inside, spotted me, and waved us away. Marty rapped on the door again. It opened a crack. "We're closed."

Marty said, "You're out of your mind." The doorman was looking straight at me as he said, "I told you we're closed to you."

Marty turned purple. He banged on the glass door with his fist and shouted, "Tell Mr. Lindy that Marty Mills will never be back again."

We stood on the sidewalk watching the doorman walk away from us. "Look, I'll catch you guys tomorrow."

Buddy said, "We'll go to the Bird 'n Hand and have coffee."

"No, really, I'm a little tired."

He grabbed my arm and pointed to the restaurant only two doors away. "How tired can you be?"

We sat at the counter staring silently at menus. I heard the revolving door turn and in the mirror over the counter I saw a man in a baggy tuxedo hurrying toward us. He tapped Marty on the shoulder. "Mr. Mills, I'm sorry about what happened. It was that dumb doorman . . . please come back. I have a table all ready for you."

Marty looked to see what I wanted to do. He answered for me. "We've already ordered, thanks." As the headwaiter left Buddy called after him, "By the way . . . you apologized to the wrong man."

Marty was looking at me, a world of disbelief and compassion in his face. "Sammy, I'm sorry. Jesus, I knew it went on, but I never figured New York. . . ."

I tried to brush it off. "Baby, keeping us out of restaurants and hotels is the national pastime. It's bigger than baseball."

"Is it always like this?"

I shrugged. "Only when I'm colored. Listen, I'm starved . . ." I used the menu as a prop and as I stared into it I knew I'd have broken my arms to have prevented it from happening—they were my friends and I wanted them to like me, not pity me— yet I was strangely glad that they saw what it was like.

My father tugged gently at the shirt cuff concealed under the sleeve of his best suit. "Always show a little linen, Poppa."

"You're looking like Saturday night at Small's, Dad."

He fixed his tie. "Well, son, you might as well know I met myself a nurse, name of Rita Wade—I calls her Peewee 'cause she's real little and neat. I'm takin' her for dinner soon as she gets off duty." He turned. "What're you doin' tonight?"

"Nothing much, just going over to the Copa to catch Frank Sinatra."

"The Copa?" His forehead wrinkled. "Listen, Poppa . . ."

"It's okay, Dad. Buddy Rich invited me. He's a hip guy, right? He must know it's okay or he wouldn't have brought it up."

I spent twenty minutes getting a perfect knot on a ten-dollar tie I'd bought at Saks Fifth Avenue that afternoon, and although the subway downtown was half empty I stood all the way so I wouldn't crease my suit. I was in front of the Copa entrance at a quarter to eleven, staring across the street at the doorway I'd stood in so many times with my father.

Buddy and his friends pulled up in a cab. As we got to the steps the doorman stopped us. "Wait a minute. Only people with reservations." He rushed in front of us. "Hey, didn't you hear me?"

"I'm Buddy Rich and I have a reservation."

"You better wait here while I check." He came right back. "They don't know anything about a reservation for you." He gave me a meaningful look, then turned to Buddy. "Maybe if you go away and come back in a little while they'll be able to find it."

Buddy blew. "Wait a minute, fat face! Are you saying that if we come back without our friend we'll get a table? 'Cause if you're saying it I want to hear it."

"I didn't say that. Now look, don't make trouble. Go away peacefully . . ."

Buddy's arm was back, cocked to swing, but I stopped him. "Look, this is ridiculous. You guys go in. Why should you miss Frank's show? I really wish you'd . . ."

He grabbed my arm. "If you say that again I'm going to belt you. C'mon, we'll find a movie or something."

We walked silently toward Fifth Avenue. As we reached the corner I looked back at the awning that said "Copacabana." I felt Buddy's hand on my shoulder. "To hell with those bastards. You'll dance on their tables someday."

My father was waiting up for me in the kitchen. "How'd it go?"

"They didn't let us in. Good night, Dad." I went into the bedroom and began undressing. He followed me.

"Look, Poppa, they never did want us in them places and they never will and it kills me seein' you gettin' yourself hurt over somethin' you oughta know by now."

"Any word from Will yet?"

"Yeah, but you ain't gonna do no celebratin' over that news, neither. We're set to play the Flamingo in Vegas. Will signed 'cause they upped us to seven hundred fifty plus pickin' up our fare out. We can't afford to turn down that kinda money, Poppa."

"Dad, I'll play the governor's mansion in Alabama if it'll help us get off the ground a little faster! *Anything* to change the way we've gotta live. I've gotta get away from it! I've *got* to!"

He was looking at my hand, at the necktie I hadn't realized I'd been holding in my fist, crumpling it into a wrinkled mess.

He shook his head slowly, sadly. "Sammy . . . you ain't gonna get away from it till you die."

Buddy said, "I talked to Frank. He wants you to call him." I looked up from my coffee. He nodded. "Certainly. I told him." He pointed to the phone booth. "Eldorado 5-3100."

Frank's opening line was: "Tonight, you are coming to the club. I'm making the reservation and you're walking in there alone."

"Look, Frank, I'd rather not. I appreciate . . ."

"That's *it!* We don't discuss it. Just be there." His voice softened. "When something is wrong it's not going to get right unless you fix it. I know it's lousy, Charley, but you've got to do it."

I dragged myself toward the Copa. Sure, Frank had made the reservation, but what if they forgot to tell the doorman? And even if it goes smoothly, forcing my way in where I'm not wanted is even more degrading than being turned away. They're wrong not to want me but they'll have a right to hate me for pushing my way in. I walked past the entrance intending to just keep going, but I could never face Frank if I backed away. In those days, Frank's career was in a slump, he needed the Copa far more than they needed him, but despite that he was fighting for me.

The doorman stood on the sidewalk, watching me walk up the three front steps.

There was a hatcheck room in front of me and I wished I had a hat to give them so I could have a minute to get my bearings. I saw people standing around a bar to the right of me. I couldn't see anything but a mirror on the left, so I took a guess and turned right. A captain smiled too brightly. "Good evening, *sir*. A drink at the bar?"

"No, thank you. I have a reservation for the show."

"The show is downstairs."

Before I could give him my name, the headwaiter snapped his fingers and a captain appeared. "Right this way, sir."

I felt as if I were a bundle of dirty laundry being taken through the dining room. He left me at a table and I realized I was so far back that I could better see what was happening in the kitchen than the action on the stage. A table captain was standing over me. "Your order, sir."

"I'll have a Coke—a-Cola, please."

The stares, like countless jabs against my skin, were coming from every direction. I lit a cigarette, and took a long drag, breathing the smoke out gently, holding the cigarette delicately at the tips of my fingers, trying to do all the suave Cary Grant moves I'd seen in *Mr. Lucky*. Two guys were coming across the room straight toward me. I put the cigarette into the ashtray. A hand moved forward. "Sam? We're friends of Frank. He said you wouldn't mind if we sat at your table."

As we talked it was clear they were close friends who'd seen the show more than once. Frank had wanted me to walk in by myself, leaning on nobody, but he had sent them to sit with me so I wouldn't feel like I was alone on an island.

The waiter brought my Coke and I reached for it but he beat me to it, pouring it elaborately, his patronizing smile informing me that he understood I wasn't accustomed to being served.

There were cards on all the tables with Frank's picture on them, and pictures of other stars who played there every year. They were all wearing the Copa Bonnet, a hat made of fruit. The brochure described it as "the laurel wreath of achievement in nightclub circles, awarded only to entertainers who have reached the peak." One of Frank's friends laughed. "Pretty ridiculous-looking hat they got 'em wearing, huh?"

"Yeah." I could see how a hat made out of grapes and oranges could look silly, but to me it seemed like a crown.

When I asked the waiter for my check he said, "Mr. Sinatra has taken care of it." We went up to Frank's dressing room. He put his arm around my shoulder. "You did something good, Charley."

The subway lurched from side to side and I swayed with it as though all the muscles and nerves in my body had been stretched until they'd snapped and were hanging limp like broken rubber bands. For the first time I could remember, I loved that ride uptown and I nestled into the restful, anonymous cheapness of it, and where it was taking me. Usually I saw just the seamy side of Harlem and resented being glued to the poverty and second-bestness of everything, but now I yearned for the peace it offered, the release from watching every move I made and from being watched. I knew that it was everything I hated and I tried to bring myself out of it. "I've been to the Copa." I kept repeating it until I heard it screaming in my ear, roaring back at me in time with the wheels. "I've been to the Copa . . . been to the Copa . . . been to the Copa . . ." But all I felt was like I'd bought a brand-new Cadillac convertible—for a million dollars.

At breakfast I lit a cigarette with a match from the Copacabana. My father spotted the matchbox instantly. "Hey! How'd you get them? Were you inside? Damn! What's it like?"

"It's unbelievable! You go downstairs and a guy in a black coat is waiting with the reservations list. Then a guy in a red coat takes you to your table. A blue coat takes your order and a waiter in a white jacket brings it to you. And when you're finished along comes a maroon jacket who takes away the dishes. . . ."

Later, I went into the front room and looked out the window, staring downtown, toward Lindy's and the Copa—two in one week—understanding what lay ahead, and that it was worse than an insult or a fight, it was a pressure chamber, and the further I moved out into the world, the thinner the air would become. Buddy and Marty were just the start, I'd make other friends, and every time they'd breeze into a restaurant for a sandwich I'd be holding my breath, waiting.

In Vegas, for twenty minutes, twice a night, our skin had no color. I went on every night, turning myself inside out for the audience. They were paying more attention than ever before, and after every performance I was so exhilarated that I really expected one of the owners to come rushing back saying, "You were great. To hell with the 'rules.' Come on in and have a drink." But it never happened. The other acts could move around the hotel, go out and gamble or sit in the lounge and have a drink, but we had to leave through the kitchen, with the garbage. I was dying to grab a look into the casino, just to see what it was like, but I was damned if I'd let anyone see me like a kid with his nose against the candy-store window. I wanted to believe that "if they don't want me then I don't want them either," but I couldn't help imagining what it must be like to be wanted.

My father spent his time around the Westside casino but I went to my room trying to ignore the taunting glow of light coming from the Strip, bigger and brighter than ever, until finally the irresistible blaze drew me to the window and I gazed across at it knowing it was only three in the morning, which is like noon in Las Vegas, feeling as wide awake as the rest of the town, which was rocking with excitement. I pictured myself in the midst of it all, the music, the money piled high on tables, the women in gowns and diamonds, gambling away fortunes and laughing.

It took a physical effort to wrench myself away. I forced it all out of my mind and kept thinking: Someday . . . , listening to records and reading until I could fall asleep, always wondering when "someday" would be.

1 1

We had a month to get ready. We found a tailor who'd make us three suits for only a hundred dollars down. We chose a beautiful plaid and ordered dinner jackets with black satin lapels and black pants.

My father and Will would go on, then I'd come out and do the opening with them, we'd do individual dances, then I'd swing into the impressions. I'd open with Frank Sinatra. I could really hook the audience with that one because I could do funny physical bits as well as the voice, so I'd have twice as much going for me. Then I'd do Nat Cole, Frankie Laine, Mel Tormé, the Ink Spots, Al Hibbler, Vaughn Monroe, and close with Louis Armstrong. He was the only one to end on because it was the strongest impression and it would be hard to follow with another singer. Then I'd switch to movie stars. I'd been using a big cigar for Edward G. Robinson and it always got a laugh. I wanted a bigger one for a bigger laugh. I found a cigar maker in downtown L.A. and paid him five dollars to roll me a fourteen-inch cigar.

I'd noticed in Vegas that half of the first impression was wasted because the audience wasn't ready for it. I went through the newspapers looking for a current event on which I might be able to hang a topical joke to use as a bridge between the wild dancing and the impressions so the audience would be settled down and prepared for the quieter stuff.

We went to the club for rehearsal with the band. The sign out front said "JANIS PAIGE," then, underneath in smaller letters, "The Will Mastin Trio."

The stage manager said, "We've only got one real dressing room, so naturally it goes to the star. The other acts change up here." We were in the attic where they stored the extra tables. One corner was fixed up with a light, a mirror, and a clothes tree. We burst out laughing.

"By the way," he said, "under no conditions can you take more than two bows. Even if the audience calls you back. It's in Miss Paige's contract."

Dick Stabile, the bandleader, also introduced the acts. He told us, "Nobody pays attention to opening acts here but I'll gag it up a little and get their attention for you."

It was Academy Awards night, so there was going to be only one show, at midnight. I had dinner early, then took a nap and a long, hot bath until finally it was time to go back to the club.

Will said, "You go on upstairs. I want to look around."

There was still almost an hour to kill but we began dressing leisurely. Will came upstairs at a run. "Well, I've seen it all now." He was out of breath from excitement. "I walked around backstage and took a peep out front. This place is loaded with the biggest names in the business from Martin and Lewis right on down the line. They all came over from the Academy Awards."

I'd known it was going to be a big opening because of Janis Paige, but I should have realized that with half of Hollywood out at the Oscars, Ciro's was the logical place for them to wind up. "What's it like down there, Massey?"

"Elegant! We never played anything like this before. It's got the French menus and the captains in tails and the customers dressed to the teeth . . ."

There is never a night when a supporting act opens anywhere that he, she, or they don't think, "This is the night. This is the time we hit that stage and the audience won't let us off. They'll stand up and cheer and no act will be able to follow us. Then, tomorrow night *we'll* be the star attraction, the headliners, and we'll close the show. And from then on, we'll be *stars*." This is the dream of every supporting act just as every Broadway understudy fancies the night Ethel Merman will be caught in a blizzard in Connecticut and she'll have to go on in her place, and she'll be so great that the critics will cheer—"Better than Merman!"—and columnists will rush to their papers to report, "A star is born!" It happens only once in a thousand openings, to only one out of thousands of performers—just often enough to keep the dream alive in all the others.

But the kind of applause that would make that happen, the kind that was thundering in my imagination, couldn't possibly come just from doing a dance or sounding like Jimmy Stewart. There had to be that extra thing between performer and audience that's so strong he gets right inside of them and they like him personally, they feel for him. I tried to picture myself in front of the audience, touching the people the way I'd watched Mickey and Frank do over and over again—but how?

Will said, "We better go down now." At the bottom of the stairs, we took a final look at each other. My father reached down and picked a piece of lint off my pants. Then he stood there for a second looking at me. "You think we're too high-class for the room, Poppa?"

As we got backstage I could hear the nightclub sounds: hundreds of forks and knives scraping dinner plates, cups sliding onto saucers, a thousand swirling ice cubes clinking against the sides of glasses, the hiss of soda bottles being opened, the sound of champagne corks popping, the slooshing of the bottles sliding into buckets of ice, cigarette lighters clicking open, hundreds of voices talking and laughing.

We were doing bits with each other to break the tension, the corniest lines in the world. "Hey, Massey, you nervous?"

"I ain't nervous."

"Well, maybe *you* ain't nervous but yo' knees sho' is."

My father asked, "*You* nervous, Poppa?"

"Hell, I ain't nervous 'bout nothin'."

He rolled his eyes. "Well, you better *git* nervous 'cause we's in a *lotta* trouble . . ."

We were lapsing into the deepest Amos 'n' Andy talk, something Negroes do among themselves when they're nervous but happy.

Once the introduction was over, my father and Will moved out into our opening number and they were never better. Eight bars later I joined them and we might have been barefoot on hot sand, our feet weren't on the stage as much as they were in the air. We'd started probably faster than any act this crowd had ever seen and we kept increasing the pace, trying as we never had before. We finished the opening number, and, characteristic of colored acts, we didn't wait to enjoy the applause before we were off and dancing again, first Will, then my dad, and then me. We were fighting for our lives and our frenzy of movement got to the audience from the moment we started until soon it was like they were out of breath trying to keep up with us. The applause was great when my father and Will finished their numbers. Then they stepped back. As I introduced the impressions my speech was perfect. I did Sinatra and they screamed. I went through the rest of the singers, and by the time I finished Satchmo they were pounding the tables so hard I could see the silverware jumping up and down. I switched into the movie stars, first Bogart, then Garfield—suddenly I felt the whole room shifting toward me. They were no longer just sitting back watching, amused. From one second to another they'd become involved with me. They were reacting to everything, catching every inflection, every little move and gesture, concentrating, leaning in as though they wanted to push, to help. I was touching them. It was the most glorious moment I'd ever known.

When we finished, after being on for forty minutes, they wouldn't let us stay off. It was as though they knew something big was happening to us and they wanted to be a part of it.

They kept applauding, and beating on the tables with knives and forks and their fists, screaming for us to come back. My father and Will stood in the wings, hesitating. We'd already taken our two bows but a man with a gun couldn't have held me back. "To hell with her contract. I ain't gonna miss this for *no-body*!!!" We went out twice more. They kept shouting for an encore. I'd already done every impression I'd ever tried. But we had to do something, so I did Jerry Lewis, which I had never done before. The sight of a colored Jerry Lewis was the absolute topper. It was *over*. When I heard that scream I knew there was nothing we could do that would top that!

We'd taken eight bows. Janis Paige was in the wings waiting to go on to close the show. She was so upset she sang off key for fifteen minutes. She couldn't even get the audience's attention.

We stayed up until eight o'clock and the three of us went out and bought every newspaper and trade paper that had just come out. We brought them back to Will's room. I turned to Herb Stein's review in the *Hollywood Reporter* and read: "Once in a long time an artist hits town and sends the place on its ear. Such a one is young Sammy Davis, Jr., of the Will Mastin Trio at Ciro's." Paul Coates's column in the *Mirror*: "The surprise sensation of the show was the Will Mastin Trio, a father-uncle-son combination that is the greatest act Hollywood has seen in some months . . . left the audience begging for more." And *Daily Variety*: "The Will Mastin Trio is a riotous group of Negro song and dance men whose enthusiasm, brightness, and obvious love for show business combine to form an infectious charm which wins the audience in a flash . . . walloping success. . . ."

Will was reading the Los Angeles *Times*. "Listen to this from Walter Ames's column: 'The Will Mastin Trio, featuring dynamic Sammy Davis, Jr., are such show-stoppers at Ciro's that star Janis Paige has relinquished the closing spot to them.' "

It was almost nine o'clock. We called Mr. Silber. "It's true," he said. "I thought you'd be sleeping or I'd have called you. Starting tonight you close the show."

As we hit the stage I could feel something going for us that we'd never had before. The audience was presold by word of mouth and the reviews, we weren't starting from scratch anymore, we didn't have to get lucky and strike that one moment in a million when you go off like a Roman candle. The night before, we'd gotten our strength from sheer desperation. This was still in evidence. We worked as hard, maybe harder, but with the added power of knowing we belonged. We weren't trying to kill the ball anymore and we gave a flawless performance.

I was hanging my jacket on a hook in our "dressing room" when I heard someone clearing his throat. Jerry Lewis was banging his fist against the wall. "I'd knock on the door if you had one. May I come in?"

"Mr. Lewis! Of course. Please!" I pulled up a chair and almost pushed him into it.

"Don't give me a 'mister.' I'm a Jerry not a mister. How can we be friends if we're misters and you'll call me up: 'Hello, mister, mister, let's have dinner tonight.' " He smiled. "I came back because I love the act and if you don't mind I'd like to give you a little advice."

"Mind? My God. Are you kidding? Please do."

He shouted, *"Get outta the business!"* He jumped up and kicked me. "I don't *need* such competition, I don't *want* it, I was doing fine. Who asked you to come along?" I broke up over him in our ridiculous dressing room, doing bits with me.

"But I really do have a few suggestions. Now listen, you shouldn't hit me in the mouth from what I'll tell you 'cause it's only good I mean you. Okay? Samele, you're a great performer, but you're making some mistakes. I'll tell you what I saw and maybe you'll change a few little shtick, it'll be nice, it'll be bet-

ter for the act the people should like you even more." He
reached into his pocket and took out a wad of notes. "First of
all, you talk too good."

"That's how I speak. What do you expect me to say, 'Yassuh, ladies an' gen'men'? Look, I appreciate your interest, but
not all Negroes talk that way . . ."

"Ah-hah! You promised you wouldn't make an angry. But
I'll forgive you. Just listen to yourself. You don't talk that
way now, in here with me. You talk nice, like a regula fella.
But I know Englishmen who don't talk as good as you did
onstage with such an accent. Sam, people don't go for that
English crap, not from you and me. I don't mean you should
come on and do Amos 'n' Andy. I just mean you talk *too* good!
Let's face it, American you are, but the Duke of Windsor you
ain't!"

"I'm not sure I know what you mean."

"Sammy, you walk on and you say, 'Ah, yes, hello there,
ladies and gentlemen.' That's an English actor! Forget it. Nobody is gonna like a guy who sings and dances and tells jokes
as good as you and who talks that good too. You want mass
appeal! You can't afford to make the average guy feel like he's
an illiterate. Bring yourself down. Not colored, but a little less
grand . . ." His "Jerry Lewis" character was gone, there was no
comic dialect. "When you figure they like you, when you've got
them, and they're thinking: 'Hey, this guy's okay, he's like me,'
then you can switch it and talk good. When they figure you're
just a simple kind of a bum, then surprise them. But save it,
hold it back, let it work for you."

As he spoke I realized I'd been saying things like "Ladies
and gentlemen, at this time, with your very kind permission we
have some impersonations to offer. We do hope you'll enjoy
them." I sounded like a colored Laurence Olivier. In trying to
elevate myself I had gone from one extreme to the other. I
wasn't leveling with the audience. Luckily I hadn't done enough
of it to stifle whatever they saw in me that they liked, but I
could see that if I kept it up my personality could become

buried beneath an English accent just as surely as it had been buried beneath "Yassuh."

"Y'know something? Tonight you didn't make a single mistake. Last night a few, but tonight your performance was letter-perfect."

I smiled. "Well, I guess we got lucky."

He was shaking his head. "That's terrible! You've got to make some mistakes on that stage. Sure, you know your act perfectly, but you can't have the satisfaction of looking like such a pro. Some things you should make look like they never happened before. The greatest thing that can happen for the guy sitting out front is if he can go home and say, 'Wow, I saw Sammy Davis at Ciro's and did he have his troubles: the mike went dead, the piano fell apart, but he kept on performing and he was great.' If he can do that then he feels like he's been a part of something. You've gotta break up every now and then, maybe blow a lyric—something! If you do they'll root for you all the more.

"Also, in the impressions where you use props, like a hat or the big cigar, you've been handing them to your father and your uncle. What are they, prop men? Don't hand them your stuff with that gracious 'Thank you, Dad, thank you, Will,' like they're your servants. Get your own cigar. Get your own hat. And put them down yourself."

He was so right. From the audience's point of view, it had to look like "This kid's making his father and his uncle wait on him. What an ingrate! They put him in show business and look how he's using them." The audiences would resent it. We'd done it because it kept the pace moving. In the old days it hadn't mattered, but from now on it was a different audience, more show-wise, more discerning. In the past no one was offended by me handing Will my hat and taking a cigar from my father. Or had they been?

"This is the greatest advice I ever got in my life. I just don't know how to thank you."

He was on his feet, glaring at me. "You wanta thank me?

Then like I said in the first place, get outta the business. *That'll* be a thank-you." We shook hands and he smiled. "Let's see each other."

Whenever any of the buddies came in I sent a message to the maître d': "Give me the check for that table. And send over a bottle of champagne." My cut of our $550 minus Mr. Silber's 10 percent was $165 but by the end of the first week I owed the club $280 for the checks I'd picked up. How Big Time can you get? I didn't care. Money was just around the corner.

I was two weeks behind in my rent at the Sunset Colonial. I dreaded bumping into the manager and getting his withering deadbeat fish eye, so I was doing some of the world's great sneak-ins and sneak-outs. But one day there was no escaping him. I went straight for him. "I'm sorry I haven't been able to take care of my bill . . ."

"Mr. Davis. Please! I'm embarrassed that you even mentioned it. I can imagine how busy you've been." He put his arm around my shoulder and walked me to the elevator. "Whenever it's convenient." He winked. "We know you're good for it."

I rode upstairs marveling. "Oh, daddy, what a life this is gonna be! It was slow in coming, but wow."

I was the star of the hotel. People who'd brushed by me a hundred times before now wanted to stop and talk. The shocker was a chick named Mikki something. Whenever I'd passed her in the hall and tried to be civil the best I could get back was frostbite. But a week after the opening I saw her in the lobby and damned if she wasn't maneuvering herself to be standing right where I had to walk, giving me an ear-to-ear and a from-head-to-toe—all that was missing was RSVP. I was the same guy she wouldn't look at last week. I had the same face girls had always laughed at, the same broken nose, but now that it was in the papers every day it was okay. Fame creates its own standards. A guy who twitches his lips is just another guy with a lip twitch—unless he's Humphrey Bogart. It was only a few days since we'd caught on, but people knew it was happening and I had begun changing in their eyes.

I ran into her twice the next day. She was tall and had a figure like forget it, with long legs and shiny golden hair hanging below her shoulders. She looked like she should star in a movie called *Goddess of the Sun* and each time I saw her she all but handed me the key to her room. I smiled politely and ran. I'd have given anything to make a move—anything but "everything." All I needed was a racial scandal to make everything blow up in my face. I wanted wine, women, and swinging by the yard, but the Sun Goddess was a threat to everything yet to come. I'd have my chicks, all right, but I'd get them from downtown. Safe ones.

As I came out of Ciro's a woman handed me a pen and piece of paper. "Can I have your autograph, Mr. Davis?" I was caught completely off balance, but I wrote something to her and signed my name while she stood there beaming at me. I handed it to her glorying in the moment, trying to act cool. She thanked me and I gave her a little Doug Fairbanks bow. "My pleasure, I assure you."

She squinted at the paper. "I can't read what you wrote here." As I watched her puzzling over my childish scribbling the image of myself as the suave movie-star type shattered.

I sat at the desk in my room writing "All my best, Sammy Davis, Jr." I wrote it again and again, until it was light outside, trying to make something I wouldn't have to be ashamed of.

Our two weeks were up and we were held over for six more as the headliners. We moved into the star dressing room and our name went up on top out front.

The classic fallacy of show business is: "Someday you'll get your break and then it'll be all velvet for you." It's a lovely dream but untrue. You can be ready for your break and not get it or you can get your break and not be ready for it. Nobody could have convinced me I wasn't ready when I came out of the Army. And playing on the bill with Mickey and with Frank and with Count Basie and Billie Holiday at the Strand, being seen in

Vegas and at Slapsie Maxie's—those had all been breaks. But there was no mystery about why we'd gone back into the dirt after each of them. Something had been missing until the night we opened at Ciro's.

I saw, as I never had before, the importance of *everything* that happens on the stage. Everything the audience sees, hears, and senses about you contributes toward forming an image which makes the difference between just another performer and somebody whom the audience cares about.

Most of what I read about us after the opening indicated that the people liked the relationship between my father, Will, and me: the two vaudevillians who knew the business backward and the kid they'd taught it to. They liked the contrast between the old show business and the new. Maybe they also understood our feelings for the business, maybe they caught our desperation to make good—there's no way of knowing all the things that contributed to the image they liked. Little by little we had changed our clothes, our jokes, our manner—everything. Whatever we were on the stage had evolved through the years until on opening night at Ciro's the combination of circumstances was finally right and it all fell in place, like when the three cherries on a slot machine all come up at once.

12

I sat in the dressing room rereading Robert Sylvester's review in the New York *Daily News*: "The best, fastest, and most furious young entertainer to come along in some time is a twenty-six-year-old named Sammy Davis, Jr. Sammy works with his old man and his uncle Will Mastin in the latter's trio at Bill Miller's Riviera. As the old saying goes, God made Sammy as ugly looking as He could and then hit him in the face with a shovel. But the young Samuel doesn't need any beauty because he sure has got everything else. . . ."

I stared at my face in the mirror. I guess I'd gotten used to it.

If I didn't have to stand still in front of the microphone, if I used a hand mike with a long cord, I could keep moving around the stage and dazzle them with so much motion that it would draw their attention away from my face. . . .

That night as we came off, my father smacked me on the back. "Hey, Poppa, that's a helluva style you found yourself."

I closed the dressing-room door. "Y'know, Dad, Massey, I've been thinking, I've got some ideas, things we need."

Will hung up his coat. "Like what?"

"Well, the first thing is our own conductor."

"Have you any idea what it'd cost to have our own man?"

"Massey, please, hear me out. I've got a lot going for me—I

dance, I do jokes, impressions, and I play the instruments, right? If one thing dies I could keep switching until I find the thing that'll entertain them. But I'm wasting my versatility by being tied to a routine, I'm not getting the most mileage out of it if I can't use each thing when it'll work best. Now, if I had my own conductor, a guy who knows the act backward, then as soon as I see what I need I'd give him a cue and wham, we'd swing right into what I need *when* I need it. Tonight was the perfect example. When I got to the impressions the people just weren't ready for them."

"Well . . . they hadn't quite settled down as much as would've been best. But once you got started . . ."

"Meanwhile I completely lost the value of the first two or three guys I did. I was dying to switch our order and do the drums in that spot and *then* the impressions. But I was stuck to the way the band had rehearsed it. It's ridiculous! I can't do the same show for a dinner crowd that I do for the hard drinkers. Every audience is different, what's great one night dies the next, so I've got to have the flexibility to give them exactly what they want at that moment. But I can't know what it'll be until I get out there and feel them."

Will put up his hands. "Hold on, now, and let's come down to facts. I'm not saying it wouldn't be dandy to have our own man. But a good conductor comes high, maybe four or five hundred a week. We've gotten by all our lives without one."

"We can't just 'get by' anymore. The people aren't going to excuse the rough edges like they they did when we were coming up. We're on the brink of being headliners and if we're gonna get inside, then we've gotta come in like we rate it. We need the little touches, the professionalism."

"You said there was a couple of things? What else?"

"A press agent. Now, before you tell me I'm crazy, take Buffalo, we've got only two weeks there, right? So we should have a good man arrive ahead of us with his hands full of our New York reviews—someone like Jess Rand, the kid who works for the press agent here—he should hit every newspaper and radio and TV guy around, setting up interviews and appearances, everything he can. Then I get to town a few days early, I make six or seven stops a day, and by the time we open, the papers are full of us."

Will was smiling. "Sammy, you're not crazy. You're just ahead of yourself."

"Massey, let's be honest, take five hundred away from the four thousand we'll be making in Buffalo and you *know* we've lived on a lot less than thirty-five hundred a week. Hey, do you realize what a guy like Jess Rand could do with a human-interest thing like that? 'The same act that got forty dollars a week and a meal returns to Harry Altman's Town Casino at four thousand per week just a few years later!' Can't you see it in the papers?"

"I can. But I'd rather see it in the bank. Now's the time for us t'put some aside in case something happens and we don't keep working."

"No! Now's the time to put on the pressure and use everything we've got so that nothing *does* happen except us getting bigger."

He was shaking his head, sitting there like an adding machine. I'd made no impression on him at all.

Our biggest boost came when Ed Sullivan booked us for his show.

In the middle of our spot the coaxial cable broke for the first time in television history and every screen in America was blacked out. Only the sound remained on. We didn't find out about it until we were off the air. My father and Will, everybody, treated it like it was a disaster. But to me it seemed that it had worked *for* us. Ed Sullivan told us he'd book us again, which was gravy, and the next day's papers were full of stories about what had happened, they ran my picture captioned "The Mystery Guest" and "The Little Man Who Wasn't There," and people all over the country were saying, "Some guy was on Ed Sullivan's program when the picture went off and I'd have sworn it was James Cagney and Humphrey Bogart talking to

Edward G. Robinson. You never heard anything like it. . . ." It drew more attention and caused more talk about us than if everything had gone smoothly.

Passing the musicians' rehearsal room between shows, I was stopped by the sound of somebody noodling on the clarinet, creative, sensitive, a man daydreaming through a horn. It was Morty Stevens. A guy I'd thought of as just a hack in a show band was a musician when he wasn't tied down to corny arrangements of popular songs. He saw me and self-consciously began drying the reed.

I sat down next to him. "You ever do any arrangements? Original stuff? I've been thinking about doing some straight singing. If I could get the right arrangement of 'Birth of the Blues' . . . you want to take a shot at it?"

Three days later I couldn't believe what I was hearing. He was such a quiet guy but the arrangement went like a madman. As I listened he suddenly became somebody I wanted to know better. The one thing I really respected was talent and he had it coming out of his ears. He'd taken my basic ideas of how I wanted to perform it and developed it with a complete understanding of my voice and my kind of performing.

Milton Berle was at center ringside, appraising, as performers will. Occasionally his head would nod like, "Yeah, that's good," and I put extra steam into everything I did, because as a performer his little nods or the lack of them told me more than a layman's applause.

I dressed quickly, knowing that he'd give us the courtesy of stopping back to say hello.

Berle lit a cigar. "Lemme suggest something. The line you did when the drunk heckled you. The way you're doing it now, it's 'If you're ever in California, I hope you'll come by my house and take some drowning lessons in my pool.' It's a cute line, but you're not getting the most out of it. Switch it around. Frame it as a straight invitation: 'If you're ever in California, sir, I do hope you'll come by and use my pool.' A guy has been heckling you and you say something nice to him? This confuses the audience, and they're waiting. *Now* you hit him with the punch line: 'I'd love to give you some drowning lessons!' The element of surprise has to get you a bigger laugh. Also, the joke phrase is 'drowning lessons,' so let those be the last words. You can't follow them with 'in my pool,' or you're stepping on your own laugh. You force them to pause to listen and if they can't laugh the second they want to you'll lose part of it.

"There's one other thing. When you get a guy who starts throwing lines at you like that, don't go for him right away. Ignore him the first couple of times. Let the audience become disgusted with him so that by the time you finally belt him they'll be rooting for you and you almost can't miss."

He stood up to leave and we shook hands. "I can't thank you enough, Mr. Berle—"

"The name is Milton. Listen, I'm going down to Lindy's. You feel like a sandwich?"

Danny Stradella, of Danny's Hideaway, a celebrity restaurant, had been coming by every night. He was waiting for me in his car with Marty Mills and Cliff Cochrane, his press agent. "You guys better go without me tonight. I'm sorry, but Milton Berle asked me to join him at Lindy's."

Marty gave me a wink. Danny said, "Hey, that's pretty good."

I sighed, "Yes, it's a little 'sit around and have a sandwich.' Just us stars."

"I'll give you a star—right between the eyes. See you tomorrow at dinner."

The doorman at Lindy's spotted Berle's limousine pulling up, rushed to the curb, opened the door, and I stepped out. Milton gestured for me to go ahead of him and I spun through the revolving door. He introduced me to the guys waiting for him, and made a place for me next to him. Everybody at the table

focused attention on me. "Caught the act." "Tremendous."
"Where do you play after the Riviera?" They were press agents,
personal managers, comedy writers, all Broadway pros who
were on close terms with a lot of stars. They knew I was just a
"kid who's moving up" but they treated me almost as if I were
already there, giving me more attention and acceptance than I
really rated. It seemed that as much as the world loves a winner
it reaches out all the more for a contender.

Suddenly Berle stood up and shouted at me. "Okay, out!
Out! I don't need you to steal my audience."

As we left there an hour later Milton offered me a lift but
the world was beautiful and I felt like walking in it. I strolled
downtown, crossed 51st Street, and as I passed the Capitol
Theater, I thought about Frank. I'd read that he was in town
and I was wondering where he was staying and how I could get
in touch with him, when I looked across the street and there
he was. I started to run after him and call out to him, but I
stopped, my arm in the air. He was slowly walking down
Broadway with no hat on and his collar up—and not a soul
was paying attention to him. This was the man who only a few
years ago had tied up traffic all over Times Square. Thousands
of people had been stepping all over each other trying to get a
look at him. Now the same man was walking down the same
street and nobody gave a damn. God, how could it happen?

I thought maybe he'd rather not see me. I couldn't take my
eyes off him, walking the streets, alone, an ordinary Joe who'd
been a giant. I was dying to run over to him, but I felt it would
be an intrusion. Or maybe I felt too much for him to want to
see him this way.

I stood in the wings watching Jack Benny's performance every
night. I think he's the only man in the world who can do nothing but gaze at the people and make them laugh. His legendary
genius for timing was akin to hypnosis. He'd mold a theater
full of people into a little ball and hold them in his hand. And

when he was ready—only when he was ready, he would open his hand and as much as say, "Okay, now you laugh."

Almost always, they roared. But by not setting himself up like "Here comes the joke, folks," by carefully not preparing them for anything hilarious, if a joke didn't work he was never left in the position of having to do desperation lines like "I know you're out there 'cause I can hear you breathing."

I saw my mistake in presenting the impressions by saying, "Ladies and gentlemen, Jimmy Cagney." If on a particular night I didn't sound exactly like Jimmy Cagney I was in trouble. Without intending to, I'd been setting myself up as Charley Impressionist and I had to be great or I was dead.

I tried it differently. "These are just in fun, they're satirical impressions of people I dig," implying that I was just doing them for laughs rather than "Look how much I sound or look like somebody." And I could feel it paying off before I'd finished the first one. No one knows better than I the impressions I do very well, the ones I do badly, and the ones which are just passing. But now when I did a "just passing," it got laughs instead of polite applause, and when I threw a good one the audience screamed. The whole key was in how I set it up in their minds.

At dress rehearsal the director said, "We're running three minutes over, Eddie." I began thinking which of our members to cut. Mr. Cantor glanced at the script. "Kill my second number."

Before we went on the air he said, "After your act you and I'll have some fun together onstage, for three minutes."

My father, Will, and I took our bows. They went off and I stayed on to join Mr. Cantor. He hugged me, took a handkerchief from his pocket, and blotted my face, beaming like a proud father. I followed his lead, and he was such a great pro that we could have ad-libbed for *ten* minutes with no trouble at all.

In his dressing room after the show I noticed a gold chain

with a gold capsule attached to it. "That's a mezuzah, Sammy, a holy Hebrew charm. We attach them to the doorposts of our homes or wear them for good luck, good health, and happiness. There's a piece of parchment rolled up inside and on it are twenty-two lines of Deuteronomy, a prayer for the protection of the home."

"Do you have to be Jewish to wear one?"

"I'm sure the sentiment is what counts. I don't suppose God cares very much which floor we do our shopping on, just as long as we go to His store. Keep that, Sammy. I'd like you to have it."

I opened my shirt and hung it around my neck. "Is there anything I'm supposed to do with it—I mean a special prayer?"

"Only what's in your heart. In our religion we're not confined to many rituals. That's a basic part of our belief—that every man should have the freedom to face God in his own way."

Finally, Frank called me at the Sunset Colonial. "Bogie's having some people over. I want you to meet him."

The butler escorted us to the living room. Bogart nodded to Frank the way you do to a close friend and shook hands with me. "Glad to see you. Come on in." He took me over to Lauren Bacall. "This is my wife."

She smiled. "I saw you on the Cantor show. You're marvelous."

Bogart said, "Come on and meet the people." He began steering me around the room. "Mr. Davis, Mr. Tracy. This is the kid I saw on television, Spence, he's been doin' me and if he keeps it up he's gonna get a knuckle sandwich . . . Say hello to the Grants . . . Mr. and Mrs. Stewart . . . Miss Hepburn . . . Mr. and Mrs. Gable . . . Miss Garland . . . okay, now make yourself at home."

I tried to seem at ease and at home drinking a Coke, listening to the conversations, but I found myself gazing like an idiot.

There was something so incredible about being in a private home, watching four people casually chatting like anybody would at a party—except they were Jimmy Stewart, Katharine Hepburn, Spencer Tracy, and Judy Garland.

I couldn't take my eyes off Frank. The dignity and the guts of the man! By all standards of show business success he was as down as anybody could be, yet, as he moved around in this incredible group of movie giants, he stood as tall as any of them.

He'd starred in half a dozen big pictures that had been completely built around him, and he'd lost it all. But he had the strength to start all over again completely from scratch. He'd just signed to make *From Here to Eternity*, accepting a secondary role, without any singing, ready to try for a whole new career as an actor. Being down in the business hadn't licked him as an individual. Maybe the whole world was saying he'd had it, but he didn't hear them or care. He was a total individual, measuring himself against nothing but his own standard.

I went into a coffee shop for breakfast. The counterman smiled. "Afternoon, Mr. Davis." I didn't know him. He began sponging the counter in front of me, even though it had seemed spotless. "I saw you on the Eddie Cantor show." A man two seats away raised his coffee cup. "Enjoyed you a lot. The whole family did."

In over twenty years of playing nightclubs and theaters nobody had ever before recognized me, cold, like that. But the right presentation on just one television show had done it.

Will was waiting for me at the Morris office. The head of the nightclub department said, "Sam Bramson just called from the New York office. You're hot as a pistol in Pittsburgh. They're sold out for your entire engagement. The club started getting calls the night of the Cantor show and they had to close reservations in forty-eight hours. That show was fantastic for you."

I stopped at a newsstand and bought a pile of papers and

movie magazines. I picked up my mail at the front desk and as I started toward the elevator the door slid open and there was the Sun Goddess in a pair of white sharkskin slacks that fit like they'd been painted on. The elevator closed behind her and she was coming straight for me, smiling. The best thing was to keep it light—do jokes with her. I shook my head. "You could be arrested for looking like that." *Exactly* the wrong thing to say.

Her smile expanded. "Well, you *can* be friendly."

Oh God, that voice! She made Marilyn Monroe sound like a bus driver. Where the hell was the damned elevator?

"I saw you on television the other night. You were wonderful."

The elevator opened and I did one of those great suave walk-aways, crashing right into a guy who was coming out. I rolled off of him, fell against the edge of the door, and stumbled into the elevator like a drunk, mumbling, "Well, nice t'have met you." She was gaping at me like I was out of my mind.

Back in my suite, I stared out the window, thinking about the rules of society. If she were colored and gave me openings like that—but she isn't. What'd I need her for? There was nothing about her that was any better than most of the girls I was making it with.

I started going through my mail to get my mind off her. I opened a manila envelope from NBC and took out a stack of letters and a note: "Dear Mr. Davis, Enclosed please find letters addressed to you in care of *The Colgate Comedy Hour*. We will forward any further viewer mail."

I cleared the bed of everything but my fan mail, stretched out comfortably, lit a cigarette, and opened the first letter. "Dear lousy nigger, keep your filthy paws off Eddie Cantor he may be a jew but at least he is white and dont come from africa where you should go back to I hope I hope I hope. I wont use that lousy stinking toothpaste no more for fear maybe the like of you has touched it. What is dirt like you doing on our good American earth anyway?"

I opened a few others. I was an idiot to let them bother me. The hell with them.

I turned the pages of a fan magazine, trying to lose myself in the Hollywood Hills, Bel Air, and Beverly Hills, trying to imagine myself owning one of those beautiful homes with a swimming pool and a convertible parked in the driveway. I stopped at a picture of a girl stretched out on a diving board. The Sun Goddess. I should have known that anyone who looked that good was out here to get into the movies. I thought of the big hellos she'd given me in the lobby and her incredulous stare as the elevator door closed. I really *must* be out of my mind. I turned down *that*? To stay in good with people who call me *nigger*?

I felt stupid for thinking I could stand in the middle of the road without getting hit by a truck. What had happened to me since I got out of the Army? I'm the guy who wasn't going to let anybody tell me how to live. But they'd started telling me and I'd listened instead of spitting in their eyes. I'd played it safe. I wanted to be a star, so I'd as much as made a deal: "You let me 'make it' and I'll play the game." But suddenly I had an eight-by-ten glossy of the people I'd made the deal with, whose rules I was following. I could never appease them. How could I not offend them by what I do when my very existence was offensive to them? There could be no end to it. Don't be seen at the same tables with white people. Stay away from white women. Don't touch Eddie Cantor. What next? I wanted to make it, but if that was the price, it was too high. If I'd just thought it out, I'd have known it couldn't work. It was spelled out in the Bible. "What shall it profit a man if he shall gain the world and lose his own soul?" I'd sold my dignity. Worse still, I'd sold it to people who never believed I had any.

I looked for her last name in the magazine. I could feel my hand getting moist on the phone while I waited for the operator to connect me with her room. What the hell was I going to say? She definitely must think I'm a lunatic by now . . .

"Hello?"

"Uh—hi! This is Sammy Davis, Jr. . . . ."

"Well, *hello!*"

"I didn't think you'd be in your room!"

"Oh? Is that why you called?"

"Look, I know you must think I'm some sort of a nut, but—well, y'see, I was in a big hurry before . . ."

"I got that impression."

"What I called about is, I thought it would be nice if . . ."

"I can't hear a word you're saying, Sammy. We have a very bad connection. I'm in 418, why don't you stop by and tell me."

The guy at the Morris office said, "There's been an avalanche of 'em. To the station, to Cantor, the sponsor . . ." The bundles of letters covered his desk. I looked at one, addressed to Eddie Cantor: "Where do you get off wiping that coon's face with the handkerchief you'd put on a clean, white, American face?"

"Well, I guess this finishes us with the Cantor show."

The Morris guy said, "The sponsors don't want bad public opinion. Even from bigots. They've warned Cantor that if this happens again they'll take him off the air."

"What about other shows?"

He shook his head, grimly sympathetic. "We might as well face the facts. These things don't stay secret very long."

When I left the Morris office, the cabdriver was staring at me in his mirror. He turned around for a better look. "I *thought* I saw you on television. You're okay."

"Thanks."

When I got back to the hotel there were five phone messages from the Morris office. I used the booth in the lobby.

"We've been trying to reach you all afternoon."

"I went to a movie. What's wrong?"

"Cantor called, Cantor himself. He wants to negotiate for you to be on all the rest of his Colgate shows for the season. I guess he's not a guy that pushes easily. God knows what went on between him and the sponsor but he's got three shows left for the year and you're on all of them at three thousand each."

Long after I'd hung up I was still sitting in the phone booth. The man was a pro before I was born and he knew exactly what he was doing when he told me, "We'll have some fun on the stage together," but he'd done it anyway because he wanted to point me up, obviously not worrying that some people might not like it.

How could you figure it? People were going out of their way to kick me in the face with nothing to gain by doing it, then along comes Eddie Cantor with everything to lose, but he deals himself into my fight and says, "They'll have to kick me, too."

The sign on the hotel said "No Niggers—No Dogs." Everybody'd assured us: "Miami Beach? You'll have no problems there. It's like New York."

Sure!

But it was the height of the season, every celebrity from New York was in Miami Beach, and if you were a top act then this is where you should be playing.

Arthur Silber, Jr., had come along as company. "We're coming to a station. I wonder where we are."

I raised my shade and looked out. "We're in a lotta trouble, that's where we are."

He grinned. "Whaddya mean *we*, colored boy?"

I did an elaborate lean-back and pointed out the window to another sign: "Everybody Welcome but the Nigger and the Jew."

He swallowed hard. "Well, yeah, Kingfish, like you was saying, we's in a lotta trouble." The redcaps passed us by, grabbing for white people's luggage. We watched one straining under a load of suitcases, followed by the people who owned it, a thick woman in a frilly cotton dress and a man in a shiny blue suit with brown shoes. My father sighed. "Trouble with some colored people is they're plain prejudiced. Now that redcap's gonna catch himself a white two bits and he ain't never gonna know it coulda been a colored five spot."

As we neared the end of the platform a heavyset cabdriver rushed past us, bumped into Will from behind, and knocked the suitcases out of his hands. "Outta my way, niggah." Will stood motionless, struggling to regain his shattered dignity. I lunged after the cabdriver but a hand caught my arm. Will was looking into my eyes. "That won't get us nothing, Sammy. But thank you." He let go of my arm and picked up his bags.

There was a sign on the wall of the station: "WELCOME TO MIAMI." Inside, to the left and right, were the waiting rooms: "WHITE," "COLORED."

The Lord Calvert was a first-rate second-class hotel in the heart of the Negro section of Miami. Eddie Compadre, one of the bosses of the Beachcomber, looked around my room. "Everything okay?"

"Yeah, sure, it's fine. Everything's crazy."

He handed me a car key and pointed out the window to a bright red, brand-new Corvette in the parking lot. "That's yours as long as you're here. Only white cabs can cross the bridge from Miami onto the Beach and they aren't allowed to ride colored guys." He was telling it to me fast, like a man jumping into cold water. "Here, I got you these cards from the Police Department. There's a curfew on the Beach for all colored people and they can arrest you unless you show 'em this card, which explains you got a right 'cause you're working there."

"But there's a desegregation law!"

He looked at me, simpatico. "Not if they don't wanta enforce it. But you'll be in the club most of the time anyway and naturally the place is yours."

Arthur came into the dressing room and handed me a newspaper. "There's a guy peddling this in front of the club." The headline was "NIGGER ON THE BEACH" and the story was titled "Stamp Out Sammy Davis, Jr." It said, "The black people are an un-American disease which threatens to spread all over the Beach . . ."

"Baby, do me a favor, see what Eddie can do about this."

It was a six-page hate sheet and as I read it my father said quietly, "You're gonna wrinkle your pants, Poppa. No point upsettin' yourself over fools like that. C'mon, we gotta go on now, anyway." The chorus kids and the backstage guys were giving me sympathy looks like, "How can he possibly do a show now?"

I did three encores. Arthur was waiting in the dressing room when we got off. "Well, the guy is gone, but who do you think chased him? Only Milton Berle. I'm walking outside with Eddie when Berle gets out of a car. He hears the guy shouting 'Nigger on the Beach,' walks over, looks at the headline, and smashes the guy in the mouth, a shot that knocks him right off his feet. The papers go flying in the air and Berle is kicking them into a mud hole. The guy runs like a thief. Berle! He was beautiful."

Eddie came back after the second show. "Whaddya say we bum around with some of the guys? We'll have some laughs." I knew he was trying to make me feel that I didn't have to run back to the hotel. He took me to a few jazz spots, where I was tuned in half to the music and half to the people around us, looking for a raised eyebrow, listening for a comment.

I fell into bed and lay staring into the darkness above me until I became aware of the ceiling turning white with the first rays of the morning sun.

I woke up around two o'clock and went down to the pool area. Nat Cole and Sugar Ray Robinson were there and the ball clubs were in town for winter training, so the Campanellas and Jackie Robinson were there too. Arthur was in the swimming pool riding Roy Campanella's kids around on his shoulders. When Arthur and Morty Stevens had checked in with us there'd been a few remarks and suspicious looks, but now nobody was giving them a second thought.

I was enjoying the crowd of chicks around me until one of them said, "Gee, I wish I could see your show." I was embarrassed to be playing a club that wouldn't let me in either if I weren't starring there, and I would never do it again, but I wasn't sorry. Every important date like Miami Beach was bringing me a step closer to the top. Someday they'd want me so badly that I'd be able to demand they open the doors to everybody or I wouldn't play.

I made a date with her for that night and we hit all the colored clubs, had laughs, champagne, and everywhere we went the MC introduced me from the stage. I got back to the room around six in the morning, dead tired, but unable to sleep any better than the night before. I kept telling myself what a swinging night it had been, but it was no good, I'd had a million laughs but no fun. It should have been, and it would have been if it wasn't being forced down my throat.

Will closed the dressing-room door. "I'm calling a meeting of the Trio. Eddie wants us back next season. He's offering . . ."

"The next time *I'm* playing Miami Beach is never! Not till they let colored people come in as customers. I don't care how much the money is, I don't want it!"

He was smiling. "I already told him no." He waved away my apology. "I'm only telling you so you can enjoy that we're in a position to pick and choose. And as long as we're all in the mood you'll be glad to hear I turned down another Vegas deal. They're up to seventy-five hundred, but they still won't give us rooms in the hotel. They offered us three first-class, fully equipped trailers parked on the hotel grounds."

"Did the Morris office say anything about the Copa?"

"No. Jules Podell, who owns the Copa, doesn't move fast. He isn't ready to come up with an offer yet."

It only takes 336 hours for two weeks to end. I finished our last show with "Birth of the Blues" as an encore. Harry Richman, the MC, was calling me back for another bow when someone yelled, "Now *you* sing it, Harry."

He shook his head. "Friends . . . you and I have had a lot of good times through all the years we've been together, and I'm not reluctant to say that it's been a lot of years. I remember the day somewhere along the line a man came to me and handed me a piece of paper, a song, and I had no way of knowing then that those thirty-two bars of music would turn out to be the best friend I ever had." He put his arm around my shoulder. "For the last two weeks I've been watching this youngster putting all of his heart and soul into what he's been giving you and I've been trying to think of a way to let him know what an old-timer like me feels when he sees someone like him come along. The only way I have is to give him something I love. So I'm turning 'Birth of the Blues' over to my young friend, Sammy Davis, Jr. He's going to go a long way and I want him to take my song with him. I'll never sing it again, Sammy. It's yours and I hope it's as good to you as it's been to me."

I knew that at that moment he meant it, just as I knew that the next day when I was gone he'd be singing it again. But I appreciated it for the gorgeous piece of show business shmaltz that it was.

I packed my dressing-room things and Arthur helped me load them into the Corvette. When we'd squeezed all my stuff in he appraised the remaining space. "Even *you* can't fit in there now."

"Then, baby, how about if you run them back to the hotel and come back and get me? I can use the time to say goodbye to Eddie and some of the guys inside."

By four o'clock the bartender had locked up the liquor and everybody was gone except me and the night man, who was making his last rounds. I called Arthur at the hotel but his room didn't answer. At a quarter to five, I said, "There's no point in your staying to lock up. I can wait outside. He's sure to be along any minute."

I sat on the curb trying to remember exactly what I'd said to Arthur. He must have had a flat or run out of gas. A taxi was cruising up the avenue. I stood up and waved to him. He slowed down and called out, "Can't ride you." Another cab slowed but as he got a closer look he stepped on the gas. I watched his taillights disappear.

I started walking. It must have been fifteen minutes before I saw another one. I rushed out into the street and held my arm up. He stopped about ten feet in front of me. I was suddenly blinded by a huge beam of light. A man ordered, "Stand right where you are." He touched my chest, waistband, and back pockets. "What're you up to? You know you've got no right being here."

"I'm Sammy Davis, Jr." He had one hand resting on the butt of his gun. "I have a card . . ."

"Let's see it." I moved my hand slowly to my inside pocket and drew my wallet out. He looked at the card. "Well, why're you sneaking around here at *this* hour?"

"I've been waiting for my friend. He was supposed to pick me up. I don't know what happened to him."

He led me over to the police car. He leaned in and told his partner, "He's in the show. Says he's waiting for somebody to pick him up."

"He can't stay here."

"Officer, if you'll call Eddie Compa—"

"Easy, boy. We'll handle this."

"What're we wasting our time for? Get him in the car. We'll leave him at the bus stop."

They put me between them. "I think my kid saw him on TV."

"What's he do?"

"I guess he tap-dances. My kid likes him. I think I read that he gets five thousand a week for being here."

"Where'd you read bull like that?"

"One of the papers."

"You didn't read that, you dreamed it. Five thousand a week! Hell! *I'd* get up and do a dance for that much."

"Officer, couldn't you take me somewhere so I could call my friend?"

"No need for that. A bus'll be along in an hour or so. But don't you go walking nowhere or we'll have to lock you up. Just sit on that bench till the bus comes and everything'll be fine."

I walked over to the bench and sat down. They didn't drive away. "Hey, c'mere, boy."

He handed me a slip of paper and a pencil. "Put your auto-graph on here for my kid."

As they drove away, I lit a match and looked at my watch. It was 5:20. An hour and a quarter later it was light out and the bus stopped at the corner.

Mama sat in a big easy chair in my dressing room at the Apollo Theater on 125th Street, holding court as she did every day for dozens of people from our neighborhood. I sat on the arm of her chair while the women stood around giggling, trying to think of things to say. "I knew you when your grandma used to wheel you in a carriage, Sammy. We'd say, 'Here comes Rosa Davis and her Jesus.' " She smiled at Mama. "Guess you al-ways knew he'd turn out to be something, didn't you, Rosa?" Mama gave her a silent, blasé nod which as much as said, "You see I did, so why do you ask such foolish questions?"

Sometimes I stayed off in a corner so I could enjoy watching her. I knew she was bursting with happiness, but she just sat there, arms folded, her mink jacket draped over the chair, nod-ding graciously, occasionally smiling and accepting the atten-tion with all the dignity of a queen completely at home on a throne.

I'd taken a room at the America on West 47th Street, and on my way uptown one morning I left the cab a block early so I could stand across the street from the theater, looking at the long line of people waiting to buy tickets for our early show. A truck went by carrying a billboard for *The Barefoot Contessa*. As hot as we were, *that* would be the capper. Ava Gardner, in person, on 125th Street. I went back to the dressing room and looked up the phone number of the Drake Hotel.

I looked out at the jam-packed theater. "Ladies and gentlemen, I'd like you to meet a lady who took the trouble to come up here from downtown. This lady is the brightest light in all of

Hollywood . . ." They were looking around, sensing it was going to be someone big. I kept building the suspense. "She is in town to publicize her newest motion picture, *The Barefoot Contessa* . . ." Then the buzzing really started and they were turning back and forth with question-mark looks, having mental arguments with themselves, like, "He can't mean Ava Gardner. It must be someone else in the picture . . ." "Well, who else could it be?" "Hell, this cat ain't about t'get no Ava Gardner to come uptown—is he?" I kept building it, and every word was like I was pumping air into a balloon. When they were all but leaning out of their seats I paused and laid it on them: "Ladies and gentlemen, Miss *Ava Gardner*!"

There was utter stillness. The Love Goddess of the World was walking toward me, a smile on her face, diamonds in her hair, swathed in a skintight gown which was not just revealing, but elegant—and at the same time so sexy it was frightening.

The audience started whistling and shouting. She put her arm around my waist and they exploded, stamping and jumping up and down in their seats until I could actually feel the theater rocking! Never before had a star of this magnitude come to Harlem and they were going out of their minds, and I was thinking, "I can die right now because I ain't *never* gonna see an audience this excited again!"

Ava was smiling as cool as ice cream, knowing what this would mean to me, playing it right to the hilt for me with her arm still around my waist, best-of-friends style.

It took a full five minutes before they settled down enough for Ava to say, "I can't tell you how grateful I am for your very generous reception. I know that we share a mutual respect for this great entertainer who so kindly invited me to come here. Incidentally, I'm in a picture called *The Barefoot Contessa*, and if you don't mind, I'd love to take my shoes off . . ." She kicked them off and that started it all over again. When they quieted down she spoke for a few more minutes, waved goodbye, and did one of those tippy-toe walks off on the balls of her feet. Every eye in the place was watching her very feminine departure and I summed up what everybody was thinking. "Well—if you're gonna be a girl, *be a girl!*"

She was waiting in my dressing room with her escort, William B. Williams, and a guy from United Artists. "Ava, I can't tell you how grateful I am. You wanta talk about making somebody a big man?"

William B. asked, "How about a little drink?"

The street outside the stage door was blocked with people standing on stoops, on cars, and literally climbing up lampposts for a look at her. With the help of twenty policemen who'd rushed over on a riot call, we were finally able to get through to her limousine.

We had a drink at the Shalimar, a nearby bar. They were going on to Birdland and asked me to join them, but I knew that word of this evening had already spread all over Harlem and I wanted to stick around and take some bows.

Jess Rand, who'd been working for us since before Miami, called me at the hotel, excited. "Sam, the editors at *Our World* heard about Ava Gardner coming up to the Apollo and they said if you can get her to pose for a picture with you they'll use it for the cover of their Christmas issue. They want you dressed up like Santa Claus standing near her while she sits in a chair with a pencil like she's making up a Christmas list. Her studio wants to build her in the Negro market, so they're writing a byline story for her to okay called 'Why I Dig Sammy Davis, Jr.'— it goes into why she thinks you're such a great performer, and all that kinda jazz."

"Well, if the studio wants it, then why don't *they* ask her?"

"Chicky, they're tickled silly she's making the p.a. tour to promote the picture and they're not asking any extra favors. But they figure if it came from you it would be like a personal thing."

She was waiting for us in her suite. A press agent from United Artists neutralized me with the Santa suit and two photographers took pictures for twenty minutes. When we were ready to leave I thanked her. "But you don't wanta give me that autographed picture you promised me at least a year ago, right?"

"I only have those glossies the studio sends out. But we can take a picture together right now if you like."

We posed for a few shots of us talking together. The guy from United Artists happened to be standing so that half of him was sure to be in the picture but I didn't ask him to move away, I felt enough like Charley Fan already. When the photographer was through I told him, "Baby, lemme have that roll of film, will you?"

"I'll develop it for you."

"Well, look, please be careful. Don't let it get into the wrong hands. It could make trouble for her."

"I'll process these shots myself. Nobody'll even see them."

I felt foolish. Here I was telling another Negro to be careful, as if he didn't understand.

13

I sat at a table on the upper level of the Copacabana. A hard light from two large, bare bulbs illuminated the room, which was a mass of plain wooden tables with chairs stacked on top of them. A man was pushing a vacuum cleaner between the tables, and another was washing the mirrored walls of the staircase. I ran my hand over the unfinished-wood tabletop. I wasn't surprised that the Copa was just a nightclub, but that I'd never before thought of it as one. I'd feared and lived in awe of it but now being there to work, seeing it without its illusion-making white tablecloths, shiny black ashtrays, the silver, the glassware, and the beautiful people, it was just another room where people come to be entertained. Okay, it was *the* club and they were *the* people but still they were only people.

Morty was running through our opening number with the band. They were playing it well—loud and flashy the way it was supposed to be. I listened to music I'd heard a thousand times but suddenly I didn't like it. It was jarring me. I disliked what it was saying.

When they finished the number, I waved to Morty. He gave the guys a break and we sat down at a table. "Morty, I want to change the opening number."

"Not for tomorrow night?"

"I'm sorry. I know it's a hell of a thing to ask, but please don't fight me on it. I don't care if I have to pay ten guys to stay up all night copying new music—I can't use that opening."

"I don't understand. What would you rather have?"

"I don't know. I only know that I don't want to come running onto this stage tomorrow night the way we always have. I don't want to come on with panting and puffing and fighting for my life like 'Is this good enough, folks?' I want to do something that no Negro dance act has ever done before. I'm going to *walk* onto the stage."

I waited for him to say something, hoping I wouldn't have to draw a picture, to explain, ". . . with dignity. I'm a Headliner. I want to walk on like a gentleman."

He was looking past me, thinking. "There's a number from *Street Scene*. It's soft, New Yorky, and it has an importance to it." He hummed it.

"That's perfect. Start off with twelve bars of what you were just rehearsing, to get their attention, then drop into *Street Scene* and I'll walk on."

"I'll ask the guys to ad-lib it right now. See if you like the way it sounds."

As I sat there listening to it I felt like a Headliner.

My father and I left our hotel at six-thirty Thursday night and I told the cabdriver, "The Copacabana." As we turned off Madison Avenue into 60th Street I said, "Driver, stop on the other side of the street." My dad and I walked over to our old doorway. I didn't have to explain what I was doing. He could appreciate the corny "show business" mood of the moment. We were five or six hours earlier than we used to be, and it was ten years later. My father was staring across the street and back through the years as I was. I remembered Buddy saying, "You'll dance on their tables someday." I tried to remember something pleasant about those years, but it seemed that the first real happiness to come out of all that time was this ten minutes of looking back on it.

My father put his arm around my shoulder and we walked across the street.

People were pouring into the dressing room, grabbing for my hand, reaching out to smack me on the back. "Tremendous!" "Great opening." "You were fantastic." But their words were shrouded by what I knew to be true. We hadn't made it. We'd stayed on for an hour and twenty minutes and I'd never tried harder in my life, I'd thrown everything I had at them, I'd dug down deeper than ever but I hadn't been able to find that extra half ounce that lifts the show off the ground. They'd given us strong applause, but they'd only been acknowledging a good, solid performance. They hadn't been cheering us for a great one.

People were filling the room, smiling, shouting how well we'd done, but I couldn't focus on their faces or listen to what they were saying. All I could hear was the big hollow where the applause had ended just below the level I had hoped for. I'd blown it. I had wanted to explode them through the roof with my performance but I hadn't done it.

Our dressing room was a suite in the Hotel Fourteen above the Copa. I was taking my shirt off in the bedroom when Sam Bramson came in with some other men from the Morris office. "You were great, Sammy. They were calling for more even after you left." I looked into their eyes as they continued praising our performance and I could see they meant it. Sam patted me on the shoulder. "Get some rest before the next show." I was grateful to him for that. I could have listened all night if it had been true. They closed the door behind them and I fell on the bed doing cop-outs to myself: it was the first time in a new room, I was nervous, it was a lousy audience, the music wasn't right. But the music was perfect and there's no such thing as a bad audience if there's a great performance. And what if it was a new room? I'm supposed to be a pro.

I went over every move I'd made. It could be only one thing: I'd run scared and tried to kill the ball. I'd stood offstage waiting for my cue, thinking, "I'm gonna give them a performance like the world has never seen." I'd reached so deep and desperately and belted so hard, I'd been so involved with making my performance letter-perfect, that I all but forgot the audience. I never created a relationship with them. For years I had known the importance of touching the audience and I had finally started doing it. Now, when it counted more than ever—I hadn't done it.

I had one more chance. The top people in the business always waited for the second show. If I could just get across to *them* . . . but I couldn't remember what it feels like to touch the people. Or how to do it. I'd never really known how. I could control the rest of my performance, but this was nothing I could try to do, it was something intangible that happened by itself between me and the audience. What if it never happens again?

The door opened. "You sleepin', Poppa?"

"No, Dad. C'mon in."

He handed me a slip of paper. "Ronnie, the maître d' downstairs, just sent up this list of celebrities that's here for the second show, in case you wants t'introduce 'em. This way you won't leave nobody out."

I looked at the first few names, Milton Berle, Red Buttons, Jackie Miles, Eddie Fisher. . . . Just what I need. I crumpled it up. "Dad, this is very efficient, but where the hell would I get off asking people like this to stand up and take a bow? Maybe for the next opening. If there ever is one."

"Whaddya mean if there ever is one?"

"Nothing, Dad. Just talk."

I turned on the television set and tried to get involved in a movie. I looked at my watch. Page and Bray, the opening dance act, were about to go on. Then there'd be a production number, then Mary Small, then another production number, then us. I had about an hour, but I started dressing so I could be downstairs early. Another feel of the room might help.

Jules Podell was standing near the cash register in the kitchen. He beckoned to me and I walked over.

"Have a drink, kid."

"Thanks, Mr. Podell. I'll have a Coke."

His eyes narrowed. "Kid, I said have a drink! It'll do you good." He rapped the bar hard with his heavy star-sapphire ring. "Bring us two scotches." He didn't even look up to see if the bartender was there. He knew he would be. Two shot glasses were placed in front of us and filled. Mr. Podell raised his. "Good luck."

I reached for mine. He growled. "What the hell are you shaking about?"

"Well, you know, opening night nerves, I guess."

"What's there to be nervous about? You've *got* the job!" I couldn't believe my ears but damned if he wasn't yelling at me. "What the hell do you think I hire? Amateurs? If you didn't belong here, you wouldn't be here. Do you think you'd be starring at the Copacabana if you were a bum! Let me tell you something, kid. Don't worry about them out there. The hell with 'em. The only one you gotta worry about is me. And my contract with you says you're a *star!*"

The last production number had ended. Morty was already out there and Nathan would be setting up the drums and putting my dancing shoes under the piano. Mr. Podell put out his hand. He was rough and gruff and hard as nails, yet he'd shown untold warmth and understanding in those few minutes.

The announcer was saying, "Ladies and gentlemen, the Copacabana proudly presents: *The Will Mastin Trio* . . ." Morty brought the band in on the button, stinging the audience with loud, sharp notes, the stage lights came up full, my father and Will slapped the stage with their opening steps and stood back exactly on beat as Morty stopped the music dead. Every sound and movement in the room stopped with it. He let the absolute silence hang in the air for a full two seconds, he dropped into *Street Scene* and the announcer said, "Featuring *Sammy Davis, Jr.*" The audience was turning around, looking, anticipating, applauding in welcome. I waited for three bars—and I walked onto the stage.

The time I was onstage might have been a minute or an

hour or my lifetime, it was as unreal, as immeasurable as a dream which covers a year but takes only seconds to happen. There were no clocks in the world, no tomorrows, no yesterdays. I was welded to the emotions of the audience. Suddenly the bond between us was snapped by a tentative crackling of applause answered by a sharp burst from across the room. Another picked it up and it began spreading, gaining urgency, ripping through the stillness like something wild breaking loose, rolling toward me with such force that I couldn't hear the music playing or the words I was singing—only that monumental roar growing and growing and finally wrapping itself around me, penetrating until it filled every inch of my being.

My head fell to my chest. My arms hung limp at my sides. When I could look up I saw a wall of people rising all around us; table by table they were getting to their feet, standing and applauding us. I was unable to feel my feet on the floor or the fingers I knew I was digging into my palms, or hear anything except one vast, magnificent roar that went on and on and on. I looked at my father and Will and the tears were pouring out of their eyes as they were from mine. After more than twenty years of performing together this was the climax, the ultimate payoff. I lost count of the bows we took and the encores we did before I was stumbling offstage, exhausted, stunned, crying for joy.

Mr. Podell had me by the arm, half leading, half carrying me toward the kitchen, waving to my father and Will to follow. The whole kitchen staff in aprons, the waiters, the busboys, over a hundred people, gathered around us. Mr. Podell led them in three cheers and said, "From now on, Sammy, you wear the Copa Bonnet."

I heard my own voice saying, "Thanks, boss," and it startled me. I'd never called any man boss. Then he was walking me back to the elevator. "Y'see what I told you? There's no amateurs headlining at the Copa." He gave me an affectionate shot on the back that flung me into the elevator and almost flattened me. I looked back in time to see him beaming like an angel as the doors closed.

The hall to our dressing room was jammed with people I'd never even met, waiting in line to get in. Jess Rand cleared an aisle through them for me. My father came rushing out of the bedroom. "Earl Wilson wants five minutes with you—he's in the other room. And Danny Stradella said come down to the Lounge soon as we're dressed 'cause he's throwing a party for us." The phone was ringing. I heard Jess saying, "You'll have to call back. He just got offstage and he can't talk to anybody."

As I walked into the Lounge a captain came straight for me. "Right this way, Sammy." He cleared an aisle for me through the crowd. Someone touched me on the arm. "Sammy, will you sign this for me, please?" "My pleasure, ma'am." . . . "Sammy, I met you in Miami. I'm a friend of Eddie C." "Nice to see you again, sir." The captain came back for me. "Please, folks, let him through." . . . "Great show, Sammy. Listen, my daughter's too shy to ask, but would you sign this menu for her?" The captain fought his way back to me. "This way, Mr. Davis." When we finally made it to the table he shrugged. "I'm sorry. I tried to bail you out."

"Don't give it a thought, baby. Can't brush the paying customers." Danny's table covered the entire length of the room and was loaded down with bottles of liquor and champagne. I leaned over to my father. "Would you believe that it just took me twenty minutes to walk across this room?"

A captain was standing near Mama, waiting for her order. When he came to me I handed him a ten. He was surprised. "Thank you, Mr. Davis." *Don't thank me, baby. You're one of a thousand lousy things that drove me so hard that I'm sitting here now and you're taking Mama's order.* "Are you sure I can't bring you something? Maybe a little soup?"

"Bring him a steak!" The captain nodded and hurried away. Mr. Podell was beaming. "You've gotta keep up your strength, kid." The quartet on the bandstand started playing "Birth of the Blues," dedicating it to me. A woman came by. "Can I have your autograph, Sammy?" A waiter put a steak in front of me.

I signed the menu she'd handed me. I reached for my fork and knife but someone else was waiting. They were surrounding me, holding out papers and pens. Danny pushed his way through the crowd. "Hey, give him a break. He's tired. He just did two shows. Let'm eat his meal." "That's okay, Danny. Thanks." I reached for another pen.

At 3:30 I thought: If I got up and left now—that would be a class move.

As I walked toward the door, the band hit "Birth of the Blues" and everybody started applauding me. I turned, waved, and went through the door.

"Taxi, Mr. Davis?" The doorman whistled for a cab and rushed to open its door for me. I gave him a ten. He tipped his hat. "Good night, Mr. Davis." And looking to see that my feet were safely inside, closed the door as though it were made entirely of glass.

As the cab pulled away I reached for a cigarette and was aware that for the first time all evening there was no one there trying to light it for me.

After I'd read and absorbed every word of the reviews, I called Will's room. "Massey? You see the papers yet?"

"We couldn't ask for anything more, could we?"

"They're fantastic! Listen, I wanted to speak to you last night but it got a little wild. The light cues weren't picked up on the split second and it hurt some of the laughs. I think the only way we're going to get what we want is by having our own man."

"Well, the truth is we could use a man to do that and to handle a lot of other things too—transportation, props, setting up. I think I know just the man we oughta get. Big John Hopkins. The fella who used to be Nat Cole's road manager. I'll take care of it." Then the all-business tone was gone. "Mose Gastin? How's it feel being a star?"

As I hung up I shifted my eyes from the cardboard coffee

cup to the waxed paper the Danish had come in, to the wooden spoon I'd used to stir my coffee, to the open closet half filled with unexciting suits, empty wire hangers, a dozen or so ties lumped together on the single hook. To the right of the newspaper reviews a hole in the gray blanket had been mended with white thread, the wallpaper across the room had buckled, probably from the heat of the uncovered radiator. I *didn't* feel like a star, but I sure was going to.

I leafed through the classified directory to "Hotels." Abruptly I was aware of being colored. I skimmed the list. The Warwick. They catered to a lot of show people, it was a first-class hotel, good location. Fifty-fourth and Sixth.

I opened the window and waited for a gust of air to grope its way in. I sat down at the phone and stared at my hand on the receiver . . . there's only one way to find out. I lifted the phone and gave the number to the operator.

"This is Sammy Davis, Jr. Do you have a suite available for me? For about four weeks."

I went to Will's room, told him I was moving to the Warwick, got a fistful of cash, and hit the stores.

I glanced at the bolts of fabric along the wall of Cye Martin's shop. He rushed from the back. "Sammy, that show you did last night—I never saw anything like it. I mean . . ."

"Thanks. Look, baby, I'd like to see Rocco. I've got an idea I want to go over with him."

Rocco was cutting the shoulder of a jacket. "Oh? You're not going to stop when a star comes in? You won't put down the scissors, right?"

He took one last snip. "Mr. Davis, how are you? What can I do for you?"

"I want you to make me some suits with three buttons down the front, a center vent . . ."

"But we're making the two-button Hollywood lounge suit with side vents. Nobody's wearing three-button suits anymore."

"I like to have three-button suits with center vents."

When I'd chosen the fabrics I asked Cye, "How long does it take to make a suit?"

"I can have these for you in—three weeks."

"No, what I want to know is, how long does the process take? I mean the actual cutting and sewing. How many hours?"

"Oh. Well, it takes maybe eight hours for a fitting to be ready, then after that there are corrections . . . figure another twenty hours to make the finished garment."

"But in my case we don't need a fitting 'cause he's got my pattern perfect from the last time, right? Fine. Then, today is Friday, so that means I can have five suits by Wednesday, right?"

"Sammy! I couldn't begin to do it in less than two weeks. The men go home after eight hours."

"I'll pay them to stay overtime."

"Bubbele, be patient. Can't you wait?"

"No. I've waited all my life. I'm through waiting."

"Well, how about if I give you three on Wednesday?"

"Give me at least five on Wednesday and the rest by Saturday."

I stood outside Sulka, sizing up the marble front and the elegant window displays.

A salesman zoomed toward me. "Mr. Davis! I'm one of your greatest admirers. What may I show you?"

"Everything."

"Splendid." I followed him to the tie department and he handed me a basket. "Just drop your selections in here."

"Why, thank you. Well, here we go gathering nuts in May . . ." I picked out a few ties. "I love the quality of these but I wish they weren't quite so wide."

"Why don't you let me take you upstairs, show you our silks and make them to order for you. There's no extra charge and that way you'll have them exactly the length and width you'd like." He smiled and led me to the elevator. "While we're upstairs I'll show you our robes and pajamas."

"Excellent. Do you by any chance have pajamas th cut a little slim? I'd love to avoid the balloony pants."

"We can easily make them to your specifications."

"You mean with a fitting? For pajamas? *Marvelous*. And while we're at it, let's do something a little different. How about a nice double-breasted pajama, cut exactly like a suit, except no pockets in the pants."

The clerk at Alfred Dunhill of London, Ltd., lifted the large silver lighter gently off the glass shelf. "We call it the 'Standard Unique.' It's a fine lighter, sir."

"I love it. I'll take two of them, please. And may I see those cigarette boxes . . . and that pipe with the curved stem. Yes, that's the one. A bit like Sherlock Holmes, isn't it? I'll take that. And will you show me that set over there, the one with a pipe for each day of the week. Charming idea. One can never grow tired of the same pipe that way. Can one? Now, what tobacco would you recommend for me as a starter?"

Big John Hopkins was in the dressing room with Will and Nathan when I got there. "Mr. Davis"—he laughed—"I believe you're the gentleman who called for a road manager. Now, I've worked for some very fine acts like Nat 'King' Cole, Lionel Hamp . . ."

I wanted to play it cool but I couldn't. "Well? Didn't I say you'd be working for me someday?"

John roared like a laughing lion, picked me up like I was a glass of water, and swung me around in the air. "You were right, boss! And I'm glad I'm here to see it." He put me down and shook his head. "What's been happening to you! Good God Almighty! Did you see where Lee Mortimer called you a miracle?" He took a newspaper clipping from his pocket.

"John, you're working for a very big star now. I mean—really, I couldn't possibly begin to read *everything* that's written about me."

He laughed in my face. "Hell, you can't con me with that bored jazz. You musta already read it. I knew you when your little bottom was hangin' out and it ain't been that long since then."

When I came back between shows a vaguely familiar-looking man, carrying a little black suitcase, was waiting for me. "Sammy, my name is George Unger and I'm glad to meet you. I've been around show business all my life and I never saw a performer like you." He opened the combination lock on the suitcase and began taking out platinum and gold watches, diamond rings, gold cigarette cases . . . "Whaddya like, Sammy?"

Now I placed him. He sold jewelry to a lot of show people and I seemed to remember him in Frank's dressing room at the Capitol. He kept pulling things out of the suitcase. I picked up a heavy gold money clip with a twenty-dollar gold piece mounted on it.

"Y'like that?"

"Yeah, it's pretty crazy. How much is . . ."

"Put it in your pocket."

"But how much?"

"What're you worrying about? Put it in your pocket." He moved around the room giving away gold chains and key rings to everyone there.

"Are you kidding with all this? Look, George, I appreciate the gesture, but I'd really rather pay."

"Will you stop it, please? You'll embarrass me."

I put the money clip in my pocket. "Okay. It's ridiculous but I'd never want to embarrass a nut who's trying to give me a present." I browsed through some of his things. "I'm in the market for a good watch."

He showed me a Patek Philippe, then a platinum Vacheron-Constantin. "Here. Look at this one if you can stand it. It's the thinnest watch in the world. Go to a jewelry store and price the same watch at eleven hundred fifty. It's yours for nine hundred."

"I'll take it. Can I pay you at the end of the week?"

"No! Not till the end of the *year*. Maybe not even till *next* year."

"You've gotta be kidding."

He threw his hands in the air. "What is it with you? I'm making statements of fact and you're asking me am I kidding. Now be a good fellow. You like something? Take it! You got any presents you have to buy people? Take 'em now. If you don't see 'em here, tell me what you want and I'll bring 'em around. I've got 'em at the store. And stop annoying me about money."

"George, you're out of your mind but if that's how you want to play, I dig this kind of a game. Hey, listen, have you got a solid-gold pen? With a heavy point? Something I could use for signing autographs?"

Standing at a window in my suite at the Warwick, looking out over the city, I felt as though I were in a John Garfield movie.

I opened the ribbon on the Dunhill box. The lighters were in flannel bags. I set one on the coffee table and put the other in the bedroom on my night table. I distributed the cigarette boxes, set the pipes up in the bedroom, and started on the Sulka boxes.

Morty Stevens called.

"Baby, I hope you've got something very important to say. You interrupted me right in the middle of putting away my gold garters. Now, if you have any class at all you'll get off the phone and be over here in fifteen minutes."

He blinked at the sight of me in maroon silk pajamas with white piping, matching robe, and burgundy velvet slippers.

"Just a little something Sulka whipped up for me." I took him on a tour of my closet and dresser drawers. "Don't get hysterical, baby. Just some of the little niceties of life. Hey, whaddya say we call room service? We can watch television and have dinner right here. How about steak, salad, and coffee?"

I got room service on the phone. "Darling, this is Sammy Davis, Jr. I'd like to order some dinner. . . . Oh? . . . Why, yes, fine. Thank you."

Morty was looking at me when I hung up. "How come you didn't order?"

"Baby, I wish you had a little more class. How can you order dinner until they send up a captain with the menu?"

We were finishing our coffee when Jess Rand called. "I've got some wild news for you. I arranged for you to have a lay-out in *Look* magazine."

"Beautiful."

"You're damned right. I set up a dinner for tomorrow night with the photographer Milton Greene."

"You're kidding. He's an idol of mine."

The operator buzzed me back as soon as I hung up. "Mr. Davis, did you want service on the line?"

I rested the phone back on its cradle, and turned slowly. "Morty, from now on when you call, it may take a while to get me." I crossed my legs and puffed on my pipe. "You'll have to give your name and then the operator'll have to tell me who it is and . . . well, who knows, I mean I can't be expected to be in a telephone mood *all* the time."

Will closed the dressing-room door. "Sammy, I want a word with you. You and your father are spending money like you're plain drunk."

"I can't talk about what my dad's doing. That's his business."

"Then we'll just talk about you. The way you're buying clothes and jewels and records and hi-fi sets all over the place and spreading yourself out in a hotel suite . . . why, you're act-ing like you believe the mint is working overtime just for you. You must've spent five thousand dollars this week."

"So what? It's only a week's salary."

"It's *five* weeks' salary. Sure, we're making five thousand a week but we're splitting it three ways and we're *supposed* to only take a thousand a week apiece in salary and put the rest aside for agents and taxes and expenses. But this week alone you've already borrowed three thousand from me in cash, plus you drew your salary, plus I know you've got a whole lot of charge accounts because you've been letting them send the bills to the Morris office. Now, I told them to go ahead and pay 'em, but you gotta cut down. I'm afraid to see what it totals up to."

"What's the difference? So it'll take me a few weeks to catch up. How many weeks a year will we be playing New York anyway? Look, I'm having a little splurge. I can cut down when we hit the smaller towns where they don't have these kinds of stores. And by then I'll have everything I need, anyway."

"I hope so. You've got to think about the future."

"I am thinking about the future."

"When you buy yourself ten suits at a time?"

"That's right. I'm a *star!* And I've got to *look* like one. When I walk down the street I want people to say, 'Hey, that's Sammy Davis, Jr.' I can't be a star just the few hours we're onstage. I've got to feel like a star every minute I'm awake."

"Sammy, what's the name of that comic who was sitting outside?"

"What's the difference?"

"*That's* the difference! You don't even know his name and you gave him a hundred dollars."

"Massey, he's a performer and a good one too. If he needed a few bucks badly enough to have to ask for it, well, I'm sorry, but I couldn't turn him down."

"I'm not saying don't help people. But you're overdoing it. Why, the word'll get around there's a damned fool at the Copa handing out money and he doesn't even want to know your name!"

"Maybe. But it would've been a long walk back to the South Side if the Wessons hadn't helped us in Chicago. And I can't forget what it was like when I had to ask B and he came through for us."

"I can't forget it either, Sammy. And it could happen again. That's why you've gotta be more careful with your money."

"Oh, come on, Massey. It's not going to happen again. We've made it for sure this time, and we're going to keep on making it. My God, we've got enough offers to keep us working two hundred weeks this year. *Nothing* can stop us now!"

"The only thing that sure is money in the bank! Don't you see that you've been working the Copa for nothing?"

"How do you figure *that*?"

"You've got nothing left, so you've worked for nothing."

"The way I see it you're the one who's working for nothing. That suit you're wearing is the same one you wore four years ago. And you're still living in the cheapest room you can get at the America, right? We're making five thousand a week and what've you got to show for it? A bankbook?"

"That's what I work for."

"Well, it's not what *I* work for. The money has never been my payoff for a week's work. Never! When we were starving from one town to another I wasn't thinking, 'Someday I'll have a pile of money.' I was thinking, 'Someday we'll make it and I'll live like a human being. I'll go where I want to go and I'll be able to do anything I want to do!' I've got no complaints about this week. I've got everything I wanted out of it."

14

The real estate broker drove me straight to the colored section of Los Angeles.

"Nothing up in the hills, in the Hollywood section?"

"Well—you see—uh . . ."

"I see."

"Mr. Davis, try to understand. If you were buying it would be a lot simpler. An outright sale—well, these things can be handled. But renting presents certain additional problems. . . ."

Obviously I wasn't big enough yet. "Will you take me back to the Sunset Colonial, please."

"But don't you want to see any of these?"

"I don't have to."

I was never again going to live in a ghetto. Not even if the wall around it were made of solid gold.

I took a cab to my father's apartment. "I'm sorry, Mama. You'll just have to stay here with Dad and Peewee for a little while until I can work this out somehow."

My father spoke softly. "Sammy, they ain't about to let you have a house up there in the hills. Not to buy, not to rent. No way. So, why tear yourself apart over it? You can't change these things."

We were booked as summer replacements for Eddie Cantor's Colgate shows, so we played clubs around L.A. and San Francisco. I'd started recording for Decca, and "Hey, There," one of my first sides with them, was starting to appear on all the record charts.

My friendship with Frank was becoming really precious to me. I could relax with him more than I had in the early days, but I was still "the kid" to him and he was still "Sinatra" to me. He took me up to the Bogarts' a few times and those were always beautiful evenings. Bogart might have been color-blind. He decided on somebody with his second level of understanding. There was no "he's a this" or "he's a that." Bogart got to know a man before he decided if he liked him or not.

I was dating anyone I wanted to, not "white girls" or "colored girls"—girls! If I saw one I liked and got the nod and she happened to be white there'd be a voice saying, "Hold it. She's trouble." Then there was another voice that answered. He was the swinger. "Go, baby. If she wants you and you want her then damn the torpedoes and full speed ahead. *Go.*" And I went, playing both sides of town, each with its little extra kick: on one side, the satisfaction of knowing that nobody was telling me how to live; on the other, peace of mind and the joy I got out of the fantastic attention my own people were giving me. I hit those hot downtown bars empty-handed, but when I left I was the Pied Piper of the Sunset Colonial, heading home with the freshest, best-looking tomatoes in the whole grocery store skipping along behind me.

The phone rang. "Sammy, I'm at the Morris office and something just came up. How fast can you get down here?"

"I'm in the middle of packing, Massey, I'm not dressed."

"Then *get* dressed. You'll be glad you did."

The receptionist led me to the room where Will and my father were waiting with one of the agents from the nightclub department.

Will said, "We're playing Vegas. The Old Frontier. And we'll be *living* at the Old Frontier! In the best suites they got!"

"You mean right *in* the hotel?"

"And free of charge besides, and that includes food and drink *and* seventy-five hundred a week."

I resented the excitement I felt over it. "I don't know, Massey, I just don't know if anything's worth crawling in there like, 'Gee, sir, y'mean you'll really let us live at your goddamned hotel?' "

"Sammy, we're not crawling to nobody."

The Morris guy smiled. "*Crawling.* It's not good business to pass up an attraction that'll bring people to the tables. To get you now, they'll break their necks, let alone a ridiculous custom."

It was a gorgeous crisp November morning as I stepped off the train in Las Vegas. My father and Will were waiting for me on the platform. I searched their faces. "Well?"

"The best."

"No problems?"

Will shook his head. "They're bending over backwards."

As we approached the hotel I saw the big marquee: "THE WILL MASTIN TRIO featuring SAMMY DAVIS, JR." We pulled up in front of the entrance. A doorman opened my door. "I'll take care of it for you, Mr. Davis." I gave him a five and he tipped his hat. "Thanks, Mr. Davis." A bellman came over. "Take your luggage, Mr. Davis?" I pointed to a cab just pulling up. "It's in that one, baby. My valet will give it to you."

The door closed and we were alone in a huge, beautiful suite. I collapsed onto the bed, kicking my legs in the air. "I don't *never* wanta leave this room! I'd sign a contract to stay here for the rest of my *natural!*" I got up and looked around. There was a large basket of flowers in the living room. The card read: "Welcome to the Old Frontier" and was signed by the manager.

Morty was rehearsing the band. I sat in the back of the room listening, and checked John out on the lights.

When Morty gave the guys a break I called him aside. "Baby, I'll open with 'Birth of the Blues.' "

"You're joking! What'll you go off on?"

"We'll use 'Fascinating Rhythm.' Look, we throw away all the rules here. The plotting of a show for a Vegas audience is different than anywhere else. For openers, the hotels are all but giving away the best shows that money can buy, so the average cat who comes in to see us has been in town for a few days and he's already seen maybe six or eight of the biggest names in the business. This same guy may never see a live show from one end of the year to the next when he's home but after a few days here he's Charley-Make-Me-Laugh. Now, above and beyond that, plus the normal nightclub distractions, if I don't hook that guy right from the start and hang on to him, I'm dead, because he'll be watching me but he'll start wondering if when he leaves maybe he should try ten the hard way. So it's like when we make records: we do or die in the first eight bars." He whistled softly. "And on top of that, where in a normal club if I start off a little slow I can always stay on until eventually I get 'em and they leave saying, 'Hey, isn't it nice the way he does those long shows,' in Vegas the headliner has exactly fifty-two minutes, including bows. They're in the gambling business here and everything's timed down to the split second: there's no dancing after the shows and your check is collected before the show breaks. Those doors lead into the casino and they want the people to walk through them *on time!* There are just so many minutes in each day and the hotel anticipates a certain amount of gambling revenue for each one of them. I can't steal any of that time to make sure I come off smelling like a rose. They pay me to bring customers *to* the tables, not to keep them away. So watch me extra carefully for the cues, baby, 'cause once I'm out there it's fight-for-your-life time."

As we stood in the wings listening to them shouting for more my father cocked his head and sighed, "I hope the word don't spread that we're bad for the heart." The three of us walked arm in arm back to the dressing rooms. "You gonna take a look around the casino, Poppa? Maybe take yourself a few bows?"

"I don't know, Dad. I'll see."

I put on a black mohair suit, a gray-and-black-striped tie, my platinum watch, folded a handkerchief into my breast pocket, and took a last look in the mirror. I removed the handkerchief.

I stood outside the casino, sweating. A security guard passed me. "Anything I can do for you, Sammy?" I shook my head. A few people coming out spotted me. "Great show, Sammy . . ."

I lit another cigarette, stamped it out, pushed the door open, and walked in.

The deputy sheriff who was standing just inside said, "Hi ya, Sammy."

I smiled back and kept walking. I was right in the middle of all the sounds I'd heard before and they took form even wilder and more feverish than I'd imagined them. People were playing blackjack and roulette and shooting craps with a deadly serious hilarity, dropping coins into hundreds of one-armed bandits which lined every wall, and the sound was like we were inside a huge tin piggy bank and somebody was shaking all the money around.

There was an empty seat at one of the blackjack tables. The faces around the table seemed pleasant enough, but how would they react to me sitting down to gamble with them?

I broke a hundred-dollar bill at the cashier's window. The seat was still open. I went over to one of the machines and dropped a silver dollar in the slot. If I win, I go to the table. I pulled the handle and watched the spinning figures slow to a halt . . . cherries . . . cherries . . . orange. There was a sharp click and silver dollars poured out.

The dealer was in the middle of a hand as I put my money on the table and pulled up the chair. Someone said something about me but I couldn't catch what it was. I kept my eyes on the green cloth. People were gathering around. I looked up. They were smiling.

I pushed a silver dollar forward and played my first hand. I won. I let the two dollars ride—and won again. I pulled back my winnings and kept playing for two dollars. A woman at the end of the table smiled. "I loved your show." The dealer glared at her. "Would you like another card?" She giggled nervously and looked back at her hand. I lit a cigarette and he slid an ash-tray toward me. He jerked his head toward the nightclub. "I hope you're as lucky out here as you are in there." The man next to me said, "That's not luck. That's talent." A cocktail waitress came by. "Would you like a drink, Mr. Davis?" "I'd love a Coke, thank you."

I began to feel some of my audience drifting away. I handed the dealer a hundred-dollar bill. "I'll take some of those five-dollar chips, baby." Without counting them I pushed a stack of blue chips forward. Someone said, "Yeah. Go, Sammy. Break the bank." I won. I let it all ride. A woman yelled, "Arnold, come over here. Sammy Davis is playing. Hurry, Arnold." The dealer was all but handing me the chips in a shovel. He looked at the mountain of them spilling over the whole table in front of me. "You want twenty-five-dollar chips for these, Sammy?" "No, thanks, baby. These are doing fine for me." The crowd was three deep around the table now. I pushed the whole pile forward. "Shoot the works."

"Oh my God, Arnold, will you look what he's doing?" "It's peanuts to him. Do you know what he makes a week?"

The dealer casually flipped the cards around the table. The crowd was silent. The ace of diamonds slid face up in front of me. I opened my down card. The jack of hearts. There was a roar behind me as if I'd just gone off on "Birth of the Blues." Arnold's wife was going out of her mind and people were pounding me on the back as the dealer stacked hundred-dollar chips against my bet and then added half again, the bonus for blackjack.

I wasn't going to top that moment. I pulled the mass of chips toward me and dropped a handful of them into the dealer's shirt pocket. "Thanks, Sammy." A woman moaned.

"You're not stopping, are you?" I smiled. "It's a definite quit while I'm ahead." As the crowd opened up for me I heard, "Hurry. Sit there, Arnold. It's a lucky seat."

I walked through the casino, both hands holding the bundle of chips against my chest . . . "Hey, Sammy, y'want some help gettin' rid of those?" . . . "How much you sock 'em for, kid?" . . . "The rich get richer, don't they?" . . . A deputy rushed ahead of me to help me with the door.

Outside, alone, I had to fight an urge to throw the chips in the air like confetti. It was such a joke. Such a big, fat joke.

On my way to breakfast, I passed a couple of the chorus kids sunbathing around the pool. I did bits with them for a few minutes, had some coffee, wandered over to the casino, and sat at the bar drinking a Coke and watching the action. A middle-aged guy with a swinging-looking blonde raised his glass and smiled. "You're the greatest, Sammy."

The manager sat down on the stool next to me. "Sammy, I hope you won't mind, but I'd consider it a favor if you'd try not to spend too much time around the pool."

I looked him in the eye, waiting for "It's not that *we* mind but you know how people are."

He said, "You saw what happened in the casino when you played last night. There were shooters playing ten times as big as you were, but nobody paid any attention to them. Whenever a star sits down at a table he draws a crowd. And it's fine, no harm there. But if you hang around the pool during the day you'll attract crowds there too, and frankly we'd rather not have you pull them away from the tables. Naturally, if you feel like a swim, fine, but we'll appreciate it if you'll keep it down to a minimum."

The pulse in my forehead began slowing to normal again. I smiled. "I don't know how to swim anyway. Besides, I've already got my tan."

I walked around, found a blackjack table that looked good,

and ran $500 into a twenty-five-dollar chip. I dropped it into
the dealer's shirt pocket and stood up. "Thanks, Sammy. Tough
luck."

"I'll get even tonight, baby."

I was dressing after the second show when one of the boy
dancers came into the dressing room. "No party tonight?"

"Sorry, baby. Gotta run into L.A. I'm doing the sound track
for *Six Bridges to Cross*."

He looked at my rack of clothes and stroked the sleeve of a
gray silk. "Crazy-looking threads."

I lifted the suit off the rack. "Wear it in good health."

"Hey, no—I didn't mean—"

"No big deal, baby. I'd like you to have it."

I heard him down the hall. "You won't believe what Sammy
Davis just did. I was looking at this suit . . ."

I felt like Frank had always looked—like a star to my fingertips.

As I stepped out of the dressing room, someone grabbed my
arm. "Whaddya say, chicky?"

"Jess, you nut. When'd you get in?"

"Ten minutes ago. How's it going?" He walked outside with
me.

"We're doing all the business in town and it's been the ball
of all time."

"What've you been doing?"

"I do what everybody else does." I stopped at the sound of
my own words, gripped by the understanding of their meaning.
I snapped myself out of it. "Listen, here's the skam. I'm driving
to L.A. to do the sound track for *Six Bridges*, I'll be back tomorrow, sixish, we'll grab some steam, then it's a little din-
din, and you can catch the show." I tapped him on the arm.
"Meanwhile, grab a chick, have some booze, sign my name,
and I'll see you tomorrow."

I took the long way around to my room, through the casino,
just for the sheer joy of walking through it. The deputy sheriff
at the door gave me a big "Hi ya, Sammy." I waved back and

kept moving through all the action. Some guys at a dice table made room for me. "Come on in, Sammy. We've got a hot shooter."

"Thanks. Can't tonight. Gotta run into L.A. Catch y'tomorrow."

I'd just finished showering when there was a knock on the door. One of the chorus chicks was standing there, smiling.

"Hey, this hotel has crazy room service." I told her, "Darling, I sent Charley around to say there'd be no party tonight. I have to go into L.A."

"I know." She stepped in. "But he said you weren't leaving till three. I thought maybe you'd like some company while you were getting dressed." I watched her disappear into the bedroom. The doors weren't only opening, they were swinging!

Charley Head, the man I'd hired in L.A., was waiting in the car. I climbed into the back seat and stretched out. The big neon sign in front of the hotel was flashing my name on and off and I lay there enjoying a delicious drowsiness. As we turned off the Strip and onto the highway I said, "Keep it under fifty, baby." I felt around my chest for my mezuzah. I sat up. Maybe the chain had opened. I reached inside my shirt, around my waist, but it wasn't there. I distinctly remembered taking it off to shower, but I couldn't recall putting it back on again. It must have slipped off the dresser, and with the chick there and in the hurry of leaving, I hadn't noticed. I was tempted to turn around and go back for it, but we'd been traveling at least twenty minutes and it would mean losing an hour.

I lay back watching the stars through the window. There were three particularly bright ones in a row, like diamond studs on a black velvet vest. The desert air was sweet and clear and it seemed a shame that all that beauty had always been there to be enjoyed but it had never looked the same through the windows of a bus. I closed my eyes. The rolling of the car increased my drowsiness, and I let myself sink deeper and more comfortably into it.

15

Why do they always say hospital sheets are cool and crisp? They were hot and sticky. And I didn't have to ask "Where am I?" I sensed it or smelled it or remembered it. The room was very dark, I turned my head from one side to the other but there wasn't a crack of light—a bulb, the moon—nothing! It was too dark just to be night. I must have been near an open window because I felt a gust of air pass over me, hot and thick like it never is at night. I heard cars moving outside. Slowly. A lot of them. I could hear a radio soap opera playing, people talking in a daytime tone and walking carelessly down the corridor. There definitely was daylight around me. I just couldn't see it.

I grabbed for my legs but my arms wouldn't move. My hands could feel iron bars on both sides of me and if I had hands then I had to have arms. I kicked my legs and heard them swishing against the bedsheets. I banged my feet together so hard that they hurt. Thank God I had feet. There was terrible pressure around my head. I stretched my neck toward my hands to feel what was wrong.

"Don't touch your bandages, Mr. Davis. Everything is all right."

It was a woman's voice. I fell back against the pillow. Oh,

God. I can't see, I can't move, and "everything is all right, Mr. Davis." "Are you a nurse? Am I blind?"

"Don't worry. Everything's going to be fine."

"But I can't see! Am I blind?"

"You have bandages over your eyes. You were in a bad automobile accident."

"*Please!* I know that. Just tell me yes or no. *Am I blind?*"

"No. You're not blind."

Naturally she'd say that. They wouldn't let a nurse break it to me. Not like this, not the second I wake up.

"If you promise not to pull at your bandages I can take the straps off your arms now."

"Thank you." I felt my legs. They were okay. There was a small bandage on the palm of my right hand. I put my hands to my face, slowly, so she wouldn't think I was pulling at the bandages. I started touching them at the top of my head but I couldn't feel my skin until I got to my mouth. I was wrapped up like a mummy.

I turned my head toward the sound of footsteps coming into the room. "Good morning, Mr. Davis. I'm Dr. Hull."

I nodded, waiting. He wasn't saying anything and I was suddenly afraid he would. "Look, Doc, I know this sounds like a B movie, but where am I?"

"This is the Community Hospital at San Bernardino. You were operated on last night."

"You operated on me?"

"Yes."

"Doctor, please—will I be able to dance? Am I . . . blind?"

"You're not blind. You're going to see. You'll be able to dance and sing and do everything you ever did. But I removed your left eye."

I distinctly heard the words, but the tone—it was like "Shall we have lunch?"

"Mr. Davis, losing an eye isn't as tragic as it seems when you first hear it."

He really *had* said it.

"Try not to touch the bandages."

I dropped my hands. I felt like an idiot. Here a man tells me he took out my eye and I'm checking to see if he's kidding.

"You're handling it very bravely."

"Doc, you'd better tell me some more about it 'cause I'm about to be the scaredest brave man you ever saw."

"We'll discuss it in detail when you're rested, but for the moment what it amounts to is that you struck your left eye against the pointed cone in the center of your steering wheel. When you were brought here yesterday morning . . ."

Yesterday? If a whole night went by, then what happened in Vegas? Who did the show?

". . . the doctors on duty felt that although the eye was severely damaged there was still a possibility of saving it, so they called me because I specialize in this sort of operation. When I examined you I agreed that it might be saved. However, from the amount of damage done, the best you'd ever have had in that eye would be ten percent vision. Although that would seem to justify saving it, we've learned that the damaged eye pulls, or leans, so heavily on the good one that eventually the healthy eye is weakened and the patient suffers what we call 'sympathetic blindness.' As a result, in a few years you might have had almost no sight at all and for that reason I recommended the removal . . ."

The bed was turning and I grabbed for the bars . . . I don't have to hold on, I can't fall off. The bed isn't really moving. I took deep breaths, trying to fight the nausea.

"With one perfectly healthy eye you'll have excellent vision. As for appearance, you'll have an artificial eye and eventually no one but you will know the difference."

"A glass eye?"

"We don't use glass anymore. They're made of plastic. In any event you'll be wearing a patch for a while."

"Aha. Floyd Gibbons, eh?"

His hand was on my arm. "That's the spirit. I know it's a tremendous shock to find that you have only one eye, but the eye is lost and that cannot be changed. You can take the attitude that everything else is lost too—and it will be, or you can take the attitude that you still have one perfect eye. You can see. You have both legs and both arms. You have a relatively small adjustment to make before resuming a completely normal life. Try to not think of what you've lost but of how much you still have."

My father was holding my hand between both of his. Will was on the other side of the bed, patting my shoulder.

"Hi, Dad, Massey. Where's Mama?"

"I'm right here, Sammy."

I asked, "Hey, how about Charley?"

"He's down the hall. His jaw's broke and he lost all his teeth, upper and lower, but he'll be okay."

"What happened in Vegas? I mean, the show?"

"Jeff Chandler went on for you last night, Poppa. He called here after the first show and he said when you wakes up to tell you the people was sitting at their tables and cryin' just thinkin' about what happened to you."

My father had walked across the room and he must have been holding his hands or a handkerchief against his mouth so I wouldn't hear him crying. Somebody kept trying to light a match and Will was clearing his throat. I was glad I couldn't see their faces.

"Well, folks—I guess this wraps us up." I waited, hoping somebody might say it didn't make any difference, that we'd be as strong as ever. But nobody said it and I'd have laughed if they had. Sure, they'd cry for me on one dramatic night. People always cry at funerals. Then they go home and forget you.

I remembered telling Will, "You don't understand, Massey. Nothing can stop us now."

The hospital was very quiet. There was an occasional pair of rubber-soled shoes making its own quiet sound down the hall. I felt around on the night table, hoping they hadn't taken away my cigarettes, but they had. I heard the day nurses coming in. That would make it seven o'clock.

My father and Will burst in.

"Aren't you guys up a little early?"

"Mose Gastin, we've been outside over an hour waiting for them to let us in. We got news like you never dreamed about."

"Poppa, what would you like to have more than anything in the world?"

"I'd like to have my goddamned career back."

"Read it to him, Will."

"Sammy, this is a telegram from the Sands Hotel in Las Vegas, Nevada." He cleared his throat. "It says, 'Firm offer for Will Mastin Trio Featuring Sammy Davis, Jr. *Twenty-five thousand per week,* first available date, please advise.' "

"They must be crazy."

My father was almost hysterical. "Crazy like a fox, Poppa. Will called the Morris office and they say clubs all over the country are breakin' their necks t'get us. They're offerin' money like we never even heard about. The Frontier's tearin' up our old contract to meet this price. We'll be lightin' cigars with what we used to make. We can write our own ticket across the country and back and all the way to London, England!"

I heard the window shades being pulled down. The nurse said, "Dr. Hull is on his way."

"Poppa, just relax yourself and get ready for when the bandages come off, 'cause Will and me'll be standin' right here with this telegram and you'll have something beautiful to see."

I'd planned to be pleasant and maybe throw a little joke at Dr. Hull when he came in but I couldn't think of one. My hands were clutching the tightened muscles of my legs under the blankets. There were five of us in the room but it was so quiet that I could hear my father breathing and the sound of the scissors cutting through the gauze, strand by strand. Then I heard the scissors being placed on a metal table. My father whispered, "Easy, Poppa." It was still dark but I knew I was okay as long as I could feel Dr. Hull's hands moving around my head, unwrapping the gauze layer by layer.

Suddenly light appeared on the right side of my head. It kept growing stronger as he unwrapped more and more, and as he removed the last layer, I had to put my hand over my eye, shielding it from the glare, uncovering it little by little.

I saw Dr. Hull's arm. My father and Will were at the end of the bed. I was shaking with laughter. "Doctor . . . thank you." I leaned against the pillow and caught my breath. The nurse mopped my face with a Kleenex. "Do you wanta know about a cat who ain't gonna take his sight for granted no more . . . Massey, call Vegas and tell 'em to get our name back up."

Dr. Hull said, "Not so fast. You've got to learn how to use your one eye first."

"What do you mean?"

"It'll be a while before you get back your senses of balance and distance. For example, you'll have trouble pouring water into a glass, objects will appear flatter than they did before. . . ."

"Doc, I don't care if *Marilyn Monroe* looks flat just as long as I can move around a stage. Hey, can I have a mirror?"

I stared at my nose. It was flatter than ever. This third break had really collapsed it, and there was a big gash across the bridge. "Oh, now wait a *minute*, Doc. I was never a debutante, but this is ridiculous!"

He took the bandage off my left eye. I'd expected to see a hole, but the lid had been sewn closed like a Boris Karloff makeup job. I put the mirror right down.

"We took thirty stitches inside and outside the lid."

"Maybe I'll break into pictures yet, Doc. I can play Frankenstein monsters."

The nurse was motioning my father and Will to leave the room with her. I turned away from the doctor but he put his hand on my shoulder. "You're entitled to a little self-pity. Just don't let yourself enjoy it too much. It won't bring back your eye but it will undermine the strength which has carried you through this so well. I'll be back tomorrow. Feel free to get out of bed, but move carefully."

I listened to him walking away. It hadn't been so bad until

he'd taken off the last bandage. I was so high from being able to see that I hadn't been prepared for it—but if it was covered with a patch, or with makeup . . . I saw the telegram propped against the dresser mirror. I'd thought I'd be able to see half what I used to see, like when I'd had two eyes and closed one. But it was less than half, almost as though they'd built a wall over my nose that blocked out everything to the left of center. I stood up, but I got dizzy and fell back against the bed. When the dizziness passed I started walking slowly across the room toward the dresser. I reached for the telegram but my hand passed right by it and touched the mirror at least three inches away. I slid my fingers across the glass until I had it. I felt dizzy again and I started back to the bed. As I turned, something struck me in the hip. A chair had been right next to me on my dead side. As I got to the bed the steel rim banged into my knees and I fell across the mattress. The telegram flew out of my hand. I groped in the air trying to catch it, but it fluttered to the floor.

The nurse walked in and helped me get under the covers and I lay there exhausted and embarrassed, wondering how much she'd seen. "Don't let it get you," she said, "it's natural." She picked up the telegram and held it out to me. I shook my head. I didn't want to look at it. I could just picture myself doing my stumbling act in Vegas. And getting a nice big round of pity.

Why the hell wouldn't she stop looking at me like she was so damned sorry for me? I tried to think of something to talk about. I pointed to the adhesive tape on the palm of my right hand. "Hey, isn't this kind of a strange place for me to get a cut? I mean, I was holding on to the steering wheel with both hands."

"That didn't happen in the accident." She opened the night-table drawer and handed me a gold medal the size of a silver dollar. It had St. Christopher on one side and the Star of David on the other. "You were holding this when you went into the operating room. We had to pry your hand open to make you let go of it. You were holding it so tight that it cut into your flesh. It's going to leave a scar."

I'd never seen it before, but I had a vague recollection of Tony Curtis and Janet Leigh walking alongside me as I was being wheeled down a hall, and of Janet pressing something into my hand and telling me, "Hold tight and pray and everything will be all right."

I gave it back to the nurse and lifted one end of the bandage and looked at the cut. It was a clear outline of the Star of David.

My father came in carrying a magazine. He seemed upset as he handed it to me. It was *Confidential* and the headline on the cover was: "WHAT MAKES AVA GARDNER RUN FOR SAMMY DAVIS, JR.?" The cover was a picture of us together. I turned to the story. The same picture was captioned: "Ava and Sammy cheek-to-cheeking it in her 16th floor suite at New York's Drake Hotel."

"Poppa—just between us—I mean, is there anything to that?"

"Dad, are you losing your mind?" I skimmed through it. "Some girls go for gold but it's bronze that 'sends' sultry Ava Gardner . . . Said Sammy after his first meeting with Ava, 'We just dig each other, that's all . . .' Ava sat glassy-eyed through a gay tour of Harlem with Sammy. Said a bartender, 'Another round and she would have been plastered.' " They'd based the whole thing on the night she'd come up to the Apollo and on the *Our World* story her studio had written. They'd capitalized on its title "Sammy Sends Me," but they left out "as a performer," and slanted all her quotes like "exciting, thrilling, masculine" about my performance onstage to make them sound like she meant in bed. Then they wrote in some smirks and left the rest to the reader's imagination. And they'd done it so well that if you didn't look carefully it sounded like Ava and I were having the swingingest affair of all time.

My father was watching me, still not sure. If he'll believe it even after I told him, then I don't have a chance. Everybody'll believe it. I called the nurse. "When you went through the telegrams and letters, was there anything from Frank Sinatra?" She shook her head. "It's very important. Are you sure?"

"Positive." She motioned toward a pile of mailbags. "I still haven't been through those."

"It wouldn't be a letter. He'd send a telegram or flowers. Or he'd call."

"Definitely not. I'd certainly remember if there'd been anything from Frank Sinatra."

I fell back against the pillow. Here's a man who's been nothing but good to me. For him to have to see this, even if he knows it's not true—it's inexcusable to have put her in a position so that this could happen to her.

I called the publicity man at her studio. "Sammy, Ava's ignoring it. If you sue you'll only bring more attention to it."

"But I've got to clear her . . . at least demand a retraction."

"Please, let it die by itself. Nobody reads retractions."

"But we can make them print the original picture. Don't you remember when it was taken? You were standing in it till they cropped you out."

"Why do you think I was standing there? I also remember the 'gay tour of Harlem' was a quick drink in a bar near the theater. But the best thing is to forget it. By the time they can print your retraction it'll be months from now and it'll be forgotten. You'll only revive it."

"Well, will you at least get word to Ava how sorry I am."

"Sammy, she knows it's not your fault."

Will had come in while I was talking. He was reading the story and shaking his head. "How'd a thing like this happen, Sammy?"

"Please, Massey, I'm too tired to think about it anymore."

My father was standing in front of me, glass in hand, laughing. "You're mighty quiet, Poppa. Hey, remember when we was stranded in Lansing? Remember that do-gooder who put us out of work all through Michigan? Guess she never figured that little kid she run off the stage would be makin' twenty-five thousand a week."

"But for how long, Dad?"

"I believe it said four weeks. Tell y'the truth, Poppa, I thought I had this business learned, but I'm damned if I ever hoped I'd live to see the day when they'd pay that to *anybody*."

"It's simple, Dad. They're buying the Will Mastin Trio featuring the World's Only One-Eyed Dancer."

"Sammy, don't say things like that . . ."

"Face it, Dad, it's true. But have you and Massey wondered how I'll do impressions and get laughs with only one eye?"

"Well, I . . ."

"All right, forget that. Even if I stink, the publicity and the shock value oughta carry us for one time around. But once everybody's had their look, what'll we do for an encore?"

Will stood up. "Sammy, you've got it all wrong!"

"Have I, Will? Then maybe you'd better explain it to me."

He walked toward the bed slowly, giving himself time to think. "Well, you're making it out like a freak show, but it's only—well, with the publicity and all, we turned into a name the people heard about. Add that to the fact that we've always been a top act . . ."

"Massey, do you believe we're seventeen thousand dollars a week better today than we were last week?"

"Well, it's not exactly we're a better act . . ." He was reaching for an answer he couldn't possibly find.

"Massey, we've got a bitch of a gimmick if we play it right. If we can get twenty-five thousand for one lousy eye, then next year when they're tired of that I'll just hack off something else. The Will Mastin Trio oughta be worth at least forty thousand featuring the only one-eyed, one-legged dancer in the world."

"Poppa, for God's sake—please!"

I had the same careening, out-of-control feeling I'd had in the accident. I saw the horror in my father's eyes but I could no more stop the words than I'd been able to stop the car. "There's no limit to it. Just think of the billing each year. Instead of 'Bigger and Better' it could be 'There's less of him than ever before, folks!' "

I felt a hand on my shoulder. "Poppa?"

"I'm sorry, Dad. I'm sorry, Massey."

"Maybe you'd better get some sleep, Poppa. Just get your rest and we'll be right here lookin' after you."

They were confused, giving me every ounce of what they had, but I was still "Poppa" and "Mose Gastin." I was dying to talk to them about what was ahead of us. I needed them to give me some concrete answers, a little logic, a plan—something. But they couldn't give answers to problems they didn't see. They were so used to thinking only of getting booked, getting our price, and doing our show that it hadn't occurred to them to wonder: What do you have to do on a stage to begin to justify twenty-five thousand dollars a week? And what happens if you can't do it? I couldn't get through to them. I could reach an audience of a thousand strangers, reach them on any level and make myself understood, but I couldn't reach my own two fathers.

"Poppa? You sleepin'?"

I heard him and Will tiptoeing up to the bed. "Hi."

"How y'feelin', Poppa?"

"Fine. How 'bout you guys?"

They smiled and nodded. My father said, "Look, maybe Will and me been lookin' at this thing all wrong. I mean we been talkin' and all we wants in this world is to see you okay. Sure, we likes the money and spendin' it and all that, but . . . well, we don't want it if it's comin' outta your heart, Poppa. . . . What I'm gettin' at is, you don't have to lay there thinkin' you gotta get up and start workin' again 'cause Will and me's waitin' to go on. We've been thinkin' maybe we oughta quit the business while we're on top. It would be damned good show business. You know what I mean? Whad-dya think of that idea, Poppa?"

"It's beautiful, Dad, Massey. But it's not for us. Look, I'm the one who was wrong yesterday, not you guys. Don't worry. We're going back. Maybe they'll think they're coming to a freak show, maybe it'll be curiosity, but they'll be there, I'll have a crack at them. I'm going to sing and I'm going to do impressions and I'm going to dance. And I'll do them all better than I ever did. I've got one good eye and I've got my legs, and this isn't going to stop us."

Eddie Cantor sat by the side of my bed doing jokes and talking show business with me for an hour. He smiled. "I see you're still wearing your mezuzah."

"Mr. Cantor, the only time I didn't have it on was the night of the accident. I'd taken it off to shower and I was twenty miles away before I realized I didn't have it. My friend searched the room and found it on the floor behind the dresser. It must've slipped off . . ." As he listened, I suspected that for one moment a question crossed his mind as it had my own, but when I finished he went on to another subject, like myself, refusing to dwell on it.

Eventually it was time for him to leave. "Mr. Cantor, the whole hospital knows you're here, and if you don't stop by the wards, there's gonna be an uprising and a mass hanging of nurses and doctors. I hate to impose on you but if you have time, the other patients would get a tremendous kick out of seeing you."

"That's not an imposition, it's a privilege." He stood up and as we shook hands his face became paternal in its expression. "Sammy, you've got a tough fight ahead of you. But you've also got great strength. Never forget what an enormous gift God gave you when He gave you your talent. Treat it as you would anything that is rare and precious. If you protect it and use it well it will carry you wherever you want to go."

There was a knock on the door. A rugged-looking man in a khaki suit and a button-down collar introduced himself as the rabbi from a nearby congregation.

"Oh, now wait a minute. A football player, yes, but not a rabbi." I suddenly realized I was doing bits with a minister. "I'm sorry. Please come in."

He pulled up a chair. The image of a rabbi with a long beard, a silk coat, and the big hat which I'd retained from my days as a child around Harlem was in total conflict with this man. After a while I said, "Rabbi, we've been talking for an hour about shows, politics, people, everything, right? Now, can we talk a little business? I'm not Jewish, but can you give me some answers anyway?"

"I'd like to try."

"Well, before you came in I was thinking I've been given something. Talent. And the way it's worked out, my talent has been a fantastic edge in life. Now on top of that, I had an accident last week and by all rights I should have been killed, but instead, I came out of it with everything except one eye. I've got flowers and prayers from thousands of people I never met. I'm getting offered more money than I ever saw in my life . . ."

He was smiling. "What's your problem?"

"I don't know . . . maybe I should just take it all and run like a thief, but I figure there's a reason for everything, and things just don't add up. On the one hand, God gave me talent. Why? Why me instead of some other guy? Very few Negroes— or whites—have been given the chance to go where I've gone. Why was I given this free ticket to a good life? Now, on the other hand, He puts me in this accident and I'm not exactly better than ever but I'm here and I'm in pretty good shape, so I start thinking, why did He put me into the accident and then save me?"

"Sammy, this talent you speak of is undeniably an extraordinary gift, but why God gave it to you in particular, I can't tell you. Nor can I tell you why He kept you on earth. The answers will only be found within yourself."

"You don't think maybe you could give me a little hint?"

"Do you want platitudes like 'God saved you because you are one of His children'?"

"I keep thinking maybe He's trying to tell me something. Did I do something wrong, did I let Him down somewhere along the line? And if the accident was a hint that there's something I'm not doing right, then I'm not anxious to wait around for Number Two."

"Sammy, you look upon your accident as a warning or a threat. I can only speak to you as a Jew and interpret it according to our philosophy. We don't believe that goodness should stem from threat of punishment. We worship God in love, not in fear. In the Talmud, which represents many centuries of Jewish thinking, it is written, 'Whom the Lord loveth He correcteth.' Therefore, 'Should a man see suffering come upon him let him scrutinize his actions.' We believe that a 'warning' such as you have had comes not to punish you for wrongs you have done but to stimulate some spiritual progress—the kind of thinking you're doing now. You're wondering what you might have done wrong. Turn it slightly. Have you done as well as you might have with what God gave you to work with? We believe that man is made in God's image and therefore is endowed with unlimited potential for goodness and greatness. But only you can know your potential. Only you have the knowledge of where you have succeeded and where you have failed, where you've quit when you shouldn't have. Only you can know if you have been remiss, just as it is only for you to know how good or even how great you might be. Are you falling short of what you might accomplish, what you might be?"

It was a strange sensation to know that a flashlight was shining into my eye but I couldn't see it.

"Do I get the new eye soon?"

"The socket is still too sore, but we can begin preparing you. During the operation we set a little plastic disc in your socket, about the size of a thumbnail. Your new eye will eventually rest on that. But first we'll use a smaller plastic ball to accustom you to having a foreign substance in there.

"Don't be surprised to find you have no control over the lid. It'll flop closed because its muscles were shattered. Eventually it will be held open by the large plastic eye, but until you build up to that you'll need to wear the patch. The drooping lid won't be attractive."

"Doc, I hate to sound like a starlet, but once I take off the patch, what happens when I look to the side with my good eye? I won't be able to make the false one look that way too, will I? I mean, it'll just stare straight ahead."

"In the beginning, yes. But in time you'll train the outer muscles to move the plastic eye and you'll be amazed at how much movement you'll get."

A nurse came skidding into the room. "It's *Frank Sinatra!* He's on his way up!"

I could hear the excitement in the halls accelerating until it was almost a roar. Nurses were running from room to room gasping, "He's here, in the hospital! Frank Sinatra!"

Frank was in the doorway, smiling. "Hi ya, Charley." He came in, flipped his hat onto a chair, and studied me. "You're going to be all right." He said it like he'd just gotten the word from "upstairs." He embraced my father and Will. The nurse was rooted to the floor, staring at him, so flustered that she didn't think to give him a chair. He smiled. "Hi ya, honey." She nodded like a drunk, with the grin and the glazed eyes.

He pulled up a chair and straddled it, arms resting against its back. "Well, what's happening with the eye?"

"I'll have to wear a patch until the socket heals, then I get a new eye." I shook a cigarette out of a pack and held up my lighter, but the flame missed the end of the cigarette. When I finally got it lit Frank smiled. "You're full of little party tricks, Charley."

"For an encore I light my nose."

He'd lit a cigarette too, holding it cupped in his palm. "How long do the docs figure it'll take you to straighten out?"

"They say maybe three months, but they're not sure."

"Do you know when you're leaving here?"

"A few days, I think."

"Come out to the Springs and spend a couple of weeks with me. Hey, what the hell are you crying about?"

"Frank . . . I can't tell you what it means to me for you to come here . . . I thought maybe the magazine thing . . ."

"So what else is new?"

"But . . ."

"Forget it, Charley. You don't even have to mention it. Have you decided where you want to open?"

"Well, that Vegas money looks great, but I've got a funny feeling about our first date. Herman Hover can only give us five thousand, but I've been thinking maybe we should go back to Ciro's, where it all began for us."

"You're definitely right. The important thing is to start strong, and in L.A. you know you have friends around you. The Vegas money'll still be there." He looked across the room. Will nodded. "Meanwhile, Charley, get your health back. Rest, don't rush."

"I wish it was that simple. Let's say it takes three months. By then, all this fantastic publicity I'm getting won't mean beans—I'll have blown all this momentum. On the other hand, I can't come back too soon and look like I'm stumbling around for sympathy."

"First of all, you've got no choice. You wait until you're ready! Second, don't worry about the momentum. They'll wait for you. The day you go back to work you'll be as hot as you are today."

"I wish I could believe that."

He raised an eyebrow. "You want to talk about comebacks?"

He picked up his hat. "I'll see you at the Springs." He put

his hand on my shoulder. "Relax. You're going to be bigger than ever, Charley. Bigger than ever."

Flashbulbs were popping and a guy with a newsreel camera was walking in close to the bed. I turned so he'd get a good shot of the patch.

"Hey, is that the morning's mail, Sammy?" He was pointing to the three tables of letters in the corner of the room.

"Have you read 'em all?"

"Hey, fellas, I've only got one eye, remember?" It got a laugh.

"Sammy, is it true that Jeff Chandler offered you his eye?"

"Yes. Jeff offered a cornea for transplantation, and I understand that I've had nine other offers since then."

"Why do you think Chandler offered to give you his eye?"

"He's my friend, and that's just the kind of a man he is."

"Have you heard that because of what happened to you the Cadillac people are redesigning their steering wheel? They're inverting the thing that sticks up in the center."

"Sammy, now that you've had almost a week to think about it, what's your feeling about what happened to you? Have you wondered, 'Why me?' "

"Baby, all I can say is that God must have had His arms around me, or I would have been killed. There was an identical accident in Oregon just two days ago and everybody in both cars was killed instantly. So if there's any 'why me?' it can only be why did He let *me* live?"

"How do you think it'll affect your career?"

"That's entirely up to the public. If they still want me I'll be there." I pointed to the letters. "It's gonna take me a long time to answer them all. You guys could do me a favor if you'd mention how grateful I am for the support they've given me. I can't begin to describe what it's like to have total strangers take the trouble to send little prayers and to tell you they're rooting for you. I'm having all those letters bound in books 'cause I don't ever want to be without them. Anytime I feel unlucky I'll just take them out and read how wrong I am."

I turned my pillow for the tenth time. When its cool freshness had become warm and soggy I sat up in the dark room and lit a cigarette. Would we really be bigger than ever, or would we go down the drain? I listened to the sounds of the hospital, the "everything's going to be all right" sounds, the anesthesia for reality. Hospitals are so safe. You're exposed to no one but well-wishers, friends who come with pocketfuls of optimism, doctors and nurses who speak encouragements, and who can stop the pain of almost anything but the future. It had been so easy to decide I'll perform like always, so pleasant to daydream that we'd be bigger than ever, that I'd be better than ever, so easy to be a hit while I was safely in bed, where success could be enjoyed just by planning it. I'd been so sure I could go out and just walk onto the stage and dance my head off, I'd already heard the applause. Now I was afraid to sleep, dreading the passing of every hour that was bringing me closer to the moment when I'd have to step outside and do it.

Dr. Hull came by early in the morning to say goodbye. "Drive the car yourself at least partway to Los Angeles. You'll be afraid, but you can drive safely if you're careful, and you must conquer the fear. In all things. The driving is only symbolic. You must walk out of here a whole man."

I tried the patch over my eye at different angles. Arthur walked with me while I said goodbye to other patients I'd gotten to know. I did bits with the nurses, like, "Anytime you wanta be in pictures, baby . . ." That kind of humor. They laughed, but they knew I was scared. Maybe it happens to everyone who walks away from death.

There was no way to stall anymore. I walked downstairs and out the front door. My father and Will were sitting in the back seat of a new Cadillac convertible, a duplicate of the one I'd smashed up.

I sat in the driver's seat. The upraised knob in the center of the steering wheel looked so harmless. I tapped it with my finger. "Well, here we go, folks. Double or nothing." Nobody laughed.

I turned the key in the ignition. My hand trembled. I looked at the car parked ahead of us. It seemed to be about fifty feet away, but I couldn't be sure. I took my foot off the brake and the car started moving forward.

16

"Can Sammy run again?" Alongside the story was a two-column picture of me wearing the patch. "Sammy Davis, Jr., is scheduled to begin a four-week engagement at Ciro's in mid-March. The announcement by Herman Hover causes one to speculate as to whether the Sammy Davis, Jr., who'll open at Ciro's can possibly bear any resemblance to the dazzling figure of perpetual motion whose career only two months ago loomed as one of the brightest in show business. . . ."

The rehearsal room was empty except for some chairs, a long mirror across one wall, and an upright piano with a record player on top of it. I didn't want Morty or anybody around, so I'd brought some records. I wasn't too worried about the singing or the impressions. My balance and sense of depth had become pretty good for normal things but dancing was going to be something else. I put "Fascinating Rhythm" on the machine and lowered the needle.

My legs shook, I had almost no wind at all, every turn brought a knife-stab to my eye, the tempo seemed faster than it had ever been. I kicked myself in the leg and tripped. I saw myself in the mirror, sitting on the floor, one hand protecting my

eye, gasping for breath, my shirt wet and clinging to me. I pictured myself falling like that at Ciro's. I'd have landed on somebody's table. I can't come back like, "Gee, isn't it great how
hard he's trying." That's death. When I come back there can be
no "He's almost as good as he ever was." I've got to be *better!*

The needle was scratching on the label of the record. I got
up, picked out a slower record and started dancing again. My
eye burned and throbbed but I didn't dare stop.

I saw Ciro's lights from a few blocks away on Sunset Boulevard, and as we drew closer I could see a line of people extend-
ing all the way around the block. "They're waitin' for you,
Poppa." He turned the corner and pulled up to the stage entrance. He came around to my side, opened the door, and
reached in to help me make the move. "You're gonna tie 'em in
a knot, son." He was looking at me hard and straight, trying to
give me the strength he knew I needed. "Come on, Poppa,
we're goin' back into show business. And this time we're
stayin' there." I couldn't answer him. I put my arm around him
and we went into the club.

The dressing room was stuffed with flowers. I changed out
of my clothes and into a robe and started putting on my
makeup.

"Hi ya, Charley." Frank was smiling into the mirror at me.
"I'm going to introduce you out there." He gripped my shoulder. "The patch is dramatic as hell. See you in the wings."

People were filling the dressing room—close people—talking, laughing. I went into the bathroom and closed the door. I
looked at my face in the mirror. Can they possibly relax and enjoy the act with the patch there to constantly remind them I've
got no eye?

Frank was speaking to the audience. Then he was coming toward me, holding out his hand, and I was walking onstage to meet him. The applause began. I saw people starting
to stand up. Frank hugged me hard and whispered, "Don't let

'em throw you, Charley. Tonight you're the only star in the room."

From one end of Ciro's to the other were the giants of the motion picture industry—the Cary Grants, the Bogarts, the Edward G. Robinsons, the Spencer Tracys, Gary Coopers, Jimmy Cagneys, Dick Powells—standing and applauding. I saw tears rolling down June Allyson's cheeks. The applause kept on and on, building until I almost couldn't breathe, and I knew that if I didn't start performing I wouldn't be able to. I put up my hands, asking them to stop, and little by little they sat down and the room became quiet. I nodded to Morty and at the sound of the first chord my strength and confidence was back as though I'd never been away. I finished "Black Magic" and they were out of their seats. I turned and bowed to Morty for the arrangement he'd done. The second I started my turn back toward the audience I realized I was spinning toward my blind side, but it was too late to stop myself and my head slammed into the microphone. There was a horrible, loud crack! The audience gasped. The pain was as though a burning cigar were being ground into my bad eye. A thousand hands that had been applauding froze in midair, and the room which had been exploding with sound became deathly quiet.

I reached out, patted the mike, and smiled. "Sorry, Frank. Didn't see you come in, baby."

There was a split second of even greater silence, then a scream of relief and I was doing the Jerry Lewis strut around the stage—half to keep the laugh going until they could relax and half so I could have a breather until the pain in my eye subsided.

When I got off I leaned against the wall in the wings listening to their roars for more. All my fears had been for nothing. They'd go whichever way I played it: if I went for sympathy, I'd get it—until I was sympathized right out of the business; or I could brush it off, kid it, and soon they'd forget everything except my performance.

I hurried back on and did everything I could think of—

every song, every dance, every gag I could invent or remember since I was five years old. I did Danny Kaye, which I hadn't done in years, and I did half the people in the room. All the show business rules of "leave 'em wanting more" fell by the wayside because it was I who could never get enough of what they were giving me.

I'd been on for over two hours, done three closing numbers, and run out of excuses to stay on. I bowed a long last thank-you and when I looked up they were standing and applauding; Herman Hover was walking onstage followed by every waiter, busboy, every cook and kitchen helper in the club. They formed a semicircle around me, the band began playing "Auld Lang Syne," and they were singing to me—led by the Chinese chef holding a long spoon for a baton. The audience fell apart, I fell apart. I just stood there crying like a baby, not just little tears, but deep, racking sobs.

Marilyn Monroe and Milton Greene were waiting for me. I'd read in one of the trades that Milton was "financing and masterminding MM's break from Fox." I'd been dying to meet her, not for the boy-girl jazz, just for the kick of knowing Marilyn Monroe, so I'd asked Milton to bring her to the opening. When the dressing room cleared, he asked, "You want to go back to my place and have a drink?"

"Not on your Rolleiflex, Milton, old buddy. I've had it with the Garbo bit. You and I are going to take Marilyn to the Mocambo, then it's a definite see-and-be-seen at the Crescendo . . ."

Humphrey Bogart opened the dressing-room door and looked in. Will beamed. "How'd you like the show, Mr. Bogart?"

"The show was great. But you're too damned old for the business. Why don't you retire? The kid's the whole show!" When you asked Bogart a question he assumed you wanted his honest opinion and he didn't do Dale Carnegie answers. "Look, I don't mean to hurt your feelings but why don't you face reality? You and the old man are doing less than you did the last time I saw you here and you weren't doing much even then. The nostalgia's wearing a little thin, y'know. The people have stopped saying, 'Isn't it nice they're still together' and if you're half the showman I know you are, then you oughta see it."

Later in the evening Frank took me aside. "You're doing great, Charley. There's nothing I can tell you about the dancing and the impressions, but about the singing: You've got to get yourself your own sound, your own style. It's okay to sound like me—if you're me. I'm only flattered that you like what I do well enough to be influenced by it, and your ear for making other people's sounds isn't helping any, but it's a dead end. No matter how good it is, no copy of anything ever sold for as high as the original."

17

The room clerk shuffled through a stack of cards, glancing at them in a way that you knew he knew he wasn't going to find what he was looking for. "I'm terribly sorry, Mr. Davis, but there's no reservation for you. And we're entirely filled up!"

Dave Landfield, who was on the road with me as a secretary and friend, didn't catch on. "But I wired you two weeks ago."

"Well, uh, we tried to notify you—but we didn't have the address."

Morty glared at him. "Why didn't you try sending it to 'Sammy Davis, Jr., U.S.A.'"

I sat in the cab between Dave and Morty, looking straight ahead while the doorman put our bags back into the trunk. There was a sharp crack. The sunglasses I'd been holding had snapped in my hand.

"Take it easy, Sam."

I looked at the cracked lens and a trickle of blood coming out of my palm. "I *am* taking it easy."

I'm a star! This isn't supposed to happen anymore.

In the dressing room my father said, "I'm sorry about what happened with the hotel."

Will nodded. "I'll make arrangements for your room in Frisco. I suppose you'll want a suite."

"Thanks, Massey, but I'm staying at the Fairmont."

"Now, Poppa . . ."

"Sammy, what's wrong with our old hotel?"

"There's nothing wrong with it, but I'll be playing the Fairmont and I'll be living at the Fairmont, because it's better than our old place, it's more convenient, and if any other star were playing there, there wouldn't be the slightest question where he's staying."

"Poppa, you saw what happened here."

"It's not going to happen at the Fairmont. If they don't want to give me a beautiful suite, then they're going to have to get on the phone and call all the people with reservations and tell 'em, 'Don't bother coming over, 'cause there ain't no show.' "

The cab stopped in front of the Fairmont. Morty and Dave got out, and I took my time paying the driver, watching the doorman who was hurrying toward us. I handed him a five. "Will you take care of our bags, please? My man will be along with them in another cab."

"Yes, Mr. Davis. Thank you."

Dave had gone in and Morty was motioning for me to go ahead. I gave him a little push. "After you, baby."

A short, thin little man, like a Donald Meek movie character, was gliding across the lobby toward us, hand extended from twenty feet away. "Oh, Mr. Davis, welcome to the Fairmont. My name is Frye. The assistant manager?" He snapped his fingers at a bellboy. "Mr. Davis' overnight bag!"

"Mr. Frye, this is Mr. Stevens, my conductor, and Mr. Landfield, my secretary. They'll be staying with me."

"Splendid." He was looking at me like he would at his boss's kid who'd just barely got over the measles. "We can go directly upstairs. You're already registered, sir." He led me through the lobby to the elevators.

Is he trying to get me out of sight fast? I felt the looks and the nudging I was causing all over the lobby. *Why shouldn't they look? I'm a celebrity.*

Mr. Frye was beaming at my camera case. "So you're a photographer too! Does your well never run dry?" He poked at the elevator bell, impatiently glancing up at the floor indicator. "So sorry to keep you waiting." The elevator doors slid open; he smiled me in ahead of him and ordered the operator, "Express to the top." He turned to me. "We've certainly been looking forward to your arrival. Your engagement will be mammoth. Absolutely mammoth. We've had to move the bandstand to create space for more tables. But I daresay that's an old story to you."

"Well, you know what they say, the old jokes are the best."

He slapped his knee. "Oh, that's charming, charming." The doors slid open and he bowed us off the elevator and ran to catch up with us. "Ah . . . here we are." He flung open the door like Loretta Young. "We've chosen one of our roomiest suites for you. We do want you to be comfortable. There's a television in every room, we've put in a small refrigerator . . ." He fluttered around showing me where the couch was. "Now, if there's anything at all that you should want, don't forget, the name is Frye. Just think of fried chicken, and think of—*oh!* Oh dear, I . . . well, good day, gentlemen." He fled.

I flopped into a chair.

Morty grinned. "You wanta do ten minutes on Mr. Frye?"

Dave asked, "Anybody hungry? I'm starved."

"Call room service for some menus, baby."

"Crazy, Sambo."

It hit me from behind like a rabbit punch. I went out the door and rushed for the elevator.

People recognized the patch. The fresh air and the smiling and waving at me felt good and I was annoyed with myself for letting Mr. Frye get to me. At least he was trying to be nice. And poor Dave. He'd have called me Sambo if I were white. I had a mental picture of him in the hall as I'd left, standing a safe distance away from me, arms outstretched, gaping at me.

I stopped at the jewelry shop in the hotel, picked out a gold watch, and gave the clerk three hundred dollars. Dave leaped out of his chair as the door opened. "Hey, look, I don't know what I said or did . . ."

I tossed the watch to him. "Do me a favor, Dave, put that on your wrist, because that chrome job you've got doesn't look like you work for a star."

"I guess it wouldn't be a benefit if we didn't get creamed chicken."

The man seated next to me on the dais laughed. "Don't complain. I do this almost every day." He put out his hand. "My name is Alvin Fine. I'm rabbi of the Congregation Emanu-El."

He got up to make the opening speech and without a wasted word or an idle thought; with just logic, sincerity, and dignity, he completely wrapped up the audience. He wasn't much older than I, but an Old World wisdom poured out of him in combination with the most modern terminology, almost hip. As he sat down I said, "Thanks a bunch. I'm not choked up about following you."

When I returned to my seat I said, "Rabbi, I had an automobile accident a few months ago, and while I was in the hospital I met a rabbi who talked a lot like you do, and I really liked what he said." I reached under my shirt and showed him my mezuzah. "A friend of mine gave me this. I wear it for sentiment, not as a religious thing, but I'm interested in Judaism, or maybe you'd call it curious. Are there any books you'd suggest that could give me the general idea? I don't mean to sound like I'm asking for Instant Judaism, I realize it's a big subject. . . ."

"If you'll excuse an anecdote, years ago a man challenged the great Hillel to explain all there was to know about Judaism, while standing on one foot. Hillel stood on one foot and said, 'What is hateful to thee, do not unto thy neighbor.' In those ten words which we know today as the Golden Rule he had recited the basic principle of Judaism."

"Well, nobody can argue with that kind of thinking."

"We've been getting arguments for thousands of years." He wrote some titles on the back of a menu. "I hope you'll find these to be interesting reading. And this is my phone number. If, after you've read the books, you'd like to discuss them, I'd be delighted to see you when you're in San Francisco again."

Our cab moved slowly through the downtown traffic, past the Golden Nugget, Horseshoe Club, Jackpot, and onto Highway 91. Dave was Charley Tourist, twisting around, looking out of all windows. "Hey, is this the Strip? Wow, what a wild-looking town! What's it like in those places?"

I stopped off at my father's room to say hello. "Any word from Mama and Peewee, Dad?"

"They called from a gas station. Oughta be here by six."

"Great. I'll arrange a table for the dinner show."

"Hey, Poppa, you pushin' the horse a little faster'n he can run? Colored people sittin' out front in Vegas?" He was shaking his head. "I hope you ain't stickin' your neck out too far."

"I'm not sticking my neck out. But I ain't pullin' it in like a goddamned turtle, either. My grandmother is gonna sit and watch me perform or there ain't *nobody* gonna sit and watch me perform." I picked up the phone and asked to be connected with the Venus room. "Hello, this is Sammy Davis, Jr. . . . Fine, thanks. I'd like a table for six for my family, at the ringside . . ."

"Well? What'd they say, Poppa?"

"They said, 'Have a great opening, Mr. Davis.' "

"Hell, don't give *me* that poker face. I taught it to you."

"Dad, they couldn't have been nicer and they're holding a table at *center* ringside. I'll invite Dave to sit with them, that way they won't feel like they're alone in the world." I stood up. "Catch you later."

The living room was jammed and I went from group to group, saying hello, soaking up the flattery. I sat down next to Mama. "You have a good time tonight?"

"Just seeing what people think of you and how they're treating you is a good time for me, Sammy. I'd better be getting my sleep, though. And don't you stay up too late neither."

I walked her to the door. "Don't worry about me, Mama. I never felt better in my life."

There were still a dozen people left. Charley handed me a Coke, and I lit a cigarette and relaxed into their conversation. Dave said, "Whaddya say we start at one end of the town and hit every place along the way?" His face was still reflecting the excitement of the evening. "I hear there's a wild lounge act over at the Desert Inn. We could start there and then . . ."

"Baby, it's late, we've got everything we want right here."

"It's only four o'clock. Come on, let's really celebrate."

"I don't know about those places, Dave." He looked at me, not understanding. "Baby, this is Vegas. It's one thing for me here where I'm working, but I'm not so sure about those other hotels. Now do you wanta see a lounge act, or a lynching?"

Somebody else said, "Are you doing modest bits or don't you *know* how big you are?"

Dave said, "He's out of his mind and I'll prove it." He picked up the phone. "Maybe years ago it was one thing . . . Hello, may I have the Desert Inn, please."

Conversation stopped. Dave lit a cigarette, crossed one leg over the other, and blew smoke rings at the ceiling. "Connect me with the Lounge, please, darling. . . . Hello, I'd like to reserve a table for about twenty minutes from now for Sammy Davis, Jr., and a party of . . ." The burst of red across his cheeks was as though he'd been slapped. He lowered the phone back on the hook.

I shrugged. "Let's not make a ninety-minute spectacular out of it." I could feel everybody looking at me, embarrassed for me. There were murmurs of "Well, if that's how they are then who needs 'em . . ." "They're a hundred years behind the times . . ."

The party was lying on the floor dead. I stood up. "Charley, get hot on the phone with room service and have them bring over twenty steak sandwiches, and tell them we'll need a case of their best champagne, quick-style. Morty, do me a favor. Swing by the casino and find Sunny and the kids. Tell 'em it's a party. Invite everybody you see that we dig." I turned up the hi-fi set. Within ten minutes the room came alive like somebody'd plugged us in.

Dave came over to where I was standing. "You okay?"

"Thanks, baby. I'm fine."

I had the feeling of having waited all my life to own a raincoat and when finally I got one the water was coming through.

I had to get bigger, that's all. I just had to get bigger.

My father took a newspaper clipping out of his pocket. "Maybe you better give this a look; that's not nice things they're sayin' in there."

The headline was: "*Is Sammy Ashamed He's a Negro?*" I sat down.

> Sammy Davis, Jr., who recently sparkled like a 14-carat gold star on the stage at the Fairmont, was a rare pleasure to us as a reviewer and a pride to us as a Negro. But, unfortunately, persistent reports of his offstage performances leave much to be desired. During his stay in San Francisco he never once came by the neighborhood where he stayed in days before he was able to make the move to the less dark, more glittery side of town. Clearly, Mr. Davis is doing nothing to discourage rumors that success has erased his memory for friends who knew him "when." His all-night, all-white, orgy-style parties are the talk of Las Vegas, where he is currently appearing. We are sorry to be the ones to remind Mr. Davis of his obligation to the Negro community, but even sorrier for the necessity to do so.

"I don't get it. Why should they want to write lousy stuff like this about me?"

"Well, the fact is you never did come by the old neighborhood . . . you had a coupla buddies from around there."

"And every last one of them was at the hotel with me almost every night. They came to me, so what was there for me to go across town for? Ask Charley. He was there every night. He can tell you there were as many colored cats as ofays, maybe more."

"Well, this newspaper didn't hear about 'em."

"Hold it. Am I supposed to send them a guest list every time I wanta have some people over? Should I mark the names 'colored, white, colored, colored, white'?"

"Sammy, you gotta go along with the fact that . . . well, right there in the other room, just look who you got around you. There ain't nothin' but ofays . . ."

"Dad! Where in the goddamned hell am I going to find colored people in Vegas? Y'want me to invite Mrs. Cartwright? Should I go over to Westside and find cats I don't know and invite 'em to a party just to dress up the room? Or maybe you'd like me to send a plane into L.A. for buddies so this paper'll be happy?"

"Well, maybe you could cut down on the parties some."

"What else am I supposed to do? I kill myself on that stage every night, I drain myself dry. Don't I have the right to unwind? Okay, I can't do it like everybody else; I can't go around town doing drop-ins at the Desert Inn, and 'Hey, let's catch the new lounge act at the Sands.' I'm not complaining, but let's not forget I'm on an island here at the Frontier. I shouldn't have to draw pictures for you why I bring people over."

My anger turned to a rotten, hollow feeling. "They don't mention that because of me, colored people sat out front in a Las Vegas hotel for the first time in history. Just that I have parties." I stared at the paper that was faceup on the floor. "I don't get it. I swear to God I don't. I'd have thought they'd be happy every time one of us breaks out and lives good."

I took the towel from Charley as I came offstage, and wrapped it around my neck. "There's no party tonight. Let everybody know."

"But I've got fifty sandwiches."

I hung around the casino for a while and then went back to my room. The door opened and Morty stuck his head in. "You feeling okay?" I nodded. "Y'mean . . ." A smile of hope was tentatively spreading over his face. "No party tonight?"

"That's right, Morty. And stop grinning like that or you'll tear your mouth."

Dave rushed in, "Hey, where *is* everybody?"

"It's a quiet night at home for old Sam, baby. Why don't you take a look around the town."

They both sat down and watched me tuning in the television set. I looked around at them. "What're you guys, a couple of nitwits? *You're* always looking for a good night's sleep, and *you're* always saying how you want to see the town. Well, this is that great come-and-get-it night. Go on, you don't have to sit around with me. I appreciate it but I really don't need a nurse."

They closed the door and I caught a local disc jockey. ". . . dynamic. I don't know where he gets all the energy. And he's the same offstage. Always going, always moving. Came up from nothing and now he's sitting on top of the world . . . the greatest Negro performer to come along since Bill Robinson. . . ." I changed the station. "Looking for the best odds in town? Try the Lucky Buck on Fremont Street. Every player's a winner." I turned it off and went into the living room. I took one of the sandwiches back to the bedroom and got into bed.

I opened a new book about the Nuremberg Trials, but the Negro press rap kept running through my mind. Isn't it *my* life? Why should I have to live by other people's rules? Who am I living for—me, or some guy who sits behind a desk and wants to tell me how to live? What makes his rules better than mine? Why should I let myself be forced into a mold? I've worked all my life toward the day when no white man could tell me how to live—now the colored people are trying to do it. I looked through the door, at the empty living room. I had no desire for it to be empty. What was the point of making it if I've got to wind up sitting alone in a room like an outcast? I didn't have to become a star to accomplish *that!*

I telephoned Charley's room. "Baby, come on over to the suite, will you please? I'm going to have some people over and I'll . . . What's the difference what time it is? . . . Yeah, right away."

The room was swarming with people laughing under the wail of the hi-fi set. Morty was standing in his doorway, hair rumpled, wearing candy-striped pajamas and a stunned look as a chick rode by on a room service table. The word had spread from hotel to hotel down the length of the Strip and the kids were arriving like volunteer firemen, all but climbing in the windows.

The train swerved sharply and Morty muttered, "Sonuva-bitch!" He caught my involuntary smile at the slash of ink his pen made across the music he was writing. He looked at the cover of the book I'd been reading. "You gonna become Jewish?"

"Baby, I'll do the jokes and you write the music." I continued reading, but I could feel him watching me, dying to say something. I put the book down. "Okay, Morty. What is it?"

"Can I ask you a straight question?"

"You're gonna ask it anyway, right?"

"Seriously. You've been hung up in that all day. You thinking about converting to Judaism?"

"Morty, I like guns, but I didn't become a cowboy, did I?"

"I don't dig. When I read that stuff it was like dullsville."

"Baby, you'd better read it again. These are a swinging bunch of people. I mean, I've heard of persecution, but what they went through is *ridiculous!* There wasn't anybody who didn't take a shot at 'em. The whole world kept saying, 'You can't do this' and 'You can't do that' but they didn't listen! It's beautiful. They just plain didn't listen. They'd get kicked out of one place, so they'd just go on to the next one, and keep swinging like they wanted to, believing in themselves and in their right to have rights, asking nothing but for people to leave 'em alone and get off their backs, and having the guts to fight to get themselves a little peace. But the great thing is that after thousands of years of waiting and holding on and fighting, they finally made it."

He was looking past me, reaching back to his Sunday school days. "I don't remember any of that."

I slipped on the tweed patch that matched the suit I was wearing and it was a definite kissing-the-mirror. It did away completely with the medicinal look of the plain black one. I set the elastic band at the most rakish angle I could get and went over to Lindy's to find someone to try it out on.

Milton Berle waved me over. "Come on to the Friars Club with me and take some steam. It'll help get rid of all that flab."

Jack E. Leonard was shmoozing with some other comics. "It's nice to see you again, Sammy—but I think I should tell you, your tweed beret slipped down over your eye." He gave me his glare. "Either that or you've got lint on your monocle." He turned on Berle. "Hello, Milton. I saw your show last night. Keep it up and one of these days you may own your own gas station!"

Berle nodded. "Very funny, Jack. Stand still, please. We were going to the gym but we'll just take a walk around you."

"That's funny too, Milton. You've got a familiar style. *Mine!*"

When they'd finished dueling they smiled pleasantly at each other; Jack went back to the comics he'd been sitting with and Milton showed me around. "We're getting a new clubhouse soon. Y'know, you really should become a Friar."

"I'd love to—but can I?"

"Why the hell not?"

"Milton, this isn't exactly a *sunburn* I'm wearing."

He grabbed my face with one hand and slapped me lightly with the other. "Repeat after me: 'I do the singing, and Milton does the jokes.' "

Jack Eigen reached out to shake hands with me as I sat down in front of his microphone. "Sammy, welcome to Chicago and thanks for stopping by. Ladies and gentlemen, I'm speaking to the dynamic star of the great show here at the Chez Paree. Sammy, it's a pleasure to meet you . . ."

I glanced across the room at my father. He winked and threw me a circled thumb and forefinger.

". . . this young man just finished his first show of the engagement and literally turned the Chez upside down. It was pandemonium, they wouldn't let him off the stage, they were jammed in like sardines but they kept calling him back . . ."

He was reporting it like Clem McCarthy doing a Kentucky Derby, screaming the winner past the finish line. ". . . Sammy, how do you feel about what's been happening to you lately?"

"Jack, I'd have to be out of my mind not to be thrilled and grateful. And I'm particularly happy to be a guest on your show."

"Thank you, Sammy, I'm certainly happy to have you."

He thought it was just showbiz "Glad to be here, folks." "I really mean that, Jack. When I was a kid, there was a time when we'd pawned everything except our radio, and we held on to that just so we could listen to your show from the Co-pacabana. I'd sit in our apartment playing cards with my father, and we'd hear you talking to Jimmy Durante, Joe E. Lewis . . . well, maybe it'll sound a little cornball, but I dreamed and prayed that someday I'd get a little closer to all that excitement."

"Ladies and gentlemen, in case you tuned in late it's my pleasure to sit opposite the most talked-about, most talented, most versatile Negro performer . . ."

I was aware of the warmth of my arms and legs taking the crispness out of my suit and wrinkling it.

"Sammy, we're all familiar with your great energy and your great talent. Let's find out a little more about you. Is there anything missing, anything further you'd like? How about motion pictures?"

"Well, sure. I'd love to make one someday."

"How is it you haven't done a picture already? I mean, now that it's out in the open, do you feel that your color has prevented you from doing a movie?"

"Wait a minute, it's not 'out in the open,' because it's never been a hidden subject. The way things have been going for us I haven't had time to even think about it, but I can tell you that the opening we had earlier this evening was everything I ever dreamed about. We'll be doing the second show soon and if the people are as fab—"

"But isn't it true, Sammy, that when a young singer has a hit record and starts getting hot, he almost automatically gets pulled right out to Hollywood?"

"I don't know, Jack. I really don't. I doubt it."

"You've had several big hits and you're a great performer . . ."

I pressed my hands against the cloth on the table and glanced at my watch, hoping it was almost show time.

"Have you had any offers from Hollywood?"

The room was quieting down to listen more carefully, they were looking at me differently. I was colored again.

"But have you had any offers?"

I leaned against the back of the chair. "No, but that doesn't prove anything, because neither did anybody come up to me and say, 'We aren't calling you to make a picture because you're colored.' " I lit another cigarette. He had asked me something but I'd missed it. I looked at him, knowing he'd repeat it.

"But they're not calling you."

"Jack, it can't be a racial thing unless you can tell me that Sidney Poitier is trying to pass." One of the ribs of the chair was sticking into my back, but I just didn't feel like bothering to move away from it. Across the room my father was staring at the floor.

"Sammy, do you feel that despite the fact that you're the most exciting Negro performer to come along since Bill Robinson . . ."

The last thread snapped. The beauty of the evening was long gone, but over and above that, words I'd heard and hated a thousand times, words I'd accepted without answering, words I'd forced to bounce off, stuck and stung me to response. "Why do you compare me to Bill Robinson?"

"Well, Sammy, I, uh, I don't believe I understand your question."

"Jack, I want to make it clear that you are not the first person to do it. I hear it all the time and I see it in the papers and in magazines, and obviously nobody means it as anything but a compliment and I'm enormously flattered by the comparison— but it's a wrong one!" He was looking at me with curiosity. "I don't kid myself that I could even begin to dance on the same stage as Bill Robinson. I haven't a touch of his greatness. But aside from that: we are not the same kind of performers. Sure, I dance, but my style is totally different from his, plus the fact that I also sing and tell jokes, do impressions, play the drums and the vibes, and act like a nut. Mr. Robinson didn't do any of those things. So if you're talking *performance* it would be much more logical to compare Fred Astaire to Bill Robinson, but I never heard *that* done."

"Well, now that you mention it . . . well, I just know that Robinson was the greatest Negro performer of his time and you're the greatest Negro performer to come along . . ."

"Hold it, Jack. Maybe it'll seem like I'm touchy, but I take exception to that too."

"To what?"

"You called me a 'Negro performer.' I'm a Negro and I'm a performer, but I don't think of myself as a 'Negro performer' any more than you think of yourself as a 'white disc jockey.'

"Why do people want to label *me* when they don't label

other people? I never yet saw a newspaper refer to Milton Berle
as 'the greatest Jewish comedian.' Sure, he's Jewish and he's a
comedian but he doesn't do Jewish comedy any more than I do
Negro humor. When I walk onto a nightclub floor the newspaper guy is automatically comparing me to everyone else he's
seen headlining on that same floor. I'm competing against *all*
performers, so if I get a rave I don't want it to be qualified, like
I'm good compared to only one small section of the business.
I'll take the knocks if I have to, but if it's good then I want all
that's coming to me.

"When I played Florida about a year or so ago I was staying
in the same hotel as Jackie Robinson, and he happened to see
some of my reviews. They were raves but they all had the
'Negro performer' bit in them. He said, 'I had it all my life. I
was always the "Negro ballplayer." Occasionally a hater would
throw a black cat on the field and yell the names at me, but
most of the time people bent over backwards the other way. If I
missed a ball or struck out they didn't boo me like they would
a white guy. Then, all of a sudden one day it changed. I don't
know how or why, but it did. I could argue with the umpire
and shake my fist at him and the crowd started booing me, but
I knew it wasn't racial. The greatest day of my life was the day
I was thrown out of a game. I went into the locker room and
cried 'cause I was finally just a plain "ballplayer" like any other
guy.'

"I guess what it comes down to, Jack, is that I want to be
looked at by the world not as Negro, white, or polka dot, or
put in a category with anybody. Good, bad, or indifferent, like
me or hate me—but measure me by the sum total of what I am
as an individual."

My father was waiting as I stepped down from the platform. He put his arm around my shoulder and we walked back
to the dressing room. "How *about* that, Poppa?" He smiled.
"The Jack Eigen show." He was saying the words, but they
didn't have the ring of happiness he wanted to get out of them.
He was shaking his head, reaching for the nostalgia we both

wanted to feel. "You got it all now, just like you always wanted." The last few words were hardly pronounced, as if in denial of their own statement.

I gripped his shoulder. "Not yet, Dad. I've got to get bigger. I've got to get so big, so powerful, so famous, that the day will come when they'll look at me and see a man—and then somewhere along the way they'll notice he's a Negro."

18

"Whaddya say, chicky? How's the cover boy of the scandal magazines?"

"You're a bundle of laughs, Jess." I pulled a chair up to his desk. "Listen, is there something happening at Disneyland tomorrow?"

"They're having the big pre-opening thing for celebrities and their families—you know, 'Mr. and Mrs. Famous at Disneyland with their little monsters.' "

"How come I wasn't invited? I'm not exactly an unknown."

He raised an eyebrow. "Well, right off the bat I can think of two reasons. First, you've got no kids. Second, they're going for the wholesome, family kind of publicity, so if there are three guys in the world they'd make a point of overlooking, chicky, it would be Rubirosa, Errol Flynn, and you."

"You're a very funny man, Jess."

"Hey, I was just doing bits." He took a manila envelope out of a filing cabinet and handed me a stack of clippings. "Maybe you don't read all this stuff but it's my business, so I have to."

The top one, a scandal magazine, another of the dozens of imitators of *Confidential*, had me and June Allyson on the cover. "Do you realize what a horrible, unfair thing this is?

Here a woman was kind enough to come backstage on my opening night at Ciro's, with her husband, for one minute to say, 'Hey, I liked your show.' So for that they smeared her. That's all she did. The only time I ever met her." I dropped the magazine into a wastebasket.

"Chicky, face it: you're a sex symbol."

"You're sick."

"Come on, cheer up. Look at the bright side of it: they're not calling you a fag."

"Jess . . . this'll kill you, but I don't think of myself as somebody who can't be seen around decent people. It's not exactly what I worked my whole damned life for."

The phone was ringing as I got to my suite in the Garden of Allah. Dave grabbed for it. "Hello? Oh! . . . yes, *sir*. One second please, he's right here." He held the phone out to me like it was hot, and mouthed the words: "It's Frank Sinatra."

"Hi ya, Charley, listen, you dig all this Donald Duck jazz. You want to go to a thing at Disneyland tomorrow?"

His children were leaning out of the back window waving to me, and the sight of them almost threw me. It had seemed impossible that he'd be going to Disneyland without them, yet, knowing how he protected them like all the gold in Fort Knox, I'd wondered if he'd let them be seen with the town monster.

The radio was on and as we drove a disc jockey said, "Now, the number one record in the country, Sammy Davis, Jr.'s 'Black Magic'!"

"Turn off that record, Charley. Get another station."

"Oh, sure, Frank. Gee, I wouldn't want to make you jealous, I mean a man with an Oscar and all . . ." I turned to the next station. "Here it is, folks, number one, Sammy Davis, Jr.'s 'Black Magic.' "

Frank smacked the steering wheel. "For crying out loud, I can't listen to anything on that radio but you!"

"You want me to change it, baby?"

"I'll baby you! Leave it."

When it was over he turned off the radio. "The records are good, Charley, but you're not singing yet. You're performing. You're doing them like you do them in clubs, but on a record you don't have the physical moves going for you, there's only one dimension to work with—the voice. On this one it comes across, but on some of them you don't. I don't mean they're not good, but they don't translate unless people can see you, so you're cutting down your percentages for a hit. But I'm not worried about you. One day you'll be singing."

The guard waved us through the gates at Disneyland, we pulled into the parking lot, and the photographers crowded around before Frank could open his door. I stayed in the car while he and the children got out. I turned my face away from the mob and tried to keep busy tying my shoelaces. I could hear them yelling, "One more with your arms around the kids, Frank?" . . . "Can you move closer together, please?"

There was a knock on the window. Frank was beckoning me with his finger. "Hey, Charley, did we come here together or not? Let's go, let's get into these pictures." He pulled me over and put one arm around his children, rested the other on my shoulder, and the photographers began shooting. I looked at him smiling at the world through those cameras, as much as saying, "In your ear. He's my friend."

We walked around the park looking at the rides and saying hello to almost everyone we passed. Frank hadn't invited me just for fun. He'd known there would be newsreels, wire services, that almost everyone in the industry would be there, and he'd wanted to give me the value of association so that some of his tremendous public favor might rub off on me. I turned to watch one of the rides and when I looked up Frank was a few feet ahead of me talking to someone. He had one arm around Tina and Frank Jr. and his other hand was unconsciously stroking Nancy's head.

He walked over to me. "What're you looking at, Charley?"

"I don't know, I was just thinking about you and the kids. Frank . . . thank you for bringing me here."

"Come on. Y'wanta be late for Donald Duck's party?"

Dave opened the dressing-room door. "There's a Finis Henderson outside."

Finis, a buddy since our early days around Chicago, stood in the doorway, holding back a smile. "Mr. Davis, I presume?"

I played it angry. "Finis, where in the damn hell have you been? I've been in town since yesterday."

He held up his hands. "Please. Don't raise your voice at me, 'cause I don't need you. I'm poor but I'm proud."

"You silly nut, come on in here. Listen, this is Dave Landfield, my secretary, and you know Morty. Hey, where're the rest of the guys?"

He looked away. "Oh, I guess they're busy or something . . ."

"*Busy or something?*" I turned him around to face me. "What the hell is *that?* On my opening night? You're lyin' through your teeth, Finis. Now let's have it."

"Well, maybe they're a little mixed up. They figure you're living over here with the ofays, when you oughta be over there. They think maybe you've gotten a little snow-blind."

"Hold it, Finis. Look at my face. I've had my nose broken too many times to hear I'm an Uncle Tom."

"Well, they read all the stuff in the papers and . . . well, they figure it must be true what people've been saying."

"And just *what* have people been saying?"

"Oh, come on now, daddy, don't put me on the rack. I came over here to see my buddy. If I want a third degree I'll rob a store."

I pulled on my jacket and jammed a silk handkerchief into the breast pocket. "Boy, that's beautiful. All they want is to drag me back to the gutter with them. Well, man, I ain't comin' back!"

The Chez was packed, and as I walked onstage, I scanned

the room as I had every night since the opening. When I got off
I sent for Donjo Medlavine, one of the owners. "Don, a
straight question: are my people getting treated okay? I mean,
your guy at the door isn't giving them a hard time or anything?"

"They're treated the same as anybody else—when they
show up. Last year we always had a couple of tables . . ."

"Thanks, Don. I'm sorry I asked. I should have known better."

The man behind the rich mahogany desk didn't like me one little bit.

"Mr. Johnson, why are you turning my people against me?"

The faint smile disappeared. "We're not trying to turn anyone . . ."

"I didn't say 'trying.' If I thought it was deliberate, I
wouldn't be here. But you're *doing* it. Not so much in *Ebony*,
but your guys on *Jet* have been bum-rapping me with little
zingies in every issue. Between your magazines and papers like
the *Defender* and the *Courier*, you've been holding America's
first all-colored lynching. Why?"

"Mr. Davis, you are the one who *makes* the news. Can you
seriously be telling me that you haven't gone out of your way
to indicate a complete disavowal of racial ties, to disassociate
yourself in every conceivable . . ."

"Mr. Johnson, I didn't come up here to do two choruses of
nobody understands me. You've been printing your point of
view. All I ask is that you listen to mine."

He settled back in his chair, not bothering to conceal his
contempt.

"A few weeks ago a Broadway column ran an item saying I
turned down twenty-five thousand a week in Miami Beach because I refused to live in the colored section of Miami. Now,
the fact is I *won't* live there, but that's not why we turned it
down. We were offered our own suites in the hotel that was try-

ing to book us. We turned it down because my father, my uncle, and I have one firm rule: we don't play where they won't open their doors to colored people. The columnist obviously didn't know about the suites, so the item came out sounding like I hate colored people so much that even for a twenty-five thousand dollars a week I won't live with them. Nice, huh? Okay, it's bad enough when an ofay columnist does this, but when I see it run in the Negro press too, when I hear the reactions and see I'm marked lousy and suddenly I'm not getting Negro customers where I'm playing—well, that hurts. I can't say it ran in any of your magazines but I saw it in three Negro newspapers. Now, I'm not looking for togetherness, but that's inexcusable."

He sat forward slowly, frowning. "You're perfectly right. It's a story that should have been checked out with you just in the hope that it was wrong."

"Mr. Johnson, when I get to a town it's not a secret. There's always a sign saying: 'He's in there.' But my phone didn't ring. I've never yet had one guy call me and say, 'Hey, Sam, this true what I hear?' Not one."

"Well, as a newspaperman I can guess what happened with that particular item." He leaned back in his chair again. "Whoever heard it was aware of your overall racial image, the item seemed to be in character . . ."

"Wait a minute. Before you talk about my image like *that's it*, lock the box, that's what I'm here for. What did I do to get that image? Let's go down the list A, B, C."

"If you insist. Offhand I remember an item we ran recently about your conductor. How do you, a prominent Negro, justify the use of a white man when you know how scarce good jobs are for Negroes?"

"Mr. Johnson, Morty Stevens is one of two white men out of seven people who travel with me, he's the best man I know of for the job, he's arranged three hit songs for me, and he's one hell of a conductor. I'm not buying his color, I'm buying his music."

"And you couldn't find as good a musician who's a Negro?"

"Maybe I could. But none of them have come to me looking for the job and even if they did I'm not about to fire Morty and hire them just 'cause they're colored and he's white."

"Fair enough. But you live in hotels not open to the average Negro; you bought a house in a restricted area of Los Angeles . . ."

"Right! I've got one of the best houses in Hollywood—and incidentally, the neighborhood's not restricted anymore. As for the hotels: they haven't yet figured out how to build one as good as I want to live."

"Sammy, there's no arguing with this kind of thinking, but you must see that it contributes to the impression which the average Negro has, that you have removed yourself from Negro life and have turned away from him."

"I haven't turned away from anyone or anything except living in the gutter."

"But your way of living, your associations . . . the man on the street can only interpret them as—well, they'll certainly never conclude that you're *proud* of your race."

"Why do they have to conclude anything? People I never even met sitting around deciding what I oughta do! They're out of their minds. The white cats are saying 'He oughta live there' and the colored cats are saying 'He oughta live here' and it always ends up with both of 'em saying 'Hell, he thinks he's white' and 'Yeah, he's ashamed he's colored.' *Bull!* If I was ashamed of being colored would I present myself at the best hotel in town and expect them to let me in? It's lousy enough when I walk into a hotel and I've gotta feel a white guy looking at me, thinking 'Why does he want to push his way in?' and I'd love to sit down with him and ask, 'Why should I *have* to push my way in?' But when I'm convicted by *my own people,* who should know better, what kind of acceptance can I hope for from the rest of the world?

"I'll tell you now. I'll be playing the Copa in New York later this year and I'm not going to live in Harlem any more than I'm going to live in New Jersey. I know now they're gonna fight me on it. The guys on the papers'll start the whole thing about me trying to be white, and the cats on the street'll read it and say, 'Yeah, how come he don't live up here where he belongs?' But, Johnny, there ain't a one among 'em that wouldn't move downtown and into the Waldorf-Astoria if he had the money and if they'd let him in.

"I'm not going to run up to Harlem and hang around to keep up appearances, either. And I know now what's gonna happen. The mass Negro's gonna bitch, 'He's not a corner boy.' And they're right. I don't go up to Harlem and just hang on the corner of 125th and Seventh. I never did it when I was a kid and there's no reason for me to do it now. I'm not about to con my own people into liking me by making regular visits to Harlem and hangin' around like 'Hey, baby—I ain't changed. I'm still old Sam. Still colored!' "

Betty Bogart called. "Sam, I know it's short notice, but we just heard you were in town and we're having a few people up for dinner tonight. Slacks style. Bring a date."

"Thanks, Betty. I'll come by alone."

It was just Frank and a date, Judy Garland and Sid Luft, the Bogarts, and me. After dinner I sat in a corner of the living room with Bogey. "You think you're pretty jazzy with the glen plaid patch."

I grinned. "Bogey, let's face it, either you're suave or you ain't. I mean, you've gotta admit it *is* just a little distingué, don't you?"

He just looked at me. Abruptly he asked, "How long you gonna keep the goddamned patch on your eye?"

"Well . . . I don't know, it's only nine months or so and the new eye still doesn't look very good."

"You got the eye underneath it now?"

"Yeah."

"Lemme see it."

I glanced around. "Let's not scare any women and children." I lifted the patch. "I'll tell you the truth, I've been thinking I may never give it up. I kinda dig it."

"It's a big mistake. Don't get caught on it. You aren't too goddamned pretty to look at, and the patch gives you a little feeling like the guy in the shirt ad. You figure it's glamorous. But you're getting to like it too much. You want 'em to say 'There's Sammy Davis' or 'There's the kid with the patch'?" He smacked the table three times and the butler came in. "Fix us another drink, please." He turned back to me. "Take it off as soon as possible. The eye'll be better than the patch. You'll be happier."

"I'm not so sure. It's becoming a trademark. I guess I'll get rid of it eventually, but I'm not in any hurry."

"Don't waste too much time. You're kidding yourself with that trademark crap. You're using it for a crutch. Don't fool yourself that wearing a patch over your eye gives you an excuse for not being good-looking."

There was no snow, no icicles on the trees or frost on the window, none of the seasonal things which had always been a part of it, but it felt like Christmas. I put on a robe and listened outside Mama's door. She wasn't up yet. I walked through the house, opened the door leading from the foyer into the garage, and smiled at the brand-new four-door white Cadillac with a red ribbon tied all the way around it. I stood back to see what kind of a first view she'd get. No good. The thing to do would be to take her outside and then open the garage door so she'd catch a look at it all at once with the sunlight shining on it.

I put a Christmas album on the hi-fi set, loud, and listened outside her door again. Still sleeping. I opened it a little and did some stumbling and coughing until I heard her moving around. I leaned over the bed and kissed her. "Merry Christmas, Mama." I handed her a little box containing the car key.

She was still half asleep. "I'll open this when we have Christmas breakfast. Then I can enjoy it."

"Okay, you get dressed and I'll get things started." I tried to lay out the things she'd need to cook with. Twenty minutes later she came in. "Mama, let's just have some coffee."

"Well . . . all right, Sammy."

"*Instant* coffee!"

She was on her second cup but she hadn't made a move for the box. I picked it up and shook it. I put it down. "Sammy, you push that any closer to me and it'll be in my cup. I guess I better open it now or you'll jump out of your skin." She held up the key. "Now what's this for?"

I shrugged. "Beats me. Let's look around and see if we can find something it fits." I tried it on the kitchen door. "Doesn't fit here. Let's go outside."

"Sammy, what're you up to? And don't tell me Santa Claus, I couldn't make you believe it after you turned three."

I ran ahead, out the front door, and called back, "Maybe we can find something out here." I turned to open the garage and stopped dead. Somebody had come by in the middle of the night with a can of paint and a brush and had smeared across the front of the garage door: *Merry Christmas Nigger!*

"Sammy, you out here?" She was just coming through the front door. I spun around and grabbed her arm, stopping her before she could see it, and pulled her back into the house. I slammed the door closed and locked it against the ghoul-ish, dripping letters. The smile that had been on Mama's face was distorted by a stunned bewilderment. "Sammy, what happened?"

"Mama. Stay inside! Promise me you won't go out." She nodded silently and I ran into my bedroom and closed the door. I dialed and waited. "Arthur . . . The hell it is. Listen . . ." I took deep breaths to keep my voice from breaking. "I need you. I want you to come over here tomorrow night. I'll be in Frisco. Bring a gun. Get a cop, someone off duty, I don't care what it costs, I want him on the hill across the road and I want you in the window . . . and if anybody comes onto my property . . . shoot him! Kill him. If anybody comes near my house or wants to bother Mama, then *kill him!* Stay here every night I'm out of town, please, Arthur, and kill anybody who comes near my house . . . that's the law, they can't come *here.*"

19

I hung up and sat on the bed staring out the same window I'd
looked through less than an hour before. Holy God! Even on
Christmas. I had to get my mind off it. I turned on a record. I
reached for a book, any book I might lose myself in. I picked
up *A History of the Jews* and opened it in the middle. The first
word I saw was "Justice." I skimmed the pages but that same
word kept reappearing. I'd read the book before, but I started
reading it again, from the beginning.

More than ever I saw the affinity between the Jew and the
Negro. The Jews had been oppressed for three thousand years
instead of three hundred like us, but the rest was very much the
same. I went through page after page, reading of their oppres-
sions, their centuries of enslavement; I traced them from one
end of the world to the other, despised and rejected, searching
for a home, for equality and human dignity, suffering the loneliness of being unwanted, surviving the destruction of their
homes and their temples, the burning of their books. For thousands of years they hung on to their beliefs, enduring the scorn,
the intolerance, the abuses against them because they were "different," time and again losing everything, but never their belief
in themselves and in their right to have rights, asking nothing
but for people to leave them alone, to get off their backs. I

looked at the name of the man who had written the book. Abram Leon Sachar. I felt like sending him a note: "Abe, I know how you feel."

I got hung up on one paragraph. *"The Jews would not die. Three centuries of prophetic teaching had given them an unwavering spirit of resignation and had created in them a will to live which no disaster could crush."* I read it over and over again, wondering what those teachings had been. What had they learned that gave them that strength?

". . . Rabbi, I read the books around the clock and it was like 'Yeah! I'm not the only one it's happened to.' I don't mean 'misery loves company' but there was something about seeing what your people lived through that made me able to detach myself from what was going on around me and measure my problems for what they really were. I came to thank you and tell you what I suddenly got out of them. They're nothing like what I expected. Maybe this'll sound odd to you but it's not like 'religion': something that on Sunday you get it over with because it's got to be done, or even if you like it, it's a once-a-week or even a once-a-day thing. It's more like basic rules for everyday living and so much of it is what I believe in—ideas I'd love to be able to live up to. It was all there, straight and familiar, confirming so much that I'd learned the hard way, like fight for what you believe in, suffer for it if you have to but don't let go of your ideas—'cause if you do, then you've got *nothing!*

"I love the attitude that man is made in God's image and that he has unlimited potential, and that 'In God's world all things are possible.' I love the idea that we can all reach for the brass ring and we can keep stretching until we're tall enough to reach it. This has been my thinking all my life and it's a joy to open a book and see that not everybody puts different people in separate cubbyholes and looks at them like 'How dare they' if they try to break out. And there's no 'Well, it's up to fate' and 'If it's meant to be.' I admire an attitude of: it *is* meant to be if you'll go out and get it done. I love your thinking about not waiting around for a Messiah to come and straighten everything out, that the Messiah is not an individual but mankind collectively and that it's up to them to create the kind of a world that'll be like a Kingdom of Heaven right here.

"I memorized certain things, one in particular, 'The difference between love and hate is understanding.' I kept thinking about it and I realized that it was something I'd found out in the Army, something I'd seen a dozen times since then, but I just hadn't known the words for it. Can you know what a hunk of truth like that does for a guy like me? If I can keep that in mind it's like a bulletproof vest. I know for a fact that when I meet someone who doesn't like me, who hates my guts, that if I sit with him for a while my chances of changing his mind are pretty good. I've just got to give him an opportunity to see what he didn't know or think about before. I realize that there are certain people who are never going to like me, not on toast or on rye. If two World Wars didn't wipe out blind hatred, then I know I'm not about to. Nor do I really care that much about trying with certain guys. If I look at it calmly and think, then I know that their prejudice is a crutch, it's an equalizer that some people need—they're getting kicked around and they've got to let it out on somebody so they find someone *they* can kick around. Okay, but when the guy calls you nigger, normally you don't smile and think, 'Relax, Charley, it's his crutch.' All you know is he just hit you over the head and you want to hit him back, and whether you do or not, it's exhausting. But now, let him hit me with his crutch. I'm wearing a steel hat. If I find somebody hating me because he doesn't want to understand me, then I'm not going to hate him, because I *will* understand him. I'm not going to let him insult me and then exhaust me, too."

The rabbi was laughing. "I've heard of personally applying a philosophy but you just made a pretzel out of it."

"Don't knock it, Rabbi. It's working. Y'know my friend with the gun, and the cop I told you about?"

"Yes."

"I hired a painter instead."

"Sammy, you seem to enjoy the Jewish philosophy. I didn't give you much about our theology."

"Well, there was some, and here's where you're going to think I'm out of my mind entirely, but as I read about the three levels of Judaism, the Orthodox, the Conservative, and the Reform—I hope you won't take offense, but it's something like the way I do my act. I do my shows to suit each audience. I give them what I feel they want. Maybe you can see how Judaism does sort of the same thing. It's broken down so that the individual can have what he needs. The religion serves the man, it's there to make his life a little better, not to tell him, 'Hey, God's over here, three shows on Sunday and you'd better catch Him or you blew it and you go downstairs.' I'm not knocking the others. Obviously they work for millions of people, but I appreciate the flexibility of Judaism. You don't put a guy in a box and say, 'Now here's how to worship God.' " I looked at a piece of paper I had. " 'God, where shall I find thee? Wherever the mind is free to follow its own bent.' "

I hated to break the pleasant camaraderie of the past two weeks but I couldn't put it off any longer. "Rabbi, we can talk openly, can't we?"

"I certainly hope so."

"Well, I've been coming to services, we've spent hours and hours talking Judaism, and I've read all the books you gave me until I was blue in the face—and y'gotta admit, with my face that's not easy—in other words, obviously I'm interested, right? But at no time in all our talks have you ever once said, or even hinted, 'Hey, why don't you convert. Become a Jew.' "

"Sammy, converting to Judaism is a monumental move. Particularly for you."

"What do you mean by that?"

"Don't be sensitive. You know there are many Negro Jews

and that I wasn't thinking about that. But you're publicity-prone. An immediate conversion might very possibly create the opinion that you're doing this as a publicity stunt."

"Oh, you can't believe that?"

"You should know that I wouldn't waste my time or thought on you if I even suspected that. I know your sincerity, but there are many who won't and they'll deride you and make a mockery of something which has begun to have significance to you.

"There's no need to rush into formal conversion. For a while be a Jew at heart. You can be just as good a Jew if you really believe in it without having a document to make it official."

"Rabbi, all my life I went in back doors."

"It's not the back door. When you've had enough time to be absolutely sure, then come in the front door. But don't rush through it. When you get back to Hollywood you should look up Rabbi Max Nussbaum. He's one person I believe you should meet in your quest for a kinship to Judaism."

He was not a man to whom I wanted to give quick answers.

"Rabbi Nussbaum, religion is something I did without for over twenty years, but in a remote way it's like a policeman or the fire department: you may not use them often but when you need them you'd better know how to find them. I don't know how much Rabbi Fine told you about how I got interested in Judaism—it was strictly by accident. But when I started getting an idea of what it was all about I kept reading and I've developed a tremendous feeling for it, and for the first time in my life I see the hope of filling the spiritual void I've always had."

"Have you given your own religion a chance to fill that void?"

"Well, my father's a Baptist and my mother's a Catholic but I wasn't raised very close to either of those faiths."

"Wouldn't you think it advisable to examine and understand what you already have before you trade it away for something else? What's wrong, Sammy?"

"Rabbi . . . I hope you won't misunderstand this, but I want to be totally honest with you. I get a feeling that when I talk about becoming a Jew . . . well, nobody seems to get too choked up about the idea."

"Sammy, if I brought a grown man to you and said, 'He hasn't been able to make a living in real estate but he's read a lot of books on show business and he's thinking about becoming a performer, so I'd like you to put him in your act'—what would you tell me?"

I felt the heat of embarrassment crossing my face. "I apologize for making an idiot of myself."

"Don't apologize. But don't be sensitive either. Race has nothing to do with our reluctance to rush you into conversion. You should know that from the reading you've been doing. I'm sure you've come across Isaiah's pronouncement 'My house shall be a house for all people.' You must have seen that one of the primary tenets of Judaism is a hospitality to differences.

"Sammy, a rabbi is a teacher. I'm here to help you find what you want, not to act as a membership committee. In your reading you must have seen that we do not urge people to convert. Would we, of all people, tell others, 'You should think our way'? But that does not mean we aren't delighted to find someone who does. We *cherish* converts, but we neither seek nor rush them. We don't want today's enthusiasm to be tomorrow's disappointment. We want Judaism to serve you, to bring you comfort, joy—everything a faith might mean to one—but it can only do so if approached properly, with the fullest understanding of what it offers. You may in a short while decide it's not all you thought it was cracked up to be. On the other hand, and I believe this will be the case, I think that your appreciation and enjoyment of Judaism, your benefit from it, will be broadened by the extent to which you understand it."

"I just hate to put off doing something I feel so sure of."

"Don't put it off. Identify yourself as a Jew. Study, attend services, associate yourself with whatever Jewish organizations your traveling will permit. When you come down to it, what *is* the act of being a Jew? It's an approach to life, an adherence to a set of principles, to a moral code, the acceptance of a standard of human ethics and behavior. Obviously much of our thinking was yours before you even met a rabbi or you wouldn't have related to it. But know everything you possibly can before you make up your mind. Read more. Take time. Come back and see me. I will always be available to you. We'll talk about what you've read and about what you think, and we'll explore what you believe in. But let me caution you not to expect to find Judaism in books. They'll only present the philosophy, its history, its evolution; they will give you knowledge which may or may not translate within you so that someday you will come to me and say 'Rabbi, I'm a Jew.' "

20

I leaned across the dressing table at the Frontier, in Vegas, and put on my patch, letting my hair hang casually over the elastic band, making Charley Handsome faces into the mirror. Morty and Dave came in.

Dave turned to Morty. "She's beautiful, isn't she?" Morty nodded. "Gorgeous!"

Between phrases of "Black Magic" I caught a woman at ringside nudging her husband, pointing to her eye, whispering, "The patch is satin, it matches his lapels." Instantly I heard Bogart again, *"You want 'em to say 'There's Sammy Davis' or 'There's the kid with the patch'?"* I signaled Morty to cut the music.

"Ladies and gentlemen, there's something I've been wearing for the last year or so and I really dig it, but I think it's starting to wear me, so it's time I got rid of it."

I slipped off the patch and tossed it to a corner of the bandstand. A woman at ringside closed her eyes and groaned. There was a gasp throughout the room. They were probably expecting to see nothing but a large hole.

"I hope you'll bear with me, but I can't wear that thing for the rest of my life." I cued Morty for the impressions.

The audience was coming out of its shock; the applause

began growing, and they began standing, table by table. The people were much too high for the impressions. I had to steamroller over them to regain control. I snapped my fingers fast, cueing Morty for "Fascinating Rhythm." The first notes burst over the heads of the audience, but it was hopeless, the music couldn't begin to climb over the continuing, growing roar.

The Frontier's publicity guy burst into the dressing room. "Sammy, I could've had photographers, wire services . . ."

"I'm sorry, but I couldn't tip you off 'cause it wasn't planned. There was no 'I'll go and make a dramatic thing out of it.' It's the last thing I expected to do."

He was looking at me with disgust. "Well, at least let's set up a shot now of you taking it off and throwing it away. I guess I can still plant it with one of the wire services."

"Baby, it won't work. It'll be phony and it'll look like it."

"Sammy, please, I know what I'm doing."

I checked the morning papers. There were stories but no pictures. I called Jess to see if the picture had broken in L.A. It hadn't.

Dave asked, "What's there to look so happy about?"

"I'm happy to know I was right. That picture *shouldn't* have run. It was posed and phony and the newspaper guys smelled it. The audience got hung up on the drama of the moment because it was real. When you're selling emotion then it better be real, daddy, or you ain't gonna sell it. The picture was dishonest. And the cat who thinks he's gonna fool the people is gonna wake up someday and find he's out of the business."

Jule Styne came into the dressing room, shy, yet bristling with energy. "Sammy, I saw your show. Fantastic! You're a great talent but you can't play nightclubs forever. You'll suffocate that talent in saloons. You've got to expand, spread out. You need dimension . . ." His enthusiasm was dizzying. "The place for you is Broadway!"

I sat him down in a chair, careful not to interrupt him.

"You should star in a musical. You *must!* You can sing and dance and do everything you do in clubs. I'll produce it and we'll get some good writers to do a modern musical comedy. We'll build the story around whatever kind of a character you feel you could play best. They'll die over you on Broadway. And the stature and prestige would be enormous for you."

I was staring at him like he was Charley Messiah.

"Jule, keep talking. But keep your distance or you may get a kiss on the lips."

"Then you like the idea?"

"I love it."

"Great. We'll get together tomorrow and discuss it. In the meantime try to think of a character you could play best."

I found myself walking around the room, smiling at the walls: if TV and movies don't want me, to hell with them—there's *nothing* that can match Broadway for stature and dignity.

I had a lunch table set up in the room and I'd put a "Don't Disturb" on the phone when Jule arrived. "I think I should play someone like me. A performer. Let's face it, that's the kind of a character I really understand, plus the fact that it gives us a built-in excuse for me to sing and dance."

"I like it. He could be a kid who's trying to make it against the odds, the racial thing . . . he's alone in the world . . . he's got nothing but talent going for him . . ." Jule's face took on a dreamy, faraway look. "Maybe he's too sensitive to fight the race thing here, so he goes off to Europe—Paris! He finds himself a little Left Bank club and he becomes the chic thing to do."

I listened to him ad-libbing a show, speaking with childlike enthusiasm—the truly creative man, forgetting past triumphs, involved deeply and only in the thing of the moment. I was swept up in his excitement and the ideas flew back and forth across the table.

We took a breather and I said, "Jule, I'm not going to try to be a writer but I do have one strong feeling about the overall idea of the show: it's got to say something racially. And, as you said, we should do a 'modern' musical. That means an integrated show with a mixed chorus. I mean *really* mixed. Not the typical thing where they have eight dancers and one of them is colored and the producer goes around saying, 'We have an integrated cast.' That's bull. Nobody's ever done it right and we of all people should be the first ones."

"Definitely. And, we should do it first-class right down the line. For choreography let's get Gene Kelly or Agnes de Mille . . ."

"Jule, people like that are fabulous, but when they choreograph a show you don't even have to look at the program to tell who did the dances—they've got their own styles, and they're great, but not for me. I don't want my audiences to watch me work and see Gene Kelly or Agnes de Mille dancing; I want them to see Sammy Davis, Jr. And I have the same feeling about the music. I've got to dance my way and do songs my way. . . ."

"Sammy, are you willing to pay half a million dollars in order to do a Broadway show?" The man behind the desk at the Morris office said, "The difference between what you can make in a play and in clubs comes to exactly $518,000 in one year. Assuming you sell out on Broadway for every single performance, at ten percent of the gross the most you can earn is $6,000 a week. That's $312,000 in twelve months. Thus, you are trading a *sure* $830,000 in firm nightclub contracts for a possible $312,000. At best, you sacrifice half a million dollars." He dropped the paper on his desk. "You can see that it's out of the question."

Will spoke gently. "Sammy, they've looked into it carefully but it's like I was afraid of."

The Morris guy said, "It's a monstrous financial loss. You can't possibly afford it."

"Forgetting the money for a minute, do you agree that it's important for us in terms of career?"

"No question about it. If the play is successful it will give you substantial longevity elsewhere."

"Then the fact is that at this stage of our careers, the prestige of a hit show could be considered more important than immediate money." I turned to Will. "How about if we compromise? Supposing we limit our run to one year?"

"Sammy, the prestige we'd get isn't worth what we'd have to pay for it."

"Massey, I'm not looking for prestige just to have prestige. I want to invest one year to grow, to build something."

"That's fine. But you can't afford to spend $500,000 to do it."

The Morris guy nodded. "He's right. You can't forget that you're over $100,000 in debt, and you have to keep earning big money if you're ever going to get out of the hole."

I turned to the Morris guy. "I'd like to speak privately to Mr. Mastin. Will you excuse us for a few minutes, please?"

The door closed and I walked slowly across the room and leaned against the desk, facing Will. "Massey, what is it you want out of life? What I mean is: you love the business and you like having your money safe in buildings and banks and things like that, right?"

"That's right."

"You've seen a lot of show business, Massey, good times and bad, and you've got a few investments going for you, haven't you?"

"Enough to carry me the rest of my life."

"And I'm glad you have them. We may not be flesh and blood, but we're as close as we can get other than that and I'm glad you've gotten what you want. You worked for it and you deserve it. Now I'm going to tell you what *I* want from life. We talked about this a long time ago but you didn't listen to what I was saying, or if you did, then you don't remember. I don't want 'nigger' written on my door. I don't want to be a buffoon because I bought a beautiful house." I took out my wallet and showed him a card I'd had sealed in plastic. "You said I'd never get this. Read it. Tell me again that they'll never let a Negro into the Friars Club." He stared at my membership card, shaking his head slowly. "This is what *I* want out of life, Massey, and I know how to get it. I'm willing to cut down on everything. I'll drop Dave. I'll live in a furnished room—anything, but I've got to do this show. You've got yours. Let me get mine. Please. Don't stand in my way."

21

Jule Styne was smiling at me from just outside the gate to the field—there was a fellow with him: about my age, a little taller than me, horn-rimmed glasses, Italian raincoat.

"This is George Gilbert, Sammy."

"Hello, George. Glad to meet you after all the talk on the phone. You look different than I pictured you." I hadn't pictured him at all but I wanted to make it warmer than how-do-you-do.

As we shook hands, humor flickered across his eyes. "I recognized *you* immediately."

Jule gave my baggage checks to a chauffeur, and we walked through the terminal building. I waved back to the skycaps and the reservations clerks; a woman coming toward us held a scrap of paper. "Would you, Sammy?" Others came over with pencils and papers, and I let a crowd form. "You in town for *Mr. Wonderful*, Sammy? My whole family's waiting for it. We wouldn't miss you." Out of the corner of my eye I watched Jule and George soaking it all up, beaming happily. I pointed to them. "Those two gentlemen are my producers. I'm sorry but I can't keep them waiting any more or they'll fire me and get maybe Harry Belafonte." It got a laugh, the crowd opened for me, and I quickened our pace so we wouldn't be stopped again.

The limousine was waiting directly out front. I looked at Jule. "In a No Parking zone?" He smiled, pleased that I'd noticed. "Jule, I'll tell you right now, if the people like us as much as I dig your style then we're going to be the biggest hit of all time." He smiled again, still seeing the crowd around me, and the three of us settled back contentedly against the cushions of the limousine as it rolled out of the airport and onto the parkway to New York.

The lobby of the Gorham Hotel on 55th Street, between Sixth and Seventh, was small, with a tile floor and furniture which had limped through the years barely making the transition from elegant to homey, and the elevator man was wearing one of those uniforms which you know wasn't bought especially for him. "Penthouse B" was a freshly painted large room with a bar at the end near a small kitchen. The bar and kitchen had been thoughtfully stocked.

"You do this, George?"

He gave me a self-conscious nod and pointed quickly to a pair of couches. "They open into beds. And this whole terrace is yours." I looked through the glass door leading onto a terrace that was bigger than the entire apartment. I smiled. "I'll use it for sunbathing."

He blushed and walked toward the door. "Well, I'll be going. I hope you like the apartment—it isn't exactly the Plaza."

"Baby, I've lived in worse, and for four hundred dollars a month it's beautiful."

"Anyway, I live downstairs and if there's anything I can do . . ." He grinned. "Like if you need a recipe or something."

I unpacked the outfit I'd chosen for the first rehearsal: a new pair of Levi's—they'd cost $3.98 plus $22 for the alterations, but the fit was worth it, a red alpaca pullover under a double-breasted alpaca sweater, a little cashmere polo coat—and they'll know a star is coming to work.

I looked around the living room of Jule's suite in the Bellevue-Stratford in Philadelphia, at the director, writers, our press

agent, the producers, manager, general manager—all linked together by a common bond: panic. One by one they'd come in,
glanced at the others, tried brave smiles and taken seats, all
with the self-consciousness of entering a funeral chapel. There
was a room service table with sandwiches, coffee, and a few
bottles of liquor, and occasionally somebody stood up and
browsed disinterestedly through it to spare themselves the necessity of speaking.

Jule looked sick as he called the meeting to order. "Well,
we're in trouble. We got one good one out of three. Sammy's
personal reviews are fabulous, so at least we've got that going
for us. And they liked Jack Carter and Chita Rivera. But on the
other side of it two of the papers slaughtered us on the racial
thing."

Somebody in the back of the room ventured, "Maybe
they're right. Maybe it's something that doesn't belong in the
theater." The one voice triggered the others: "It's dangerous." . . . "Like they say, let Western Union deliver the messages." . . . "Yeah, the racial thing should be softened." . . .
"It's touchy." . . .

I stood up in the middle of the cross fire. "May I say something? If we take the racial theme and just sweep it under the
carpet, then we'll have no reason to exist."

The room sank into a fuzzy silence of uncertainty and inde-
cision. A voice broke through. "I think that if we change the
basic story line we take the heart right out of the show."

The room burst into action again: "Our point of view is to
stay alive." . . . "Sammy, you're new to the theater, it's a different art form." . . . "We know what the critics will buy." . . .

I felt the helplessness of a man getting mugged by a gang.

The stagehands were striking the scenery and hauling it into
New York–bound trucks before we'd taken our last bow. I
changed clothes and George and I waited for Johnny Ryan, our
stage manager, and his assistant, Michael Wettach, to finish seeing the last of the stuff onto the trucks. Then the four of us and

Johnny's wife, D.D., went for supper at our usual place, a little
Italian restaurant a few blocks from the theater.

George was staring into his plate, quietly humming something from *Pal Joey*. I glared at him. "At least you could hum
one of *my* hits." Johnny made a whole production out of
breaking a bread stick exactly in half and buttering the end of it
like he was painting the Mona Lisa. D.D. said, "Sammy, as
soon as we're in New York I'll get you some of that verbena
soap I was telling you about."

I nodded ruefully and looked from face to face. "In other
words, nobody wants to discuss the corpse, right? They're completely out of their minds. They threw out scenes and put new
ones in so fast that nothing in the whole show makes sense
anymore."

"Don't complain. At least no one suggested they call in
Donald O'Connor to play Charley Welch."

"You don't want to be serious, right?"

"Well, I don't *want* to be, but if it'll make you feel any better the fact is we've still got something left—"

"I'll tell you what we've got left, baby: the last half hour of
the show, the Palm Club scene—a twenty-five-thousand-
dollars-a-week nightclub act that I'm now doing for *six* thousand."

Nobody argued with me. We started back toward the hotel,
walking in bleak silence, all of us knowing that the story was
shot, morale was shot—that we were nothing more than a
patched-up mongrel held together by string.

We passed a theater where workmen were pulling down the
signs for *My Fair Lady*. "Do you think this show's as good as
they say?"

George shrugged. "We'll see soon enough. They open a few
days before us in New York. I know that they didn't have anywhere near the advance we had here."

I stopped in front of the Latin Casino. "The last time we
played here you couldn't get in with a shovel and a wedge.
There were people piled up on the sidewalk. I must be losing

my mind. I actually gave up all that for this." We continued walking. "What the hell am I doing a show for? If nobody can possibly respect what we're trying to do then why the hell am I doing it?"

George buttoned his overcoat tighter around the neck. "Please. I've got my own troubles. I own a beautiful hotel in the mountains, the Raleigh. I can take all winter off and be in Florida, instead of freezing my . . ."

"Cheer up, you guys." Johnny put his arm around my shoulder. "We've still got better than a fighting chance. The fact is that in addition to the Palm Club scene we've got lots of entertainment, lots of flash, some good songs, dances, jokes. . . ."

"Yeah, Johno—everything but integrity."

The clock on the Paramount Building showed three o'clock. In a few hours the whole city would know we were a flop. George was sitting at my bar. He poured himself another scotch and stared at the bottle. He picked it up and started reading the label. Our eyes met but there was no reason to speak, we'd said it all: the cliché cop-outs like "They didn't understand what we were trying to do" when both of us knew too well that they *had* understood. Maybe the techniques were different on Broadway, but it all boiled down to the one thing that worked anywhere—honesty. The lights of the city became hazy as tears began filling my eyes. I was aware of George watching me and I hid behind a Garfield bit. "Sure, sure . . . y'see those lights up and down Broadway? Well, I'll give 'em to you for a necklace, I'll have this town on its knees." I shook my fist out the window. "Big town, I'll get you yet!"

I heard George blowing his nose. He'd seen that movie too. "If you'd done that onstage maybe we'd have been a hit."

"Man, them mothers didn't use up *any* of their good words, did they?" I read aloud: " 'If you want to see "Mr. Wonderful" we suggest you get over to the Broadway Theater this week. He won't be around very long . . .' "

"Well, thank God at least *you* got great personal reviews."

There was no point explaining that I could find little satis-faction in seven critics discovering I do a good nightclub act; that I'd come to Broadway to accomplish something and I'd been told, "Stay in nightclubs where you belong."

"I suppose you'll be going back to clubs."

"I signed a contract to be on Broadway for one year, and I intend to stay for one year." I crumpled the reviews into tight wads. "The votes aren't all in yet."

"Sammy, even if the afternoon papers are good . . ."

"I don't mean the critics. I'm talking about the people."

He was looking at me sympathetically. "I know how you feel, but it's impossible. You can't beat the critics. Nobody ever did—except *Hellzapoppin'* and that was only because Walter Winchell decided to plug them every single day. He made them a hit, but we don't have him . . ."

"Baby, I know everything you're going to say, so don't bother. I'm hip that when the critics come out against you everything changes—all the heat comes out of you. I'm hip that where just last night we could call our shots with the press, now we'll have to fight for every inch of space we get."

"The world hates a loser."

"The world doesn't hate losers, George, it just has no time for them." I walked over to him. "But did you ever see a guy get beaten bloody and then get up off the floor and start fight-ing? Did you ever see what happens to the crowd when he starts *winning*?" I felt the cool edge of excitement biting through the sogginess of failure. "Our show is going to run. I came to Broadway to get something and I'm not leaving with-out it."

The next day the kids began straggling into the theater at around seven o'clock. They weren't due until "half hour" at eight, but when you're a flop there's no fun in hanging around the show business bars. At the theater, they had refuge from the embarrassing sympathy of friends, and the smug looks from people who are glad there's no reason to be jealous anymore. By the second night of a flop you're tired and sick like you've got a hangover, and there's no one you want around except maybe someone else who has one.

I asked Johnny Ryan to have the cast gathered onstage at ten minutes before curtain. I deliberately didn't change into my first act costume, which was designed to make Charley Welch look like a loser. I wore my own clothes, my own jewelry. I wanted them to see success talking.

They were standing around like lost souls, clustered in little groups of defeat. I walked to center stage. I remembered a scene from *The Great Dictator* in which Hitler made Mussolini sit in a very low chair so that he had to look up at Hitler and subconsciously got the feeling of looking at strength. I motioned for them to sit on the floor in front of me.

". . . I've got no plans to be Charley Flop Came to Broadway. But either we play like we're the biggest hit in the world or we're going to die, because with the people presold against us we're only as good as what we give every song, every line, everything we do on this stage for every audience. Now, nobody can keep the people away from what they like and want to see. And they like *me* or they wouldn't pack the nightclubs to see me. I can bring them into this theater but I can't entertain them without you. So if you give me the word, if I can count on you, I'll go out and get us audiences with my bare hands; I'll go on television and radio, I'll use every friend I've got, I'll do every interview, from the network blockbusters to if there's a cat on Broadway and Fiftieth with a megaphone I'll be his guest. The people will come to see me and if we work a mile over our heads, if we kill ourselves to entertain them, they'll talk about us and I guarantee that we'll run. . . ."

One of the boy dancers jumped up. "We're with you all the way." Another was on his feet. "We'll work our heads off . . ." The mood swept through the crowd, catching them up in it until all of them were standing and cheering, straight out of an M-G-M musical. They were shouting and waving their fists in the air, a pack of losers changed into fighters. It had turned into a cause.

I'd just finished doing the impressions in the Palm Club

scene when a woman in the audience stood up and shouted, "The critics are crazy. We love you, Sammy." I threw her a kiss. "So tell your friends!" The audience cheered. It was eleven-fifteen and I was ready to go into the last number but I cued Morty and I did an extra thirty minutes.

Mike Goldreyer, our company manager, was waiting in the wings, wringing his hands. "Sammy, it's no good. It's no good. We can't keep the stagehands so late. We have to pay them overtime. . . ."

Jule Styne burst through the fire door between out front and backstage. "Sammy, that business of 'tell your friends.' It's terrible. *Terrible.* It's not 'theater.' You can't do it."

I closed the dressing-room door behind us. "Jule, for the last few months I've listened to everybody telling me how to do a show: writers, directors, producers, chorus boys' parents, out-of-town critics—everybody! But that's all over. From now on I do it *my* way. Maybe I didn't do the chic thing out there but I didn't see anybody walk out, and I sure as hell heard a lot of people yelling bravo when we took the curtain calls. So don't tell me about overtime or 'theater.' I'm not in the 'theater' anymore. I'm back in the entertainment business!"

The elevator opened into the reception room of the Morris office. I waved to the girl behind the desk, "Darling, will you tell Mr. Bramson I'm on my way in, please." I smiled at the performers waiting to see their agents, pushed the double doors open, and walked down the corridor to the television department.

"We've *been* talking to Sullivan, Sammy. We knew you'd want that exposure for your show . . ." Sam Bramson looked down. "But he doesn't want you."

"You're joking!"

"It's not exactly that he doesn't want you . . . Look, why don't you speak to him yourself. I'll get him on the phone."

Ed said, "Sammy, I can't use your father and your uncle.

Naturally, I'd love to have you on the show, but I want you alone. I'm sorry, I really am, but if I buy you and put aside eight minutes for you I don't want that time split up. You're what my audience will tune in to see and that's what I want to give them."

"But, Ed, we've always been a . . ."

"They're dead weight, Sammy. I admire your loyalty to them, and there's no reason why you still can't split the dough with them if you want to, but from a strictly show business point of view, frankly, it's becoming uncomfortable."

"You don't understand . . ."

"No, Sammy, I'm afraid it's you who don't understand. You're not the first performer who had a situation like this. It was the same with Willie and Eugene Howard, and Al Jolson and his brother Harry. Al had the big talent, so Al worked alone. But it wasn't easy for him. You'd go into a town where an Al Jolson movie was playing and across the street from it there'd be a vaudeville theater with a marquee saying 'Jolson' in the biggest possible size, then over it in little tiny letters it said 'Harry.' Al had his problems too, but he never let them interfere with what he did on the stage."

When I hung up, Sam Bramson said, "Steve Allen's been after us for you. He's fighting hard to compete with Sullivan and he's offering ten thousand instead of Sullivan's top of seventy-five hundred."

"No. Sullivan was the first network show I ever did and he's always been a gentleman to his fingertips. I can't just run for the money. Keep trying. Maybe he'll change his mind."

When I got back to the hotel, there was a telegram for me: "WELCOME TO NEW YORK. PLEASE DROP IN AND VISIT US. ED WYNNE, THE HARWYN." I called George at his office. "What kind of a place is the Harwyn?"

"East Side supper-clubbish. It's the hot place. Whatever *that* means."

I read him the telegram. "That's damned nice of them."

"Well, really! You *are* the star of a Broadway show."

"Baby, I admit I'm one of the great stars of our time. I even admit that I'm adorable. But I'm not exactly in demand around the chic nightclubs." As I spoke, the tone of his voice caught up with me and I realized that he'd understood; I could picture him smiling, but he was considerately playing it cool. "Anyway, the least we can do is accept the man's invitation, right? Will you have your secretary make a reservation for me for twelve-thirty, baby?"

"Sure, *baby*."

"And call Johnny and D.D. and Michael and tell them we'll all go over to Chandler's after I get off tonight—I've got the Barry Gray show—and then we can swing over to the Harwyn and be chic and East Side-ish."

Barry Gray, New York's most influential talk radio star, gave the show an enormous plug as he'd been doing every night since we'd opened. Then we got down to the interview. "Sammy, do you mind if I get personal with my questions?"

"Anything you like."

"Is it true that you've become a Jew?"

A hush fell over the restaurant. The people were leaning in, listening. "Yes, Barry, I am a Jew."

"Welcome aboard, landsman. When did this happen?"

"I think I have always been a Jew in my thinking and my own undefined philosophies which I found so clearly spelled out when I began reading about Judaism a few years ago."

"How will people react to Sammy Davis, Jr., being a Jew?"

"I guess everybody will react differently, if they're going to react at all. And judging from the past—they'll react. I don't think my departure will set Christianity back. As for the Jewish community, I'm aware of the possibility that they might be offended by a Negro becoming a Jew. Maybe it'll turn them against me, I don't know. It's a pretty frightening thought, because they make up more than fifty percent of my audiences. But I've found something in Judaism, and I'm not about to give it up. I have to believe they'll accept me according to Jewish law and custom which sees no color line or any lines other than between belief and nonbelief."

"I've heard it said that you wanted to be a Jew because all your friends are Jewish."

"Barry, Frank Sinatra is my closest friend and I never yet saw him wear a yarmulke. I'll admit he eats a bagel every now and then . . ."

"I read a joke in one of the columns that said you were playing golf on Long Island and the pro asked you for your handicap and you told him, 'I'm a colored, one-eyed Jew—do I need anything else?' How do you feel about the Sammy Davis, Jr., jokes?"

"They're a hazard of the business and the fact is you're glad people know your name well enough to do jokes about you; but some I despise because they are destructive and insidious."

"Can you remember—or would you rather not remember— any you'd classify that way?"

"I'm not about to forget them."

"Would you tell us one?"

"Yes. But in order for it to serve a purpose I'd like to say something first. I believe a very large chunk of the racial thing is a question of changing the images that remain in people's minds and *certainly* not contributing to them. You've noticed that there are no Stepin Fetchits anymore, no more Parkyakarkuses, none of the characters which were caricatures of entire groups? It didn't happen because they weren't fine performers, but pressure groups went to work and they asked Hollywood, 'Hey, don't use a Stepin Fetchit anymore. Let's not have any more kids growing up thinking of Negroes as slow, lazy, shuffling characters.' Groups like the American Jewish Committee fought against stereotyping Jews as greedy, grasping, and money-mad, just as the NAACP got Little Black Sambo, and all those damned pancakes he ate, out of the schoolbooks and out of our lives.

"Now, I get myself to the point at which I'm able to own a

beautiful home, we keep our house and grounds looking well, and although I certainly didn't buy the house as my contribution to racial harmony, it's a beautiful extra to know that the neighbors can see a colored family and they've got to say, 'Gee, it's not really true they live eighty of them to the room.' The next thing I know a guy tells me a joke that's circulating: One of my neighbors tells her husband, 'Strange about the house next door: The maid comes and goes all the time, but the people who live there never leave the house.'

"Now, I'm not so hard-nosed and bitter that I can't see the humor in a well-constructed joke. But I have to detest humor predicated on the assumption that all colored women are maids. My grandmother *was* a maid, and a lot of guys dug ditches until they became president of the company or until their families made it and pulled them up with them. There comes a time to forget humble origin. Mr. Armour isn't a butcher anymore, right?"

"Sammy, did you rap the guy in the mouth, I hope?"

"No. He wouldn't have known why I was hitting him. Most of the people who tell these jokes are not haters; they'd never yell a dirty name, they'd get sick if they saw a mob throwing rocks at a colored kid trying to go to school, they'd be repelled by racial violence, yet—intentional or not—they are perpetuating the legends which perpetuate the prejudice which causes the racial violence.

"Charley Joke Teller doesn't understand that violence is the smallest part of prejudice. He's standing in the middle of a social revolution, telling his little jokes, thoughtlessly assuring people that we all carry knives and steal and lie, until it's hardly any wonder that when we try going to school with you, some guy who's been convinced is ready to crack open our skulls to prevent it.

"As awful as violence is, at least it's out in the open where it can be recognized and handled and eventually it's ended. But the jokes keep on, quietly, subversively, like a cancer, rotting away the foundations of hope for the Negro, stealing the dignity on which we can build respected lives.

"And as bad as the jokes are the words—the put-down words like 'nigger,' 'kike,' 'chink,' 'wop,' 'spick.' I hear them used between buddies, good-naturedly, but anyone who thinks he's above prejudice, so he can use them affectionately or humorously, is missing the point: If a person sincerely desires to stamp out a sickness he can't keep a few of its germs alive just for laughs. Before we can reach a utopia in human relations those jokes and those words and the legends they perpetuate must die."

In the cab to the Harwyn, Michael asked, "And where did all *that* come from? You sounded like Harriet Beecher Stowe."

I nudged George. "And what about our producer? Doesn't he have some kind word for his star who just turned out to be a public speaker?"

"I was trying to remember if I've ever told a racial joke. I'll even be afraid to listen to *Amos 'n' Andy* from now on. When I think how much I used to like Stepin Fetchit and Willie Best . . ." He sighed. "Little did I know what I was doing. Every time I laughed I probably sank a ship."

The Harwyn's doorman held open the cab door. "Nice to see you, Mr. Davis." He moved quickly to open the front door for me. I let Johnny, D.D., George, and Michael go in first.

A tall, good-looking man extended his hand. "Sammy, my name is Ed Wynne. Thank you for coming in."

The dance band started playing "Mr. Wonderful"; people all over the room were smiling and waving at me; Ed led us to the only unoccupied table in the room and called over the table captain. "Mac will see that you have everything you want." A waiter brought a bucket with champagne bottles in it. "Compliments of Mr. Wynne."

I leaned back against the soft banquette and smiled at the group. "That's how it is when you're with a star, folks. It's a definite First Cabin all the way."

Mac was handing out menus. They were in French. I said, "Thanks, but I know what I want, a steak about an inch thick. . . ."

A vaguely familiar-looking guy, one of those faces you see

around Vegas and New York, came over to the table. "Whaddya say, Sammy?"

"Hi, baby. How y'doing?"

"I'm gonna come by and see your show."

"Be sure to come backstage and have a drink with me."

"Hey"—he smiled—"thanks, Sam. I will. How's Thursday?"

When he'd left George asked, "Who's that?"

"I don't know, he's a guy."

"And you're going to have drinks with him?"

"I'm not going to spend the night with him. But what'll you bet he'll be at the box office tomorrow? And what'll you bet he'll bring friends? Now, am I Mr. Wonderful or not?" He looked pleased. "You see, George. Colored people aren't really lazy."

When I called for the check the waiter said, "Compliments of Mr. Wynne."

I learned toward George. "Baby, give me a twenty for the waiter and ten for the captain, will you? I'll catch up with you Friday."

Ed walked me to the door. "Thank you for coming in, Sammy. Now come back soon. Please. Think of this as your home."

We left Johnny, D.D., and Michael getting a cab and George and I started walking toward Park Avenue. When we were far enough away from the club I grabbed his arm and hung on it like a half-hysterical nitwit. "Do you want to know about a small Negro lad from Harlem who just saw his first chic supper club and the owner told him, 'This is your home'?" I did a few Bill Robinson steps up the stoop of a private house.

George shrugged. "Now really. What's the big deal?" But his face was bursting with concealed pleasure for me and I danced back down the steps and gave him a shot on the arm. "You rat fink."

"Ow."

"I'm a star and it's in my contract that I can hit my producer anytime I feel like it."

The next morning I walked to Fifth Avenue, thinking about D.D. and Johnny, remembering the surprise of seeing his name, John Barry Ryan III, in Cholly Knickerbocker, and learning that a guy who worked as a stage manager and dressed like he couldn't afford to get his name in the phone book was Charley Social Register. Johnny and D.D. invited me over for Sunday dinner, and he'd said it would be informal. With anyone else that would be Levi's and hamburgers, but with them it might be a sit-down dinner with only three forks instead of five.

I walked to Tiffany and pushed the revolving door slowly, trying to get my bearings before I was inside. A store detective smiled. "Hello, Mr. Davis." The showcases sparkled as though every time a customer touched one a hand came out and polished it.

As I stepped off the elevator, into the silver department, a saleswoman approached me. "Mr. Davis, so nice to have you in the store. May I help you?"

"Thank you, yes. I'm interested in two things . . ." I selected a silver water pitcher to bring Johnny and D.D.

"You said there was something else, sir?"

"Yes . . . it's a favor I'd like to ask of you. Just between us, I don't know the first thing about the different kinds of silverware and I want to learn. I thought about looking it up in Emily Post but then I figured that she must have learned it *here*."

She laughed, pleased, and lowered her voice. "You wouldn't believe how many people don't know an oyster fork from a bouillon spoon. Come along, Mr. Davis, it will be my privilege to show you."

22

I slept late Sunday and took the package from Tiffany out of the closet. I slid the string off the outer wrapping and opened the large blue box. The pitcher was in a flannel bag. I re-wrapped it exactly as it had been. A few dozen roses would be more appropriate for one dinner, but Johnny and D.D. had been great to me on the road. I could always play it as though it were in return for the books on fine art they'd given me. I dressed in a gray tweed suit, an eggshell shirt, a black knitted tie and a vicuña polo coat.

A strong gust of wind from the East River almost knocked the box out of my hand as I stepped out of the cab in front of River House. I gripped the box securely and walked toward the building. As I reached the front door, a doorman stuck his head out. "Delivery entrance is up the street." He closed the door.

My phone was ringing as I got home. I called the desk and asked that no calls be put through. George was back and had asked them to let him know when I came in. I told them to ask him to come up. "But be sure to tell everybody else that I'm out."

George breezed in. "Weren't you supposed to be having dinner with Mr. and Mrs. John Barry Ryan III, cha, cha, cha."

"Something came up, baby."

He sat on the couch and glanced idly at the box that was with my coat on a chair. "Who lives in *there?*"

I put it into the closet. "It's just something I bought."

George walked into the dressing room and gaped at a line of bulky sweaters hanging along an iron pipe rack. "My God. What is *that?*"

"They're for the kids."

He inspected one of them. "You bought seventy-dollar sweaters to give away? For no reason?"

"I'm not giving them away, I'm going to wear them onstage, a different one every night, to help keep the kids from getting bored." I heard Johnny Ryan's voice in the hall.

"Sam? Are you okay? You weren't sick last night?"

I turned around. He was standing in the doorway. "No, John. I'm fine. I'm sorry about dinner, baby, but something came up."

"Oh . . . okay."

I went after him and stopped him in the hall. "Look, Johno . . . I'm sorry. I didn't forget. I just couldn't make it."

"Sammy . . . D.D. spent the whole day cooking a turkey for you. Couldn't you at least have called?"

"I'm sorry, John. I couldn't. I really couldn't."

His eyes became veiled, just as surely as if a stone wall had risen between us. "All right, Sam. We'll do it some other time." He turned and I stood there watching him walk away from me.

I smiled with satisfaction at the first line in Earl Wilson's column: "The B.W. and I had dinner with Jack Benny, who is as tight as Sammy Davis, Jr.'s pants." The pants were on their way to becoming a trademark for me. I opened an envelope of newspaper clippings. The top few were from the Negro press. The first was a three-panel cartoon: two colored guys were standing near a lamppost, which said "Harlem." One of them was asking, "Howcum we never see Sammy Davis hangin' on the corner up here?" The other was shrugging. "You crazy, man? Sammy ain't colored no more."

After a while I looked at the next one, an article: "Sammy Davis, Jr., Starring in 'I'd Rather Be White.' " My thoughts kept drifting to the pride Mama had taken in me. I didn't want to think about her seeing these, but I knew she would; she read the Negro papers religiously, looking for stories about me.

I kept going through the clips. I stopped at a Robert Sylvester column from the *Daily News:* "Dropped in to see Sammy Davis, Jr., in *Mr. Wonderful.* Sorry, but I just can't get excited over him. Maybe it's me, because throughout his night-club act—the last scene—Mr. Davis' talents were not lost on the rest of the screaming, applauding audience."

I called Jess on the Coast. "Baby, when we first played the Riviera, can you remember what Bob Sylvester said about the act?"

"Yeah . . . he said you were ugly as a shovel but you could dance like a son of a bitch! Something like that."

"Do you still have the clipping?"

"It's in one of the albums. Want me to send it to you?"

"No. I'll hold on till you find it."

It was a rave, just as I'd remembered. I hung up and stared at Sylvester's name. What the hell had happened?

Cliff Cochrane was Danny's press agent and I'd hired him to help me.

I lit a cigarette and watched his face as he reread the recent Sylvester clipping. "I've read worse."

"If Bob Sylvester saw my act for the first time and he didn't dig it, I'd say, 'Crazy, you can't win 'em all.' But Sylvester *used* to like the act. And the act hasn't changed! You were there when we opened at the Riviera. I did everything I do now except I'm technically better than I was then, I'm more polished, more mature. And I've got to assume that Sylvester's taste hasn't changed, either. Let's face it, he was a pro then—it wasn't like he was seeing his first nightclub act and got carried away by the excitement. So, if the act didn't change, and Sylvester didn't change—what did? There's only one thing left. Me! My image."

"I don't see the connection. The man was reviewing the *show*."

"Cliff, there's no separating a performer's public and private life—not with a 'personality.' It all weaves together. Whatever people believe I am from what they hear and read *must* have an effect on what I'm trying to say as a performer. The constant 'wild kid' bit has been hammered at so often that it's hardened into fact and created an image so strong, so vivid and distasteful, that a guy like Sylvester doesn't like me anymore."

The next evening I took Cliff to Danny's for a meeting with the top press agent Billy Rowe.

"I don't know where I went wrong with the Negro press, Billy. I cherished their acceptance when I had it, but I sure lost them somewhere along the way. Like Evelyn Cunningham. Cliff, this woman is our Hedda and Louella put together but with a little Dorothy Kilgallen thrown in. Now, I never even met her, but for some reason I happen to be her personal choice for president of the White Citizens Council."

Billy nodded painfully. "The general impression around the Negro press is that he's got it made and he just doesn't give a damn. Maybe we should start off our campaign with them by having a little get-together. Let them see how you feel. It might break the ice a little before you tackle them individually."

"Beautiful. We can do a special thing just for them—family style. No business, no interviews, none of the 'Hey, put my name in the paper' jazz. Strictly a thing for us all to relax, have a little booze, a little food, and get to know each other."

Evelyn Cunningham's column jumped up out of the *Courier* and slapped my face.

Dear Sammy,

Right off I can't think of anything I dislike about you. Not only are you one of the greatest entertainers in the world but from what I hear and what I see you also seem to be one of the nicest. In a way I'm as proud of you as I am of Ralph Bunche, Thurgood Marshall and the rest of the guys who will be written about in history books.

So, when you invited me to your press party I was real tickled to get a chance to meet you. I didn't expect that you and I would get to be boons on sight or that you would even remember my name after we'd met. All I wanted was the kicks of being in close quarters with you and maybe getting a small idea of what makes you tick. You see, I'm a 14-karat fan of yours. Anyway I got the most awful sinking of the stomach when I got to the party and saw at a glance that it was a press party for people on the colored papers. My stomach turned over again when I suddenly realized that it had been a long, long time since I had been through this type of all-colored press party in New York. Seems they went out with ankle strap shoes.

But I'm crazy about you. So after my stomach turned up I made excuses. I said to myself he's got something special to say to us that's exclusively for us or something really big is coming because this doesn't make sense. Nothing came. You were charming, gracious and entertaining. You hopped from guest to guest and you went to the trouble of engaging in small talk with us. But you weren't happy. Neither were we. Every now and then I got the feeling that you were embarrassed, that you didn't think the party was such a good idea after all. And then you made a short talk. You said with great sincerity that you were deeply appreciative of the Negro press and the Negro patrons who were helping to keep *Mr. Wonderful* running on Broadway. You intimated that despite the negative reviews of the show when it opened, Negroes were in a large measure responsible for making it run. For this, thanks. But Sammy, wouldn't it have been a gasser if you had said the same thing at a press party to which you had invited people from both the daily and weekly papers. It wouldn't have offended the daily boys. In fact I've got an idea they would have respected you even more. Don't get me wrong. I don't want you running down to Montgomery and jumping on buses or yelling and screaming about your civil rights. But in many, many quarters integration is fashionable and chic and you have access to these quarters. In short I don't think the press party was necessary, but I love you anyway. Love and kisses,

E.C.

P.S. Ain't it rough being cullud? There's always something!

I got Billy on the phone. "Did you see what that bitch wrote? Did I have to throw a party for *that*?"

"Sammy, she's right and we were wrong. Read the column again and you'll see it."

"Holy Toledo. Is it against the rules to be friendly and just say hello? Isn't 'Have a drink and let's be friends' enough of an announcement? What the hell does she want from me?"

Joe E. Lewis gazed around the jam-packed Friars Club roast in the ballroom of the Delmonico Hotel. "It's wonderful being up for lunch . . ." He had the mike against his mouth. "I sound like the all-clear signal at a floating crap game."

Walter Winchell heckled from his seat on the dais. "Speak into it. Don't kiss it."

Joe E. continued: "I don't want to interfere with the fun. I'll just introduce my fellow Friar, one of the greatest entertainers of all time, Sammy Davis, Jr."

I stood up. Red Buttons shouted, "Sit down, you shmuck!" He stalked over to Joe E. "You're supposed to introduce *me!*"

Joe E. nodded. "Gentlemen, I wasn't supposed to introduce Mr. Davis—you're catching me on a losing streak. I want you to meet Mr. Davis' nephew, Red Buttons."

Red took the mike and gestured toward me. "We're gathered here to honor this runaway slave. . . ." He waited for quiet and spoke seriously. "It's a happy thing for the Friars to be throwing a luncheon for someone we love and who has accomplished something important in our business." He looked at me. "Don't get a big head, you bum." He smiled at Winchell. "Walter, it's nice to see you take a few minutes off from fighting with people. I have a few telegrams here. This one is from Adam Clayton Powell: 'Sammy, if you vote for Adlai Stevenson you'll never play the Apollo again.' Here's one from *Confidential* magazine: 'Dear Sammy, You made us what we are today.'

"For our first speaker, I want to introduce Eddie Fisher, one of the finest singers to come along in three or four months."

Eddie took the mike. "Gentlemen . . ."

Jack E. Leonard shouted, "Is that your closing remark!"

Eddie composed himself. "As I was saying, before I was so rudely interrupted . . ."

Jack Carter heckled, "Work without the mike, Eddie. You're better off."

Eddie grinned. "I'll try again."

Jack E. called out, "I want to wish you luck with your comeback!"

Joe E. groaned. "Three-to-one he won't sit down."

Eventually, they let him say a few words to me, then Red took the floor again. "I'd like to introduce some members of the press who are in the room . . . Earl Wilson, the great columnist from the New York *Post*." Red looked nervously at Winchell. "Walter, I'm sorry, but I've got to do these things. . . . All right, he's *not* such a great columnist." Still getting no smile from Winchell, he threw out his hands. "The hell with this. I'm quitting the business."

Jack E. was on his feet. "I've got a big shock for you. You were never *in* it!" He took the mike and looked from Winchell to Red. "I just want to say, Red, I certainly enjoyed watching the end of your career today." He stared defiantly at Winchell. "Mr. Winchell: I like Ed Sullivan! Seriously, Walter, you're doing a great job on your TV show and you're a very clever fellow but I just want you to know that soon you'll be off the air with the rest of us."

Alan King began his turn at the mike: "I have nothing bad to say against Mr. Winchell because I'm just getting started in this business whereas all these other guys are through. . . ."

The hilarity of the afternoon could not, at least for me, overwhelm the warmth which motivated not only the jokes but the presence of the men who were telling them. I looked around the room and up and down the dais remembering a kindness with almost every face, and I could think of no greater satisfaction, no sweeter pleasure, than the approval of my own kind of people, show people.

The luncheon was drawing to a close, the heckling ended, and Walter Winchell took the mike. "Sammy, I join all the others who have saluted you and honored you here today with quips and insults. You know we are all devoted to you and respect your art and talent. Damon Runyon once wrote that the word 'class' is difficult to define. But once you see it you recognize it, and once you've recognized it you'll never forget it. Class, he said, was something you might find in the grace of a ballerina, the lift of a Thoroughbred's hoof, or the flip of a champion's glove. Gentlemen, Damon must have meant— Sammy Davis, Jr."

As I walked to the microphone the entire assemblage was standing, applauding me, and I looked toward the table where my father and Will were sitting with George, Michael, and Charley Head. There was confusion in Will's eyes, and I could imagine the turmoil within him: the tug-of-war between wanting to enjoy what he'd never believed he would see happen, to believe it was real and okay, with no strings attached, and the fear that something would happen to prove it all a lie. But the layer upon layer of emotional scar tissue which had taken a lifetime to develop was impenetrable, and I knew he could never see it as I did and enjoy it as tangible proof that a Negro could gain acceptance at least somewhere in a white world.

I didn't have to know the room at Sardi's to know we'd been seated in the back of the bus. "Well, it's another 'Welcome to Broadway' for old Sam by the chic theatah people."

George said, "Sammy, I forgot there was an opening tonight. If Richard Rodgers walked in here at this hour without a reservation . . ."

If I were Richard Rodgers it wouldn't matter. I sensed heads all over the restaurant turning and staring at us like, "Hey, look where they stuck Sammy Davis, Jr."

Burt Boyar, a Broadway columnist friend, said earnestly, "If you look around the room, the fact is the really important people are sitting back here."

I shook my head. "You lie beautifully, baby."

"Well, anyway," he said, "when people see you sitting here they'll assume the chic section was moved. Just think how uncomfortable you're making all the little nobodies who thought they had good tables up front."

Chita asked, "Would you feel better if we left?"

"Darling, you've got a lot of talent and a big heart but you've got a few things to learn about being a star; we play it with smiles and chic talk like we couldn't care less 'cause our every move is being watched—like the man said: 'The curtain never falls.' Also we don't order anything that'll keep us here too long. One drink, then a casual exit, and home, sweet home."

Michael asked, "What about the Copa and the Harwyn?"

"Another time, baby. Old Sam's had it for tonight. We'll go back to the hotel. We can sit around, get to know each other better. . . ."

George groaned. "My God, how much better can we know each other?"

I turned on the television set and sat behind the bar. "I admit we don't have caricatures on the walls, but we have records, television, books, magazines, and guns for those who wish to practice their draw. Now, the first thing we'll do is make a little call to the Stage and get some delicacies sent over. . . ."

Burt said, "Here's that pass you wanted for your father."

"Thanks, baby. He'll get a big kick out of this. I'll go down and give it to him now."

My father smiled at the words "Working Press," fanned the little slips of paper for each day of the racing season, and hung the pass on the lapel of his pajamas, beaming. "Poppa, I'll be the first man standing at the gate in the morning." He winked. "Wait'll some of my pals sees me with *this* hangin' from my jacket."

I got out of the cab in front of the Gorham and told Burt and his wife, Jane, "Catch you guys at Danny's. Sixish." As they drove away, my father pulled up in another cab. I made a production out of checking my watch and giving him Oliver Hardy looks through the window. "Oh, no. Oh . . . I don't believe this. You ran out of the money by *three o'clock?*"

He stepped out of the cab, looking brokenhearted, like he'd lost his shirt. "You have a bad day, Dad? You drop much?"

"No. I just didn't feel much like stayin' around."

He started into the hotel but I held his arm. "I don't get it. Why?"

He hesitated. "Y'know that pass you gave me?" Tears started coming to his eyes. "Well, when I got to the gate the guard looked at it and then at me—and he made me take it off.

He said, 'This ain't yours. Ain't no nigger reporters on the New York papers.' " His shoulders sagged as he pronounced the last few words and he kept looking past me up the street, avoiding my eye.

"Look, Dad, the guy was a bastard. Burt'll get you a new pass and he'll speak to the track so it can't happen again."

He was shaking his head. "Thanks, Poppa, but don't bother. What the hell. I appreciate it and all but it wouldn't be no fun anymore. . . ."

I stayed with him at his apartment for an hour or two, then went upstairs to dress for dinner. I was tired and I dressed slowly, waiting for the usual adrenaline, the charge of excitement I could always count on to surge through me at the prospect of meeting new press guys and beating their preconceptions, neutralizing them, winning them over. It was always there for an audience, for an interview—the greater the challenge, the greater the extra voltage—but it wasn't happening, and I had to drag myself downstairs and into my car.

As I checked my hat at Danny's, Cliff Cochrane put his arm around my shoulder. "We got a bad rap in the *Amsterdam News,* a thing about you always eating here instead of going uptown. Billy set up a dinner with the editor for next week. At least he's willing to meet with us and get to know you."

Cliff filled me in on who was waiting for me at the table. I started toward them, trying to remember the names he'd just told me, trying to get myself in the right frame of mind. George and Burt and Jane were already there. I shook hands with the people and started smiling.

I did ten minutes of chitchat to loosen everybody up, then somebody asked, "Sammy, you live on Fifty-fifth Street, don't you?"

"Yes, ma'am."

She tried to conceal her surprise at something she had known but couldn't really believe. "Well . . . isn't that interesting . . . I mean, it's much more convenient for you."

As I worked the table my guests laughed, were trying to be

nice, to keep it social—but they were testing, weighing, judging, and with every answer another layer of doubt seemed to fall away from their faces, and I knew that soon I'd see the look that would say, "Gee, he's a human being," and I resented my eagerness to see it, to be so goddamned glad to get what should have been mine to start with. A guy across the room was staring. I'd been aware of him from the moment I'd sat down. I turned back to the people I was there to meet, but I could feel his eyes on me. Why doesn't he eat his dinner and get off my back?

George and Jane and Burt were helping me carry the ball. They had to be bored to death but they were going along with it for me, playing it charming and interested. Why did I have to impose this on them? Why should it be necessary for me to use my friends as props and scenery?

"Sammy, I've been curious about your becoming a Jew. As a matter of fact, when we first read about it my wife said, 'Doesn't he have enough troubles?' I mean, what with having one eye and being . . . uh, a member of the"—he lowered his voice—"Negro race."

"Well, sir, the truth is I never *did* get invited to be in the St. Patrick's Day parade. Now they've got two reasons."

I could feel people all over the room looking at me, and I was aware that as usual I was watching myself, making all the right moves so nobody could point a finger and say, "Well, what do you expect?" I was so tired of being tested and judged, of doing the right things for the wrong reasons. Why couldn't I have good manners because I *want* good manners? Not because I *need* them because I'm colored. Why must I always keep proving myself? Nobody else has to. Why me? Why must I always prove what I'm not before I can prove what I am?

The son of a bitch across the room was still staring. I looked around our table, from face to face; the woman was completely won over, her husband was on the fence, skeptical, but one more question and answer and I'd have him on my side too. I turned to him. I could feel the hate-filled eyes from across the room still boring into me as I heard my own voice being charming, sensible, witty, humble. . . .

Is all this doing any good? Am I accomplishing anything? When does it end? I can't meet the whole world, I can't neutralize everybody one by one. I can't even make a dent. What am I doing here? Fighting, always fighting, always begging people to like me. The faces at the table came into focus again and I saw them looking at me like I was supposed to say something. They were waiting and I remembered somebody had asked me something but I couldn't remember what it was. Everybody at the tables around me was talking, the whole room was talking, but I couldn't hear what anybody was saying, there was just a great big drone like a car horn that was stuck and wailing at me, growing louder, droning on, screaming, screeching, surrounding me, pushing me. . . .

I was standing in the middle of the room. Danny was in front of me, worried. "Hey, maybe you'd better sit down. You feeling okay?" I stepped around him. "I've got to get out, Danny. The walls are closing in on me."

I started driving uptown.

Maybe in Harlem I'd be able to breathe, to get a reprieve from the grasping for quicksilver acceptance, from the constant looking over my shoulder, the listening, waiting—the endless vigil.

I passed 110th Street—I was beginning to feel better, looser. I turned west on 125th, drove over to Seventh Avenue, and parked.

I walked to the corner. This is where they want me. Okay. It's easy. I'll hang on the corner. Anything. I let a crowd form around me. They were shoving to get near me, excited, calling down the street to their friends. But they didn't give a damn that I was Sammy, that I was home, standing on the corner. I was just another celebrity, that's all they saw—that and my car and my clothes. They were shoving and crowding and their voices were getting louder and louder—the same mass of noise as downtown. I broke through the circle, pushed my way

through them, and got back in my car. I drove further uptown
toward Mama's old place, speeding, suddenly afraid it might
have been torn down.

I put my hand on the banister, trying to feel as I had when
Mama was in the kitchen and I could race up the stairs for dinner. The rich warm smells of the food Mama was cooking, the
home smells, used to be all the good things in the world to me.
I looked around me at the walls, the stairs, the banister—not
really surprised at finding it no different, but not the same. I
thought of going upstairs and standing in front of our door.
Somebody'd come by and say, "Aren't you Sammy Davis, Jr.?"
and I'd nod. "I used to live here." They'd ask me in and I'd sit
in the easy chair next to the window and the whole family
would come in and watch me. "That's Sammy Davis, Jr., he
used to live here, right here in this room." They'd be poor like
we were, and when I left I'd find the landlord and pay up their
rent for a year. But I knew that I was only torturing myself, ro-
mancing my unhappiness, playing a corny scene—that I didn't
even feel like I was home.

Perhaps I didn't belong at Danny's yet, and Mama's place
was yesterday, but I'd made my choice a long time ago and the
years and all they contained had closed the doors behind me.

I headed downtown to the theater. I had to keep playing it
the way I'd set it up. If it worked out, then someday I could
stand on the corner or sit in Danny's—I could be anywhere and
still be home.

23

George did a mock groan. "*Must* we sit up so close? I feel like I should get up and sing or something."

I gave him the glare he'd been expecting. "The biggest opening in ten years, but you couldn't possibly just say, 'Hey, Sam, this is a wild table.' There's got to be a zingy, right?"

He blushed. "That's my policy."

Jane asked, "Did you see Earl Wilson's column today?"

I'd seen it. "What'd he say, darling?"

"He said, 'If you want to see Sinatra at the Copa speak to Sammy Davis, Jr. He's got a ringside table for ten every night.' "

I touched my father on the shoulder. "I'm going back and say hello to Frank." I passed Sugar Ray squeezing through the crowd on his way back to my table. He shook his head. "They usually put four ropes around me when I fight." As I moved through the club it reminded me of Ciro's—a famous face at every table.

When I got to the dressing room Hank Sanicola told me that Frank had gone out for a walk, by himself. If ever there was a time for a performer to be alone, this was it. The strength to face that fantastic audience could only come from the same place that he'd drawn the power to attract them. I went back downstairs, not envying him this hour. It's great to know that the world is out there waiting for you, but who could know better than Frank how easily you can close your eyes to bask in the flattery and the admiration of millions of people and then when you open your eyes they can be gone. It's great to be the absolute hottest thing in the business but how do you live up to being a legend?

The lights lowered and a single spot shone on the microphone in the center of the stage. The music started, only the brass and the drums, like a signal, an announcement. I glanced toward the stairs. Frank was standing motionless, looking straight ahead, waiting.

It was all there: the sound, the confidence, the distinctive hands, the shoulders, the cigarette cupped in his palm, the slight stretching of his neck—everything, and within three songs he'd more than lived up to the legend, he'd surpassed it. As he rolled from song to song dictating every emotion of his audience, I vividly remembered that night on Broadway in '53 or '54: the same man, walking by himself, hands in his pockets, coat collar turned up—nobody recognizing him. To see him come back from that, not only a better performer but bigger than ever, was a sight to behold. And he'd done it alone. The women were gazing at him with greater adoration than ever, and now even the men were giving him a beyond-envy kind of respect, leaning in toward him, approving, nodding like *Yeah!* because Frank was the guy who was living, being, doing, accomplishing it; he was the guy with the guts to walk alone, the guy who'd fought the odds and won, the man who stands on his beliefs, "Like me or not," but he stands on them, who professes to be no god, from whom there is no "Look at me, I'm a pillar of society," but who is a man, and like a man, all the mixtures are there: the good guy, the bad guy, the actor, the father, the businessman—every known facet of his offstage personality had fused with his performance, and his atmosphere was lifting everyone to that peak of excitement which surrounds a performer as he stands on the ultimate plateau.

On Wednesday morning I read the grim, giant headline: "HUMPHREY BOGART DIES."

Julie Podell called. "Sammy, Frank can't go on tonight. I've got Jerry Lewis for the first show. I need you for the second."

I was back in a nightclub again. I didn't have my father and Will on the stage with me, there was no chorus, no supporting cast, no story; I was alone—making it on my own again.

Frank was back the next night and I was at ringside. As I cut into my steak a voice behind me snarled, ". . . little nigger in front of me." I continued cutting my food and glanced around my table. They hadn't heard it. The voice demanded. "Waiter, let's have the captain over here." Then he was saying, "You got any authority around this place?"

"Is something wrong, sir?"

"Damned right there is. I want a table without such a lousy view." A woman was trying to quiet him down. Jane glanced past me, then at me, smiled nervously, and went back to her food. George took a shot glass of scotch in one swallow and closed his eyes as it seared through his chest. The captain must have signaled up above because I heard Bruno asking, "Can I help you, sir?"

I kept cutting away at my steak.

"Maybe you can do better than your flunky here. You look like a man who knows right from wrong." The voice softened, becoming fraternal, conspiratorial. "It's obviously some kind of a mistake. I come in here thinking I'm spending my money in a first-class place, so you can understand my surprise when I find my wife and I seated behind that little jigaboo. Now I'm sure that you . . ." The words ended in a gasp. I turned. The table was empty. Bruno and the captain had the man under each arm and were already halfway out of the room with him. A woman was hurrying after them. People all around us were leaning together, whispering, looking toward me, speculating on what might have happened.

My group was limp. They were doing self-conscious smiles of relief, not knowing if they should look at me or away from me. A hand was on my shoulder. Julie Podell was looking at me simpatico. "The bum is out on the street where he belongs."

The kids were starting to get their wind back and they were talking, but their voices were like a record being played at the wrong speed. Michael had said something to me. "I'm sorry, baby, what did you say?"

He blushed. "It wasn't worth repeating. It was just something insipid, like 'Keep a stiff upper lip, things'll be better someday.' "

I sympathized with their impossible position, but I hated my own. "Baby, if you'll excuse a little well-earned bitterness: colored people don't really have big lips, we just look that way from *keeping* them stiff for so long."

I sat behind my bar looking through the mail, autographing pictures, occasionally glancing up to see how George, Chita, and Michael were doing. The bell rang and Michael opened the door for Jane and Burt. I waved. "So the wandering journalists are home after another glittering night of gathering tomorrow's news today, eh?"

Jane slipped off her shoes and walked over to glance at herself in the mirror. George asked, "And where were Mr. and Mrs. Manhattan *this* evening?"

"The usual." Burt's voice came from the closet. "There was an opening at the Plaza . . . we looked into Morocco . . ."

"Don't knock it," George grumbled. "These four walls."

I listened to them talking, realizing that it had been weeks since we'd been anywhere except Danny's for dinner. It was always the benefits, a drop-in at Barry Gray's show, then straight back to the apartment, to the island I'd created, to the few people I'd allowed to live on it with me—like a recluse, avoiding aggravation. Not only had I given up everything I'd come to New York for, but by doing so I was giving sanction to the idea that I had no right to it. It was frightening. I was the guy who comes home from the office and goes for a dip in the ocean,

closing his eyes, luxuriating in feeling the tensions and pressures easing—unaware that he's drifting from shore, further
and further . . .

"Burt."

"Yes, Sam?"

"What's it like at El Morocco?"

He thought about it for a moment. "I guess it's about the
best place of its kind in town, probably in the world. It's lively,
sophisticated-type crowd, glamorous . . ."

"But you're never going to take me there, right?"

"Just say when."

"It's only one o'clock. Let's go tonight?"

Chita jumped up. "You really mean it, Sammy?"

"How long will it take you to get home and change your
clothes?"

She rushed for her coat. "I'll be back in less than half an
hour."

Michael was already out the door and ringing for the elevator.

When the door closed I told Burt, "Maybe you'd better
make a reservation . . . tell them I'm in your party."

He dialed a number. I opened a window, got a camera and
started making shots of the lighted buildings, appreciating the
tripod which kept the camera steady, concentrating on the methodical clicks of the shutter that cracked across the room like
gunshots until they were drowned out by the sound of Burt's
voice, angry, pinched, straining to be calm, but vibrating with
emotion. The skin was pulled tight around his jaw, the muscle
in his cheek throbbing; Jane started going through her purse,
George picked up a photography magazine which he'd already
looked through earlier. I heard the phone being set slowly on
the receiver.

"They don't want me, right?"

He sat down, stunned, his face totally drained of color,
chalky. I walked over to him and gently pinched his cheeks.
"Baby, it's okay to be white but you're overdoing it." I sat be

hind my bar. "Well, I went for broke and I got it." I looked at Burt. "Well, let's hear it, don't leave me in the dark. Oops. What do I mean by *that?*"

He was shaking his head slowly, staring at the phone, holding a cigarette in one hand and a lighter in the other, not moving to bring them together. He looked at me blankly. "It was unbelievable . . . he started to say they didn't have any tables but he didn't go through with that—he knew I'd know that's ridiculous at this hour. Then he said he wanted to speak to John Perona—he's the owner. I don't know if he actually did or not but he came back and said, 'We'd rather not.' I told him we weren't asking if they'd rather or not. Then he asked me what you looked like."

"What I look like?"

"He said . . . 'He's very black, isn't he?' Then he started copping out: 'I mean he's not light-skinned, I mean it's awfully dark, isn't it?' Then he asked me to hold the phone again and came back with a new idea. He said you've been in *Confidential* and the scandal magazines and that's the reason they don't want you—because they don't want to encourage people like that. . . . I was so dazed I . . . I just hung up."

"Did they actually say, 'No. He can't come here'?"

"No. That's against the law. They just said that you won't be treated nicely if you do."

I ground my fist into my hand, drawing my fingers tightly over the knuckles, watching my skin changing color under the pressure, overwhelmed for the millionth time by the great goddamned difference people saw in it, disgusted by my incredibly naïve optimism that had survived so many moments like this and had, again, inexcusably, suckered me into going for the rare chance that maybe this time it would be different.

"Sam?"

I looked up. "As he was saying you weren't welcome, just as I hung up—the dance band was playing 'Mr. Wonderful.' "

"Well, folks. It's a small world. Particularly if you're colored." I stood up. "Okay, let's forget it. It was a bad idea and it ain't gonna get any better with you guys giving me the June Allyson smiles." I looked around the room at Jane, Burt, and George. "At least you've got to admit this is the first funeral parlor you ever saw with TV, hi-fi, and booze." The doorbell rang.

George groaned, "Oh, God . . ." I stood up. "Well, somebody's got to answer it."

Chita was framed in the doorway, dressed to the teeth, posing *Vogue* magazine style. She yawned. "I left my *large* diamonds in the vault." Michael was behind her, all smiles.

I bowed them in. "This way, dear friends. Services will begin in a few minutes."

24

When I got up I called George. "Come on. Let's go spend some money and *be* somebody."

"Sammy, I'm in the middle of a meeting."

"Don't tell me your troubles, baby, 'cause I'm colored and I've got my own. Now, if you're not in the middle of this lobby in half an hour your star may get so upset he'll develop laryngitis."

As we walked across town I stopped at an antique-silver place and gazed through the window at a large silver goblet resting on a piece of red velvet. "Hey, George. Dig."

He shrugged. "I guess it's okay if you're Henry the Eighth."

"Or Sammy the Second."

We walked to Madison Avenue, and at Lefcourt's I showed Lloyd, my salesman, the shoes I wanted to see. When at least a dozen boxes were piled alongside me George said, "My God, isn't that enough? Even a train stops!"

"Baby, do you mind if I get a little pleasure out of life?" A crowd was forming outside the window, watching me. I swung the show into high gear. While Lloyd was trying a shoe on me another salesman was on the run for more styles. The crowd kept growing and so did the pile of shoes until I was almost hidden by the boxes.

We walked up Madison Avenue. George said, "I thought you were so broke."

"I ain't half as broke as I'm about to be. Now just up the street, with a little turn to the left and a turn to the right, we have A. Sulka and Company, where you will see a truly creative man destroy himself. Then we follow the yellow brick road to Gucci."

George was almost punchy as we left there. "Six suitcases for like a hundred dollars apiece—and you're not even going anywhere, Sammy, I'll see you later. I really can't stand watching this. You're doing *Lost Weekend,* but with money." He hesitated. "Look, I'm not trying to be staff psychiatrist, but whatever your reasons are you're only causing more trouble for yourself with all this."

"I know."

"You *know?*"

"I've been making big money for a long time. Baby, I know everything wrong that I ever do—and I don't need a psychiatrist to tell me why I keep doing it."

"But if you know it's wrong . . . ?"

"I'm not looking to be right. Just to be happy."

He was shaking his head. "You're too smart to mean that."

We were at the corner of 52nd Street and I saw a song plugger I knew get out of a cab and waltz into "21" like he owned the place—and I knew that no matter what I ever accomplished I could never hope to go into one of those places and feel like that. It was all so stupid, so unimportant—except for the fact that I knew I would never be able to really grasp it, and that after all these years of looking in a mirror and seeing a man, I finally had to accept that it might as well be a trick mirror. I looked away. "I don't know, George. I'd like to be as wise as I am smart—but I just can't swing it."

Because we'd stopped walking, a few fans appeared and offered me pieces of paper to sign. One of them stared at George with curiosity. "Are you anybody?"

He scowled. "I'm a famous madam."

I steered him away, and we continued walking. After a while he said, "I guess it's none of my business, and I know it's not a Lucky Strike Extra to be colored, but if there are a few places and a few idiots . . . well, how can you let them bother *you?* I could understand if the average 'colored cat'—whatever *that* is—complains, but you're a big star, people stop you on the streets, you can go almost anywhere and wherever you *do* go you get treated better than most people ever hope to be treated." He continued, uncertainly. "I mean, you've got to admit that it *is* a lot better for *you.*"

"Yeah, baby, being a star has made it possible for me to get insulted in places where the average Negro could never *hope* to go and get insulted." I was surprised by the edge of bitterness in my voice, but I liked it. "Things are so beautiful for me that maybe by 1999 I'll even be able to rent an apartment in one of those buildings where they throw parties in my honor. But, all things being equal—and they never are—until then I'll keep reminding myself I'm a star in the only way I know. And if you're going to be a drag then go back to your meeting, 'cause if I need a drag I'll call an agency."

We kept walking down Fifth Avenue, neither of us speaking for several blocks. As we reached Saks he looked at the windows and mumbled, "My God, when I think what a wardrobe I could have if only I were colored."

I laughed. "But, baby, where would you wear it?"

That night, after the show, George came into the dressing room. "There are two limousines downstairs. One says he's supposed to take you to a benefit in Great Neck and the other one says you're supposed to be somewhere up in the Bronx." He was looking at me like, "They're not *both* right? *Are* they?"

"Tell the guy from Great Neck to follow us to the Bronx. He can wait for us and then take us to Great Neck."

"But this makes ten benefits this week. Sammy? This afternoon—all the money you spent—didn't it help?"

I laughed, to get it light. "It's like a Chinese dinner, baby."

As I put my feet on the jump seat he gave me a vicious look. "Oh? Settling down for a long winter's rest?"

I loosened my collar. "Yes, said the little brown bear."

He muttered, " 'Where does he get all the energy?' "

I finished the show in Great Neck, got back into the car, and held the second plaque against my shirtsleeve. "George, do you think these are too big for cuff links?"

"Well! The little brown bear certainly revived himself."

"I guess *that's* where 'he gets the energy.' Driver, you can drop us in New York at the Harwyn, please. But don't drop us too hard, because I'm pregnant."

George fell back against the seat. "The *Harwyn?* At this hour?"

"I've got a few people meeting us."

George gaped at the twenty-foot-long table running down the center of the back room. "What did you do? Run a call for a general audition?"

"Baby, bear with me. They're just some kids from *Bells Are Ringing* and *Fair Lady*." I sat down at the head of the table. After about thirty minutes, I spoke quietly to George, Michael, and Jane and Burt. "Let's split and go back to the apartment."

Burt said, "Sam, I think we're going to go home."

"Hey, it's only four o'clock . . ."

"Well, I've still got the column to do and we're getting up early tomorrow to be at the record session."

"Holy Toledo, baby, I'm not worrying about it and I'm the one who's got to sing."

Jane said, "Sammy, don't you think you should get some sleep too?"

I gave her the withering stare. "No, Jane. I *don't* think I should get some sleep. But far be it from me to keep you guys up one second later than you want to be. See you at the session tomorrow." I turned to George and Michael. George said, "Well, it really wouldn't hurt you to get some sleep." Michael yawned and started to make an excuse but I cut him off. "Don't even bother. So the family's deserting me again. Okay. See you all when you have time for me."

I tapped my glass with a fork. "Drink up everybody and it's a definite move-the-party-over-to-the-Gorham."

My eyes felt gritty, and my throat was tight. I finished the hot tea I'd sent out for and walked over to the mike in front of the window of the control room. Milt Gabler pressed his talk-back button. "Let's go for it this time, Sammy."

The red light went on. The orchestra started playing and I waited for my cue, my right hand cupped behind my ear to catch the sound of my voice, hoping the tea had done it some good. But one cup of tea can't beat only three hours of sleep and I barely climbed in under the big note.

While the band ran through the next number I walked over to a bunch of the kids who'd been at the apartment the night before. "Sammy, that was fantastic. Beautiful." . . . "If that's not a hit then I never heard one." . . . "Great sound . . ."

"Thanks, kids. We'll see what the public wants to buy." I went over to the group. They all smiled at me.

"It was very nice."

"Don't strain yourself, Michael." George made one of those pleasant faces. Burt gave me a George Gilbert look.

"And what about *you*, Jane? What's *your* opinion?"

"Well . . . you *are* tired . . ."

"Everybody's a critic, right? Well, it's very strange that *you* didn't like my voice, because the president of Decca Records is inside that control room and *he* didn't seem to mind it."

George murmured. "That's showbiz."

"What's that, George?"

"I said, 'I'll have a gin fizz.' "

I called out to the other kids. "It's a definite one o'clock at Sam's place tonight."

Burt said, "Sam, you look kinda beat. Get some rest tonight."

"Hey. I don't remember asking how I look. And I have no desire to get some rest."

I sat behind my bar watching all the action, digging the

party sounds. One of the chicks from *Bells* was wearing tight
Levi's and she had my twin holsters slung low on her hips. She
wasn't trying to draw, she just dug walking around, flinging her
butt out as she leaned her hands against the guns. One of the
other chicks was on the phone rounding up some of her friends.
The "family" was sitting at the bar like there was nothing going on around them.

Jane saw me pouring a Coke into my silver goblet. "What is
that?"

"That, my dear lady, is my glass. I'm a star, and I don't
drink out of the same sort of a glass that the common people
use."

"Oh. Well, I'll settle for some ginger ale in a common
glass." She walked behind the bar.

"Jane! Get out from behind my bar." She looked up, surprised. "That's right. Out out out! You can have anything you
want, but just ask for it." I poured a glass of ginger ale for her.

George said, "That's his toy; you know you're not allowed
to play with it."

I nodded, sipping from my goblet. "You can go to El Morocco; I sit behind my bar. Now, if my friends, the inner circle,
are through finding fault with me . . ."

The doorbell rang and George glanced vaguely over his
shoulder at the throng of new arrivals. "Anyone you know?"

I looked away from him. "Michael, it's time for a little
Stage. Order about forty roast beefs and corned beefs, will you,
baby?"

"You're not going to *feed* all these people?"

"Michael, please, just order the sandwiches, like a buddy?
Don't give me any raised eyebrows, no 'Well, really!' Okay?"

George came over to me as I was doing gun tricks for a
group of kids. He said, "Well, it's '30' for tonight. The Big Producer is going to sleep." Within fifteen minutes, he, Jane and
Burt, Chita, and Michael had gone.

I sat behind the bar watching the chick with the holsters
slithering toward me, smiling.

"Darling, whatever you're auditioning for—you're hired."

I called Arthur Silber on the Coast. "I didn't wake you, did I, baby? . . . Crazy. Listen, Arthur, I'll be back in L.A. soon and I don't have a swimming pool. Will you get moving on it for me? . . . Arthur, what in hell do I know about swimming pools? I don't plan to hold the Olympics in it, but on the other hand I don't want a bathtub. . . . Fine. And figure on a little cabana too. You know, out-of-their-slacks-and-into-a-bikini, right? As a matter of fact you'd better make two dressing rooms with showers, one for the guys and one for the chicks. Y'know, baby, the more I think about it, we ought to make it like a Playhouse, a self-sufficient unit, so when I have parties I won't need to worry about the kids running all over the house bothering Mama. We could do a thing where the dressing rooms are at one end, y'dig, and the rest of it is one large room, as wide as you can make it and maybe thirty feet long so we could even show movies. . . . Arthur, what am I working for if I can't have a little joy out of life, the niceties? Now look, put a bedroom in there too, so in case it's late at night and I don't want to go back to the house I'll be all set. Or I can use it for a guest room. . . . Well, then build a second floor. Hey, that's wild. Put the bedroom over the dressing rooms, and make the main room studio style—two stories high. And you'd better give me another bathroom upstairs so it's a complete suite. . . . Hey, let *me* worry about that, please! I'll get it from somewhere. As long as we're going to do this, let's do it right. You'd better write all this down: Put in a slate floor and a bar with a refrigerator and all the jazz with maybe six comfortable stools, with backs and arms and leather padding, right? And use cork walls so if we're a little noisy we don't get heard all over the hills. And about the movie setup: I want it so I can sit on a big curved couch in the center of the room, in a smoking jacket, press a button and zzzzzz a screen comes out of the ceiling; I press the next button and the lights go out; I press another button and the guy in the projection room starts showing the movie. And get two projectors, hooked up so we go directly from one reel to the next. I don't want one of those Mickey

Mouse setups that you have to wait ten minutes between reels. And find the best sound system that we can wire into every room, including the three johns, and give them each their own volume control and turnoffs . . . You know the kind of stuff I dig. Make sure the johns all have full-length heaters in the wall so when people get out of the shower it's not goose pimple time. . . . What's the difference? If you're gonna be a star, be a star! And make sure the pool lights up at night."

When I hung up I beckoned to the chick with my holsters. "I dig you. What's your name?"

I woke up around noon, went to the kitchen for some tomato juice, and almost broke my neck on a high-heeled shoe someone had left behind. I opened the blinds. The sun spotlighted dozens of half-filled glasses with cigarette butts floating in them, used coffee cups, and little pitchers of cream with wrinkled yellow skin on top. There was a scotch bottle on the floor under a stack of my record albums that had been strewn around like old newspapers, and everywhere I looked there were overflowing ashtrays and twisted pieces of bread. The place smelled like a garbage pail. It hadn't seemed that bad when I went to sleep.

Cliff called. "Sammy, have you seen the columns today?"

"What is it this time?"

" 'Sammy Davis, Jr.'s long-unpaid bill at a midtown bookshop now totals $1,460.' It's none of my business but—"

"Cliff, I don't mean to be rude, but between Will Mastin and the Morris office I've got all the damned managers I need."

"Okay. Just don't be surprised if a lot of this kind of item starts to break. I've been hearing it all over town for months. People love to say 'Sammy Davis owes me . . .' "

Once it started becoming public it would destroy the illusion, the atmosphere of a star. I pulled a suitcase out of the closet and began opening the hundreds of bills I'd stuffed into it as they'd come in. I put all the dangerous ones in a pile and totaled them. The very least I needed would be about $40,000. I called the Morris office and told them to set up Steve Allen and all the variety shows they could. Then I got busy on the phone with a few out-of-town clubs and lined up $25,000. I dialed the Copa and waited for Julie Podell. I was clean with him and borrowing money now would mean committing myself to play there in the spring, only a few months after we closed the show. After so much exposure on Broadway I'd planned not to play New York for a full year. But I had no choice. Better to have to fight to draw crowds than to have a lousy name to do it with.

The night man at the desk called out, "Mr. Davis, your father said to stop off at his apartment no matter what time you come in."

He was sitting in the living room, wearing a bathrobe and slippers, waiting for me. There was an almost empty scotch bottle on the table next to him but he was cold sober. "Sit down, Poppa. I've got something to say."

"You okay, Dad?"

"I'm fine. Sit down."

I took off my coat and pulled up a chair.

"I'm leavin' the show, Sammy. I'm quittin' the act and I'm retirin'." He looked straight at me. "Don't you think it's time, Poppa?" There was no sympathy seeking, no hidden hope that I would deny it—just the calm of a man offering the intimacy of honesty. "Poppa, I wish I could go to Will and tell him: Let's both quit, and we could do it right, maybe take an ad in *Variety* sayin' how we're puttin' you out on your own—that'd be good show business and I'd love to go out that way—but you know Will and you know he's got the same damned sickness I had all these years only he's got it worse: he's gotta be on, gotta see his name up." He paused. "Maybe when he sees me out of the act he'll get the idea and quit too. But I know if I was to tell him I'm quitting, he wouldn't let me, he'd talk me out of it. So I've got it in my mind how I'll do it but it's best you don't know. Only reason I'm telling you is so no matter what you hears about me in the next coupla days, you don't worry . . ."

He looked at me straight. "I hears the jokes about Will and

me. And they're right. I knowed it the first time we opened Ciro's. I watched Will do his dance and then I did mine and I stood back thinkin' we was really somethin' else. Then I watched you and I saw what you was doing to the people and I knew we'd moved into a show business that was over my head, that I didn't have no right to be on the same stage with you, and I shoulda been happy sittin' out front or standin' backstage and lovin' you 'cause you was mine, instead of being in your way, makin' it harder for you."

He poured himself a drink, took it down straight, and slowly shook his head. "I just didn't have what it takes to quit, Poppa. I liked the fuss everybody was makin' over us and I liked the money and I figured: Well, I'll just hang on a little bit and enjoy bein' big for a while before I bow out. But the more I got of it, the harder it was for me to walk away. You know what I mean?"

As he spoke, I could remember knowing it was wrong for us to remain a trio, but none of the reasons seemed important compared to the pain on his face, the longing he'd feel for our way of life, the finality of the exile to which he was sentencing himself. "Dad, maybe it isn't wrong. Who the hell knows. We're doing good . . ."

"Poppa, please. Leavin' show business is the toughest thing I ever done." He got up and took something out of a drawer. "You know what these is, Poppa?" He was holding a pair of shoes on the palm of his hand. "The first shoes you ever wore to dance in." He sat down, smiling nostalgically. "It was back in '28 or '29, you was three years old and there was this amateur contest at the old Standard Theater in Philadelphia. . . ."

Two days later the newspapers reported that my father had suffered a mild heart attack and his doctor had ordered him to retire from show business.

A stagehand was centering cards on an easel and a cameraman was focusing on them: "Mike Wallace"—"Night Beat." I was sitting in what they'd started calling "the hot seat."

"You've already achieved more than most men ever hope for. You have fame, you earn a fortune, you wear fine clothes, drive the best cars, own a magnificent house—why can't you sit back and enjoy life? Why does Sammy Davis, Jr., remain a controversial figure?"

"First of all, I don't think of myself as a controversial figure—I know that I am but I don't *feel* controversial. I never woke up and thought: 'Today I'll shake 'em up. Let's see now . . . what convention should I defy?' I do what you just suggested: I try to sit back and enjoy the life I've been able to make for myself. I choose my own friends, live where I like, and do whatever I feel I have a right to do. Now, unfortunately there are people who disagree about what my rights are, so I become controversial."

"But you're not the only Negro who's ever been in the limelight. How is it the things *you* choose to do become so public? Your dating of white women, your conversion to Judaism."

"Mike, I never yet went on radio or television and said, 'Hi there, folks, I'm dating a white chick,' or 'Yoo-hoo out there in television land. Guess what? I just turned Jewish.' On the other hand I'm not going to go out of my way to hide what I do. I keep the Talmud on my night table—I like to have it there. When friends come up I don't slip it under the pillow. They see it and I guess because it's me they mention it to other people. From time to time it's come up in an interview and I'm not about to say 'No comment' or tip the guy off in advance: 'Let's not talk about that.' "

"Sammy, is this determination to live your own life motivated by a desire to do so for the good of the rest of the Negro people?"

"No. It would be nice to get medals like 'He's a champion of his people.' But what I do is for me. Emotionally, I'm still hungry, and let's face it, paupers can't be philanthropists. I can't do anybody else much good until I get *me* straightened out. However, I know that my people will benefit from what I do, because every time someone moves downtown—not just to a hotel, but in all ways—he opens the door a little wider for others to follow. Look what Jackie Robinson went through as the first Negro pro ballplayer. But he just dug in and played harder. Now, I don't know who he was doing it for but I do know that he made it a lot easier for guys like Willie Mays to follow him. In my case, I'm totally aware that if I break down a barrier, others will benefit, and although I can't claim that as motivation, it certainly gives meaning to some very unpleasant moments."

"To balance those unpleasant moments in the struggle to be Sammy Davis, Jr., have there at least been rewards?"

"Definitely. I never went to school but I can stand in front of a thousand people and just talk to them and make them laugh. That's something I couldn't do years ago and wouldn't be able to do today unless I understood my audiences and could speak on their level of sophistication. I don't have to rely on 'colored' or 'show business' topics to get laughs. I can reach them because I understand them."

"Sammy, despite your fame, do you also pay by feeling a certain amount of discrimination as you travel through what is predominantly a white world?"

"I've had my moments."

"Even here in New York?"

"Mike, let's not kid ourselves that prejudice is geographic. Down South they lynch you and kill you—up North most Negroes die before they ever really lived at all. How much difference is there between preventing a man from earning the money to buy clothes and ripping them off his back? Either way, the result is he's standing there naked.

"If you steal a man's dignity, does it matter if you rob or embezzle it? The crime is the same—only the method is different. Down South they do it openly; the restaurant puts up a sign: 'No colored people allowed.' Up here they use raised eyebrows to accomplish the same thing. You don't see many or *any* Negroes lunching or having dinner in ninety percent of the good restaurants below 125th Street. And this isn't because all the colored people got together and said, 'Hey, let's boycott all the best restaurants and the best hotels in town.' "

"Could it be explained, at least partially, in terms of economics? Just the simple cost of going to these places?"

"Sure, for ninety-five percent of the colored people that might be the answer. But what about the other five percent, the guys who make the dough? All them cats in Harlem cruise around in block-long Cadillacs complete with radio, TV, and kitchens, they wear diamond rings on every finger—and then the white cat rides through Harlem on the commuter special to Westchester shaking his head: 'I can't understand these colored people; they live in tenements like animals but you always see brand-new cars parked out front.' How else can they spend it? They can drive it and they can wear it. Period. They'd prefer to eat balanced meals, but if the meat store is the only one open then they've got to make a whole meal out of steak. They can't go join a golf club and spend an afternoon shagging golf balls, or say to their wives, 'Happy birthday, darling, let's celebrate, we'll catch the show at the Waldorf or the Plaza.' There's no 'Where do you feel like eating tonight?' They *know* where they can eat and it's not listed in *Cue* magazine. So they're buying all the things they shouldn't because they can't do half the things they should.

"Why does a man buy his wife a big diamond ring, Mike? Because it's beautiful and he loves her and he wants to make her happy. But isn't it also because he wants to look at that ring on her finger and be able to feel that in her eyes and in the eyes of the world he made it, he belongs, he's somebody? But if every day of his life someone jumped up and told him, 'You *don't* belong. You're *nobody*,' if every place he went he saw that he doesn't even cast a shadow—imagine how big a diamond he'd need."

He was looking at my clothes, at the gold cigarette case I'd just opened, then at my face. Leaning forward, his eyes probing mine, he seemed to have forgotten that we were on the air, and I caught a glimpse of a man hooked on the contradiction between fact and reason, involved in it, feeling the frustration of it. He got a time signal from one of the floor men, and surfaced. "Sammy, one last question. I asked you earlier what it is you're looking for. Could it be summed up in one word: acceptance?"

"That's as good a word as any."

"You want people to like you."

"Yes, but that's the frosting on the cake. In its simplest form: I don't want people to *dis*like me before I've earned it."

25

George leaned against the wall of my dressing room. "We're going to gross fifty-nine thousand this week." He dropped the words like a jeweler spreading diamonds on velvet. "The word is all over town that you've single-handedly beaten the critics."

I let myself sink back against the chair, floating on the pleasure of the moment. "We did it. We really goddamned did it." The countless interviews, the television shows, radio shows, the handshaking, the appearances at parties and clubs, the month after month of pushing uphill—all the strain of it was washed away in that one glorious moment.

"Can you appreciate what this means? It's like *for the first time!* You've made Broadway history." He sat down, smiling. "When you said that you were going to beat the notices . . ."

"Yeah . . . remember that night? God, they really knocked the wind out of us, didn't they?"

He nodded and we sat in silence, remembering that night and all the nights that had brought us to this moment. I felt a craving for the "family," our little in-group I'd chased away these past few weeks with a quantity of near-strangers to help me fill the dead hours.

"Hey, look, I've got no benefits tonight. I'm clear. Whaddya say we get Chita and Michael, we'll find Jane and Burt, and we'll go someplace and celebrate. I'll have the elevator guy at the hotel get rid of everybody. We'll really make a night out of it."

"Michael's already left with some people. And I know that Chita's got some boy she's going with . . ."

"Well, how about you? We can take a walk down Broadway. Look, I know it's corny but I just feel like doing it."

"Well, I have . . . wait a minute, maybe I can cancel an appointment I've got . . ."

"Never mind, baby. Look, it's not such a big deal."

"Sammy, I . . ."

"Hey, we're grown men, right?" I started putting on my shoes. "Look, if it could've worked out it would have been pleasant but it's not life and death."

"We can up the year's gross by thirty thousand if you'll accept this Miami offer . . ." Sam Bramson sat across the table from me and Will in the boardroom of the Morris office, holding a sheet of lined yellow paper with penciled-in dates, names of clubs, and figures, plans for after the show closed. His voice was tentative. "They've agreed to a beautiful suite . . ."

"What about letting colored people in to see the show?"

He looked down at the paper, avoiding my face. "Well, that's the only problem, Sammy. It's not that they don't want to go along with you but the custom down there . . ."

"The custom stinks. We've been through this before, Sam. I don't play to segregated audiences."

Will nodded. "That says it for me too."

Sam held up his hands. "I'm with you a hundred percent. I'm just telling you what the offer was. Now, Julie Podell says you've agreed to go in there in the spring."

Will grunted disgustedly. "Sammy, the dumbest thing you could've done was to go borrowing money from Julie Podell and committing us to play for him this spring. That's hardly three months from now. Who's going to come and see us?"

"I know, Massey."

"We shoulda stayed away for a year. Six or eight months at

least. Here we're gettin' offered the best money from clubs that we've ever got—and I credit the show with that—but what good is it if we can't cash in? If Julie Podell'd had to come to us, we could've sat down and set a new price with him just like we're doing with everybody else—not countin' those clubs you used for banks."

"Massey, I've already said you're right. Can we forget it, please? It's done and it'll work out."

"Maybe it will and maybe it won't. Either way it's time you stopped leaning on your talent and used your head."

I stared at his indignant, angry face. "Yeah, Massey. You're right. I really should use my head."

One of the Morris guys said, "Sammy, the fact is, your uncle is right. But it's not just borrowing money, it's a lot of things. I don't know if you're aware of it but the publicity you've been getting, well, it hasn't been good. You really ought to do something about it. For your own good . . ."

I wandered over to the Stage Delicatessen, pushed a door marked "Pull," and sat down at a table.

Jack E. Leonard came over. "Hello, Sammy. I didn't recognize you all by yourself." I smiled, not enjoying the joke. He became serious. "Your old man's okay now, isn't he?"

"He's fine, Jack. Thanks for the flowers you sent him."

"Things work out. Let's be honest, it's time you were doing a single."

"Well, it's not exactly a single. Will's staying with the act."

"You mean, just you and him?" I nodded. "But it's still the Will Mastin Trio?" he asked knowingly. I nodded. "I see." He gazed into his coffee cup. "Who the hell knows? Like they say: *The Saturday Evening Post* comes out on Wednesday and they're doing okay."

I'd been so glad to see everybody leave, but now I wished I'd told one of the chicks to stick around. Which one should I have kept? I couldn't remember any of their faces. They'd all evaporated into air like the laughs, leaving nothing behind.

I looked through a drawer in the kitchen and found the slip of paper a kid named Betsy had given me, and propped it against the phone. Why couldn't I call her and have her come up, just for company, or take her for a walk—the city's beautiful at this hour.

Her voice sounded sleepy and I'd have hung up but I didn't want to frighten her. "Betsy, this is Sammy."

"Sammy who?"

"Sammy Davis, Jr. . . ."

A few minutes later I opened the door and she walked past me into the apartment.

"Hey, I told you I'd meet you downstairs. What if I'd had some chick up here?"

She smiled. "Then you wouldn't have called me, would you?" I took a windbreaker from the closet. "Sammy, it's too cold for walking." She opened her coat. She was wearing only a bra and panties.

She'd dropped the coat to the floor. I put it around her shoulders. "Thank you, I appreciate the gesture, but you're not the type for this kind of jazz." She stood helpless and vulnerable, the coat hanging from her shoulders, gazing at me blankly. "Now, listen, Bets, I didn't mean to hurt your feelings, you're a gorgeous kid and I dig looking at you—it's taking every ounce of strength I've got to stay away from you—but you don't have to impress me that you're a swinger. Now, be nice. You're young, you've got a lot of living ahead of you . . ."

She tossed off the coat. "Sammy, I voted last year. And I'm not sorry for anything I've ever done. Now, may I have a drink? Scotch and water, please."

I mixed it for her and stayed behind the bar. She sat across from me, caught a look at herself in the mirror behind the bar, and smiled, satisfied, then raised her glass. "Well, here we are."

I smiled, looking straight at her face so as not to encourage her by letting her see me enjoying the sight of her body.

She asked, "You won't be in New York much longer, will you?"

"Just another month or so."

"You can play any club you want to, can't you?"

"Yes."

"I read in *Variety* that you signed a million-dollar contract with the Sands in Las Vegas. They must want you pretty badly."

"Well, it's over a period of five years. . . ."

She came behind the bar and put her hands on my shoulders, flexing her body, posing, inviting. "Sammy? I'd love to work in the line at the Sands; the girls make great money out there; if you mentioned my name to Jack Entratter he'd give me a job. I'll never get anywhere on Broadway; I know I haven't got any talent. But I've got the looks for Vegas, haven't I?" She put her arms around my neck.

At least when a drunk gets rolled he has an excuse.

As I turned away from her I saw my face in the mirror: the nose, the scars, the dead eye, the features jammed together—it looked so vastly different than I had felt.

I tore my gaze away and was confronted by her face again, the looking glass in front of which I'd primped and pranced, gorging myself on the joy of playing Sir Galahad, Lancelot, and Walter Raleigh, all rolled into one big clown.

I lifted her arms off my neck, walked past her, out from behind the bar, and dropped her coat over her arm.

"You don't want me?"

"Some other time. I'll take care of Vegas." I walked to the door.

"You're mad at me."

"Darling, I love sirloin steaks but I don't have to consume every one in America. I'm tired. It *is* seven o'clock in the morning, right?"

She put on her coat and closed it around her, smiling like she'd made the phone call and gotten her dime back too. "Okay, but whenever you're in the mood I'll be available. Aren't you going to take me home?"

"I never take anybody home. Here's twenty for a cab. I'll let you know about Vegas."

I poured a Coke and watched the foam rise above the edges

of the silver goblet, hang in midair, then run down the sides and form a puddle on the bar. I touched my finger to it and wrote "Sammy Davis, Jr." on the bar top. I sat there staring at it. It no longer seemed like the name of a person.

I set a stack of my own albums on the record player. I put on a silk robe with a large "SD Jr." monogrammed across the breast pocket. Then I walked behind the bar and faced myself in the mirror; I ran my finger slowly along the scar which circled the bridge of my nose, I touched the eyelid that was drooping like a dope addict's. "You're ugly. You've got nothing going for you except your talent and the fact that you're a star. You didn't see any chicks running after you when you were hungry and you haven't gotten better-looking since then. They want to hang around you because you're a star and they dig being around success. That's all they care about. So take what you want without ever looking back. They're getting theirs and you don't owe them nothing! Just never kid yourself why they're here. Say it every day: you're *ugly*."

I began putting on my makeup. Charley Head, my dresser, was packing the things I wouldn't be using again, putting a year of my life into boxes. George came in and looked around the dressing room at the stack of telegrams, the flowers, the table of little gifts from the kids, and the *World-Telegram* that was opened to our "Last Performance" ad. He leaned against the wall and spoke to my reflection in the mirror. "I hear some of the brokers were getting a hundred dollars a pair for tonight."

"That's a pretty nice send-off for the unwanted child." I looked up. "You're coming to the Harwyn, aren't you?"

He nodded. Then: "I'll have to hire someone to call me in the middle of the night and wake me up."

"You're not going to change, are you, George?"

He gazed at the floor. "I'm rotten to the core."

As I waited to go on for the last scene, there was a gasp of surprise from the audience and I looked onto the stage. The Palm Club set was packed with tables of celebrities, stars of other Broadway shows and of every important nightclub in town. Walter Winchell was seated at "ringside," next to him were Judy Holliday and Sydney Chaplin, Jerry Lewis, Tony Bennett, Shelley Winters. George, dressed in the headwaiter costume, was ushering a customer to a table: Jule Styne, wearing Ruth Dubonnet's mink coat.

In the middle of my act the entire choruses of *Fair Lady, Li'l Abner,* and *Bells Are Ringing* arrived from their theaters and seated themselves on the stage; Edward G. Robinson, who was appearing in *Middle of the Night* down the street, walked on with his cigar, the slouch hat, his hand in his pocket, Little Caesar style. He took the mike out of my hand, cased the stage. "Kid, you're making a big mistake, see? Y'got a good setup here, see? Lotsa dames. Of course we got dames over at my place but they're all old married dames." Jerry Lewis sprang from his seat and began dancing around the stage, still wearing his makeup from the Palace, where he was doing his first "single." It was the hottest ticket in town, the talk of the city. I waved. "Hi ya, Jer. What're *you* doing in town?"

It got a laugh. He said, "I just finished my show at the Palace. And, Sam"—he paused—"*I'm* not *closing!*"

The audience screamed and he did his strut around the stage heckling everybody. I could ad-lib with Jerry because he could hit back. I folded my arms, Jack Benny style, and watched him with mock impatience while I was looking for the right line. My father had come back to the show for closing night and he and Will were in their usual places. I motioned toward them. "Jer, I've still got *my* partners."

Shelley Winters got up from a table and took the mike. "Ladies and gentlemen, all these people sitting up here came over after doing their own shows to pay tribute to a great performer and it's been a lot of fun but you'll have to excuse me for adding a serious note because there's something that should be said. Sammy made something important happen on this stage for the past year. *Mr. Wonderful* is more than just a hit show. It's the first show in which both Negro and white performers worked together on the same stage and after five minutes nobody cared or even noticed the difference."

As I finished my closing number, row by row, like waves popping up on an ocean, sixteen hundred people stood, applauding. The cast gathered around me, we took twelve bows, and the audience was still applauding and shouting "Bravo" as the curtain fell on *Mr. Wonderful* for the last time.

"You really did it, Sammy." "Fantastic personal triumph." "Tremendous accomplishment!" "You really made it." I moved from table to table through the Harwyn, which I'd taken over for my closing night party. The higher the hilarity rose, the more impossible it seemed for me to reach it. I kept moving, trying to soak it up and feel it as everybody else could, hoping that if I heard it over and over again it would numb the doubt, and the joy of the evening would flow into me too, and I'd be able to taste what they were all telling me was mine. . . .

Jane and Burt were getting up from my table to dance. I spoke quietly. "Let's go to El Morocco."

"*Now?* In the middle of your own party?"

"Just for a little while, then we'll come back."

I told our chauffeur, "El Morocco," and I sat back in the seat. Here we go, daddy. The frosting on the cake or a pie in the face.

We were approaching the blue-and-white awning I'd passed so many times, and the doorman, dressed like a guy from the French Foreign Legion, symbolizing the gaiety inside. Burt, Jane, and I did a wordless grasping of hands. The doorman opened our car door, we stepped out, and went through the revolving door.

Two headwaiters stood at the entrance to what seemed to be the main room. Burt smiled pleasantly. "Good evening, Joe, Angelo. We're three tonight."

They didn't look at me but at Burt, and there was a word-less, vacant look in the eyes of the two men, a look conveying the hurt of betrayal. "This way, please." At least the words were right, they hadn't embarrassed me, and I was walking to a table at El Morocco.

The motion with which the room was alive seemed to veer and change course and accelerate into a more frenetic kind of action; heads were spinning. I walked behind Burt, looking straight ahead, but seeing the nudging and leaning, the blinking and staring, the simple surprise at the presence of someone with my skin color who wasn't wearing a turban. Then smiles began breaking out here and there like beacons across a dark field and I got little four-finger waves, and a "Hi, Sammy" murmured discreetly as I passed a table of six. I kept walking, experiencing an awareness of myself that I'd never felt before an audience of five thousand people. As the maître d' led us past the dance floor, the people swayed back and forth, maneuvering for better looks at the drama of the moment.

He stopped at a table against the wall, drew it out, and the three of us slid behind it. He bowed slightly and left. It was no moment for "stage waits" and the three of us plunged feet-first into conversation. "Did you enjoy the crossing?"

Jane tossed her head back. "Oh, rather. I do prefer the Italian ships, though. The English are so stuffy, don't you think?"

"Quite."

"How is your dear Aunt Agatha?"

"Haven't seen her of late. Dead, y'know."

"Really?"

"Rather!"

A table captain took our drink order. Waiters were going out of their way to walk past our table for a look at me. The guys in the band hadn't broken into "Mr. Wonderful" but they were welcoming me Secret Service style, playing all the other songs from the show. People at other tables smiled, and al-though the three of us were still playing "Oh dear, Morocco again? Such a bore," the tension began softening under my awareness of the incredible fact that I was actually sitting at a table in the place I'd read about for years as the most sophisticated club in the country.

When the waiter had served our drinks I leaned closer to Jane and Burt. "Hey, this is *okay*, isn't it? I mean, they're not even doing the slow service bit. Let's be fair. I'll admit they didn't toss flowers at old Sam but it's better than the last time, right?"

Burt smiled. "Yes. It's fine." But the muscle in his cheek was working itself back and forth.

"Baby, if something's wrong I think you'd better tell me."

"Nothing, Sam. Really."

I looked at Jane.

"Okay, fellas, let's have it."

Burt hesitated. "It's not important, but we're on the wrong side of the room. The tables they consider best are on the other side of the dance floor. It's ridiculous but . . ."

We all knew that in this case it was not ridiculous, that it was the stone wall between acceptance and rejection. I had thought that they'd resisted me by habit but once I was there, once they had seen me, they'd accepted me. But they were fighting me with the nuance, the veiled insult. Everyone in the room had known I was being insulted, that even a semi-name would immediately have been given a table on the other side. I found my hands fumbling with something. I took out my pipe and tobacco pouch to use as a prop, and I filled the pipe slowly, deliberately, trying to appear as though that was all I was concentrating on in the world. As I struck a match the maître d' seemed to materialize in front of our table.

"We don't allow pipe smoking."

I put the pipe down quickly. "I'm sorry, I didn't know."

He smiled, like: Of course you didn't.

Burt said, "Casually turn your head to the right and look at the swinging door, the one to the kitchen. That's John Perona."

The owner of El Morocco, a legendary figure in café society, was hiding behind that door, peering out through a little window as though trying to figure out what I was.

I looked away. "Tell me when we've been here long enough so we can leave."

Burt told the chauffeur to take us to the Harwyn.

"Baby, do me a favor. Drop me at the Gorham. Pay my respects at the party, and I'll see you guys at the apartment whenever you can get away."

Jane put her hand on mine. "Sammy . . . you worked a whole year for this . . . it's your party. Don't let this ruin everything for you."

They couldn't understand that there had been nothing to be ruined, that Morocco had only failed to contradict what I had known: I hadn't gotten what I'd come to New York for. The people at the Harwyn were celebrating the fact that I'd made a show run for a year but that was not what I had wanted to celebrate on my closing night.

"Darling, I'm fine, really. I'm just shot. It's been a long day." I smiled. "The marquee is out and so is he."

The apartment was dark except for a haze of light coming in through the windows. I sat on the couch, too tired to unbutton my overcoat or to reach for the lamp only a few inches from my hand. I hadn't done it. I really hadn't. And now I was at the end of a long, long road, standing in front of a stone wall a whole world high and a whole world wide.

26

As I passed through the kitchen on my way to the wings, a waiter carrying a tray with bottles of scotch and setups called out, "We missed you like a son, Sammy, welcome home." Sure, welcome home. They love you *better* than a son. You're Santa Claus come to deliver the big tippers. Just don't let the deliveries slow up. The chorus kids had come off and as they passed me one of them swung her satin-covered bottom at me. "Rub it for luck, Sammy."

Will was standing in the wings. He nodded happily to me, then turned back to the audience, drawn to them—unconsciously lifting one foot and buffing the already gleaming leather shoe against the sock of his other leg—waiting to go on with all the ready-to-go of a Major Bowes contestant.

The announcer's voice blared: "The Chez Paree proudly presents the Will Mastin Trio starring *Sammy Davis, Jr.*"

Will rushed on.

I watched him doing his old-hat number, selling it as though it mattered, "giving the people what they want," and my distaste for the ludicrous picture became mixed with resentment toward my father for leaving me with this, instead of just once standing up to Will and saying, "It's over. I'm quitting and so are you." The one time I'd needed him to come through for me he'd come up empty. All I'd gotten was a dramatic scene, a lot of tears, and a pair of baby shoes.

I walked on, took the hand mike, and began singing over the applause:

> "Hello, Joe, whaddya know
> I just came out of a Broadway show
> and it feels wonderful . . .
> It feels *wonderful* . . . to be back in
> a nightclub again.

> "Give me a saloon every time.
> Maybe it's hokey but I like it smoky,
> tell me I'm choosy but I dig it boozy,
> show me a guy with a broad. . . ."

"Seriously, folks, that song speaks for how I feel. Sure, we had an interesting year on Broadway and I won't say it wasn't a joy beating the critics, but I don't kid myself I'm Rex Harrison: Let's face it—I'm a saloon guy." I paused for the applause. "With your very kind permission I'd like to make mention of a gentleman who isn't with me tonight as he has been all my life. That gentleman, as most of you know, is my father, who was taken ill during *Mr. Wonderful* and was forced to retire to California, where he's enjoying a well-deserved rest from a lifetime of supporting me on this stage . . ." I smiled Charley Good Son during the applause, then switched to Charley Modest. "I just hope that my humble efforts may satisfy you as well in his absence as when he was here to help and guide me every step of the way." I held my hands up, preventing more applause. "If I may impose upon you just a bit more, may I say that the gentleman to the right of me is the man whose wisdom and show business teachings are so much a part of everything I do on this stage, the man who has given so generously of his vast experience and taught me all the tricks of the trade which he knows so well, and which in my humble opinion account for whatever small success I may have had. I wish you'd help me thank him for his kindness and generosity in remaining on with me, providing me with the support I need so much . . . ladies and gentlemen, my uncle, my teacher, and my friend: Mr. Will Mastin. Take a bow, Uncle Will." I led the applause and turned smilingly toward him, respectfully, devotedly, thinking: You ridiculous figure.

I waded through the crowd in my suite at the St. Clair and found George and Jane and Burt. George waved to the crowd, smiling derisively. "Hello, Chicago."

I folded my arms. "Okay, let's have it, George. You know what they say: only his best friends'll tell him."

He shifted uneasily on the couch. "Well, if you must know, I could've lived without that 'saloon' song." He glanced at Jane and Burt, like they'd all been talking about it, then he faced me and shrugged. "Aside from the fact that I think you're far beyond the point where you need special-material opening numbers—"

"You don't have to soften it, George."

"Well, I just think that song is in the worst possible taste. It's phony and patronizing. I kept waiting to find you were kidding, but the whole show had the same attitude, all those little digs about Broadway—I don't know about the rest of the audience, but *I* don't go to nightclubs to have the performer put me down."

"Baby, you don't understand. You're taking it personally but I need a song like that; it breaks the ice for me. I'm back in clubs and I can't have Charley Square feeling like I think I'm so goddamned chic now that he can't be in the same room with me. The second I walk onstage he's got to know I'm gonna tummel around like the Sammy Davis he always knew."

He looked at me dubiously. "It's a little hard to believe that you have to do anything except be a good performer." He shrugged. "But what do *I* know? Nobody's standing in line to see *me!*"

"Right, baby. So you produce the Broadway shows and let *me* worry about the nightclubs."

His face flushed and he reached for his glass. "I'll tell him when he comes in."

A comic playing one of the other clubs pushed his way through the crowded living room toward me. "How's the skinny Farouk?" He gazed around at the girls, playing it awestruck. "How am I going to adjust when you're gone? Every night with women hanging from chandeliers . . . Hey, she's got to be joking with those footballs under her sweater." He grinned at me. "This is a regular Fort Knockers! I asked a cabdriver where I could find a girl and he brought me *here*." He scanned the room. "You cornered the market on 38s."

"Help yourself, baby. Excuse me." I called Charley aside. "Get 'em all outta here, will you? But y'see the one standing next to Morty? With the boobs. Tell her to stick around. And the one next to her—the red satin with the long swingin' legs—have her here tomorrow at noon."

"Twelve o'clock?"

"That's when noon usually is. Unless somebody changed it."

"But you know you won't be getting up till three or four o'clock. Why have her sit around for nothing?"

"Charley, if I feel like keeping some money in the bank do I need your okay?"

I slipped out of the room and into 3 a.m. on Dearborn Street, relieved to be away from all the fun I wasn't having, the laughs that were gloss and veneer, that were only mechanical and blah, like a second helping of dessert. The weeks had dragged by, a mass of days without definition, their oneness broken only by the hours I was onstage. Between those periods of oasis, I shopped, had parties, dinners, interviews, let crowds gather around me on the street for my autograph—all the things that had always been the ponies on my personal merry-go-round which I still kept spinning, although it wasn't very merry anymore.

There was an empty table in a corner of the Latin Casino. My glance kept being drawn to it throughout the show. There was another one the next night. And the next. Then it got slightly worse. The dinner shows were strong but there were always three or four empty tables at the late shows.

It didn't figure. I'd been away from Philadelphia for over a year.

Arthur came into the dressing room. "It's a morgue downtown. Nobody's in Vegas except a crowd of Texans on a convention . . ."

He was pressing to sound casual, to give me a good reason why I wasn't doing capacity business, but nobody ever figured out a good *enough* reason. Or a cure for an unidentified sickness. And night after night the symptoms were there, grim and threatening: I was playing Vegas for the first time in over a year, I was at a different hotel, and I should have been bigger than ever, but something was choking off the customers just short of capacity. Neither Will nor the club owners paid any attention to what was only a slight dip in business, but to me those few empty tables represented not the dozen or so people who weren't there but the hundreds who had not been turned away; the difference between an act that's on the way up or on the way down.

Like the young, athletic-looking guy who's indulged himself in all the foods he knew were wrong until finally he looks in the mirror and can no longer kid himself about the jowls and stomach he's built slowly and surely by piling one layer of fat onto another, I had to face the fact that I'd stretched my luck and talent too far, and all the mistakes had begun to catch up with me: my lousy press, the lunatic spending that had caused the debts

which everybody in the world seemed to know about, and the
need to make desperation moves like wrong bookings and
grabbing for quick money from every variety show on television—until every time anybody turned on his TV set, I was
standing there doing Louis Armstrong.

I started to call the Morris office but it would be more dramatic, more effective to fly to L.A. and see them in person.

Sy Marsh sat on the edge of his desk. He was about my age,
which was young for top man in the television department.

"Sy, don't book me on any more variety shows for one
year."

"That's a hundred thousand dollars you're throwing away.
Can you afford it?"

"No." I lit a cigarette. "Neither can I afford to blow eight or
nine hundred thousand a year from clubs. And if the Morris office can't see what *must* happen at the rate I've been doing variety shows, at least I can: the day's gotta come when I'll get to a
town and instead of people breaking the doors down, the reaction'll be: 'Oh, him. Why pay to see him when we just saw him
sing, dance, and do the impressions on television last week?' "

"God forbid."

"I'm hip." I stood up. "Sy, you weren't with the office when
I used to come in here begging them to get me dramatic television, so we'll start from scratch: Get it for me or I'll get an
agent who can. It's chips-down time! I've got to protect my
nightclub business, so I'm cooling it with the variety shows, but
I can't become America's Secret; I still need a medium that
brings me to the public. I can't let the people in Chicago and
Philly and all the towns I play wonder whatever happened to
Sammy Davis until I get there once a year or I ain't gonna do
they're-lined-up-in-the-streets kind of business. That means I
must have the importance and the impact of major exposure
and that can only be one of three things: A big record? We
know that's the maybe of all time. A motion picture or dramatic television? We forget pictures 'cause it's been like we've
got the Ku Klux Klan running the motion picture department

here. Obviously they figure I'm not as big or as talented as *Tab Hunter!* Okay. I've never made a picture, so I can't argue with them about box office. But when it comes to television I've got a history of accomplishment going for me. It's right on the record that I lifted the rating of every show I was on. And those ratings were in the South as well as the North, so there's no sponsor who can intelligently say I'm not one bitch of a good buy." He was staring silently at his desk. "Sy, one thing: don't tell me it's touchy."

"Screw *touchy*. It's plain goddamned stupid that you're not on a million shows right now. Here they're fighting like dogs over names half as big as you. . . ." He shrugged. "Well, I guess we both know that the heroes are *on* television, not *in* it. But I'm sure there are guys in the business who won't go along with that crap." He picked up a manuscript from his desk and dropped it, thoughtfully. "The one tough thing'll be to find parts for you. I'll talk to some of our own writers."

"This'll kill you, but how about a Western?"

He nodded. "You were right. It killed me."

"Baby, I'll play anything except an Uncle Tom, but don't brush off the Western thing so fast. Aside from the fact that I happen to be better with the guns than most of the Schwab's Drugstore cowboys they're using, it also happens there were a lot of colored cowboys."

"You serious?"

"The guys who wrote the history books happened to be white, and by a strange coincidence they managed to overlook just about everything any Negro did in and for America except pull barges up the goddamned Mississippi. But I've got books on the early West, I can sit here and do an hour on authentic stories about Negro cowboys, an entire Negro regiment in the Civil War, dozens of things that have never been used—a wealth of fresh stuff. But let me ask you something: why do I have to play the part of a Negro?"

He looked at me blankly.

"I'm dead serious. Why do I have to play a part that depends on color? Why can't I play something where the fact that I'm a Negro has no bearing on the script in any way? Why must a special part be written for a Negro? Or else an entire script switched so they do *Abie's Irish Rose* with an all-Negro cast? Y'know something? I *die* every time I read in the papers about some cat on Broadway who says, 'What we need is integrated theater. Authors should write in more parts for Negroes.' That's not integrated theater. *Really* integrated theater will be when an actor—colored or white—is hired to play a part. Period. Not when a Negro actor is hired to play the part of a Negro who's in the story strictly *as* a Negro, like when they're doing a scene in a Harlem bar and the producer tells Casting, 'Send up one Negro bartender, one Negro bar owner, and some Negro extras for cus-tomers.' " I pointed to a script on his desk. "For example, who's the central character in that?"

He smiled. "An aging film actress."

"Okay, baby, what about the one underneath?"

"A mobster."

"Why can't I play *that*? Is there anything in the script that makes it necessary to the story line that this guy is white?"

"No."

"Then isn't it wrong that they'd never think to call a Negro to play him? Or a cop, or a doctor, a soldier, a judge, or a lawyer—with no emphasis on color, no mention of it? I don't say do illogical or far-out things like showing a Negro doctor making a house call to a white family—although God knows it would be beautiful—but certainly if there's a scene in a hospital and you have doctors and nurses walking around, why not cast it as it *is*, with colored doctors and nurses too? If you're doing a hospital *do a hospital!* But they don't. According to dramatic television there are almost no colored people in America. And that's about a twenty-million-person difference with what the census shows. How's *that* for being overlooked?"

"It's ridiculous. But I guess the reason is that the sponsors aren't going to stick their necks out and take a chance on jar-ring customers in the Southern markets."

"Baby, have you any idea how jarring it must be for about five million colored kids who sit in front of a television set hour after hour and they almost never see anybody who looks like them? It's like they and their families and their friends just plain don't exist."

About an hour later we were shaking hands and he was saying, "I'll really try for you. Somehow we'll get you on," and I left there hoping I'd finally found a guy who'd go to bat for me.

I hated for Frank to see me doing anything short of landslide business. As he watched me from ringside, his face changed from relaxed-and-laughs to curious as he sipped his drink, smiling at all the right times, but watching, studying me.

He closed the dressing-room door behind him, sat down on a wooden chair, and lit a cigarette, holding it cupped in the palm of his hand the way he does when he's tense or when something's bothering him. I wiped off my makeup and kept talking but I could feel him watching me. I glanced at him through the mirror. His eyes narrowed slightly, causing lines to appear at the edges of them. "What the hell's eating you, Charley?"

I slid my tie up to my collar. "Everything's swinging, Frank. I'm a little tired maybe. Why? Did it show?"

Slowly he shook his head, then, as though he'd tried a door, found it locked, and walked away from it, he said, "This won't do you much good right now but I'm making a picture in about a year or so, and I want you in it. It's called *Ocean's Eleven*, about a bunch of guys who try to heist Vegas. I hadn't planned to talk about it yet, but you can count on it. As soon as I clean up some other commitments, we go into the movie business. I'm going to pay you a hundred and twenty-five thousand."

He tossed it off like "Here's a scarf I picked up for you." There was no "We'll have to do a screen test." None of that jazz. He didn't know if I could say hello on film and make it sound convincing, yet he was willing to lay his money and his picture on the line for me. And he knew he could have gotten me for $1.98.

From town to town the dance floors grew larger and the aisles between tables—aisles through which waiters once had to walk sideways—became broad avenues crisscrossing the clubs, linking New York, Philadelphia, and Vegas to Reno, San Francisco, Detroit, and L.A.—a string of nearly filled nightclubs, of people not breaking down doors to get in. And of endless wondering: Why? I was stretching the shows from the usual hour and twenty minutes to an hour and thirty, forty, sometimes two hours, doing everything I knew how, hoping that maybe word of mouth would start filling the gap. I think I stayed on, too, because, wondering if they were ever coming back, I hated to let them leave.

Then, when finally there was a break in my luck, when Max Youngstein, president of United Artists, called me in L.A. while we were playing the Moulin Rouge, offering me the male lead opposite Eartha Kitt in *Anna Lucasta*; when miraculously this lifeline appeared, I could grab for it with only one hand. The shooting dates for *Anna* conflicted with our next run at the Sands. I never wanted anything as much as I wanted to cancel Vegas but my debts were somewhere between a quarter and a half million dollars—there was no counting them anymore, it would have taken a month to even figure out the fantastic borrowing from one guy to pay another and then from another to pay him, the complex web of advances from clubs, record companies, unpaid taxes, and corporate debts—and there was never a day without at least one pressure thing, at least one guy who wouldn't wait any longer. My piece of the $100,000 from Vegas was already promised to eight different people and my third of the $50,000 movie salary just wouldn't be enough. The shooting dates couldn't be changed, so the only solution was to do the picture and play Vegas at the same time. I'd have to leave Vegas every night after my second show, sleep in the car, and arrive in L.A. in time for the morning call. Shooting would be over by five and I'd grab a plane back to Vegas for the dinner show.

The last thing in the world I wanted was to make my first picture without being able to devote myself to it. But here it was again, more damaging and wasteful than ever: my future irrevocably owned and controlled by my past. At a time when I needed everything going for me my mistakes were in control.

Will was standing in the doorway of my dressing room at the Mou, dressed for the show, wrist in the air, eyes riveted meaningfully to his watch. "In another few minutes I'd've had to tell them to hold the show."

I tossed my shirt and tie onto a chair. "You ever know me to miss a performance?"

"Where were you?"

"Vegas."

"*Vegas?*"

I sat down. "Look, Massey, I went to Vegas to talk to Eartha, to make sure she's happy. God knows it's going to be tough enough without having *her* fighting me. So big deal: I sent her some flowers, flew down, we had dinner, I played it like 'You're a pro 'cause you've made pictures and I'm just an amateur,' I asked for her help, she was flattered, I'll send more flowers—she's in my corner. Now, is there something wrong with that?"

"What's wrong is you're running yourself ragged like a fool, making special trips to Vegas to talk about a picture you've got no right doing in the first place . . ."

I began putting powder on my face. "Massey, I've got no time to talk now."

"You mean you don't *wanta* talk."

"Whatever you say."

"I say you're wearing yourself down to nothing. Can't you see this is no way to make a start in movies?" Will was enjoying the role of the wise old showman straightening out the novice with pearls of wisdom.

As though independent of my control my hand slammed down on the dressing table and the powder burst out of the open box and onto my pants. I glared at Charley through the mirror. "Don't just stand there gaping. Get me another pair." I turned to Will. "I don't need you to tell me how good I'll be. I'll do the best I can. And not you or anything in this world is going to stop me from making that picture."

"Your health'll stop you."

"If you're so worried about my health then how the hell come you don't tell me to cancel Australia? How come I don't hear you saying that thirty-six hours in a plane each way and ten stops in ten nights isn't worth the seventy thousand dollars?"

"Don't you raise your voice to me."

"I *have* to raise my voice because you must be deaf! Or you're blind. Can't you see anything but what you *want* to see? Can't you see past your name out front? Don't you know what's happening around you?"

He blinked, confused. "What's happening around me?"

"Massey, I've got to go entertain the people. Or would you like to do it alone?"

He looked at the floor for a moment, then turned and left.

I paced the room, trying to relax. As I passed the mirror over the dressing table, I saw the skin pulled tight across my jaw, the good eye blazing with so much resentment that it made the phony look more dead than ever. As loathsome as the face was, it perfectly matched what I felt. I heard the opening act's music and I laughed out loud at the thought of myself onstage, being Charley Nice.

I'd done an hour and fifty minutes, I'd had no sleep, and I was exhausted but I couldn't bring myself to leave the stage. The taunting snow-white tablecloths, combined with a strange incompleteness I'd begun to feel at every performance, drove me to do more. I called for the vibes and drums, did a twenty-minute jam session, and then cue'd Morty into "Birth of the

Blues." As I reached for the big note a searing pain cut across my torso, like a hot wire around my back and my chest and I knew I was having a heart attack and I thought, "Oh, God I'm going to die."

I knew I should stop singing and walk off. I knew it was ridiculous but I had the dramatic picture of myself collapsing onstage and the papers reporting, "He died as he lived: performing. Death took him from the people he loved: his audiences." As corny as it was, if I had to go that's how I wanted it to be. My head cleared, I heard the music behind me, and I reached desperately and found the strength to finish the last bars.

As my feet touched the stone floor backstage I felt myself falling . . .

I was on a couch in the dressing room, rigged up to an electrocardiograph machine. My father and Will were there, and a stranger was sitting next to me. "I'm Dr. Weiss. How do you feel?" The doctor explained that I'd had a mild heart attack, "a warning that you've got to be careful. With an athletic heart you can't keep burning the candle at both ends as I understand you do . . ."

When he'd left, my father closed the door and sat on the edge of the couch. "Poppa, this tears it. You've gotta cancel out Australia and you gotta take your choice of *Anna Lucasta* or Vegas. Will and me'll go along with either one but you can't do 'em both. Truth is you really oughta take a month's time and do nothin' but sit around the house gettin' your strength up." Will nodded.

I gave them a round of applause. "Beautiful M-G-M musical, folks: the performer gets sick, takes time off, and the whole world stops till he's ready; music, curtain, have some popcorn. But I'm not Dan Dailey, I need the picture, I need the Vegas money."

Will began pacing. "At least you gotta cut the shows back to normal, maybe even down to an hour." He nodded in agreement with himself. "An hour's plenty."

"Is it?"

He stopped walking. "Sammy, I don't want to fight with you." His voice was quiet, his face a combination of compassion and confusion. "But I see you onstage for over two hours breaking your back to do everything you know how, going past good showmanship, making mistakes you knew better than to make when you was a boy. I watched you tonight and I didn't know you. In all my years I never saw a performer trying to eat an audience alive like that. You couldn't find enough to do for 'em, like you wanted to open up your veins and give 'em your blood too. Don't take my word for it. Big Sam here'll tell you. And you're acting like that movie's the last one that'll ever be made; and as far as your debts go, you know I don't approve of owing money—I never did and I never will—but paying bills don't come before staying alive." He hesitated. "All I mean to say is you can't keep on like you've been doing, or you're going to kill yourself."

My father nodded and I looked from one to the other. All they saw was "debts" and "he wants to be in a movie."

"Massey . . . the only time I'll kill myself is when there's nobody out there waiting for me to go on."

I parked my motorcycle in the driveway of the Beverly Wilshire Hotel and went to the penthouse suite. I'd met Elvis Presley on the set of his second picture, *Loving You*. Both of us were rebels in our own ways and we'd gravitated toward each other. We both had motorcycles, I had a cut-down Harley and we ran together whenever we were in the same town. Up in his living room he was at the piano. Nicky Blair, Nick Adams, Natalie Wood, Dennis Hopper, and some kids not in the business were there.

Elvis started doing Ray Charles. He was a marvelous impressionist. I could do Ray but not with the piano. Elvis did the best white Ray Charles I've ever heard. I said, "Okay, pal of mine, I've got one for you. Dr. Jekyll and Mr. Hyde." Elvis went over to a couch and the kids who'd been standing around him at the piano all took their places to watch me.

I was wearing my hair very long and I roughed it up and strung it out like the mad Mr. Hyde. I took out my bridge, and my eye, and I did the crazy eyes and bent over. I did the heavy breathing that Fredric March did. I leaped onto the couch next to Elvis, screaming, "I'm free . . . I'm free . . ." He cringed. "Don't touch me." He was really upset, so I came out of the character. He was still half nervous. "Put your teeth back and your eye and comb your hair." Then, when I looked like me again, he relaxed. "You've gotta put that in the act."

A few nights later I was in my dressing room at the Mou getting ready for the second show when I was told Elvis was ringside. I told Big John Hopkins, my road manager, "Elvis is here and I'm gonna do something. Be in the wings to catch me 'cause I'm gonna come off flying in the air."

I did the whole show, did the impression of Elvis with the white shoes and the guitar. Then I said, "This is for my man." I did about two minutes of Jekyll and Hyde dialogue, ending in screaming, "I'm free, freeeee . . ." and I ran and leaped high into the wings and John caught me. Blackout.

The people were still yelling when I came back onstage. Elvis stood up at ringside and we shook hands.

A few days later when I arrived to hang out with him at the Beverly Wilshire he said, "Stanley Kramer has a script he's going to make. The two leads are chain-gang prisoners who escape but they're chained to each other. One is colored, the other is a white Southerner, and they hate each other's guts, but they have to tolerate each other because they're chained to each other and being hunted down. By the end of the film they develop a deep respect for each other. The title is *The Defiant Ones*. He's been thinking about me for the white guy but he didn't have any ideas about the colored guy till he saw you at the Mou a few nights ago. He saw us shaking hands and he liked our chemistry . . ." Elvis was looking at me hopefully. "Whaddya think? Would you be interested?"

"*Interested????* I'm dying to do something like that."

"Oh Lord, me too. I'm up to here in these beach-and-bikini pictures." I knew that Elvis idolized dramatic actors like Marlon Brando, Rod Steiger, and Jimmy Dean. He said, "I'd really like to act, do something serious. Mr. Kramer's sending me a script. Why don't you tell the Morris office you're interested and have them get him to send one to you."

After all the begging and cajoling to get my agents to find a movie for me it happened because of a handshake in a nightclub at a moment when Stanley Kramer happened to be there with his mind on a script starring a white and a Negro.

The hundred pages of everything I wanted in the world arrived within twenty-four hours and after my late show Elvis and I read the script out loud. It was real heavyweight drama. Dynamite. Our chemistry on the screen and in the press would be sensational.

Elvis was elated. "I'm gonna be an actor! Hey, do you think the kids'll be interested in me without the guitar and the tight pants and the pompadour?" His high level of animation lowered. "Course, I'll have to talk to Colonel. He's really got the say about what I do." Colonel Parker was not in Beverly Hills with Elvis. "He'll be here in five days," Elvis said. "I'm not going to tell him about this on the phone. I do better with him face to face."

"You think he'll go for it?"

"The only thing I can guess against it is he may not see as much money in it with Stanley Kramer as when we do the teenage pictures, plus which they sell records."

"Will he see the value of a change of style, I mean the dramatic thing to prolong your career?"

"I sure think so. Colonel's smart. He's never made a bad decision. And the great plus is that he likes you. He respects you. We're a sure thing. Let's read it again."

I still had a few days in L.A. before I opened in Las Vegas. And during every free moment we had, Elvis and I read our scenes. Colonel Parker arrived in town on a Friday. Elvis said, "He's in his room sleeping. I'll get him at breakfast."

When I woke up there was a message for me to call Elvis.

He said, "Can I come over and see you? Or can you come over here?" The second I walked in I knew it was bad news. "Colonel's against it."

I sat down. "Did he say why?"

"Like what I guessed, about how it wouldn't be something that would sell records, and we probably can't get the kind of a deal from Kramer for me as an actor as we get when I do the fuckin' musicals."

I saw tears in his eyes and tried to comfort him. "Hey, you'll get your chance. There'll be another . . ."

He started sobbing. "It's not that. It's that you're my friend and I'm bullshitting you. I'm sorry, Sam. The real reason is because he says that all those people out there who buy my albums, among them are lots who won't want to see me chained to a colored guy and end up liking him."

Tony Curtis came over to me in the wings at the Beverly Hills Hotel as I was waiting to go on at a benefit. We hugged hello and he whispered, "How was Australia?"

I knew he wouldn't fly, not even to Las Vegas. "You've *gotta* go see for yourself. You're very big down there."

"No kidding?" Then he gave me a look. "Very funny. Listen, come on by the house later, we're having some people over for booze and coffee."

I knew almost everybody at the party and Janet was introducing me to the few I hadn't met before. She led me over to a group in a corner of the living room.

Kim Novak held out her hand and smiled. "I'm awfully glad to meet you. I admire your work tremendously."

The next afternoon Arthur came into the Playhouse and sat down at the end of the bar. I was listening to one of the new sides I'd just made for Decca. When it was over he said, "I never thought you'd hold out on me like this."

I slipped the next side onto the turntable. "Like what, baby?"

A mysteriosa smile. "You know what I mean. Don't do bits with *me!* It's all over town."

"*What's* all over town?"

"You and Kim Novak. Didn't you see the papers today?"

"Certainly I saw them, but they didn't say nothing about me and no Kim Novak."

He showed me one of the columns. "Kim Novak's new interest will make her studio bosses turn lavender . . ." I'd skimmed past it earlier, never imagining it meant me. I started to tell him that we'd hardly spoken twenty words to each other, but as I saw the admiration in his face I smiled, shrugged noncommittally, and turned on the record machine.

When he left I got her home number and called her. "Kim, this is Sammy Davis, Jr."

"Hi. How are you?"

"I'm feeling horrible over a rumor that's going around."

"I heard it."

"I'm calling to say I'm sorry as hell and I hope you know I didn't have anything to do with it."

"Of course I know that."

"We can handle it any way you think best. I realize the position you're in with the studio."

"The studio doesn't own me!"

"Well, but they'll probably feel—"

"Don't worry about what they'll feel. *I* don't. Listen, I'm cooking some dinner. It's not much, but would you like to join me?"

I called Arthur, and I was dressed in Levi's and a leather jacket when he got to the house. "Now, here's the skam: I'm going to Kim's house for dinner." I caught his smile of satisfaction. "Obviously I can't leave my car parked in her driveway, so I need you to drive me over in your car, to play it safe."

Half a block from her house I said, "I'll get out here. Now, check your watch with mine. At exactly ten o'clock, to the second, I want you pulling up in front of her place. I'll be running out of there on schedule and I don't wanta have to stand around on the street and get picked off by no photographers or neighbors. And have the car door open for me." I pulled up my collar, slipped out of the car, and ran the last half block, ducking behind trees and slinking across her lawn. I rang the bell. Instantly the door opened. I slipped inside.

She'd made spaghetti and meatballs and as we were eating I thought: "Wouldn't the papers give their eyeteeth for an eight-by-ten glossy of me having dinner with Kim Novak?"

She smiled conspiratorially. "About an hour after we spoke I got a call from the studio. They wanted to know if we'd ever met."

"What'd you tell them?"

"The truth. I said, 'Yes, I met him at a party. He's such a delightful man.' "

"Then what?"

"Then there was what the scripts call a moment of stunned silence while the studio gathers itself together and, in a voice tensely casual, asks, 'Is that the only time you've seen him?' I told them we hadn't met since then." The amusement left her face. "Oh, how I loathe people interfering in my life. Do you know what I mean?"

"Sort of."

She smiled, simpatico. "Well . . . at least you don't have an entire studio checking every move you make. I mean, they must really believe they *own* me."

"But let's be honest, it's not *all* bad."

She sighed. "You're not much fun, are you?" Then, dramatically: "I'm using you. You're a wall of wet paint."

"And all the signs say 'Don't touch.' "

She nodded, pleased.

I'd known it the moment she'd invited me to dinner. Through me she was rebelling against the people who made rules for her. And wasn't I doing the same thing? We'd spent a few hours in each other's company at a party, and when we'd

"The same goes for me Sam—all the way. Affectionately, Frank"

Sammy, with Will Mastin and Sam Sr., on the evening of his first performance without the eyepatch, 1955

Will, Sammy, and Sam Sr. in *Mr. Wonderful*

Sammy and May Britt on Broadway, 1964

Nancy Wilson, Sidney Poitier, Eartha Kitt, Sammy Davis, Berry Gordy, and Marlon Brando at Martin Luther King's funeral

With American soldiers in Vietnam

Campaigning for Bobby Kennedy

The notorious Nixon hug

When Altovise and I were married, there were no friends or family present. After a few years, we decided to get our families and friends together,
and Jesse Jackson tied the knot a bit tighter

If you want to get known as a swinger, you hire five sexy chicks and let them fight over you onstage

Las Vegas, 1967

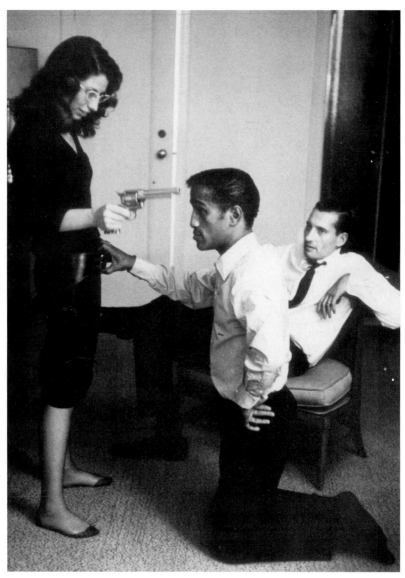

Burt watches Sammy give Jane a lesson in quick draw, 1961

said good night there'd been no slipping of private phone numbers, no thought of getting together again. I was impressed by
the glamour of a movie star and she was impressed by my talent, but she hadn't thought about me any more than I had
thought about her—until it was forbidden. Then we became
conspirators, drawn together by the single thing we had in
common: defiance. I'd sensed it on the phone and in the way
she'd been waiting behind the door, playing it like a B movie,
and I too had been doing everything but wear a cloak and mustache.

At exactly three seconds before ten I opened the door and
dashed to the street. Arthur was just pulling up; the car door
swung open as I reached the curb and before he'd come to a full
stop I was inside and we zoomed away. Even he was caught up
in the intrigue, like he was driving a getaway car.

I rented a beach house at Malibu so we could meet secretly, and
Arthur was driving me there for the sixth night in a row. As we
got close I said, "Baby, it's still light out, so pull over and let me
get in the back. I'd better stay flat on the floor and under a
blanket 'cause the way the rumors are flying, them cats on the
papers may have movie cameras set up all along this road."

The floor smelled lousy. There was a clump of dirt a few
inches from my head. From one second to the next the game
ended. I saw myself huddled on the floor of a car, hiding, like
an animal. For what? So I could say, "I showed them." What
was I showing them? They were saying, "You're not good
enough to be seen with a white woman." And I was hiding on
the floor of a car, confirming their right to say it.

Arthur whispered, "We're almost there."

I couldn't answer him.

"Hey, I said we're almost there." He looked in the rearview
mirror and saw me sitting up in the back seat. "You crazy? It's
broad daylight."

"Keep going. Don't stop at the house."

"You spot somebody?"

"Just keep going."

"Okay, but I don't get it."

"Drive downtown—anyplace." I rested against the back of the seat.

As we passed through the skid row of Los Angeles we stopped for a red light and a bum with a week's growth of beard and filthy clothes staggered up to the car. He looked at me and then asked Arthur, "Buddy, can y'give a guy a little help?"

I started to reach for some money but I stopped. Why should I? Underneath all that filth his skin is white: he'd been given a pass through the world and he'd blown it. I stared at the wasted life holding out his hand and I had a weird, ridiculous picture of Kim arriving at a movie premiere, dressed to the teeth, escorted by this old rummy wearing the same clothes and no shave and everybody smiling and applauding as they walked in. He could be a pimp or a dope peddler but still he'd be okay. Eccentric, but okay. There's nothing he could ever do to get himself as low as me.

"C'mon, buddy, be a pal," he whined at Arthur. "Whaddya say, just a few cents?"

I took a hundred-dollar bill out of my pocket, folded it, and rolled down my window. "Here." He stared at me, hesitated, then took the money. "Thanks a lot, mac. Damn white of ya." He stuffed it into his pocket without looking at it and stumbled away. He probably thought it was a single. He'd put it on a bar and get change for a dollar. He would never know what he'd had in his pocket.

The usual crowd was jamming the Copa dressing room when I got upstairs between shows. I went into the bedroom. "Charley, get out there and close that goddamned window. And make sure the radiators are up."

"But you've got people there . . ."

"I didn't ask for a guest list. I said close the window."

He was shaking his head. "You always said I should make guests comfortable. Well, they were too hot."

"I *want* it hot in these rooms. That's how I like it, that's how it'll be. Right?" I put on a robe and went into the next room, poured a Coke, turned on the TV set, and sat down in a chair facing it. I could see some of them were disappointed. Tough. If they want entertainment let them go downstairs and pay for it.

After about twenty minutes one of the guys said gingerly, "Sam, it's kinda warm in here." He'd opened his collar and his neck and face glistened. "Y'think we could open the window for a minute?"

"I'm sorry, baby. The heat's good for my throat."

"Oh. Sure! Of course."

"But you go downstairs if you're uncomfortable. I'll catch you in the Lounge after the second."

"No. It's not that bad. Really. I don't mind at all."

I watched him cross the room and explain it to his girl. Her face fell. She caught me looking and smiled over. I lit my Sherlock Holmes pipe and watched them out of the corner of my eye. They're unbelievable. I'm ignoring them, their hair is curling from the heat, their clothes are getting wrinkled, they're suffering, but still they don't leave, they just sit here staring at me. They're like moths around a flame. They get singed, burned—but still they come back for more.

As I opened the second show, a cloud of cigar smoke billowed toward me from the table at center ringside. I smiled at the guys boozing and making out with chicks while I was performing. A few tables away a man had his back to me and was eating his dinner. It's your money, buddy. I cued Morty for a ballad to quiet the room, to lure attention, but the conversations kept humming over the sound I was making. . . .

I stood in the wings waiting for the applause to build before going out to take a bow. I mopped my face, stalling, and as I heard the sound diminishing I knew I couldn't leave them on *that*. I ran on, taking no bow, as though the show hadn't been over. I cued Morty. The guys in the band gaped and hurried to reopen the music. I glared at them and smiled to the audience. "We'll now do a few bars of 'The Search.' "

I started with a jam session and began building, selecting numbers carefully, using only the sure things, trying to lift them out of their seats if only by sheer strength, digging down deeper than ever before to entertain them, to get them involved, to get a response—but it was as though I were playing handball with an orange. No matter what I did I couldn't find the power to gather them all up in one lump the way I'd once been able to. I'd done an extra hour and twenty minutes, the longest show in my life, when I finally cued Morty for "Black Magic." As I roared through the number, straining every muscle and nerve in a last effort to reach the people, searching their faces for a touch of the excitement that used to be there, I saw a man looking at his watch.

Will was in the wings as I came off. "Sammy"—it was half gasp, half whisper—"you did two hours and thirty minutes."

"You don't like it? You're the manager. Fire me! And you can tell Morty Stevens that I don't need him to second-guess me. Until his name is out front he'll let *me* decide when the show is over."

I lay on the bed in the dressing room, still dressed, staring at the ceiling. Big John opened the door a crack, came in, and closed it behind him. "Y'know what you oughta have?"

"A lock on my door?"

"No fooling, Sammy, I was thinking you should have it in your contract sayin' the waiters can't serve while you're on. Hell, all the big stars got it. They don't have to put up with guys bangin' knives and forks around while they're performing . . ."

This big gruff man was trying to make it sound like something he'd thought of for no particular reason. I was grateful for the loyalty that had brought him to my defense. "Thanks, John. I'll give it some thought."

"Yeah. No reason for you to put up with drunks talking and calling for more booze—hell, you're a great artist." He smiled awkwardly. "Well . . . see you tomorrow night, boss."

"Good night, John."

I lit a cigarette and sat on the edge of the bed remembering all the years they'd been so engrossed in my show that it had never occurred to them to eat or drink while I was on. Then I heard again the lack of excitement downstairs, and for the hundredth time in a month I reviewed every move I'd made on stage. Point by point I was as good a technician as I'd ever been. But I wasn't touching them anymore.

I called John back into the room. "Tomorrow night I want you to tape the act. From the beginning to the end. I want to hear some of the off-the-wall stuff I do. As a matter of fact, do both shows."

He gave me the tapes the next night. I went straight back to the hotel, alone. I threaded the machine. I poured a Coke, lit a cigarette, and stared at the "Play" button until I gathered up the nerve to press it.

"Ladies and gentlemen, I'm thrilled to be back at the Copa . . . the one place I really think of as home . . . your kind attention to Mr. Mastin, whose teachings and unerring advice . . . and now our humble offering of . . . with your very kind permission may we beg your indulgence during our humble rendition of . . ." I was stunned, repulsed by what I was hearing. It went on and on—the nauseatingly humble this and humble that until even an idiot would know it was pure arrogance, reeking of insincerity, of "Charley Star" putting the audience down. I was being totally dishonest.

I listened to the second tape, finding it impossible to associate myself with the mechanical man gushing sentimental statements without a shred of real sentiment attached to them. Every word sounded tinny, every emotion was a sham. I waited painfully for the songs and dances as reprieves from the fraud, but the voice kept coming back in a relentless drone of "show-biz sincerity," out-and-out phoniness, that cut through me like a knife. Obviously the audiences couldn't put their fingers on what was missing as I could, they wouldn't analyze it and say "Hey, this kid's a phony," but they didn't have to know *why* they weren't excited or *why* they weren't telling their friends, "You've got to get over to the Copa and see Sammy Davis."

All the desperation for dramatic television and movies was like giving vitamin pills to a man who'd been cutting his own throat.

I rewound the first show and turned it on, listening clinically, writing down every hokey or insincere line.

I taped the shows the next night and locked myself in my room to hear them. The sound of my voice hit me like a wet towel: whap! All the phony things I'd memorized and been careful not to say were gone, but unwittingly I'd invented new ones.

Night after night—the same hollowness. No matter how many words and phrases I eliminated, they were replaced by other words, other phrases, equally phony and equally damaging. No matter how carefully I guarded against them, no matter how sure I was that I'd succeeded in stamping them out, the tape caught them, saved them, and threw them back at me. It wasn't my act that had changed, it was me.

I'd become a Jekyll and Hyde character.

Whatever happened offstage, I looked forward to my shows like another man waits for the weekend or a summer vacation, knowing that when I was in the wings waiting to go on, I'd first begin to feel whole and that finally, in conjunction with the audience, I would come alive. When I walked onstage, when I stood amidst my audiences and saw their faces and knew I was home, where they liked me, I could relax—it was as though I could take off a coat. Then, when I had to leave that warmth and acceptance, when I had to leave the stage, I put on the coat again.

But no one can remain two distinct personalities. No one can sneer at people all day long and then for a few hours a night separate them and say, "But these are 'audience,' so they're different." You can only con people if you have no respect for them, and the more you con them and get away with it, the less respect you have for people in general. Phoniness, the lack of respect, had become a habit, a reflex, and there had been a transition within me, a shift of balance so slight that I hadn't seen it happening and the "con man" began creeping onstage until gradually but inevitably he overpowered the honest performer and I was no longer able to take off the coat. I had stopped playing the role and become the character.

I remember becoming aware that I wasn't the "nice kid" that had always been my stock-in-trade. I knew that I had to make the audience believe that I was nice, humble, warm—any number of things which once I had been but was no longer, and to accomplish it I'd reached for everything that had worked for me in the past: they'd always liked the relationship between my father, Will, and me so I'd grabbed for it, using the same words; I played "the kid," I flattered the audience—I did a dozen things I'd done when we were coming up and I did them exactly the same as I'd done them when they'd worked, when the emotions had been real. But as I acted them out, the people recognized the difference. I tried to change, to make it real. I heard about a bellboy in the hotel whose wife needed an operation and I gave him a thousand dollars. Will hadn't been feeling well, so I flew a specialist down from Boston to examine him. I made a list of people I knew cared about me and I called them all over the country just to say hello. But even as I did these things I knew they were pointless: nothing I could think to do was for anybody but myself, no compassion I felt was for anybody but me, and each audience was perceptive enough to recognize a kind of honesty that wears a mask. And I had to wear a mask because they would never accept what I really felt.

Night after night there was nothing I could do but sit by myself after the shows, staring at the foot-high stack of tapes—the coffin of anything good I had been—listening to my own voice destroying everything I'd built. Show by show it got thicker and deeper, and the more I tried to struggle out of it, the more honest I tried to be—the more dishonest it came across. It had grown onto me like a barnacle and it was eventually going to pull me under.

I threw no party on closing night. I stayed alone in my $100-a-day suite wondering how long it would be before I couldn't afford this kind of luxury, looking through the penthouse window, immune to the majesty and beauty of the city below, trying to anticipate the future like a man who's been told he's got two years to live. If I was lucky and if I played my cards right and didn't come back to the same places too often, maybe I could even stretch it into three. It wouldn't happen overnight—I had too much name, too much momentum—but it had to happen.

I didn't need to play the tapes anymore to hear the tinniness, I could see it in every face at every club at every stop along our swing from New York to Los Angeles. I unpacked some of my books on Judaism, books I hadn't looked at in almost a year. "Humility depends upon both thought and action. A man must be humble at heart before he can adopt the ways of the meek. Whoever wishes to conduct himself humbly without being humble at heart is only an evil pretender and in the company of those hypocrites who are the bane of mankind." It was like a finger wagging at me, telling me what I knew was wrong, but not how to fix it.

Rabbi Nussbaum asked, "Why, Sammy?" It was the first time he'd spoken for at least an hour.

"There're a hundred reasons."

"Give me just a few."

"I want to make a change in my life, in my thinking—a complete overhaul."

"And you sincerely believe that conversion would be the thing to do it for you?"

"Rabbi, it's *got* to!" I was embarrassed by the loudness of my voice—the desperation it revealed. "Rabbi, I'm not going to bore you to death with my problems but I've got to have something to grab ahold of, something solid I can depend on." I stood up and leaned across his desk. "I know what I am and I don't like what I am; I know what's in the books and I *like* what's in the books. I want to change but I can't do it alone. I've been trying to be a Jew in my heart but that's not enough. I can't stay on the outside looking in. I've had that all my life, Rabbi, and I just can't go that route anymore. I've got to get on the inside where I can feel it and participate in it. I know there's more good in people and in life than I can see and I've got to find a way to see it, to make contact again. I've read and I've studied and I've called myself a Jew. Everything you said. I've tried to feel like a Jew, I really have, but I know it can't work until I know I really *am* a Jew. Please. Don't turn me away."

I sat down and leaned my head against the back of the chair, staring at the ceiling. There was a long silence, then I heard the desk drawer open and close. He wrote something on a sheet of paper and slid it across to me. It said: "Sammy Davis, Jr., is a Jew." He'd signed it. He wasn't smiling or waiting for me to laugh, as if it were a gag, yet obviously it wasn't the real thing. I read it again, stalling, trying to understand. "I don't get it, Rabbi."

"Do you feel any better? Different? Does this solve any of your problems?" He crumpled the paper and dropped it into a wastebasket. "I hope you'll forgive the dramatics, Sammy. I was only trying to illustrate that I cannot make you a different person merely by signing a piece of paper."

"Then it's a turndown, right?"

He stood up and looked out the window for a moment. "The first time we met I told you not to expect to find Judaism in books. I warned you they would give you the philosophy and the theology but that it was up to you to translate them into religion. Remember?"

"I think so. I'm not sure."

"Well, I'm sorry to say that it hasn't happened. Further, you're looking to Judaism as a quick cure for your problems. You're coming to me for a bandage to cover a sore, a crutch to lean on, a pill to remove a headache. But Judaism is not a symptomatic cure. It cannot be taken internally like a tranquilizer. On the contrary, it must start from within and work its way out. Judaism is a philosophy, an approach to God and to life, a way of thinking, a state of mind. As a scholar of that philosophy I can help you to understand our principles, I can lead you to them, but only you can adopt them as your own. A rabbi is only a teacher. I don't speak to God any more than any man can speak to Him. I can't put religion into you. All I can do is help you to find it and then sign a paper attesting that in my opinion you have found this particular approach to life. But I cannot make you a Jew. Only *you* can do that. And you have not yet done it."

"But I think I have."

"Sammy, that is your desperation speaking, not your intellect. You didn't walk in here and say, 'Rabbi, I'm a Jew because I think and feel as one.' You didn't ask me to certify something which has already taken place, you've asked me to make it happen."

I avoided his eyes, knowing he was right, that I'd kidded myself it could work and taken a wild stab, like everything I'd been trying. It was embarrassing and I tried to laugh it off but the sound I made wasn't pleasant. I didn't feel very pleasant. "Well, I guess that's it, folks. It's turn-in-the-books time."

His voice softened. "Sammy, it's entirely your choice, but you have such a feeling, such an understanding for Judaism that it would be a pity to have come this far, and then abandon it."

"Rabbi, I don't have much time left." I hated the melodramatic sound of that. "What I mean is I leave for Vegas in a few days. You don't suppose we could swing it by then?"

He sat down behind his desk. "Isn't it time for you to stop fooling yourself?" I looked away. "Sammy, think back over our conversations. You've told me about friends you should have but have not, about happiness you should have but have not. We've talked for hours and you've itemized all the points of your life, ticking them off one by one. And what do they add up to? A twenty-four-hour-a-day vacuum with the single exception of your career. Hasn't it yet occurred to you why your life is like this? Isn't it likely that your career is the only thing to which you have given of yourself, that your audiences are the only people you have ever placed before yourself? By your own admission you've bought most of your friends and you've never had a relationship with a woman that was based on anything but carnal desire. You've built a gaudy house of cards and now you look around in surprise at seeing it topple. You see chaos but I can be more objective. I see justice. You've worked hard at your profession, you've been true to it, and you became a star. But you gave no thought or consideration to anything else, so you have nothing else. Should I let you approach Judaism in that same way? Would I be doing you a favor if I were to help you create another vacuous experience? And this one would be the worst of all. Where would you turn when your last resort has failed?"

"I've got a better question. Where do I turn now?"

"To yourself."

I stood up. "I've been there. There's nobody home."

"Try again. You're the only person capable of shaping your life. Don't just read the books. Practice them. Don't just come to services and say prayers which are pointless unless they reflect a life which emulates the ways of God. I shouldn't have to tell you these things. You know them. If you believe in our philosophy then follow it, give it a fair opportunity to serve you."

"Rabbi, there's nothing I'd like better. I've been trying for years but it doesn't seem to take. I must be in pretty bad shape."

The car seemed to be moving up Sunset on its own. I'd stopped for a light and I found myself staring at graying walls and the unlighted front of a building on which a cheaply painted sign advertised *Available for Bingo and Banquets*, and as the maze of thought cleared I realized I was looking at Ciro's. I tore my gaze away, not wanting to see the club dead but it was too late and I saw the phantoms of a great couple of years: people who had once stood in line along that block, the image of myself on that stage, a figure with hope, strong and alive with the vigor of success, energized and propelled by the love of being loved. The light was still red but I pressed my foot on the gas and as the car roared away the image of what I used to be was joined by a Halloween-like figure jerking convulsively up, down, sideways, racing furtively in a circle which kept growing smaller and smaller. . . .

27

The day we got to Vegas, Will told me, "Sammy, I'm quitting the act. I had another examination in L.A. and the doctors say I can't keep up. Truth is they told me I should stay home and rest but I'll keep traveling as manager."

I'd expected it and I'd planned we'd open an office in L.A. or in New York and save the $20,000 a year in travel expenses for him. "Massey, maybe you should listen to what they say. If they think you should stay home . . ."

"No. Doctors don't know everything about a man. They don't take into account that if I had to stay away from show business I'd have nothing to live for . . ." Abruptly he snapped himself out of it. "Everything'll be the same as always. We're still the Will Mastin Trio except I won't be on the stage. You'll be doing a single."

It should have been the greatest day of my life, but no outside force could make things better or worse, no pleasure I might have had could survive the constant question: But for how long?

I was starting to drink. For the first time in my life I was using hard liquor, trying to get drunk. I tried Frank's drink, Jack Daniel's, and it was working. If nothing could help me make it with the audiences at least there was a way to forget them, to remove myself from the pressure of shows which I couldn't make come alive no matter what I did.

I was in the middle of a dance when my legs felt tired and I had to switch to a comedy piece to give myself a rest. It happened because I'd stayed up all night, but it made me feel I was getting old; going without sleep had never affected my performance. A few nights later I was doing a jump-up onto a piano—it was just a baby grand, only about four and a half feet high, and I'd always made an "effortless" leap in the middle of "Me and My Shadow" and finished with a soft-shoe on the piano top. I went for the jump and my toes landed barely an inch or two past the edge and I had to dig in to stay up there. I was lucky and made it look graceful and nobody noticed it, but I knew how hard I'd strained and that there'd come a night when I'd miss. I cut it out of the act.

Age catching up with me was frightening because I'd created my own monster—perpetual motion. I'd thrived on "Wow, where does he get the energy?" Now I had no choice but to slow down the act, and it was the ultimate threat; if I didn't die one way I'd be devoured another.

And the papers kept grinding away: "Sammy Davis, Jr., has been warned by top Chicago gangsters that if he ever sees that blonde movie star again both his legs will be broken and torn off at the knee." . . . "The boss of a certain moom pitcha company has a photo of SD Jr. on his office wall. Flings darts at it." . . . "Sammy Davis owes—"

The rumors and innuendos trailed me across the country, but these things, which would have bothered me at another time, were like mosquitoes buzzing around a man being pulled down by quicksand. Everything was drowned out by the drone of the tapes as they continued telling the only story I cared about: "Sammy Davis is losing his talent . . . losing his talent . . . losing his talent."

One night a friend of mine—a very well-connected friend of mine—was waiting in the dressing room. He said, "We gotta talk." I took him into my makeup room and closed the door. "Sam, you've got a problem with the guys."

"No, babe, it's okay. Thanks, I appreciate it, but I talked to Sam in Chicago and that was just phony shit in the columns. Anyway, that relationship is over."

He was shaking his head. "I'm not talking Chicago. I'm talking L.A. West Coast. Harry Cohn's mad as hell about you and Kim Novak. There's a contract out. To break your legs. But these guys have a habit of crushing kneecaps with a sledgehammer so they never mend. They enjoy hurting people and they could decide they should balance off your eyes too." I sat down, my legs unable to support me. When this man spoke it was fact. "We can protect you while you're here in Vegas, you know that. Nobody's coming in. You're safe here, Chicago, Miami, New York—we'll be there, we can protect you. But don't go back home unless you straighten out with Cohn."

"How do I do that?"

"That's between you and him. But, talkin' as a friend, if I was you I'd think of something."

My father had come in from L.A. for the weekend, caught the show, and came back to the dressing room. "Poppa, I've gotta show you what they're writin' about you in our papers. Mama saw this one and it made her feel real bad."

> Sammy Davis, Jr., once a pride to all Negroes, has become a never-ending source of embarrassment. The legend of Mr. Davis' amours trips gaily from one bedroom to another, leering out at us from the covers of endless scandal magazines, dragging us all through the mud with him. Perhaps Errol Flynn can prosper from this sort of publicity but on one of us it doesn't look good. Mr. Davis has never been particularly race conscious but his current scandal displays him as inexcusably *un*con-

scious of his responsibility as a Negro. Look in the mirror, Sammy. You're still one of us.

I dropped the paper. "I don't need a mirror to remind me I'm colored. There's *nobody* in this whole goddamned world who'll let me forget it."

Will glared at me. "All my life I did a clean act, but the way you're rolling around in the mud there'll come a day when people stop bringin' their families in to see us." He stalked out of the room.

"Poppa, I . . ." There was a long silence. Then: "Hey, whaddya say we get us a little somethin' to eat? Just you and me?"

"I'm not exactly hungry, Dad."

"Well . . . I guess I'll stop by the casino. . . ."

He was at a crap table. "Glad t'see you, son."

"You're sure it's okay for me to be in here now? I mean, you don't think maybe the papers'll get upset and call me Uncle Tom or nigger rich?"

"Sammy . . ."

"Catch y'later, Dad." I wandered over to the cashier's window. "Baby, let me have five thousand." I sat down at a blackjack table and put five hundred on the line.

At least fifty people were gathered around me, groaning as I went down hand after hand. I signed the slip for another five thousand and kept playing. It all seemed so silly: I sign my name, a man gives me a stack of chips, I put them on a table, and another guy takes them away. "You'd better get me another five, baby." A cocktail waitress came by. "Coke, Sammy?"

"That's last year's publicity, darling. It's Jack Daniel's now."

I walked over to the crap table and tapped my father on the shoulder. "I thought you'd like to know, Dad. I just lost thirty-nine thousand dollars!" I waited for him to be shocked or get angry but he just looked sad, his eyes got watery, and I wanted to kill myself.

I did my second show, got boozed up in the Lounge, and

stumbled into my car. When I didn't feel like driving anymore, I got out of the car and looked around. The lights were blazing, music was coming at me from all directions, I was in front of the Silver Slipper.

The bartender grinned, "What'll it be, Sammy?"

"A little Daniel's, old buddy, a little double Daniel's for old Sam to make up for lost time."

The show had ended and the girls were coming out front. . . . One of them was walking toward me. The body looked familiar . . . but I couldn't place the face.

"Hello, Sammy."

"Don't I know you . . . I *know* I know you . . . Oh, for God's sake, hello, Loray. Whaddya drink?"

"I'll have a glass of champagne."

"That's right. Now I 'member. Barkeep! Champagne for the lady, and more red-eye for old Sam. Hey, where've you been, Loray?"

"Right here at the Slipper. I played some places in South America . . ."

"Rio, or Mississippi? Oh God. C'mon, we'll find a table in the Lounge and get comfortable. Y'wanta gamble?"

"No, Sammy. I don't think you should gamble either."

"Hey! Hold everything. No one tells *me* when to gamble. I'm a star, remember?" I took out a roll of bills. "Y'see this? Thousands!" I winked at her. "I feel lucky tonight." I gotta be lucky, tonight. Something's gotta be going for me. I gave her a handful of bills and steered her over to the crap tables. "Let's *be* somebody."

I got on a winning streak right away but I couldn't get interested. "C'mon, Loray, this is a bore."

She gasped. "You're crazy. You're *hot*."

"I'm hot and hot-blooded." I gathered the chips that had piled up in front of me and stuffed them into my pockets. I looked down at my legs. "Goddamned tight pants bulge." I took out some and handed them to her. "Buy a hat."

We went back to the bar. "Y'know, you're one swingin' chick, Loray. How come we stopped going around together?"

"You just disappeared, Sammy."

"Yeah, I remember. What a lousy thing to do to a nice chick like you. We had a good little thing goin' for us. Nothing fantastic—but it was kinda nice, right?"

"*I* thought so."

"Sure . . ." Oops! It suddenly came back to me. She *had* thought so. She couldn't play it for laughs and catch-you-next-time-around. I'd smelled a cottage small by a waterfall and I'd run like a thief, left town without even calling her.

Maybe that was stupid . . . maybe a wife's what I'd needed all the time, maybe that's what I need *now*. If I had a wife, I'd belong. I could relax, the papers would get off my back. I looked at Loray. She's beautiful. Better-looking than ever. Hey, this is a beautiful chick, Charley. She understands the business, she's a lady, knows how to dress . . . I bet she still digs me.

"Y'know, Loray, if I had any sense I'd marry you. Hey, this is no joke! Y'think I tell that to everyone I meet? Y'know I don't have to do this jazz to get a chick. Never been more serious in my life. Just 'cause I made a mistake once doesn't mean I have to keep making the same one all my life, does it? Does it?"

"I don't mean to be ungracious but you're drunk, Sammy."

"Sure I am, but I know what I'm doing. Whaddya think I came in here for in the first place? Hey, have another drink, Loray. What're y'drinkin'?"

"Still champagne."

"Waiter, some champagne for the lady and booze for Sam. Cert'n'y, Loray honey. Whatsa matter, they don't have booze at the Sands? I didn't exactly have to come here to buy a drink, y'know."

"Please, maybe this is laughs for you, but I don't want to play."

"Hey, cool it! Did I ever ask you to marry me before?"

"No, but—"

"Answer the question. Did I ever ask me to marry you before?" I knew I'd screwed up the words.

She smiled. "Okay, I'll play. I accept your proposal."

"You do?"

"Yes."

I leaned back to focus on her. This is a natural. Just what I need. A nice girl to come home to, someone I can be proud to introduce as my wife; I'll come across to the public as Charley Straight. The Negro press'll eat it up like a hundred yards of chitlins. There'll be hugging and kissing and front pages with come-home-son-all-is-forgiven.

"C'mon. We'll announce it." I led her over to the bandstand. The idea kept getting better all the time. The music ended. Here goes Charley Single. I took Loray's arm. "Scuse me, guys. Got a li'l 'nouncement to make." The room quieted down immediately. "Ladies and Gentlemen, your 'ttention, please, if I may . . ."

Arthur was standing close to my head. "Sammy? You up?" What the hell's he whispering for? If I'm awake why doesn't he just talk? But if I'm sleeping then leave me alone. "Sammy? You awake?" I waved my arm at him, but he wouldn't go away. "Sammy, your father's on the phone. He wants to know about your engagement to Loray White."

Oh God. I started to sit up but I grabbed my head and fell back onto the pillow. I sat up, slowly. "I'll call him back. And, Arthur, gimme a Coke, with a lot of ice." I rested, trying to piece the evening together. "What'd my father say? How'd he hear about it?"

"It was on the radio at five o'clock this morning. That's when I first heard it, and it's in all the papers today. Front page here in Vegas. When'd you start seeing Loray again?"

"Baby, cool the questions. I've got to think."

"Whaddya mean? Isn't it true? What happened?"

"Arthur, how the hell do *I* know? I asked a girl to marry me. I got drunk and made a total fool of myself."

"You're joking. But you haven't seen her in years. Not that she isn't a hell of a nice girl . . ."

"Arthur, she's a lovely girl. So is Eleanor Roosevelt, but I'm not in love with *her* either."

"Then you're not going to marry her?"

"What do *you* think? Loray and I were all over two years ago. Do you really think I'm about to *marry* her now?" My head killed me when I yelled. I whispered. "Don't be an idiot with ridiculous questions when I'm trying to figure out what in the hell I'm supposed to tell her."

"Maybe it's not so serious. Loray's a smart girl. She's probably waiting to see if you still mean it now that you're sober."

"I'd like to believe that." I looked up. "Maybe you're right. She knows I was gassed out of my mind."

He gave me a stack of phone messages. "You'll have to think up a statement. All the L.A. papers have been trying to reach you. The Negro press has been on the phone every ten minutes. *Jet*, the *Courier*, some woman in New York—someone Cunningham."

"*Evelyn* Cunningham?"

"Yeah, that's her. They're all excited about the wedding and when it'll be and when'd you meet Loray? . . ."

I flopped back on the pillow. That's it. This does it with the Negro press. Even if Loray lets me off the hook they'll wrap this around my ears: He was just using her for publicity, he doesn't want her because she isn't white. Before they're finished there won't be a colored cat in the country who'll talk to me.

Arthur was answering the phone. "Yes, he is, Mrs. Cunningham."

I hissed, "I'm still sleeping."

He put his hand over the mouthpiece and whispered frantically, "But I already said you're awake."

"What the hell was I waving my arms at you for?"

"But she's already called three times."

He knows I don't know which way to turn and he puts me on with the toughest columnist in the whole Negro press. I shook my fist at him and took the phone. "Hello, Mrs. Cunningham, so nice to hear from you."

"Hello, Sammy, I believe congratulations are in order."

She said it as if it was a test question. All I'd need is to say: Congratulations for what? I took the plunge. "Thank you very much, Mrs. Cunningham. Very kind of you."

"Then it's true?" I could feel the phone warming up. "You and Loray White *are* engaged?"

The nails were in the coffin. "Yes, ma'am. Last night."

"Well, this is wonderful." It was as though she was thinking: Could we have been wrong about him? "When will you be married?"

"We haven't set the date. Soon, though, I hope."

"Will Loray keep up her own career?"

"Well, we haven't discussed it, but I certainly wouldn't object—she's a very talented girl, you know."

"Perhaps she'll want to do an act with you."

Another partner. "Well, that's certainly an interesting idea. . . ."

Arthur was gaping at me, mouth open, as I hung up. "Sammy, I'm sorry. I know how important those papers are to you, so I thought you'd want . . ."

I told Arthur, "Call Loray and ask her to come over this afternoon."

He hung up. "She'll be here at five. What're you gonna do?"

I couldn't breathe without causing waves of nausea. "I'll explain it, ask her to go along with me. We'll get married, make it look good for a while, and then we'll get divorced."

"Y'know you didn't treat her so well that she oughta be looking to do you any favors. And another thing: once a chick becomes Mrs. Sammy Davis, Jr., she's not going to let go so easily."

"Arthur, may I assume this is *all* the good news you have for me today?"

"What I mean is, maybe it's not worth it. You've been in trouble with the press before."

"Of course it's not worth it! But this is one time I can't afford trouble with them. If I back out now, I'm dead."

"I don't know . . . it just doesn't seem right, I mean going into marriage like this."

"Arthur . . . is that your considered opinion?" I started dressing. Will arrived. "This true, Mose Gastin?" He hadn't called me that in years. He looked confused, which, all things considered, was as good a way to look as any other.

"It's true."

"Do you love this girl?" He searched my face. "You get her in trouble?"

"Not the kind you're thinking of. Massey, I got drunk and asked her to marry me. It's that simple. What's worse, I had to get up on the stage at the Silver Slipper and make sure everybody knows."

"Well, then, you gotta come out and say it was all a mistake."

"Sure." I turned on him. "I'll take full-page ads in the *Defender*, the *Amsterdam News*, and the *Courier*: 'Sorry, folks, old Sam got loaded. Heh, heh, heh.' Massey, there's no other way to handle it." I walked into the bathroom to get away from him but he followed me in with Arthur right behind him.

"Sammy, nothing is as bad as if you marry someone you don't love." He was speaking carefully—like I was a mental case.

Arthur nodded. "I agree with Will, Sammy."

I glared at him. "*Do* you, Doctor?" He backed up. "Now look, you guys, it's my life. Whatever happened was my fault. Mine. *I* did it and I've gotta straighten it out."

Loray sat stiffly erect on the couch, waiting, expecting me to tell her it's all a mistake. "Loray . . . I need your help."

"You don't have to marry me, Sammy."

When I'd finished explaining it, for about three long minutes she just stared at me, then she stood up. "Fine."

My father tried to talk me out of it; everyone knew what was best for me. I made arrangements for the ceremony. The sooner the better.

On the night of the wedding I did only one show at the Sands. Loray was at ringside. I introduced her and did all the shtick the audience expects from a guy who gets married. I had a few shots of bourbon with people who'd come to the dressing room, but I couldn't keep up the front any longer. I sent them ahead to the party with Loray. I don't know why they thought I wanted to be alone, but they winked and grinned and left. I locked the door. I couldn't have taken it to see them nudging each other: "Look, he's so happy, he's crying."

28

From the day of the wedding everybody knew it was a phony. They didn't know why or how, so they grabbed for the most obvious reasons and the papers broke loose like I was World War III: "A blonde movie star just lost 20 lbs. No diet. Simply begged the love of her life to marry another to save her career and now she misses him. Boo-hoos herself to sleep every nite" . . . "The facts: Mrs. Sammy Davis, Jr., has a six-month contract with her husband. The deal: a flat $10,000 and no options" . . . "SD Jr. moved his new wife into a house on a hill overlooking Hollywood. Close friends say he overlooks her too" . . . "Insiders say Harry Cohn paid $50,000 to guess which song-and-dance man, to take the heat off Columbia's top box-office property."

Almost everything I read about the marriage was wrong except for the single truth that nobody was fooled by it.

For the first time in my life I dreaded facing audiences. It was degrading to know I was selling a performance but they were buying a display. As I walked onstage there were women at the ringside looking me up and down, like: What's he got? And the guys were grinning and winking like I was the swinger of all time, even more than they had after the Ava Gardner story. I was so genuinely miserable that I couldn't begin to hide it, and that was probably the first honest emotion I'd communicated in at least a year. As I sang, my fists would clench and I'd pound my leg or my side, and they connected the songs to Loray or to the rumors—whatever they were thinking it brought tears to their eyes. That was the final, sick joke: to touch them but for the wrong reason.

Sam Bramson reached me by phone in Toronto. "The Eden Roc in Miami Beach has met your terms: thirty thousand for ten days, suites for you and Will—and the doors are open to everybody. I never imagined it could happen. You've broken down a tremendous barrier."

I slept as late as I could to cut down the hours I had to sweat out every afternoon, wondering: Is this the night they'll stop coming?

Then the ordeal of arriving at the club; the painfully casual question "How're the reservations?"; the momentary relief at hearing "We're sold out"; then the nauseating awareness that tomorrow is another day, and the overriding absolute that "tomorrow" would come in a week, in a month, in a year, that it was irreversible.

Throughout the first week at the Moulin Rouge I kept watching the faces, waiting, half hoping they'd finally look away from me and get it over with. But they wouldn't. Night after night they jammed the club, prolonging the agony of the death vigil.

By the end of the second week I couldn't stand to hang around the dressing room between shows or after, to hear what great business I was doing, to face the backslappers, loud, laughing, transparent, and ugly: "How's Loray?" . . . "Hey, the show was a gas." . . . "Never saw you better. Man, what drama." . . . "What business you're doing!" . . . "For a second show—on a weeknight!" Loray's and my divorce was already in the works. Their voices scraped my nerves raw. Whose dressing room will it be tomorrow?

As I turned off Sunset and started climbing the hill to my house I could actually feel the atmosphere changing, softening, and as I made the turns near the top of the hill and saw the lights of Los Angeles miles away they seemed only peaceful and beautiful.

I unlocked the front door. The racket hit me like a wet cloth in the face. My father had recently married his longtime lady friend and, with her, taken in the children of a friend. Now he was yelling at her, and the kids were crying. I leaned against the wall in the foyer. Their voices droned on, grinding each other to pieces. I'd recognize the sound of those arguments anywhere— the single overriding tone of discontent. It was ugly. Violently ugly. And the kids were right in the middle of it all, always being exposed to it, feeling all the pain and confusion that kids shouldn't feel. I listened, saddened by the same old clashing and complaining, the knowledge that nobody was satisfied, nobody was happy, and it was costing a fortune to be keeping them like that. Is this what I've accomplished? To have provided money for people who can't live together in peace, who can't be happy? To be perpetuating *this?* Maybe even to be causing it? It's bad enough that *I* can't be happy. But them too?

I stepped forward to let them all see me but nobody stopped even long enough to say hello. I backed away and ran out of the house. As I started the engine of my car I knew what I was going to do. Why not? No matter how fast I ran I couldn't get out from under the cloud that hovered over me. It kept chasing me, moving with me, always hanging over my head, and one day it was going to drop and smother me. Why wait? If I'm not doing *anybody* any good then why keep running? Who'll miss me? Who'll really give a damn? Why not go out while people think I'm still on top? Why suffer through more months, maybe even years, of sinking into oblivion, and then endure the rest of my life as a loser? Better to go out now.

The perfect spot was off the side of the cliff past Rising Glen where an eagle sits on top of the hill. There's an empty space between the houses and a sheer drop of at least five hundred feet.

I was gunning the motor, roaring around curves at sixty miles an hour, then sixty-five, steadily pushing my foot down further, gripping the wheel with both hands, planning to hold tight to it as I went over the cliff, imagining the feeling of nothingness beneath me as I'd ride out the drop. The wheels were screeching around the curves. I pressed more gas into the engine until the pedal touched the floor and I kept it there, watching the road growing shorter ahead of me and the needle reaching just past seventy as I got to Rising Glen. I braced myself, turned the wheel sharp, and held on.

The car stopped, like I'd hit a wall! I kept my foot on the gas, gunning and gunning and gunning the engine. The tires were screaming over the roar but the car wouldn't budge, as though a huge hand had reached out and was holding it, preventing it from going over.

When I opened the door the smell of burnt rubber gagged me. I turned on a flashlight. The transmission had snapped in half and was jammed into the ground like an anchor.

God had had His arms around me again. Nothing else could have saved me.

How had I come to love life so little as to want no more of it? What had I wanted and failed to find that had been more precious than life itself?

Each question drew a response too quick, too automatic to trust, and as I held them against the light of logic and fact they began opening like the petals of a carnivorous plant, revealing the skeleton of the fantasy in which I had tried to live.

I was the man who'd committed the monstrous indignity of becoming a star to become a man; who'd waited and worked, planning to surprise Hatred by proving I was its equal. I was the man who'd looked to the magic of stardom, to religion, to everything but the absolute of my own worth.

I was the man who'd missed the smiles of a thousand, obsessed by the sneer of one; who'd focused on the faces of Hatred in close-up, a hundred times their size; who'd tried to find everything I desired by searching for everything I did not.

There had been no harm in the dream of a boy—"I've got to

be a star"—until it hardened and fastened itself onto a man as a necessity, blinding, obstructing maturity, preventing reevaluation. No white man could ever have been the enemy to me that I had been to myself: he was often guilty of unkindness and stupidity, but I had wasted my life and my talent to win a victory over that stupidity. I was the man who'd opened the door and let Hatred come in, and presented my case to a madman.

I was the man who'd paid tribute to Hatred with every breath of my life.

Rabbi Nussbaum said, " 'It is difficult to make a man miserable while he feels worthy of himself and claims kinship to the great God who made him.' "

"Lincoln."

"Yes. Sammy, life is not designed for 'no problems.' But there are men who cringe from their problems and others who face them, as you have begun to do, looking toward the satisfaction of surmounting them. Look at the design of life. When a man makes a mistake, he loses what he had tried for but at least he gains wisdom. If he's young and he breaks a bone it heals and becomes stronger than before. You're still young, Sammy—"

"But, Rabbi, do you know how many mistakes I made?"

He smiled. "Imagine how wise you must be. Don't dwell on your mistakes. Correct them. And don't hold a grudge against them; they've taught you almost everything you know."

I looked at the scar on the palm of my hand, the Star of David. It had faded and it would probably disappear someday, but my need for Judaism was permanent and I was grateful now that I'd been prevented from rushing into it. I knew that the comfort and self-detachment it had already given me was only the beginning, and I was eager for it to develop slowly, but well. There was so much changing for me to do, within me, but I felt ready and able to do it. It didn't matter how long it might take before I could approve of myself without reserve. All I wanted was to know that next year I was going to be better than I was last year.

I began dissecting, until I understood mistakes I could never make again: the using of color as a cop-out for any impulse I'd felt like indulging; the incredible lack of human understanding—from *me* who wanted to be understood; the scorning of people's weaknesses, using them; the grabbing, taking, drawing everything I wanted out of everyone who came near me; accepting kindness and generosity as though they were owed to me.

And what I'd done with my talent—milking it for whatever I'd wanted, hiding behind it, using it to fill my closets, caring only that it was there, never asking why God had chosen my body in which to place the awesome gift, never seriously trying to understand what I was supposed to do with it. I remembered planning to think about it when I'd come out of the hospital and it was frightening to look back and see that once the panic had passed, as soon as things had started swinging again, it had been strictly: I've got talent, I'm a star—and I'd just grabbed it all and run.

Maybe it was too late. Maybe I'd used it all up, milked it dry. But if I still have another chance what do I do with it?

29

Samuel Goldwyn stood in the doorway of my dressing room at the Moulin Rouge, his hand extended. "Mr. Davis, you are Sportin' Life. The part is yours."

The Morris office pushed back all my nightclub dates that fell during the six-month shooting period. I came in off the road and the picture began moving on a clockwork schedule. The day after I finished recording the sound track I was due for costume fittings at the wardrobe department.

Irene Sharaff handed me a suit she'd created for Sportin' Life and as I started toward the dressing room she called out, "I don't want anything underneath those pants. Nothing!"

"Miss Sharaff—I've got to have a little *something* . . ."

"Nothing!"

As I started to close the dressing-room door she held it open with her foot and gave me an Eve Arden cynical grin, "You won't mind if I make sure, will you? I don't want anything underneath those pants except your skin."

"You're joking. You mean you're going to stand here while I—"

"Put on the pants."

"Look, Miss Sharaff, I don't wanta be Charley Modest, but . . ."

"Relax." She waved her hand, bored. "I've seen half of Hollywood undressed. Just put on the pants." She was standing there, arms folded, foot in the door.

"Okay, but I feel like a stripper."

She grinned, "Tell the truth. If I wasn't standing here like a cop, you'd sneak in a little pair of Jockey shorts, wouldn't you?"

"Well, I'll admit it crossed my mind."

She nodded. "Put on the pants!"

They fit like skin. It was all I could do to close them. "Y'know, I wear tight pants, but this is ridiculous."

She called the tailor. "Make them tighter. I want those pants so tight that you'll see him move all over his body." She handed me a coat which buttoned down the middle and closed completely in front from top to bottom. She shook her head. "No good. Split the coat at the bottom. I want them to see everything he's got."

I broke up. "You've got to be kidding. I've heard about this jazz with the glamour girls—but with *me?*"

A month into shooting I went to Mr. Goldwyn's office. He sat forward at his desk and peered at me over his glasses. "You're a *what?*"

"I'm a Jew, Mr. Goldwyn, and I can't work on the High Holy Days."

"You mean this? It's not one of your little jokes?"

"No. I'll do anything in the world for you, Mr. Goldwyn, but I won't work on Yom Kippur."

"You're a real Jew?"

"Yes, sir. I converted several months ago."

"You know what it'll cost to suspend production for a day? Twenty-five thousand. Maybe more."

"I just learned today that I'm scheduled to shoot on Yom Kippur, sir. I came up as soon as I heard."

He threw out his hands. "Sammy—answer me a question. What did I ever do to you?"

"Sir, you've been wonderful and I feel terrible about the problems I'm causing you, but I've gone to temple a lot less often than I would have liked because people still look at me like they think it's a publicity stunt, but I must draw the line on Yom Kippur. It's one day of the year I won't work. I'm sorry. I really am."

He took off his glasses. "Sammy, you're a little so-and-so, but go with your yarmelke and your tallis—we'll work it out somehow." He sighed, and as I left his office he was talking to the four walls: "Directors I can fight. Fires on the set I can fight. Writers, even actors I can fight. But a Jewish colored fellow? This I can't fight!"

I looked around my suite at the Eden Roc and went into the bedroom to begin unpacking. "Murph!" My new dresser, Murphy Bennet, didn't answer.

He was sitting on a chair in the living room, crying.

He looked up and smiled, embarrassed. "I know I look foolish, Sammy, it's just that I never thought I'd walk in the front door of a Miami Beach hotel. And when I gave the bellmen the tip"—his eyes flooded again—"they said, 'Thank you, sir.' "

I felt myself starting to go under with him. "Murphy, you're working for a star and we go First Cabin all the way. Now let's get this jazz unpacked so I can do a show or we're gonna be *living* in a cabin!"

I'd told the stage manager not to announce the act in order to avoid the ludicrous moment after "the Will Mastin Trio starring Sammy Davis, Jr.," when only I appeared.

Morty hit the first few bars of "Mr. Wonderful," which had become a signature for me, then a fast rhythm thing, an exciting mixture of drums and brass. He kept repeating it, building suspense, and because there was no way of knowing when I'd be coming on, the audience was forced to keep watching the wings. I walked on. I didn't wait for the applause to stop. I started singing right over it.

I was in the middle of the show, taking a breather, chatting with the audience; I'd just done Louis Armstrong and I was still holding the oversized handkerchief I used as a prop. I dropped it over my head like a hood and spoke through it. "And there'll be *another* meeting tomorrow night!"

Laughter started tentatively in the back of the room and gathered momentum, completely stopping the show.

Will burst into the dressing room. Murphy left, fast, and Will locked the door. "Sammy, now I *know* you're crazy."

"What's wrong, Massey?"

"Don't what's-wrong-Massey me. You tryin' to get yourself lynched? In all my years around show business I never heard a colored man stand in front of a white audience and do *those* kinds of jokes. Never!" He looked at me, aghast. "I can't believe I really heard you doing jokes about the Ku Klux Klan. And in *Florida!*"

"Take it easy, Massey. Sit down. You want a drink or something?"

"Sammy, what got into you? How'd you even *think* to say those kind of jokes on a stage?"

"I never thought about it at all. But they screamed. You heard them. And there was no race riot. On the contrary. Maybe it's because Little Rock is on the front pages every day and the racial thing is all anybody talks about, but the fact is that by bringing it out in the open it was like I'd bridged a gap that had been between us like it *always* is between *any* colored guy and white guy until one of them acknowledges that there's something standing there between them."

I began adding more racial humor to the act, and they were accepting it, giving me standing ovations at almost every performance, and each time it happened, each time I watched those people standing to applaud me, I wondered if maybe things are happening faster than we can see from within all the chaos. Granted the audience had only a small percentage of native Southerners but still—it was happening in Florida and it couldn't possibly have happened five years ago.

I sang, "Georgia . . . Georgia . . . ain't goin' there." The laughs kept building. "No, sir, if them cats in the sheets want *me* then they gonna have to come and *get* me.

"Ladies and gentlemen, if I may be serious for a moment—thank you for being able to laugh with me at these things. Maybe there are some people who'll say, 'Hey, how can he kid about a serious situation?' but I think you feel as I do, let's bring it out in the open where it can be seen for how ridiculous it is."

The audience applauded like they understood what I was doing, that the jokes weren't just to get laughs. I smiled. "*However*, needless to say, I ain't goin' to Mississippi to do this." They screamed.

"I mean it! I'm not even on the maybe list. Martin Luther King is not only a man I admire to the fullest possible extent but I have the good fortune to call him my friend. I had a few days off after I finished shooting *Porgy* and he was in L.A. and he said, 'Look, why don't you take a rest, a little change? Come on home with me. You'll spend a few days with me in Atlanta.' I almost *hit* him!"

A man at ringside drawled loudly, "I'll say one thing for you, boy, you've got a sense of humor."

"Thank you, sir. I need one." Despite an occasional guy like that, oddly enough the people who laughed the hardest were Southerners.

30

I was having lunch at the Fox commissary when a tall girl with long blond hair walked in and sat down at a table by herself. She was in costume and wearing makeup from a picture. Her hair was very straight and I dug the dramatic way it framed her face, which was unbelievably beautiful. I nudged Barbara Luna, a friend of mine, who was working on a remake of *The Blue Angel.*

She followed my gaze across the room. "That's May Britt."

"Now that's a girl! Yeah. I mean that's a *girl.*"

"Forget it."

"I saw her in *The Young Lions* and she was wild-looking, but in person she's unbelievable."

"Forget it."

I looked around at Barbara. "Hey, wait a minute. Whaddya mean, 'forget it'? A beautiful girl walks in and I just . . ."

"For-get-it! I see her on the set every day, she's nice but she doesn't do anything but work. She goes nowhere with no-body!"

A few nights later I was in my Jag on Santa Monica, not sure where I felt like going for dinner. I stopped at a light. May Britt was walking across the street. She was wearing a bluish-gray skirt, a man's shirt, and a jacket. She stood very straight and walked with a driving energy. There was an older woman with her, probably her mother. I watched them buy tickets at a movie theater.

There was a loud knocking on the roof of my car. A cop was leaning in my window. "Shall we dance, Sammy?" The light had changed and the cars behind me were honking their horns. "Excuse me, Officer." I grinned like an idiot and drove away.

I pulled into the parking lot at Patsy's Villa Capri. Maybe I'd bump into Frank or some of the buddies. I looked around inside. Nobody I knew. I took a booth and sat by myself, talking to the drink I'd ordered: How's this for being a star? A whole city of people and I'm sitting here with *you!*

I saw Judy and Jay Kanter and waved for them to join me. We were buddies and I didn't have to be "on" with them.

Jay asked, "You got troubles?"

"Nothing serious, baby, just a case of the humbles. I just feel like sitting here and having a little booze with you guys."

Judy asked, "How's your love life?"

I came alive. "Listen, I saw a girl tonight . . ."

Jay got interested. "Who'd you see? Who is it now?"

"It's not a who-is-it-now. Her name's May Britt and she's . . ."

Judy threw out her hands. "Forget it."

Jay said, "You haven't got a prayer. She's so straight that nobody even goes over to say hello to her. And the best have tried. She's not interested in dating, parties, nothing! Strictly work. She's getting a divorce from some kid who's got millions and she won't take a nickel from him. Sam, this is an unusual girl."

"Now *you* hold it. You don't think maybe you're exaggerating just a *little* bit?"

They wouldn't even bother to answer me. They gave me you-poor-fool looks, smiled at each other, shrugged, and turned back to their veal parmesan. I sat there watching them eat, trying to think of some way to open the conversation again. I took the fork out of Jay's hand. "Baby, let's talk sense. I've been around this town a few years too, right? Now, there just can't be a chick that looks this good that ain't swingin' with *somebody!*"

He gave me the blank stare and shook his head like: You wanta be an idiot? Okay. Be an idiot.

"Who's calling?"

From her voice *alone* I wished I had on a heavy sweater. "This is Sammy Davis, Jr."

"Oh, hello there."

I gave her the Orson Welles voice, resonant, full of timbre: "Miss Britt, you don't know me . . ."

"I know that." Oh, swell.

"Miss Britt, I'm having a little party—I mean a large party, at the Cloisters, Thursday night, and I wonder if I might have the pleasure of your company."

"I'd like to come but my mother's visiting me from Sweden."

"I'd be delighted to have you bring her along, if you like."

"If you wouldn't mind. Thank you very much. That will be fine."

I spent the next few days planning every move, inviting just the right people to dress up the party. I invited no attractive single guys. I cast it like a schoolgirl setting up her sweet-sixteen party.

The show was about to start when I saw her walking in. She was with George Englund, who'd produced *Odds Against Tomorrow.*

I walked over to greet them. She looked unbelievable. I put out my hand. "So nice to see you."

She smiled. "My mother was tired. Do you know Mr. Englund? I hope you don't mind my asking him."

"Mind? Delighted to see you again, George." If you'll believe *that*, you mother, you'll believe anything. I walked them to the second table. "Do you care for champagne?"

She smiled. "I hate it."

"Oh. Well, how about some vodka? Scotch? Bourbon?"

"No, thanks. I don't drink. I'll just have a plain tonic, thank you."

"Schweppes or Wildroot?" She didn't react. "Well, heh, heh . . . those are the jokes, folks." She looked blankly at me, not understanding what in the hell I was talking about. Very smart, Charley. "Well, enjoy yourselves . . . catch you later." I retreated to my table.

After the show, while I danced I kept watching May and Englund at the other table. They had their backs to me. Beautiful.

If she were dancing I could cut in but I wasn't about to risk walking over there and getting "I'm sorry. I don't dance." When the party was ready to break up I went over to her. "Everybody's coming to the house for a nightcap. Would you like to join us?"

"Nope."

"Well, don't let anybody tell you you're not direct."

She smiled and put out her hand. "Thank you for inviting me."

I waited a few days and called her. "I'm having some friends up to the house tonight—running a few movies—would you like to come by?"

"I'm sorry, I'm going out for dinner."

"Well, how about after dinner?"

"Give me your number and I'll call you when I'm through."

At ten o'clock I sat down at the bar near the phone.

By midnight I saw myself as I was: an idiot sitting in front of the phone waiting for it to ring. I sat down on the couch in the middle of the room. Nobody's *that* good-looking. The phone rang.

May Britt said, "Hello there. I'm coming over now. Will that be all right?"

Now it got to be a party. May was wearing slacks and I wondered if she'd gone home and changed specially, or if she'd been someplace casual for dinner. I could've spent the whole night just watching her move. She walked like an athlete, but oh, was she a *girl* athlete!

It was time for me to stop calling her Miss Britt. "Would you care for a drink, May?"

"What do you have that doesn't taste like whiskey?"

"Do you like oranges?"

"I love them."

"Orange brandy. It's very sweet and fruity-tasting."

"I hate sweet drinks."

"Hey. Don't hate it till you taste it." I poured a small shot for her. She sipped it, smiled, held out her glass, and I poured a little more.

She said, "This is darned good. I love it."

I looked across the bar at her. "You either hate or love *everything*, right? I mean, there isn't anything that's just in between?"

She lifted her head and smiled. "Nope."

I guessed that she was twenty-three. She made me feel very mature. She was so definite, so sure of everything. It was such a youthful, attractive thing. She took another slug of the orange brandy. "You know what else I hate?"

"What's that?"

"I don't mean to embarrass you."

"Go right ahead. Please."

"You called me May."

"Oh. Well, I beg your pardon. I'll call you Miss Britt."

She gave me the blank look of all time. "All I mean is that it's spelled M-a-y but it's pronounced 'My' not 'May.' My real name is Maybritt Wilkens. In Sweden, Maybritt is a common name. I shortened it to May Britt, for films."

"I'm sorry, I didn't know."

"That's okay. I hope you don't mind my telling you."

"No. Not at all. I'm glad you did. I really am . . ."

We got hung up on it and started laughing. Her glass was
empty again and I filled it. For a chick who doesn't drink she
was belting the hell out of my orange brandy.

Rudy Duff, a man I hired in L.A., started the second movie.
In the middle of it May excused herself. She came back,
watched a little of the movie, and then left the room again. I began to get the picture.

I whispered, "I'll take you home." She smiled gratefully.

I walked over to Arthur's kid brother-in-law, Pepe. "Baby,
do me a favor. I'm going to drive May home in her car. You follow us in mine and bring me back."

I drove May's Thunderbird toward the beach. She sat next
to me, silent except to give me directions. She guided me
through Malibu Colony to a large estate on which she rented
the guest house.

We walked through a creaky wooden gate into a large garden. There wasn't an electric light anywhere. We were surrounded by what seemed like a jungle of foliage. I looked up at
the full moon and saw, against the sky, the silhouettes of gigantic trees, bent and leaning, like they'd been standing there for
hundreds of years. It was exactly the spooky sort of a setting
where you'd expect a mad scientist to jump out from behind
the bushes and leer: "Come to the laboratory with me. I need
your brain."

"The pool is a few feet to your left. Be careful."

I wanted to kiss her good night but I knew it couldn't
be like with other chicks with grabbing and squeezing
and what-could-I-lose? Do I ask, "May I have a kiss?" like
Andy Hardy? She stopped at her door. I held out my hand.
"Thank you very much for coming tonight. I hope you feel
better."

"Thank you."

"I'm going to Las Vegas the day after tomorrow . . . may I
call you?"

"I'd like that very much." As she smiled she cocked her
head in such a way that the moonlight shining on her face lit it

so beautifully that I felt a weakness pass over me. She had freckles and her skin and hair looked more lovely than anything I'd ever seen or imagined. The moment was something apart from all moments through all the years of my life. She lowered her eyes, turned, and went inside.

31

The sign in front of the Sands was a classic, as marquees go, for nightclub shows:

FRANK SINATRA
DEAN MARTIN
SAMMY DAVIS, JR.
PETER LAWFORD
JOEY BISHOP

A few months before, when we'd made our plans to shoot *Ocean's Eleven* and play the hotel simultaneously, the newspapers had been filled with stories about Eisenhower, De Gaulle, and Khrushchev planning a Summit Conference, and Frank had joked, "We'll have our own little Summit meeting." One of the papers printed it, others picked it up, and it stuck.

Within a week after our "Summit" was announced there wasn't a room to be had in any hotel in town. People flew in from Chicago, Los Angeles, New York—from all over the country—weeks before we got there, to be sure their rooms weren't sold out from under them. We'd been in Vegas for a week, and still people were pouring into town, arriving without hotel reservations, sleeping in lobbies, cars, anywhere, hoping to get rooms.

The Sands was the hub and you could hardly push your way through the lobby and casino. Hundreds of people crowded the entrance to the Copa Room, fighting for tables.

After the shows we sat in the lounge while the crew set up cameras so we could begin shooting when daylight broke. Frank's presence in the hotel created its own atmosphere. Everybody was having a better time, looking for laughs, kicks, as though they felt they had to live up to his reputation. The hotel kept eight security guards around him to prevent the crowds from turning into a mob scene. Almost anyone else would be at his wits' end because of the money involved in the picture—his money—and all the details and aggravations plus the two shows a night. But he was doing jokes with me and the other guys, the same kind of bits we'd have done if he'd come down for a weekend.

We finished shooting around four every afternoon and the five of us met in the steam room at six, when it was officially closed for the day. Frank came in one evening carrying a bundle of newspaper clippings and we sat there passing around soggy clippings, from England, France, South America—everywhere, astounded by the incredible worldwide attention we were getting.

Peter said, "Listen to this one: 'The quintet of Sinatra, Martin, Davis, Lawford, and Bishop moved into Las Vegas in the form of an attack force with Sinatra as the nominal leader of their clan.' "

"I don't want to be the leader. One of you guys be the leader."

Peter jabbed the paper with his finger. "Sorry, Frank, but it says here *you're* the leader."

"Hold it," I said. "I wanta go on record that I ain't belongin' to nothing that's called a *clan*."

Dean sighed. "I don't know, pally." He nodded toward Frank. "You'd better discuss that with the leader."

I shook my head. "Maybe he's *your* leader but *my* leader is Martin Luther King!"

The papers had been developing the "Clan" and the "Rat

Pack" image of us as five guys who buddy around, have laughs, and in their spare time make a movie and do shows at the Sands. We were amused by it but no one could understand better than we how silly it was. I never discussed it with Frank but he, being an astute showman, must have thought: Dean's good box office, Sammy does great in clubs, Peter has a television following—why not make a picture.

It was not unlike what was done years ago when Hollywood teamed stars like Katharine Hepburn and Spencer Tracy, Walter Pidgeon and Greer Garson, William Powell and Myrna Loy, Cagney and Raft; and although each had been tremendous on their own, when they came together in a picture it virtually exploded at the box office. In the last ten or fifteen years the studios had stopped doing it, but now Frank's idea had so captured the public's imagination that movie theaters all over the world were ordering a picture that wasn't even finished. Recognizing the potential in our combination, he formulated the Five-Year Plan: assuming things continued as it seemed they would, we'd make five pictures together, one a year.

There was only one star dressing room at the Sands, so all five of us used it together. As we were getting ready for a second show, Frank told us, "JFK is going to be out front."

We always had celebrities in the audience. The five of us were onstage and we'd introduce them round-robin, each of us taking one, always saving the biggest for last, as is normal. That night Frank stepped back to where we had a bar on the stage and as I was pouring a drink he said, "Smokey, you introduce the next President."

Frank threw that to me. Instead of taking the glory for himself—which I would have done if I'd been that close to the man—he gave it to me. He was still pushing me up front.

Later the senator and his party came upstairs and had drinks with us. Everybody was calling him "Number One." After a while one of his aides said they should go so he could get some sleep because the plane was leaving in six hours. He was enjoying himself. "Don't worry about me. I'll sleep on the plane."

Peter whispered, "If you want to see what a million dollars in cash looks like, go into the next room; there's a brown leather satchel in the closet; open it. It's from the hotel owners for Jack's campaign."

I never went near it. I was told there were four wild girls scheduled to entertain him and I didn't want to hear about that either and I got out of there. Some things you don't want to know. Like when gangsters are talking and you're sitting there, you don't want to know those things. I'd be sitting in a booth with Julie Podell at the Copa and he'd have some very heavyweight visitors, like Frank Costello. I'd stand up. "Excuse me, gentlemen . . ." "No, sit down, kid, you can listen," and they'd shrug at each other: "Who the fuck is *he* going to tell? Siddown, Sam."

With the President you'd hear rumors, you had your suspicions, but you'd rather not know. I'd go out to Santa Monica to Peter and Pat's house and there'd be three or four chicks running around. And the President was due to arrive. Well, you don't have to be Dunninger to figure out why they're there. Did I see them humping? No, I did not. Did I see them kissing on the lips? No, I did not. But I also know they ain't there to play shuffleboard.

When we'd settled into our shooting schedule, I called May.

She said, "I hear it's fantastic there."

"Come down for the weekend and see for yourself."

"I'd love to. But do you think you can get me a hotel room?"

I played it like the King of France wandering through Paris in disguise—the classic scene in which the loyal, deserving subject whose wife is wrongfully imprisoned asks hopefully, "But do you think you can possibly get my case to the attention of

His Majesty?" and the King smiles behind his disguise and chuckles: "I believe I can manage it."

I was so delighted with myself it was practically incest.

She was the fifth person out of the plane. She paused at the top of the ramp and I couldn't decide if she was playing "Mary Movie Star Arriving in Las Vegas" or if she was looking for me. As she came through the gate she smiled and her face was like sunshine. She put out her hand. "Hello, there."

"Hello, there, yourself." I took the makeup bag she was carrying. A lady was standing behind her and I had a sudden horrible moment of recognition: the same woman who'd walked into the movie theater with her in L.A.

"I'd like you to meet my mother, Mrs. Wilkens."

"I'm so glad you could come, Mrs. Wilkens." For that statement alone, my nose should have grown twelve inches.

"My mother is going back to Sweden next week and I thought she'd enjoy seeing Las Vegas before she leaves."

They went to their rooms to unpack, and I headed to the health club. *Now* she brings her mother. To a party in a nightclub—*then* she doesn't bring her. No. She waits for a weekend in Vegas!

Frank was alone in the steam room. I sat down next to him. "Will you do me a favor?"

"Sure, what is it?"

"I invited May Britt down for the weekend. She's got her mother with her, but with all the press in town I want to be absolutely sure nobody connects us. I don't want to louse her up with her studio, so will you cover for me? Would you let it be known that she's your guest?" As I was asking I realized that I was imposing on him, but he just looked at me with a penetrating curiosity.

"Sure, Charley, she's my guest."

I introduced May from the stage with the other celebrities, and her mother beamed with pride. I met them in the lounge after the second show, we gambled a little, had a bite to eat with Frank and the guys. I didn't have any scenes the next afternoon, so I took them sightseeing, showing them downtown Vegas and everything I could think of that her mother might like to see. As we drove back across the desert from Lake Mead, May said, "My mother's a little tired. I think we'll have dinner in our room so she can go to sleep early. Can I come to see your second show alone?"

"Of course. I've got a permanent table. There'll be some of my friends there, so you won't have to sit alone."

As soon as I got off I sent Murphy to escort her backstage.

"Hello, there. I liked your show." Murphy did a sneaky-foot out the door like one of the discreet men of all time.

She was wearing a bright yellow dress. A sunburn highlighted her freckles, and her hair was hanging long and golden over her shoulders. We smiled wordlessly at each other.

"Would you like something to drink?"

"No. Thank you very much. But you have one if you like."

"No, thanks. I don't feel like one either."

"The club was really packed."

"Yeah . . . things sure are swinging. . . ."

I was desperate to make conversation, but I'd never really *talked* to a girl before. It was always laughs and pow! into bed or not. She walked over to the TV set and stood there, glued to it. I stared at it too.

It was impossible to believe. Here's a girl I could get drunk just from looking at, she's just seen me do the show of my life, she's in my dressing room, the door is closed—and we're standing like idiots watching a twenty-year-old movie, then pretending to be hung up in the commercial.

I looked at her beautiful face. She glanced up as she sensed me staring at her. The haughty look she'd had in *The Blue Angel* and when we'd first met was completely gone, her cheeks were flushed, and she seemed self-conscious. I walked the two steps over to her, put my hands on her shoulders, and kissed her.

She was tall. I asked, "Would you mind taking off your shoes?"

She laughed and kicked them off. I kissed her again.

Suddenly it was easy to talk. I remembered the closed door and opened it and as I turned I caught the trace of a smile of satisfaction on her face.

The airline was announcing her flight over the loudspeaker. I said, "Thank you very much for coming."

She put out her hand. "Thank you for asking me." She tilted her head a little. "So long." She turned abruptly and started toward the plane, walking with the brisk, purposeful stride which was so distinctly her.

As the ground crew rolled away the stairs I had a sense of relief. From the first minute to the last it hadn't worked the way I'd expected it to. I'd asked her down like: Here's a crazy-looking chick and I dig having her around. But it hadn't been that superficial. I'd done forty-eight hours of keeping doors open and inviting people to be with us; I'd looked forward too eagerly to seeing her every day; I'd been too willing to just sit quietly and look at her and listen to her Swedish accent; I'd been making all the high school moves hoping to please her mother, and I'd taken pleasure in them.

I sat in my car watching the plane taxi down the runway, then circle Vegas, gaining altitude heading west toward the mountains, and I urged it on in its crawl against the sky as though every inch of the way was drawing me that much further out of the involvement. I felt as if I'd been walking backward and turned around just in time to see that in a few more steps I'd have fallen over a cliff.

I went back to the hotel. I didn't feel much like gambling and it was too early for the steam room. What I needed was a chick. I called an old standby, one of the kids from the line. But as soon as she got to the suite I sent her away. I didn't feel much like that, either.

32

From the moment I met May I felt like a different man. I invited a bunch of people over to the Playhouse and while they were watching a movie May and I sat outside near the pool, talking.

"What's your next picture going to be?"

She smiled. "I couldn't care less. I like making films but, oh boy, do I hate all the other stuff that goes with it! The fuss, the press things you have to do, getting pushed into crowds, and being nice to people you can't stomach—it's such a lot of baloney!"

"You don't care about being in pictures?"

"Not particularly. My sister is a nurse in Sweden. That's what I wanted to be."

Arthur had come out of the Playhouse. "Am I intruding?"

"Well, you're not exactly vital, but sit down, baby."

"I just got the greatest idea you ever heard. Look, you've got ten more free days. Let's hire a boat and take a cruise down to Mexico."

"Arthur, what in hell would I do on a boat for ten days?"

"You'd rest. Look, I know of a yacht with a captain and crew. We'd keep it down to 'family' . . . it's got a living room, we could bring a projector and show movies at night."

I turned to May. "You're not shooting, so you've got the time. And before you answer I'll tell you this: if you don't come, then there ain't gonna be no boat trip and everyone'll be mad at you." I played it like I was kidding but I knew that I wasn't about to spend my vacation away from her.

The morning after we got back I woke up at around eleven, put on a robe, and went into the kitchen. After a few slugs of coffee I ran the shower good and hot, did a chorus of "Pagliacci," made the big note, and started dressing. It was mid-March and May's birthday was on the twenty-second. We were shooting interiors for *Ocean's* and this was the only day I had free to go downtown and buy her a present. I knew it was going to be a piece of jewelry but I wanted plenty of time to select just the right thing. I'd invited her over for dinner on the twenty-second, only the two of us: a little candlelight, a jug of wine, and I'd hand it to her when her birthday cake was served.

The front doorbell rang and I heard my housekeeper, Etheline, talking to Berney Abramson, the photographer who does my darkroom work.

He was in the living room holding a package of enlargements. "Your yachting pictures, Commodore." He tapped the package. "That May Britt's a wild-looking chick!"

I pulled it out of his hands and walked into the bedroom. He followed me in. "Sammy? What's wrong?"

Berney'd handled pictures of countless girls I'd photographed. Maybe a hundred times he'd made similar friendly remarks and I'd only been pleased. How could he know it would steam me this time when I wouldn't have known it myself? I gave him a friendly shot on the arm. "Everything's fine, baby. No problems. Thanks." I walked him to the door.

I separated May's pictures from the others and spread them out on the floor. I'd had them made up eleven by fourteen and they were incredible. From every possible angle she was beautiful. I picked up the nearest one, to study it more closely, and as

I held it I was struck by the contrast of my thumb against her arm.

I went into the bedroom. I forced myself to look in the mirror at my broken face, at my bad eye, the scar across my nose . . . I thought of her beauty, of the hundreds of desirable men she could have. Still, she'd come to Vegas, she'd made the boat trip . . . Sure, Charley, she needs *you!* You want to fool yourself that you're Charley Dapper, Charley Star? Well, you go right ahead, keep forgetting you're colored and you're short and you're ugly—until you get reminded. Better still, throw yourself in front of a truck! It's quicker and it'll hurt less.

I couldn't cancel our date for her birthday. The thing to do would be to go through with it, playing everything down until I could bow out gracefully.

On the twenty-second when we broke for lunch I called Etheline and told her to pick up a birthday cake. There was no point in being rude. We finished shooting early and I headed home. I felt rotten having no present for her. She had no family over here . . . maybe I'd get her something silly, something that doesn't mean anything. I drove to Beverly Hills and browsed through the Toy Menagerie, looking at joke-type presents like a giant stuffed giraffe. But I didn't want to give her a giant stuffed giraffe.

I stopped at Si Sandler's and gazed at the rings and clips and pins in the window. I'd never wanted anything like I wanted to give her one of them. But she was no "chick" who'd accept an expensive gift from a guy she wasn't really serious about.

What could I lose? I was in so deep that I couldn't walk away from her anymore. She'd have to send me away.

I raised the lid of the box and set it down on the coffee table in front of her. It contained a simple diamond cocktail ring, one that couldn't possibly be mistaken for an engagement ring. "Okay. You can open your eyes now."

She looked at it. She didn't speak or move.

"Look, not everybody likes jewelry, so I won't be offended . . ."

She lifted the ring out of the box and put it on her finger. Her voice was a whisper. "Thank you."

After dinner she said, "The studio gave me some rotten news today. They assigned me a new picture. *Murder, Inc.* I can't afford to go on suspension, so I have to take it." She looked away. "I have to go to New York next week. We'll be shooting most of it on location there."

I couldn't bring myself to ask for how long. "Do you know where you'll be staying?"

"The Sherry Netherland. I'll have to be there for a month."

We spent every possible minute together for the little time that was left and on Sunday I drove her to the airport. As we pulled up in front of the TWA building, she said, "I hate saying goodbye." She got out of the car, ran inside, and was gone.

I had a quiet dinner and killed the next few hours going over my lines for Monday morning's shooting, until I knew she'd be at her hotel and I could call her. I knew I couldn't give my name. Maybe because it was Sunday I thought of the characters in "Peanuts," the comic strip we both liked, and when the hotel operator asked who was calling, I said, "Tell her it's Charlie Brown calling Peanuts."

May was laughing as the connection was made. "Tell me, Sharlie Brown, are you somebody I just left a few hours ago?"

I kidded her about the way her accent slid over the "Ch" sound, softening it to "Sh," and, maybe to take the emphasis off the fact that I had to use a code name, I laughed a little harder than it was worth.

When we finished shooting on Monday I browsed around a flower shop for almost half an hour. I enjoyed choosing what I thought she'd like, and it occurred to me that since I'd been a star I'd probably sent out twenty, maybe thirty thousand dollars' worth of flowers, but this was the first time I'd ever been in a florist's shop.

We spoke on the phone as often every day as we could. I

had scenes to shoot all week and at night I forced myself to go to sleep early. On Sunday I called to say good morning and we spoke until afternoon.

I knew that if I had a brain in my head I'd get busy on the phone and have the place swarming with chicks. But I had no eyes for all the chicks in Hollywood put together, it was too late for that. There was no suddenly saying, "This is the woman I love," yet it was impossible to imagine the day I'd ever stop seeing her, and I knew that compared with what was coming, I'd never had a problem in my life.

What do I do when she becomes aware of how much I love her and she says, "I'm sorry. I like you, maybe even love you, but I . . . well, I never dreamed you were thinking of marriage."

Even as the world's greatest optimist, how can I hope for anything else? Let's say she loves me. It's one thing to have quiet dinners together, go on private boats, come to Vegas with her mother and with Frank covering for her. She thinks she doesn't care about her career, but how will she feel when they take it away from her? How can I expect her to face the world and her family and say, "This is my husband. He's a little dark, folks"?

Night after night I placed my calls, waiting anxiously while the operator connected us and then, finally, relaxing as the warmth of her voice spread through my entire being. Then, after each call, the fears and the doubts gripped me again and I lay stretched out on the bed, staring at the ceiling, hating myself for breathing life into a relationship which I'd known was condemned before it was born.

After shooting on Thursday I went to Romanoff's with Frank, Dean, and Peter. Right after dinner I went home.

We'd been on the phone for almost an hour, she'd been telling me how she hated being away, we'd counted the days she'd been gone, and I just said, sort of wistfully, "Wouldn't it be great to be married?" The instant I heard my own words slip out I hurried to make a joke of it. "Listen, at these prices on the phone two could live cheaper than one."

She said, "It sure *would* be great, wouldn't it?"

I was unable to continue talking. I told her I'd call back and we hung up. I sat on the edge of the bed, my hand still on the phone, hearing her answer over and over again.

But she was in New York and I was in California and she couldn't see my skin through the phone. Had she considered that after marriage comes children? And with us they might be colored? Was she prepared for that?

I called her back an hour later and after we'd talked for a while I said, "You know how I love kids. Won't it be great when we're married and have lots of little brown babies?"

"I'd love to. Lots of them. Sammy? . . . Sammy, are you there?"

"Yes."

"Don't *you* want little brown babies?"

Her picture was on the front page of the New York *Journal American*, captioned "Going Steady?" I put down the paper. "Darling, I've been thinking that with your divorce not final until September, we have five or six months before we can be married, so we've got to cool it with letting it be known we're going together. God knows I'd love to announce, 'This is the girl I love and we're going to be married.' But if we do that then there's going to be six months of a publicity free-for-all, with will-they-or-won't-they, and you certainly don't want that, do you?"

"Oh boy no. I'd hate it."

"Then that's it. We cool it." She nodded agreement. "Darling, do your parents . . . do they know about us being serious?"

"Yes. I've written them all about you. And I know my mother has told my father how much she liked you."

"I'll be playing London in June and you mentioned you might visit your folks in Sweden around then—is there any chance you could come over to London with your father? That way we could meet and get to know each other. It would be beautiful if we could get his consent."

"Hey, that's a great idea."

We watched television, cooked some steaks, and talked. "I want you to know what you're getting into. This kind of relationship is a first for me. I don't begin to know what marriage is going to be like. Not only have I never gone steady with a girl, I've never even done light housekeeping." She looked puzzled. "That's an expression for when a guy has a girl and he pays the bills. What I'm saying is, I've never had a day-to-day relationship with a woman. I've never even spent a whole night in bed with a woman."

"Seriously?"

"Never. When it was time to sleep either they'd go home or I'd fall asleep on the couch or on the floor. I haven't slept in bed with anyone since I was a kid and my father and I used to share a bed on the road. I don't begin to know how to be around a woman like a man is around his wife or someone he cares for dearly. I've had thirty-four years of one-way living. I make a lot of money and I'm big in the business because of three things: I've got talent, I've worked hard, and every bit as important, I have let myself remain an individual. Something has stayed in my mind since the first time I read *The Picture of Dorian Gray*. Oscar Wilde had a theory that when you love someone it must take away from you as an individual. I never before loved anybody enough to feel they're as important as I am or more important so for their happiness I'll change. But now that I'm in that position I can see that I've got to be extra careful. I've seen so many marriages where the husband or wife blended into each other until there's no way to tell them apart except he buttons his coat from left to right and she buttons hers from right to left. One has changed the other and maybe it's fun—but for me it would be death. I live in dread of the day I turn around and find I've lost my individuality.

"Let's be honest. I'm a showman first, last, and always, in everything I do, and I've got to admit that I dig the kick of the combination of personalities so that when we walk down a street it won't be just 'There's Sammy and his wife' but it'll be 'There's Sammy Davis and May Britt' and there's an extra excitement to it. I love you for all the dozens of things you are— and being May Britt instead of Maybritt Wilkens or Maryjane Smith is a part of what you are. By the same token I expect you to love me, in part, for my professional self. I spent my whole life trying to become a star. I started off in the world as fat, bone, and a gallon of water and I think it would be ridiculous to expect you to love me for *that* or for what I was when I was twenty. I love you as I want you to love me: for the sum total of what I've made of what I started with."

We went to a few parties at Frank's, and at Tony and Janet's, where I knew there would be only close friends and I could be sure nobody was going to slip into the other room, grab the phone, and do a "Hello, Louella."

Hugh Benson called. "Why don't you and May come over for dinner tomorrow night. Diane and I are inviting some of the kids, Peter Brown, Nancy and Bob Culp . . ."

I thanked him and hung up, appreciating the way he'd anticipated my thoughts and had casually given me a guest list.

I picked up May and as we neared Hugh's house she asked, "Sammy, can we tell them?" Her face was aglow. Seeing my hesitation, she said, "After all, they're friends."

"Let's see if the right moment presents itself."

Throughout dinner the conversation seemed constantly to arrive at "kitchens," "babies," and a dozen other topics that were perfect cues for me to tap a glass and say, "I have a little announcement to make," and as each opportunity arose, May turned to me expectantly but I looked away, scanning the faces at the table, wondering. Hugh's thirteen-year-old son Jeffrey was at dinner with us, and even if the adults reacted as I hoped they would, it was almost a sure thing that Jeff's youthful honesty would expose an immediate reaction—a glance from May to me and the almost-out-loud thinking, "But she's white and he's colored." I wanted to spare Hugh and Diane the embarrassment of fumbling for cover-up lines, and May the pain and shock of hearing them, but each time I switched the talk away from marriage I saw the eagerness fade from her face, and by the time we were halfway through dinner the bright-eyed excitement she had radiated was completely gone, shrouded by a bewilderment which caused mechanical smiles when she was talking and a near-glumness when she thought she wasn't being watched.

At my next chance I said, "Look, we've been keeping it quiet because we don't want a whole publicity thing, but you're all friends, so May and I would like you to know that we intend to be married."

Jeff's face brightened. "Hey, that's great. Wow . . ." and from all directions the air filled with the warmth of good wishes as people stood up to kiss May, to shake hands with me, and to offer toasts. She was blushing happily and I smiled, accepting the congratulations, resting against the chair, completely exhausted.

Jim Waters, who worked for me in his spare time, picked May up at the studio and as she walked in the door I took her by the arm and escorted her to the couch. She sat down, watching me, sensing I had something exciting to tell her.

I bowed low. "I take pleasure in informing you that your fiancé has this day been invited to appear at a Command Performance before the Queen of England." Her eyes widened with delight.

"Here I am, the world's greatest nut for castles and moats and 'Ah, yes, m'liege,' and 'By your grace, m'lord,' and I get an invitation from Buckingham Palace."

33

I turned to my dresser. "Baby, before I forget, call Sy Devore and tell him we need a complete list of my measurements. And when you get them, shoot them right over to the Morris office so they can cable them to London."

He went to make the call. "I'll be wearing my own tux for the show but I need tails for the presentation to the Queen. They said I could bring my own or they'd supply them. And one thing I know, England is England and if I get my tails from the Royal Tailor, or whoever they use, there'll be no question about looking right. I don't want no 'Hmmphs' from them cats in the bowlers."

From the second I set foot on British soil I *felt* English. I smiled and said, "Thanks awfully," to the British customs inspectors. I wasn't putting it on.

Al Burnett was waiting for me and as we walked toward the car he said, "I've taken the liberty of arranging a press conference. Your arrival has stimulated strong interest here and the press is eager to meet you personally."

The Pigalle was one flight downstairs, like the Copa. I skidded to a halt at the sight of what awaited me. It seemed there were twelve million of them. I nudged Al. "Are these the reporters or the readers?"

They cleared an aisle through their midst to the center of the stage. Al introduced me, then stepped back as though removing himself from a fight, leaving me in the ring.

The questions exploded like fifty feet of Chinese firecrackers.

"Is there anything between you and May Britt?"

"I sincerely hope so."

"Do you intend to marry her?"

They had English accents but they were no tea drinkers. "Who wouldn't want to marry May Britt? Imagine some guy saying, 'No, I don't want to marry the most beautiful girl in the world.' Now, whether or not she wants to marry *me* is something else."

They laughed and the questions kept coming. "Mr. Davis, we in England have read of your amorous affairs with the glamorous women of the world. What do you have that makes you so desirable to these fabulous creatures? If I may say, without intending to be insulting, you know, you're not the most attractive man."

I looked around the room, thinking: Well, here they are, the British press, tough, mischievous, skeptical. I gave him the Jack Benny stare, stalling. If I say why I think I'm attractive I come off like I believe I'm Cary Grant. If I say I haven't the faintest idea, it has to sound like false modesty. Further, to steam me into being foolish he'd added the zingy about me not being good-looking. Who in this world doesn't see *something* attractive in himself?

I asked, "Are you married, sir?"

"Why, yes, I am."

"Is your wife pretty? I mean, is she beautiful—attractive?"

He was uneasy. "Yes, I think she's *most* attractive!"

"Well, if I may turn the phrase around—ever so slightly— y'know you're not exactly Sir Laurence Olivier. What attracted her to *you*?"

The doorman at the Mayfair Hotel opened the car door and smiled pleasantly. "Good afternoon, sir," and I had a feeling he didn't know who I was. We crossed the lobby to the front desk and as I registered I sensed cordiality.

Al took me to dinner at Les Ambassadeurs. I waited a while before getting around to "How're the reservations?"

He answered with both eyebrows. "Enormous. Jack Benny, Judy Garland . . . virtually every American performer who's been here has added to the legend that you're quite the most extraordinary thing in America. Frank Sinatra, for one, was asked whom he thought to be the best entertainer in America and he said, 'Sammy Davis, Jr.!' " He smiled. "His exact words were: 'He can do everything except cook spaghetti.' And, incidentally, it was a superb piece of timing playing the Command Performance on your second day. You couldn't hope for a better introduction to England."

The morning papers had me on page one, and the stories read like a kiss on the lips. I looked across the breakfast table at Murph. "Baby, your employer and friend has successfully run the British Blockade." I went into the bedroom to dress. I looked over my clothes for just the right rehearsal outfit . . . light gray slacks, a six-button blazer, and a white, button-down-collar shirt.

As we walked into the theater a buzzing began among the performers. Morty went backstage and Arthur and I sat in the back of the theater. Nat Cole was onstage. This was his second Command Performance. Most of the guys I'd seen the day before were shooting pictures and writing things down. They waved hello to me and I waved back and mouthed the words "Thank you."

I sat back and watched an act do a beatnik sketch, and they were sensational. Bruce Forsyth, the MC, walked onstage and started in with lines and stories and ring-a-ding-ding, and he was brilliant. Talk had always come back from London: They're old-fashioned. They're square. Like hell. They are solid, fine performers with no old-fashioned connected with it. There could be no thinking: They don't have what we have. Everybody's got it. And I'm hip that if I went to India there'd be a guy there doing it, and as hip as we are here he'd be that hip there.

This was show business at its best. It was Broadway or Hollywood with all the dignity of the old vaudeville in which I'd been raised. I always knew that London had to have great performers if for no other reason than variety had lasted twenty years longer in England than in America, and it's still going strong.

A man onstage peered out into the audience, "Mr. Davis? You're on next, sir. Rehearsal, please."

I walked down the aisle and rather than making a leap onto the stage as I would at home I went around through the door which connects the backstage to the audience and walked onstage. Everyone, from the performers and the stagehands to the maids and cleaning women and the people from the office, the press and performers' friends, had taken seats. As I reached for the microphone the performers began applauding. I never had that kind of courtesy in my life. A performer doesn't know what courtesy is until he goes to London.

Murphy had ordered dinner sent upstairs at the hotel. I couldn't look at it. I had the colds, the hots, and I was shaking like a leaf.

When I got to the theater, the backstage doorman said, "You're dressing on the third floor, sir. Mr. Cole asked us to put you with him."

At each landing kids leaned out of dressing rooms, calling to me, "You'll be a smash tonight." "Don't worry about a thing."

Nat was already in the dressing room with his man and Murphy, and George Rhodes. Murphy had my clothes and makeup laid out. Nat was sitting across from me, not saying a word, doing some quiet drinking. I looked at the bottle next to him. "Nat, you don't drink scotch."

"I'm drinking it tonight."

"I don't drink scotch either. Lemme have some." I filled a

water tumbler with straight scotch, and dumped it, neat. Whack! I felt it land in my stomach but it might have been tomato juice. I looked at Nat. "I ain't *never* been this scared before!"

"Take it easy, we've got three hours to kill."

Arthur burst in. "The place is packed. People are standing in the back, they're out in the streets. . . ."

The show was starting. I could hear the music. Nat was on the bill before me, closing the first half, and he started dressing. When it was time for him to go downstairs I wished him luck, and stood on the third-floor landing to listen.

Nat is the personification of sophistication and calm. When he walks on, whatever nervousness he may feel stays inside of him, it never shows, and it was comforting to hear his smooth, mellow voice—like a touch of home. Then suddenly he cracked. "Oh, God!" Nat Cole has never cracked in his life! He has perfect control under any conditions. Even when he's hoarse, he knows how to play with his voice so that it doesn't come out rough, it becomes even more resonant, a little lower, and richer—never cracking!

He came back upstairs, dripping wet, shaking his head miserably. "I don't *never* want to do *that* no more! Not *ever!*" He collapsed into a chair and pulled his tie open. "Man, they is *out* there tonight!" He beckoned to his valet. "Give me a drink."

I was Charley Trembles but ten times worse than before, like I had a vibrating machine in my mouth. "Whhhhh . . . wwwwwhaddya mean 'they is out there'?"

He looked at me. "Get yourself another drink and sit down. Everybody else get out." He closed the door. "Now listen good. When you get out on the stage you *go* for it. Don't hold back nothin', 'cause they's *ready!* There ain't *nothin'* happened down there yet. You is *it!* They is waitin' fo' *you!*" He'd been talking "colored" to emphasize his point, and to relieve some of the urgency, but now he settled down to business. "When you come on, take your bows slow and easy. Don't let anything rush you. Remember what that cat told us about don't look at the Queen? Forget it! *Damn* protocol. You give her a little peek out of your good eye, or you'll be looking for her when you should be worrying about your song. And at the end of your act they're going to try to rush you off. Don't let them. Just take your time and tear them apart!" He took another shot of scotch but he was cold sober. "*And*, if you don't kill 'em, if you don't, I'm gonna take my fist and beat you to death.

"Now, when it's over and you do your bow, bow to the Queen last. Bow here, here, here, and then give her one of them—I know you know how to bow with all that gracious bull you do—so you've got nothing to worry about."

"What did *you* do, Nat?"

He reached for the bottle again. "I didn't do *none* of that. That's how I know you should do it."

By the grace of God I never performed better in my life.

Cheers and applause roared up at me, crashing all around me, and I stood limp, absorbing the beauty of it. As Bruce "carried" me offstage he whispered, "You were magnificent. Wait in the wings. You were magnificent."

Pandemonium was building out front. A stagehand screamed, "The Queen put down her fan and applauded!" Another answered, aghast, "She did. She really did." Bruce was at center stage leading the applause, motioning for me to come back on. I hesitated because we'd been strictly warned that nobody takes an extra bow. A stagehand pushed me. "He's the boss. Out you go. Can't keep the Queen waiting, y'know."

I was waiting at the gate as May cleared through customs. She smiled, surprised to see me, and I became aware of the boldness of what I'd done. As we walked toward the Rolls-Royce I'd rented, I realized that since my arrival in London I'd seen so many African students, with the bushy hair and the tribal claw marks on their faces, walking down the streets with white women, and nobody so much as looking around at them, that my built-in caution had relaxed, I'd instinctively known that nobody would care.

Her arrival hadn't been mentioned in the papers yet, but in

their own mysterious way her fans had found out that she was in town and there was a crowd of teenage girls waiting with scrapbooks and pictures for her to autograph. She started signing and as the crowd grew she gestured to me, "I'm sorry," and I waved back, "Stay. Crazy. Make it."

The kids spotted me and gathered on both sides of the car shoving pencils and papers to us through the windows.

We cruised around London sightseeing and talking, walking along Savile Row, stopping to sign autographs, experiencing nothing but warmth and kindness.

"When do you figure I should meet your father?"

"As soon as he gets in."

"Yeah. Sure. The sooner, the better. No doubt about it. Look, better still, why don't you bring him to the club for the first show and then we can go out and have supper together."

She was looking at me tenderly. "You don't have to impress him with your talent before you meet him."

"Oh, now wait a *minute* . . ." I was caught like a rat. "Look, I just want him to like me."

"Sammy, I love my parents, so I hope my father likes you and I hope you like him, but if you don't or if he doesn't, it won't change how I feel about you."

"Darling, that's good to hear, but you'll still come to the club first. Anything I can have going for me is just that much gravy, right? And I warn you—you're gonna see a show like I've *never* done. And at dinner I'm going to be so sweet, he may get diabetes. It's a definite 'Sammy Davis, Jr., starring in *The In-Law.*' Hey, listen, what about the suite? Is it okay? You think he'll be comfortable there?"

"The suite is beautiful." She smiled. "Stop worrying so much." I got out of the car at the hotel and she continued on to the airport.

I had a four o'clock appointment with a newspaperman in my suite, then I had an appointment in the hotel bar with a man from one of the English television networks. I dashed out of the suite, twenty minutes late, and headed downstairs. The elevator door opened onto the lobby, I rushed out and collided

with a distinguished-looking gray-haired gentleman. His hat
flew off his head. We both reached for it and bumped heads together. I grabbed the hat but so did he. I tore it out of his hands
trying to give it back to him. When it fell again I made such a
lunge for it that I crushed the crown entirely. I kept bungling
and apologizing and clutching the hat, like a slapstick comic. I
heard a familiar laugh and I froze, bent over, afraid to look up.

"Sammy, I'd like you to meet my father."

May sat next to me at supper and her father was across from
us. Throughout the meal I'd been rephrasing the question in my
mind: Sir, I'm sure you know that May and I want to get married. . . . Maybe I should wait? Not push too much? Maybe let
him get to know me for a few days? We were having our coffee
and we'd still done nothing but chitchat.

He put down his cup and said, "We have so far spoken of
all but what we wish most to say. Sammy, we know much
about you. Maybritt has written us many letters . . . we will be
proud to have you for a son."

"You mean it's—it's all right?"

"Perhaps you thought we would care that you have a different skin. I will speak candidly because you will be my son. When
Maybritt told us her desire to marry you we had fear for the
hardship such a marriage faces in America, where you will make
your home. But we believe that if your love for each other is
strong enough then there are no important problems which cannot be overcome. Your skin is not important to us." He touched
his heart. "We care what is here. The happiness in Maybritt's letters is in her face. And we have never seen it there like this before." He smiled warmly. "You make us all very happy."

I had to excuse myself from the table. Through all the excitement of the Command Performance and the opening, this
had always been there—the wondering what he'd say, how he'd
feel when he finally saw me face to face.

I hid in a hallway near the kitchen unable to hold back racking sobs. I felt May's arms around me. "Sharlie Brown . . ."

I gave her my handkerchief. We pulled ourselves together and started back to the table, but her father had already paid the check and was waiting for us in the lobby.

I still had my late show to do and they were going back to the hotel. I walked them to my car and shook hands with May's father. "Thank you." He drew me toward him and embraced me. "God bless you, Sammy."

One of the London papers ran a short piece: "Is May Britt to Wed Sammy Davis, Jr.?" As the days passed, people sent me others from American papers—the same sort of thing, but rough: "The gasps around London are over Sammy Davis, Jr., and May Britt and their 'we don't give a damn who knows it' attitude."

I told May, "I think the best thing we can do is announce it quickly and kill the 'are they or aren't they?' jazz before it starts in heavy. If we come out and tell 'em, 'Yes, we're engaged,' it'll get a flurry of attention and be forgotten. People love to speculate, but once they know something for sure they'll lose interest."

We called a press conference to put the matter to rest and answer everybody's questions: "Ladies and gentlemen, Miss Britt and I have been subject lately to newspaper items questioning whether or not we are seeing each other and if we intend to be married. You asked me that yourselves when I arrived here. At that time I could not properly say 'yes' because I hadn't yet met, and received the approval of, Miss Britt's father. However, I am now at liberty to tell you that I have that approval and we are engaged to be married.

"I hope to impress upon you that I would not call you all here to make this announcement as if I believe it to be earth-shaking news. You've been overwhelmingly generous to me and I wouldn't have the audacity to impose upon you for publicity's own sake. We hope you will publish it for the one reason that we are anxious to avoid the unnecessary and sometimes vicious public speculation . . ."

"When do you expect to be married?"

"Probably in October."

"How long have you known each other?"

"We met in Hollywood several months ago while I was filming *Ocean's Eleven* or just about to . . ."

An American reporter from one of the wire services stood up. "Sammy, how do you think this'll go over in the States?"

"I don't think it's something that should have to 'go over.' "

"Well, uh, whaddya think's gonna happen when you get back home? Do you think you'll ever be able to work there again?"

"I can't imagine that my career is so flimsy that it could be ruined by marriage, but if it is, then it's really not worth having, is it?"

He sat down but he wasn't satisfied. Throughout the questioning by the English reporters, simple, pleasant questions such as where we'd live and how many children we hoped for, he kept shooting the zingies at me: "Are you announcing it over here because you're afraid to do it at home?"

"No, sir. We're announcing it here for the reason I stated clearly at the beginning of this conference."

"I see . . . Well, let me ask you this: What happens if you find you can't go home?"

The English press elbowed him out of the way with their own questions but soon he was back again.

"Isn't this the first marriage between a Negro man and a blond, white movie star?"

I could feel the muscles in my face tightening. "Perhaps. I don't keep track."

Again the English press came to my side. They'd already asked everything they needed to know and it was obvious they were just re-asking questions trying to nose this guy out, hoping he'd lay off, but he wouldn't.

"Isn't it kinda rough sledding at home on mixed marriages? I mean, the chances of making them work are . . ."

"Wait a minute. I don't know what America *you're* talking about, but I know something about mixed marriages. There are many of them and eighty-five percent of them work. Eighty-five percent. That's higher than among people who are so-called 'suited' for each other racially and religiously. They work better because nobody who's faced with it would step out of his or her race to marry unless the love was so great that they felt they could not be happy without it."

"Well . . . what about the children?"

One of the English reporters said, "For crying out loud, he's already said they hope to have many healthy, happy babies. If you missed the exact wording I'll be delighted to give it to you. This isn't a trial, you know."

"But he still hasn't told me what I want to know about the kids . . ."

Out of at least fifty reporters he was the only one who had been attacking, looking for trouble, and I felt a mixture of dislike for him and embarrassment that it had to be an American. "What *about* them? Exactly what would you like to know?"

"Well . . . what about them? . . . You know what I mean . . ."

He was gutless, and I wasn't about to make it any easier for him. "Exactly what are you driving at?"

"Well—I don't know. I mean, well . . ." He looked at the floor. "What do you figure they'll look like?"

An English reporter murmured, "Oh, now really!" and a heavy silence settled over the room.

I said, "We expect them to look like babies."

"No, you know what I mean . . . Do you have some kind of preference about color?" He finally squeezed the words out. "Uh . . . how would Miss Britt feel if her kid turns out to be black—you know what I mean?"

"Buddy, I've known what you meant for forty-five minutes. Now as far as our children are concerned it would not matter to us, in terms of our love for the child, if it were white, brown, or polka dot. We don't think in terms of color. All we care about is that if God graces us with a child it will grow up to be healthy and love us as much as we'll love it from the moment its life begins."

I was leaving the hotel to do some shopping when I felt Arthur staring at me.

"Arthur. What in the *hell* are you looking at?"

"I'm not quite sure. You'll think I'm putting you on, but since you've been over here—you've become good-looking."

Murphy said, "He's right, Sammy. You look different. You really do. There's something about your face . . ."

I had an idea what they meant and how it had happened. I had stopped thinking of myself as a Negro. The awareness wasn't there because the constant reminders were gone: there were no El Moroccos I couldn't go to; I wasn't invited to "the best private clubs which accept Negroes," I was invited to the best private clubs, period. I could go anyplace that was open to the position I'd earned in life, and without the automatic evaluating: Do I dare? Is it worth the aggravation? I could walk down a street with May and enjoy the simple pleasure of feeling her hand in mine and knowing that I was walking down a street with the girl I love; there was no wondering who was revolted or infuriated, or frowning, or tolerating us. My face wasn't tight. The jaw had relaxed. The skin lay smooth on my face. I hadn't been aware it was happening. It just sneaked up on me like a gentle sleep for all the nerves and reflexes.

When we finished shopping I went to the Dorchester for an appointment with some picture people at the American Club.

The moment I entered I felt the old familiar atmosphere. The awareness returned. I sat there watching them watching me. They weren't cold, they were friendly, but they were appraising, measuring, discussing me, and I was listening over my shoulder again, on guard. I'd merely walked through a door and I was back in the vise.

And this was only the road company. In a week I'd be going

back to the heart of it, back to the cooker, back to the constant anticipating of problems that might or might not materialize— the eternal war of nerves. And suddenly I thought: Why should I? Why drag May through pointless agonies? Why not live in London and be treated magnificently? Why not travel half the world free of unnecessary burdens? I can accept any one of countless English offers, stay over on an extended visit, and return to the States for a few months every year—nobody'd even realize what I was doing. I projected to the day when we'd have our first child. Why sentence children to a life of built-in scorn and hatred? Why pass as close to hell as man can get when there's another road?

When I was able to make an exit from the club I hurried to the street like a man groping for air. A workman in a pit popped up. "Oh, I say . . . would you mind terribly if I asked for an autograph?" I gave it to him, thanked him, and continued down the street, smiling back at people who recognized me. An English bobby stopped me on the corner. "Mr. Davis, may I impose upon you, sir? Saw you on the telly." "When's the happy day?" "Have a big family, sir. That's the best kind." "No offense, sir, but your fiancée, Miss Britt, is such a beautiful lady." . . .

I burst into the living room. "Murph! Get busy on the phone and place a call to Will. Tell him I'm not coming home. Tell him to cancel out everything. I'm staying in London."

He nodded slowly. "Okay, Sammy."

"Well, don't just sit there. Get hot on it."

"Sure, Sammy. I'll take care of it right away." But he didn't move off the sofa. He just smiled like Charley Philosopher.

"You son of a bitch. You think you know me pretty damned well, don't you?"

It had felt good to get it out of my system, to rebel, but I knew I was far from ready to put my country down to adopt another.

I looked through the window at the garden of the hotel where I'd thought May and I would be married. If I got married in England I'd be running, just as surely as if I moved there permanently. I couldn't start off by ducking the first problem that faced us or it would be one compromise after another.

At Siegi's, after we'd ordered dinner I talked it over with May.

As our car approached the club the chauffeur said, "There seems to be a commotion outside the Pigalle."

A truck with loudspeakers on top of it was in front of the club. Pickets wearing swastika armbands were carrying signs: "GO HOME, NIGGER." . . . "SAMMY, BACK TO THE TREES." . . . "GET DIVORCED FIRST, SLAG." . . .

The chauffeur said, "Mosley's men."

"Who's Mosley?"

"He's got the Nazi party here."

"I didn't know there *were* Nazis anymore."

May asked, "Do you know what they mean by the word 'slag'?"

I shook my head.

She asked the chauffeur. He didn't answer immediately. "I'm sorry, ma'am, it's a slang word for a white woman who associates with Negro men."

The sound-truck driver spotted us and followed our car to the stage entrance, his loudspeakers blaring savagely, venomously.

In the dressing room May picked up a magazine, sat down, and began to leaf through the pages. "Have you got a Salem, Sammy?" I gave her the cigarette and lit it for her. "Thank you, Sharlie Brown." She continued reading.

"May?"

She looked up.

"Doesn't it bother you . . . what happened out there . . . ?"

"The only thing that bothers me is that maybe it bothers you."

"It could have been worse, I guess."

"Okay."

She was smiling as she read, but I saw the moisture around

her eyes. She had all the guts in the world, but it was heart-breaking to know that she had no preparation for this, no experience to help her through it.

Cassandra, the most widely read columnist in England, ran a front-page editorial in the *Daily Mirror*:

> CASSANDRA WRITES
> A LETTER TO SAMMY DAVIS, JNR.
> Dear Sammy Davis,
>
> I don't know you. You don't know me. I have never seen your show and I assume you have never seen mine. All I know is what I read in the papers.
>
> But this is just to tell you that the beastly racial abuse to which you were subjected outside the Pigalle Restaurant, when Mosley's louts followed you waving banners with the words "Go Home, Nigger," has nothing to do with what English people feel and think.
>
> I, and maybe I can speak for a few others (say, 51,680,000 minus 100 of the population of this country), feel revolted, angry and ashamed at what happened.
>
> Yours sincerely,
> Cassandra

The Mosley thing was a forecast. For me hate held no unknown quantity. It might take a different form but essentially there was nothing they could do or say that hadn't already been done and said, and above all I had the experience of surviving it. But could May withstand its pressures? She'd shrugged off the friends who'd stopped calling, she'd absorbed the Mosley thing, but would she be able to absorb constant disapproval, suddenly closed doors, expulsion from movies? Sure, she's a strong girl with a mind of her own, but no man, no matter how strong he is, can step into the ring for his first fight and take on the heavyweight champion. I had to protect her from as much of it as possible. I had to keep all of my strength and experience constantly at her side. I had to be thinking ahead of them, running interference, blocking, shielding, anticipating, softening anything that might be waiting for us at home.

34

Mr. and Mrs. Ernst Hugo Wilkens
request the pleasure of your company
at the wedding reception of their daughter
May
and
Sammy Davis, Jr.
on Sunday, October Sixteenth
Nineteen Hundred and Sixty
at six o'clock in the evening
Beverly Hilton Hotel
L'Escoffier Room

"It's beautiful," I told May. "Incidentally, I spoke to Frank and asked him to stand up for me."

"What did he say?"

"He knew it before I asked him. It was just a formality."

I glanced through the morning papers. Louella Parsons: "His best friends have been unable to talk Sammy Davis, Jr., out of the May Britt marriage. The reception will take place at one of the Hollywood hotels."

We were in every column. Approval and disapproval. It's a strange thing to find that your engagement is a case history, something to which each person was attaching his own significance—ten different things to ten different people, each starting from the point of seeing it as an interracial marriage, each viewing us as either hero or villain, none seeming to grasp the basic point: you can hate by color but you can't love by it; that I'd asked May to marry me, I had not said, "Will you intermarry me?"

Mama's driver and companion, Rudy Duff, brought in the mail. The usual assortment of letters from strangers—the few who took the trouble to let us feel their support, and the envelopes with no return addresses, the hate letters. One was addressed to both of us and I wondered if May was getting any of them at the studio.

"Rudy, while I'm out of town, May is going to be coming in and out of here with the decorator. Please check the mail carefully. Make sure none of this filth is lying around."

I had the day free, so I called May.

"Sammy, guess what? I was passing a store on Wilshire and there in the window was exactly the kind of dining set I was telling you about. Six chairs. It's *beautiful!* I'm in the store now. How would Sharlie Brown like to drive over here so we can look at it together?"

"Darling, I'd love to but I can't . . . I've got a heavy day. But if you like it then go ahead and order it."

"No, I want to be sure you like it too." Her excitement had paled. "Do you think maybe you could make it tomorrow?"

I hesitated, despising the situation that was forcing me to refuse her such a simple pleasure, stealing what any engaged girl was entitled to. But what could be gained by giving her the pleasure of looking at some furniture if in the middle of it somebody cuts her in half with a lousy look or an out-and-out insult? "Darling, I'll tell you what. It's in the window, we'll run over there tonight and take a look."

"Okay." There was a pause, then: "Hey, that's a *great*

idea!" Her voice was overcheerful. "Oh boy, I like that idea *much* better. If we do our window-shopping at night we can have privacy, we won't be bothered by a lot of autograph jazz. Gee, I've got a brilliant fiancé."

I hung up heartsick that she was beginning to catch on, that it was inescapable, that the atmosphere of fear and caution and compromise, of walking on eggs, was surrounding her, slowly dragging her into the web, stifling all that love for life—forcing it into the prison of my skin.

35

"Dear Nigger Bastard, I see Frank Sinatra is going to be best man at your abortion. Well, it's good to know the kind of people supporting Kennedy before it's too late. [signed] An ex-Kennedy vote."

The already stale news that Frank would be my best man continued making the front pages and too often, by "coincidence," alongside it were stories about Frank campaigning for Kennedy.

I too was devoting all my spare time to campaigning, in Los Angeles, in Watts, in some twenty large cities. I went with Ethel Kennedy, or Bobby, and on some occasions with John. The Broadway and Hollywood columns were alive with political humor: "If Kennedy's elected his problem is: should he appoint Sammy Davis, Jr., Ambassador to Israel or the Congo?" . . . "Public opinion experts say that when Frank Sinatra appears at Sammy Davis, Jr.'s interracial marriage it will cost Kennedy as many votes, maybe more, as the crooner has been able to swing via his successful JFK rallies."

I hadn't been in Vegas twenty minutes when I got word that the bookmakers were offering three to one that Frank wouldn't show at my wedding. Frank, Dean, and Peter had come down for the weekend and I was in the steam room with Frank. He asked, "How's she standing up under all the garbage?"

"So far so good. But the momentum keeps growing. At least if I could be with her—but I figure the less we're seen together until the wedding, the less they'll have to work with."

When I spoke with May between shows she said, "Frank called me a little while ago. Just to say hello and find out how I am."

I saw him the next afternoon. "I talked to May last night, Frank. Thanks."

"See you at the wedding, Charley. I'll leave Hawaii a day early to make sure I won't run into weather."

When I got to the dressing room I looked through the mail. Somebody had sent me a clipping, a two-panel cartoon. The first was a picture of me dressed as a butler, grinning and serving a platter of fried chicken and watermelon to John F. Kennedy. In the second panel I was sitting at the table eating it with him. The caption was: "Will it still be the *White* House?"

After the shows, I put a "Don't Disturb" on the door of my suite and sat in the living room by myself. Fair or not, my wedding was giving the Nixon people the opportunity to ridicule Kennedy and hurt him at the polls. I could imagine the pressure Frank must be under: eighty guys telling him, "Don't be a fool. You've worked hard for Kennedy, now do you want to louse him up?" And it was understandable. If he stood up for me at a controversial interracial marriage only a few weeks before the election there would be votes he'd lose for Kennedy. And the innuendo and publicity so far was only a hint of what would happen after he appeared at the wedding and they had a piece of hard news to work with.

How can I call myself his friend when I'm keeping him in this kind of a bind? If he's holding out for me like this, how can I not be equally his friend and take him off the spot?

But aside from the fact that I couldn't imagine being married without him present at my wedding, at this point if Frank did not appear it would backfire. They'd make it look as if Kennedy's staff had suggested it. Maybe he'd regain the bigot vote but he'd lose some of the liberals and a lot of the Negro vote.

There was only one way to take the pressure off. Postpone the wedding. I knew he was at the Springs with Peter.

"Hi ya, Charley, what's new?"

"Frank, we're going to have to put the wedding off. You wouldn't believe the problems a poor soul has trying to get married: there's a hitch getting the Escoffier Room for the reception, the rabbi's booked for a bar mitzvah . . . I don't know when it'll be but I'll give you plenty of notice."

"You're lying, Charley."

I hesitated, but it was pointless. "Look, it's best that we postpone till after the election."

There was silence. Then: "You don't have to do that."

"I want to. All the talk . . ."

"Screw the talk."

"I know, but it's better this way."

When finally he spoke again, his voice was almost a whisper. "I'll be there whenever it is. You know that, don't you?"

"I know that, Frank."

"I'd never ask you to do a thing like this. Not your wedding. I'd never ask that."

"That's why it's up to me to be saying it."

"You're a better man than I am, Charley. I don't know if I could do this for you, or for anyone . . ."

"You've *been* doing it, haven't you?"

I heard him put down the phone and then Peter was on the line. There were no jokes. None of the usual insults we do. He said, "Frank can't talk anymore." If he got that choked up now, if he could break down in the middle of a phone call, then the pressure must have been greater than I'd imagined.

"Charley?"

"Yes, Peter?"

"Charley, I . . . it's beautiful of you."

I stared at May's picture on my night table. What could I say to her? "We're postponing our marriage because it's so repulsive to some people that they won't want to vote for Kennedy." How does a man explain this to the one person above all others from whom he wants respect and admiration?

I got into my car and drove aimlessly around downtown Vegas, racked by the picture of her excitement of the past few weeks, rushing around and getting the house ready, waiting for her parents to arrive from Sweden, sending out invitations, fitting her dress . . . I went into a drugstore and sat down in a phone booth.

"May, I have something important to tell you, but before I do I want you to know that this is the first and only thing that concerns us both that I'll ever do without consulting you." As I explained it, I knew by her silence that she was hurt. "Darling, it boils down to this: during a period of over twenty years Frank has been aces high, aces up—everything a guy could be to me. Now he needs something from me, so there can be no evaluating, no hesitating, no limit. It's got to be to the end of the earth and back for him if he needs it."

"I understand," she said, "and I agree with you. There was nothing else to do."

Rogers and Cowan, who were handling my public relations, sent an announcement to the press: The Sammy Davis, Jr.–May Britt wedding has been postponed due to a legal technicality in Miss Britt's Mexican divorce from her previous husband.

That was the lie and that's how we told it.

There were bomb threats on my opening at the Huntington Hartford Theater in Los Angeles: "We've got guns and we've got hand grenades and we're coming to blow up the place." "Is that black bastard still going to open there? There's a bomb in the theater right now." The stage manager had called the police and they were searching the building. Another call came in: "We'll fix him and we'll get his nigger-loving girlfriend too."

I called May. "We've had some threats and I don't want you here tonight."

"Are you going to do the show?"

"Yes."

"Then I'll be there. Nobody is going to frighten me away from you."

I called the sheriff of Los Angeles County and hired ten off-duty detectives to be sitting in front of and behind her seat.

Murphy brought me a folded sheet of paper. "Somebody slipped this under the stage door." A bullet was drawn in the center of the paper. Below, it said, "I'm going to shoot you dead during your show. Guess when?"

Cranks, sadists, idiots. Yet among the empty threats could be the one that might materialize. I walked to the wings. Policemen were stationed all over the backstage area. I looked through the curtain, scanning the audience. How do you entertain them while wondering if a bomb will explode? How do you do two hours of singing, dancing, and jokes, distracted by the thought that at any moment a lunatic might shoot you?

On the day of our wedding, people were leaning out their windows all the way up the hill with telescopic lenses trained on my house, crowded onto the porches of the houses above us. Reporters and newsreel men clustered in front of the door. Photographers were perched in trees to get a free line of sight to the doorway.

"Sammy and May, you are standing in front of me to join your lives even as your hands are joined together, and custom dictates that I, as your rabbi, give you some advice. Your marriage is something more than just two people in love, and it is most certainly that or I have never seen two people in love in twenty years of the ministry. But as you come together as man and wife something more is involved. You are people without prejudice. You represent the value of the society that many of us dream about but, I suspect, hesitate to enter. As such, because you are normal in an abnormal society—society will treat you as sick. To be healthy among the sick is to be treated as sick as if the others were healthy . . ."

The day after our wedding the manager of the Geary Theater in San Francisco called me at home. "Mr. Davis, we've had a number of bomb threats and threats against your life."

May was still resting. She'd been up late packing for San Francisco, our first trip together and what we had planned would be the honeymoon we lost when we postponed the wedding.

I sat on the bed. "Darling . . ." I forced the words out. "I'm sorry but you can't come to San Francisco. We can say it's wrong, it's lousy, but that's not going to change it. In the days of King Arthur, or the days of the Romans, they'd have a trial by ordeal: they'd say, 'We'll put him in with a hungry lion,' and if he survived he was set free. It's going to be like that with us. If we can survive the first year then I think we'll have it made."

"Do you really think it will take a whole year before they'll leave us alone?"

"I don't know. But I do know that I have to protect what I hold dear. We'll adopt a security procedure that we'll follow until the pressure is off. You won't arrive in any city with me. I'll go ahead and get a feeling of what's up. When it looks safe I'll be on the phone telling you to grab the first plane. Meanwhile I've hired someone who'll stay here while I'm gone. Rudy'll be here too, but it won't hurt to have another man in the house."

"A guard?"

"He's a private detective."

"Do you think . . . do I really need that?"

"No. Nor do I expect the house to burn down but I carry fire insurance against the remote chance that it might."

The threats and hate mail continued heavily in San Francisco. I told May not to come. "Maybe Reno."

I called her from Reno. "I'm sorry but you can't come here . . ."

And then a few weeks after that I told her, "I'm sorry but you can't come to Chicago . . ."

The applause increased, kept growing louder, but I could only think of it as an ideal shield for the sound of a gunshot.

Despite the plainclothesmen spread all over the Latin Casino in Camden, New Jersey, despite every possible precaution, I found myself unable to devote myself fully to each song, each dance: I was looking for hints of trouble, studying hazy faces as far as I could see into the lights. As I did the impressions, my mind's ear wasn't tuned entirely to Cagney or Robinson, and as I sang, only half of me was absorbed in the words of the song while the other half was praying that somebody hadn't left a window or a door unlocked at the house. Somewhere out there, in this audience or the next, was the guy who'd make trouble. Or was he in Hollywood creeping up to the house planning some horrible revenge against May?

Suddenly I wasn't so sure where I could best protect her. Even with a professional security man there was always the human factor. Maybe it would be safer to have her where I could be on top of her security. And I wanted to see my wife. So far, more than ninety percent of our marriage had taken place on the phone. I took a chance and brought her to New York.

Earl Wilson reported, "The Sammy Davis, Jr.'s are expecting. If it's a boy they'll name him Mark Sidney, or Tracey if it's a girl." Hundreds of letters arrived at the Copa: "God will strike you down for what you are doing. You have sinned against God's will." "What about the children?"

May pulled back the curtains excitedly. "Look. It must have snowed all night." I put my arm around her and we stood at the window of our suite in the Sherry Netherland admiring the beauty of Fifth Avenue. "Sammy, can we go walking in the snow?"

"Darling, may I tell you something?"

"Sure."

"That's the *worst idea I ever heard!* A woman takes a singer who dances—a dancing singer—and wants to turn him into a ski instructor? First of all, have you any idea what happens when a small colored fella like me goes walking around in snowdrifts? Right away people point and yell, 'Hey, look, it's a penguin, it's a penguin.' "

I stood at the window watching the snowflakes swirling through the trees in Central Park, wishing I could take her out and we could run around like a couple of nitwits. I had bought her a mink coat at Maximilian. Knowing I couldn't afford it she'd insisted I return it, but I wouldn't. It was for self. It was a way of compensating, a way of saying, "It ain't *all* bad. You're locked out of this, you're locked out of that, you've lost your contract at Fox, they don't want you anymore, you're a nigger lover, but look—I can give you this." I yearned to take her out in it—window-shopping along Fifth Avenue, going into some of the stores and buying things together. We'd had dozens of nice invitations I didn't accept. Even the idea of taking her to Danny's or the Harwyn, where it was as safe as any public place could be—still, the hotel and dressing room were safer. Nobody could insult her there or do icy stares from across the room.

May was putting on her boots. "I'm going for a walk around the block. I've got to get some air."

"Why don't you wear your mink coat?"

She was surprised. "I'm saving it to wear for the first time with my husband."

I wiped the frost off a window and watched her as she turned the corner at 59th Street. Paul Newer, my bodyguard, was a few yards behind her. It had been more than ten days of confinement to the club and the hotel. There'd been "How come we don't go to Danny's?" and "What's the Harwyn like?" and I'd covered with trumped-up reasons why we had to be at the hotel: an interview, business meetings, exhaustion . . . The frost was re-forming on the glass, blurring the outside, reducing the world to the rooms of our suite.

She stamped the last of the snow off her boots, her face pink from the cold, smiling as though she'd opened a safety valve and all the tension had been released. I helped her off with her coat. "How was it?"

"*Beautiful.* There's hardly anybody on the streets and the snow is so fresh . . ."

"I got four tickets for *Camelot* for the matinee tomorrow."

She beamed at me. "You mean my husband and I are really honest-to-God saying to heck with meetings and stuff and going to a matinee?"

"And I've asked Jane and Burt to come with us." Apart from being friends whom I know she liked, having another couple with us, a white couple, would dilute the impact of just the two of us together.

I woke up afraid. I felt it physically, like whirring motors in my stomach, down my legs, and an ache in my heart for her when she finds out she's not a beautiful girl going to a matinee with her husband, but a "nigger lover." It was out of the question to risk it. I knew I couldn't protect her forever but I had to wait until I could be sure that we had enough background together so that the threads of our marriage could absorb the shock of the abuse that was waiting for us outside.

She was moving around quietly, believing I was still asleep. She'd washed her hair and had a towel around her neck. I didn't move. I heard her open the bedroom door, then close it softly. Her mink coat was hanging outside the closet door. Under it was an orange dress and pink beads. Her boots were on the floor directly under the coat. It was one o'clock. It seemed like a long time before I heard the door opening.

"Sammy? It's one-thirty."

". . . five minutes, darling, just five more minutes . . ." I heard the phone ring in the other room.

"Sammy, that was Jane and Burt. The traffic is heavy and we should be waiting downstairs or we'll miss the overture."

I rolled over, keeping my eyes closed. "Five more minutes . . ."

"But, Sammy, if you don't get up now we'll miss the show." I could smell her perfume. I didn't want to look at her and see her all dressed and ready with her makeup on. "Well, if you're this tired you'd better sleep for another hour or two." I was aching to tell her, "Darling, I don't want to sleep away our day.

I love you and I want to see you happy. I don't want to keep your beauty locked in a closet. I'd give anything to be able to take you to the show, to take you anywhere, but I don't dare." I stayed in bed long after she'd left the room, certain I'd done the best thing, yet what was it costing?

I stood in the doorway of the living room, wearing a robe and pajamas. May got up and hugged me. I held her tight. Jane and Burt were sitting on the couch. "I'm sorry, guys. I just couldn't have gotten out of bed if my life depended on it."

Burt shrugged. "We've already seen it."

"Look, I've been doing two shows a night and three on weekends and I plain ran out of strength."

May poured a cup of coffee for me and looked at Jane and Burt. "Coffee?"

Jane smiled pointedly. "No, thanks. We're already awake."

"Hey," May said, "he's my husband and if I'm not angry at him, then you guys have no right to be."

They didn't care about the show. They were annoyed and puzzled by the way I was treating May. There was no way they could understand without my telling them and it was better that they didn't understand and couldn't pity her. I played it Charley Cheerful. "I've got a swingin' idea for dinner tonight. Instead of ordinary room service we'll have a dinner party. The guys'll wear black tie and the girls long dresses. We'll order caviar, lobster cocktails, steaks or maybe some duck. Then for dessert we can have a soufflé, cordials with our coffee—we'll do it banquet style for two hours and we'll keep a waiter and a captain here to serve the whole meal . . ."

Jane and Burt left to get dressed and sent flowers. I'd ordered a magnum of champagne and poured drinks for the four of us. The evening went off with the luxury I'd planned, but all I'd accomplished was to raise the level of the prison.

The mail brought our invitation to John F. Kennedy's inauguration. I felt May watching me and I was embarrassed to be so proud of receiving the invitation. I copped out, "These are not exactly being sent to every cat on the corner."

She squeaked out, "I'm very impressed . . ." Tears were streaming down her face, which had a huge sunshine smile on it.

"Hey, don't cry."

"I'm not crying . . ."

"Well, then you've sprung a helluva leak."

"I'm so happy for you, Sharley Brown."

We sat there in a happy funk, allowing the moment to press back some of the twisted muscles, to knead them soft and back into shape. Then I said, "Tomorrow it's a definite Bergdorf Goodman and buy the most elegant, most knock-their-eyes-out gown you can find. That will be for the Inaugural Ball. Frank's putting together the show and I'll be performing. You'll also need something afternoony, a Chanel suit, for the swearing-in ceremony."

"Sammy, I thought we were going to be on an economy drive."

"Darling, if when I was a kid in Harlem somebody had told me, 'You'll be performing at the White House,' I'd have saved my money for your dress. However, as I just got this news today . . . Look, don't worry about it, we'll save money later. Which reminds me, I'd better call Sy Devore and get a new tux made."

"But you have fifteen or twenty tuxedos."

"Would I be so crass as to wear a previously worn tux to entertain the President? And after I wear it at the White House it's going into mothballs."

The Philadelphia *Inquirer* ran a story: "Sammy Davis, Jr., will be among the luminaries attending the presidential inauguration parties. The singer-dancer's performances at the Latin Casino in Camden will be canceled for the night of January 20."

Three days before the inauguration I was in my hotel room when Murphy woke me at eleven in the morning. "Sammy, President Kennedy's secretary is calling . . ."

It was Evelyn Lincoln, JFK's personal secretary, whom I knew from the campaign. "Mr. Davis . . . Sammy . . . the President has asked me to tell you that he does not want you to be present at his inauguration. There is a situation into which he is being forced and to fight it would be counterproductive to the goals he's set. He very much hopes you will understand . . ."

I felt a torrent of words bubbling up in my throat: "No, don't ask me to understand. Don't do this. Don't humiliate me. Don't cut me in half in front of my wife. In front of all the people I've told about it, my family, my friends, my audiences. My God, my wife called her parents in Sweden! If John can do this to me, then tell him I hate him. Please!! I have goals too. I campaigned, I earned better . . ."

But I didn't say any of that. I said, "I understand. Thank you for calling."

Murphy was looking at me fearfully.

"Cancel our reservations to Washington, Murph. And tell them at the club that I won't be needing that night off."

I knew that Murphy was hurting more for me than I was, and *I* was just short of bleeding. "But, Sammy, you worked hard for him—he told you 'Thanks,' I heard him."

"They don't want me, baby. Now let's not make a three-act play out of it." I lay on my back trying to understand it. The election was over. The votes were in! We'd all worked so hard for Jack to be President . . . and throughout those moments you're never aware of the difference. I was with May at some occasions. I'd introduced her to them. They had seen me with white women and black women, and there were never any raised eyebrows. They were sophisticates in every sense of the word.

Obviously my presence would be bad for him. I knew that I was expected to understand that. I was supposed to be worldly. To understand. My hurt and embarrassment turned to anger at my friends, at Frank and Peter: why didn't they stand up for me? But I knew they had, to the extent they could.

Murphy opened the door. "Peter's calling."

"Sam . . . Pierre told me what happened. They talked the President into it. They said, 'Look, this is our first time out. Let's not do anything to fuck up. We've got Southern senators, bigoted congressmen. They see you as too liberal to start with. Peter Lawford's an actor, we've still got residue from 'The Clan's Taking Over the White House.' If we have Sammy here, is he going to bring his wife? We can't ask him not to bring her.' The President said, 'Okay, then dump it. Call Sam. He'll understand.'

"Bobby argued for you, 'That's bullshit! The man campaigned.' But he was overruled. He got so angry he walked out of the rest of the discussion."

I suppose I was pleased to hear that about Bobby, but I had the desire to slam the phone so hard it would go through the floor. How could I tell May? What could I do to soften it, to make it less embarrassing? To not have her feel sorry for me?

36

A man is not complete until he sees a baby he has made, and by the grace of God I stood there looking at mine, seeing her tiny face and hands, her whole delicate self. I watched the nurse taking Tracey away until she was out of sight. I wasn't ready to go downstairs and talk to people. I went into the waiting room and I prayed that by the time our baby was grown she would live in a world of people who would not care about a layer of skin. But was that possible? Ever? Are people willing to change? Would they ever be willing to understand a child's innocence? I gazed out the window, grateful for the talent I had been given and because of it the thought that perhaps I could have something to do with affecting the world so that someday my children, or maybe only my grandchildren, would be able, finally, to stop fighting.

I never lost that feeling. One night, when Tracey was a little girl, May and I made one of the most rewarding decisions of our life together. Candles were burning on the dining table, which was set for just us. "I've been thinking that if God allows us to have more children, that's wonderful, but I'd like to adopt some Negro children too. There are too many colored kids that are orphans, they have nobody that wants them, nobody comes to get them . . ."

"Ohhh, Sharley Brown, I agree with you so much! Maybe we can start with a big brother for Tracey."

I was relieved that she was enthusiastic about adopting Negro children, that some of the wars we had been through had not weakened her, made her lean toward an easier road.

Soon we adopted Mark. He and Jeff (whom we adopted a year later) are every bit our sons, and we have always loved them as much as any parents, biological or otherwise, could love their children.

I was at home between dates when I got a call from London inviting me to play the Royal Command Performance again. It coincided with my date for a one-man show at the Prince of Wales Theater. I described the elegance of the evening to May: ". . . with the Queen and the royal family and all those cats wearing sashes and medals. Darling, you are going to see a small colored lad perform so good that the Queen's gonna say, 'I ain't leavin' here to go to heaven.' "

"Sammy . . . I'm dying to be with you in London, and to see that performance . . . but I don't see how I can go."

"Why not?"

"I can't leave Tracey."

"We'll bring her with us."

May shook her head. "She can't travel."

I didn't realize how serious she was, so I kidded it. "Darling, it's no problem. There's a new law that until you have a tooth you don't need a passport."

"Seriously, Tracey's too young to travel all the way over there and to live in a hotel."

"Then we can leave her home. We'll get a great nurse. Mama will be here, and my dad can look in every day."

"No. I want her to know the walls of her nursery and to hear my voice and your voice, to never have a moment when suddenly there's a nurse she doesn't recognize. If we give her that kind of security at the beginning, then if she has some rough times later, hopefully she'll have all the feelings of self to help her over them. And it's not just racial. We talked about this before we got married: I want to raise my own child. I'm not going to be one of those Hollywood mothers who stop by the nursery for ten minutes a day. I want our daughter to know us."

"Darling, I agree, but can't Tracey start getting to know us when we come back from London? My life, which I can't change, is traveling. When are we going to see each other?"

"Whenever we can during these early years. Sammy, it's not how I'd choose to be married, but we made a commitment to an unborn child—to give her whatever she needs—so if anyone's got to bend, it has to be us."

I stepped off the plane and onto the front pages of four London newspapers. Not a little box saying "Sammy Davis is back again," which would have been plenty considering I hadn't done anything yet, but front-page photos with "S.D. Jnr. Is Back," "The Prince of Wails," "Mr. Wonderful," that kind of thing. Of course, I didn't exactly hurt my case by stepping off the plane in a British-cut double-breasted suit, wearing a bowler, and carrying a tightly wrapped umbrella. It was all the sadder that May wasn't with me. After all the downers we'd been through, I wished she could have seen her husband flying.

I called her at twelve every night after the show, catching her at four in the afternoon Los Angeles time. On closing night she said, "Tracey and I have been sitting here eating birthday cake and waiting for you to call. I'll put her on."

"No. Stop! Look, I love our daughter but I am not having a phone conversation with her for at least twelve more years."

"Well, then will you sing 'Happy Birthday' to her?"

"I'm not singing 'Happy Birthday' to a one-year-old. Just tell her Dad says, 'Have a Fabulous First.' Or tell her I'm sending a birthday card."

"Sammy . . . don't you know the words?"

I tried to whisper. "May, listen, I'm calling you from my dressing room. I'm in the back room. Out in the living room is

Noël Coward, who's giving a party for me tonight in his town house. And all the muckety-mucks are here with him. Sir Laurence Olivier, Albert Finney, Peter O'Toole, Michael Caine, Stanley Baker, and the cream of the British theater, plus the Duke and Duchess of Kent or York—I can't remember. I've just received a standing ovation with oak-leaf clusters, with the audience singing 'Auld Lang Syne' to *me*. Fifteen hundred people. Now, are you going to make me have them hear me singing into a telephone like a Western Union man?"

"I think it would be sharming. 'The great star is just a loving father at heart.' "

"May, please . . ."

"Tracey and I both have our ears to the phone."

I sang "Happy Birthday" to a one-year-old.

A star. What is a star? In the same way that live performance is an impermanent art, a star is an impermanent illusion who lives only in the memory of those who have seen him and then dies with them. He is carried on people's shoulders and he falls on his face, all within a minute. He is an insecure egocentric, a tyrant, and a teddy bear. Is the mike right? The music good? Hey, what are those musicians doing reaching for cups of water while I'm singing? A star is the fool who'll try anything in public and the genius when it works. A star has a thick skin that you can pierce with a frown. Draw me happy, draw me sad. He has been gifted with talent, with the ability to see deeper, hear wider, laugh harder. Also to cry more easily because he bruises more easily. And he was given the hunger, the need to excel. He is amazed by his fame, thrilled by applause, made incredulous by the money. And a thousand times he has wanted to ask, "Dear God, I don't deserve all this. Why *me?*"

It was a strange time, the sixties, a strange feeling suddenly being "black." Yet overnight thirty million "colored people" and "Negroes" had become "blacks." It was difficult to think of myself as a "black" after all the years of hating "black bastard," "black motherfucker." Nobody ever got called "Negro bastard" or "colored motherfucker." It was always "black" and the word was nasty and hard. Only a few months earlier I'd heard someone say, "This black guy . . ." and was offended by it. I berated him: "I've never *seen* a person with black skin. I've seen people with brown skin, tan skin, but never black."

But riding on the mood of social change, James Brown recorded "Black Is Beautiful," in which the lyrics urged, ". . . say it loud, I'm black and I'm proud . . ." and suddenly we didn't loathe the word "black" anymore. It was no longer a sneer, but an anthem. ". . . say it loud, I'm black and I'm proud . . ." One song found the pride of a scattered people, one song straightened our backs and raised our heads and drew us together more than we had ever been, uniting us all into blacks.

In the dressing room, Murphy handed me the telephone. Finis Henderson was a Chicago friend from the old days. I said, "Come on over, babe."

"I'm with some of the brothers, over in Westside."

"Bring 'em along. Use my table for the second show."

"I'd love to . . ." He was backing away from it.

"Don't worry. I'll leave your name. There'll be no problem."

"I know that, Sam, and I appreciate it, but, frankly, it's heavy. Y'know what I mean? I just wanted to say hello, hear your voice. I'll catch you in Chicago or someplace . . ."

I sat behind the bar. Black Power! What a joke! We were still impotent. In my mind's eye I saw my dinner-show audience: there had been no black faces out there. Black people did not come to see me in Las Vegas because if black people didn't arrive at the hotel with the special safe-conduct of "Sammy's guest," they didn't get in. And who wanted *that?*

I called Jack Entratter and went to his apartment. We sat down on a couch. "Jack, I've got to see some of my people sitting out there."

"Sam, you know you can bring anyone you like. Your family is always welcome, your friends . . ."

"I know and I appreciate it but that's not enough. The doors have to open to *everybody.*"

He sighed, like Oops! "Sam, we still have the boys from

Kansas City; why do we call the line the 'Texas Copa Girls'?
Because we get a lot of high rollers from there."

I understood but could not accept the magic wand that
okayed anything because "It's business." It wasn't the Texans
alone, or the boys from Kansas City. Las Vegas was an inveter-
ate prejudiced city, built by Southerners and Northerners *from*
prejudiced cities: Detroit's Purple Gang, the guys from Chicago,
Kansas City. But that was a lot of sit-ins and pray-ins ago.

"Jack, keeping black people out is now illegal and it's
morally wrong. Plus, it's unkind." He nodded. "Then you'll
agree that it has to stop. And we should be the ones to do it.
We're the starters, the doers and movers . . . we've got to let
black people come see the shows and make them comfortable
doing it. And we've got to put black people to work in this
town, and where they will be visible. Things are changing, Jack.
Even Mississippi is getting ready to change . . ."

"Sammy, antagonizing our high-rolling Southern clientele is
not smart business. But lemme talk to the board. I'll try to
come up with something to at least get us started."

Ethel Kennedy invited me to lunch at Hickory Hill, their home
in Virginia. I was performing at the Shoreham Hotel in Washington. Jane and Burt were visiting. It was a small gathering:
Peter and Pat, Pierre Salinger, General Maxwell Taylor, and Art
Buchwald.

I was grateful to Bobby for reaching out to me, for as much
as saying, "You're welcome in *my* house."

After lunch, while Ethel and I watched Bobby, Max
Taylor, and Jane and Burt playing tennis, she said, "Sammy,
that business about Jack's inauguration, I hope you know
we had nothing to do with it. Bobby was outraged by what
they did."

"I knew that then. Peter told me. You didn't even have to
mention it, but thank you."

Before it was time to leave, Bobby walked me around the
house for privacy. "You're not popular with the Klan," he said,

"or the White Citizens Council. You're on all of their lists. Whenever you plan to appear in public at anything controversial, anything to do with civil rights, be sure to call me a day or two in advance and at least I can have a couple of men there looking out for you."

Sy Marsh called me from California while I was in New York playing the Copa. He asked, "Sweetheart, do you remember Clifford Odets' picture *Golden Boy*? A producer named Hillard Elkins wants to make it into a Broadway musical starring you as the fighter. He's got the rights and he's got Odets himself to adapt it for the stage."

In my dressing room Odets said, "I'll write it out of your mouth . . ."

Hilly Elkins was a few years younger than me, he had big, wide-open eyes, and he was all enthusiasm. "One of the major conflicts should be that you're in love with a white girl. I think we can do something important racially."

For a white man to think that way was remarkable. "And, Hilly, what about a really integrated cast, not just a couple of token black kids in the chorus?"

"Fifty-fifty. Which is more than equal, but it's time for the pendulum to swing a little too far the other way."

"And why not a black musical conductor, for the first time? George Rhodes, my pianist, has been conducting for me and writing arrangements. He's a talented, experienced man."

Hilly agreed with everything. We sat up until dawn talking about it. He said, "I saw you in London about two years ago and I thought of *Golden Boy* and you, and I haven't thought of anything else since. I got Clifford, I've got financing . . ."

"And you've got me."

"New York?" May was less than receptive to the idea. "But we've just barely moved into this house. I don't know about the schools for Mark in New York . . ."

I'd been premature telling it to her on the phone. I should have waited until I was home but I'd wanted to share it with her.

"How long do you think we'll have to stay there?"

"Hilly's asking me to commit to three years."

By the time I got out to the Coast, May had sold herself on it. "Boy, Sharley Brown, three years together. We're finally going to have a real family life."

Harry Belafonte called me. "Sam, we're planning on you in Washington."

"Of course I'm going to be there. How many people are you expecting to march?"

"If ten thousand show up it will be a success. Twenty thousand would be unbelievable."

Two days before the March on Washington, Bobby Kennedy called me. "Sam, you've been moving up on the White Citizens Council's 'Ten Most Wanted' list. If you're coming to Washington, stay in the mainstream, and when it's over, don't hang around. I'll have some agents identify themselves to you and take you out to the airport and stay with you till your flight . . ."

I was playing the Elmwood Casino in Windsor, Ontario. Murphy and I left Windsor at five in the morning and flew out of Detroit to get to Washington by ten in the morning. Already thousands had arrived before us. They were walking toward the Washington Monument and the Lincoln Memorial, clustered in bunches of whites and blacks. Everyone looked tense, apprehensive. Policemen were stationed on street corners, looking hard-nosed and nervous. There had been many threats to disrupt the march. There were no thoughts of assassination yet. But the threats of violence were there.

I stood on the steps of the Lincoln Memorial looking toward the Washington Monument, looking over all the heads, into the faces, and then, as if the sun burst through the clouds, all at once people were *smiling* and it was "Hey, man . . ." and you knew there wasn't going to be any trouble, as if a happiness virus had spread among all those men and women. I watched little vignettes of people touching, holding hands; black people who had never touched white people before; a black woman handing a handkerchief to a white boy who was crying from emotion. Ten thousand? Twenty thousand? There were three hundred thousand people there and everybody felt the same way. Twenty-four hours before and maybe even twenty-four hours later they might have killed each other, but for that suspended, isolated few hours in time there was more love in that mall than the world has ever known.

Civil rights leader A. Philip Randolph introduced Martin Luther King as "the moral leader of our country." And from the Lincoln Memorial, looking out at three hundred thousand Americans, Dr. King began: "I have a dream . . ."

In November 1963 Frank, Dean Martin, and I started making *Robin and the Seven Hoods*. Bing Crosby was guest-starring and the studio had said, "Bing will get third billing." Frank said, "No, he won't. Sammy is over the title with us. The billing is: Frank Sinatra, Dean Martin, Sammy Davis, Jr."

"But, Frank . . ."

"That's *it!* Give Bing a separate box."

I told May, "Come out to the set. Hang out with the guys."

"I'd really rather not."

Something was wrong. "I don't dig."

"Frankly, I can't stand your relationship with Frank, the way he treats you, the jokes, the way you kowtow to him . . ."

"Darling, Frank and I go way back, to when he was 'Sinatra' and I was 'the kid.' Even though we've become best friends, and I'm a star too, that relationship will never change. Like with Abe Lastfogel. He's my agent, I pay him a fortune in commissions, I could call him 'Abe,' but I don't. He'll always be 'Mr. Lastfogel' to me. And I'll always be 'the kid' to Frank and he'll always be 'Sinatra' to me."

"I don't mind him being 'Sinatra.' But I can't take it when he treats you like 'the kid.' You're a grown man . . ."

I knew that by "kid" she really meant "lackey." And I knew too that I sometimes gave that impression when I was with him. But that was my doing, not his.

My morning plane from Las Vegas was delayed and as I arrived on the set Frank greeted me: "You're fuckin' late. We had to shoot the first scene without you."

"Francis, come on . . . you know I'm workin' your joint."

He grinned. "I told you not to play the fuckin' place. We did the opening scene without you . . . Who needs ya, Smokey?"

I really didn't mind the jokes. But I was just as glad my wife wasn't there the afternoon when we were shooting a graveyard scene and got the news that John Kennedy had been shot.

As I went over to see Frank he was stepping out of his trailer and onto the set and I stared after the figure of a man walking in a cemetery. I stood in the doorway watching him grieve for the man who broke his heart when he'd publicly refused to stay in the "Palm Springs White House," a four-bedroom, self-contained home which Frank had built for the Kennedys. I'd seen a sign on the door: "Palm Springs White House"; he was that sure that JFK was coming. But Bobby fought John's going there because of Frank's alleged connections in the underworld, and because Sam Giancana had slept in his house. Presidents have a lot of license. And he went up the hill and stayed at Bing Crosby's house. It broke Frank's heart. It became public knowledge. In all the gossip columns.

I have never heard Frank say a bad word about John Kennedy. I've heard "I don't want to discuss that," but I've never heard him do one minute of ". . . that so-and-so . . . I did this . . . and he did that . . ." And I resolved that whenever I had the occasion to be in Washington, I would take flowers to John Kennedy's grave and pay my respects. He had not been a friend of mine but he had been the President I and my people needed.

37

When Robert Kennedy campaigned for the office of United States senator from New York, I was in New York City rehearsing *Golden Boy*. Sarge Shriver called. "Bobby says you might be willing to help."

Bobby was a humanist. He was not a do-gooder, but a good-doer, a knight of old in a button-down-collar shirt, a man who wanted to right wrong. I wanted Robert Kennedy as a senator making my country's laws, and then to run for President. Bobby had been the strength in the Kennedy family. John was always "raised eyebrows," thinking about the next advantageous move; the "piano player" who sat out front with the spotlight on him. The other cat who kept time was the drummer, who never got the spotlight, never took the solos, but he kept time, he kept the beat going. Bobby was the drummer.

He'd shown it as Attorney General when he'd used his power to allow the marches to happen and to protect the demonstrators. It would have been a different civil rights movement without Bobby Kennedy.

We showed up a number of times in the garment district, usually during lunch hour so as not to take people away from work. For an hour or so the police blocked off Seventh Avenue between 36th and 37th Streets, thousands of people came out of the buildings to see Robert Kennedy, and I'd introduce him to "my people." We went to Harlem the same way: 125th Street at the corner of the Teresa Hotel. "I'm here pullin' on your coats to introduce a man who we *know* what he stands for . . ." Harlem knew that Bobby Kennedy was special for them.

We were on the road with *Golden Boy* for twenty-two weeks, longer than most plays run on Broadway, because we were afraid to come in. We opened in Philadelphia and got rapped badly. We had four weeks there to fix the show before our next out-of-town tryout in Boston.

In Boston, Elliot Norton, their most astute critic, cut us to shreds. Hilly invited Norton to lunch and picked his brains. He subsequently got William Gibson to rewrite the show, and he replaced our director with Arthur Penn.

Arthur tried to approach me as an actor who had studied acting for twenty years. He'd say, "Prepare."

"Prepare? For what?" I'd put my makeup on and "Let's go. Ready!"

"Okay. As you cannot prepare, then bring to the stage whatever you experienced that day, bring that emotion; up, down, whatever it was. Don't try to act. If you're angry at something and you play angry it will be honest and the audience will see sincerity."

As we ended the first week in New Haven, Hilly said, "We're not ready to go into New York from here. We need more work. I'm booking us into Detroit."

Detroit was in the middle of race riots. The onstage kiss between Paula Wayne and me outraged some people and Hilly got threats. "We're gonna cut off that whore's tits. And the nigger's balls." Paula had to be given a bodyguard. I already had one.

We were changing dialogue, putting in hunks at such speed that one night I didn't remember if I was playing a violinist or a piano player. I worked so hard that I had no voice and had to whisper my songs.

Hilly brought in a throat specialist. "You have polyps on your vocal cords. Stop smoking, stop drinking, and above all stop using your voice. Close this show for a month or two and rest, or you may never sing again."

There was no way to close down, not even for three days.

May called daily. "I've been looking into schools for Mark and I'm leaning strongly toward Ethical Culture and Dalton. There are others where he might get better athletic programs because they're not in the center of New York; on the other hand . . ." She wanted to include me as "father" and "husband" to consult and share decisions, but I could not focus on anything except the show and survival.

By the time our scenery arrived at the Majestic Theater in New York, we had a whole new and polished show. Our opening number exploded on Broadway, stunning the audience so they felt they were in—not just watching—a boxer's gym: fighters working the bags, skipping ropes, sparring, feinting, jabbing to the music; slowly at first, then faster, savagely, a boxers' ballet: jab, feint, cross; jab, feint, cross; every sound, every move sliding click, click, bam, bam; precision, style, pace, all riding on that extra inner strength that starts in the gut and comes through the heart and turns craftsmanship around the corner into art.

The morning papers came in at midnight. ". . . a knockout." ". . . this year's heavyweight champ." "They've broken new ground on Broadway." "Something daring and important is happening at the Majestic . . ." We were a solid hit.

"My God, what do you have in here?" May was struggling under the weight of a package about a cubic foot in size. "It's from Abercrombie and Fitch."

"That's my bowling ball. I'm taking the cast bowling tonight after the show. Against the other shows."

"I've never bowled, but I'll try it."

"Darling . . . it's a togetherness thing for the kids and if you're there I can't be all over the place making it into a party."

"Oh. Okay."

"But come to the dressing room during the show, hang out, then take the car home and I'll be along in an hour or two."

"No, that's okay. I'll stay home."

"Don't be silly, come on down."

"Sammy, frankly I'd rather stay home. The dressing-room jazz isn't much fun. It's not like we're together or I get to spend any time with you. In fact, it's boring as hell."

"You're kidding."

"No. I can understand it's fun for you. People come back and tell you how great you were. That's your business. But waiting around all night . . . I'd prefer to wait for you here, or if we're going out, to meet you there after you've done what you have to do with visitors."

I was astonished. To me the dressing room was the hub, the fun place to be. But from her point of view I suppose it was like watching me onstage without the music or the sound, just seeing me moving around entertaining others.

On Friday, Tracey climbed off her chair and pulled me by the hand. "Dad, you're having dinner with us tonight."

I stroked her silky hair. I knew I'd promised to take part in the Sabbath dinner. "I'm sorry, Princess of the World." I kissed her and Mark. "Daddy has work to do . . ." and I explained that I had a 6 p.m. photo session with *Life* onstage.

May walked me to the door, burning. "You could have told me!"

I hadn't because I didn't want to disappoint her about dinner, and there was always a chance that the photo session would be changed. "Darling, also, they need to bring a photographer over here on Sunday for some family shots." As I said it I knew that was largely why I'd put off the conversation.

"But the article is about you and *Golden Boy*. The children and I have nothing to do with it. And I don't believe that kids should be brought up seeing their faces in magazines and get-

ting the idea they're something that they're not. Can't *Life* magazine understand that people would like some privacy?"

"I'm thrilled that they can't. We have a good life because
people are interested in me. I don't have the moral right to say,
'Sorry, fellas, this is my home, no press,' ignoring the fact that
they have a job to do and that by doing their job through the
years they've done me a lot of good."

Passing Saks Fifth Avenue on my way to the matinee, I told my
driver to stop. "Pick me up around the corner at the Forty-
ninth Street entrance." I took a closer look at the ski outfit I'd
seen in the window. What had attracted me was a bright red
knitted cap, scarf, and mittens. I went inside and told the
saleslady, "Send them to Miss Tracey Davis . . ." I gave her the
address and wrote a card: " 'Cause I love you. Daddy," and
had them sent to the house by messenger.

When I got home after midnight I went upstairs to see the
kids. It was dark in Tracey's room and as I leaned over her bed
to kiss her my hand touched something woolen on her head.
She was wearing the cap I'd sent her, and the mittens.

Crossing New York in my car, I listened as Bull Connor and
Jim Clark, the sheriff of Selma, Alabama, were featured on another bloody news report of police brutality, beatings with
rubber hose covered with barbed wire, and stymied voter regis-
tration for Selma's black citizens.

Hilly was waiting in my dressing room. "Belafonte called.
There's going to be a protest march in Selma. They want all the
celebrities possible, to focus the press attention on what's happening there."

"You shouldn't go." The color had drained from May's face.

Gently, I pinched her cheeks. "At this moment you're a little
whiter than absolutely necessary."

"It's not funny. I've seen Bull Connor on television. And Jim Clark. They'll kill you. Or hurt you. Sammy, haven't you done enough?"

I had done a lot. I'd been marching since I was seventeen. Long before there was a civil rights movement I was marching through the lobby of the Waldorf-Astoria, the Sands, the Fontainebleau, to a table at the Copa. And I'd marched alone. Worse. Often to black derision. But had I done "enough"?

The air was hot and heavy in Alabama and as we crossed the tarmac I recognized Bull Connor at the gate staring at us all.

Medgar Evers' brother was waiting for us with a Buick station wagon. He said, "Put Sammy in the middle," and I sat between Murphy and Joe Grant, my chauffeur-bodyguard. As we drove toward Selma the radio was on and we listened to the news of our arrival. The broadcast signed off: "This is ABC, the *white* news."

On both sides of the small-town-looking street stood the local people glaring at us, resenting us, angry, fear in their eyes. There were no jeers, no insults, they watched us in silence, despising us. The National Guardsmen, local boys, there to protect us, were little comfort. My stomach trembled. My legs were weakened and I walked heavily. But I was glad I was there. Those who watched us walking across their city recognized that our presence was causing cameras and printing presses to record what was happening, to bring our protest to tens of millions of other Americans. And they saw an era fading, a way of life coming to a close.

My children were in the backyard playing on a jungle gym I'd bought them at F. A. O. Schwarz. It was noon, I'd had breakfast, and I was free until four o'clock. May and I went into the living room and I read the theater section of the *Times* while she gazed out the window at New York's version of a blue sky. "Sharley Brown?" I looked up. "Let's make a picnic basket, take the kids and find a woods somewhere and rough it for lunch."

I was in my town house, wearing a Sulka robe, holding a Steuben glass filled with bourbon and Coke. "Darling, rough it? You know what's my idea of roughing it? When Murphy's not here and I've got to make my own drink. Also, there's not enough time."

"Okay, okay. It was just a thought." She picked up the newspaper. "Anyway, it's sure nice to have a few hours together."

At 3:30 I was dressed and ready to go down to CBS. "Got the cast party tonight, darling. I'll be home a little latish." She kissed me goodbye and nodded sadly. Her expression stayed with me on the ride downtown.

It was a crisp, wintry Sunday–in–New York morning and as I was settling into the Sunday *Times* I heard, "Sammy, we've got the whole day free, let's take the kids to the zoo."

"May, I can't walk in Central Park *by myself*, let alone with you and the kids. It'll be a crowd scene with autographs and staring, and you're not going to enjoy that, and the kids aren't going to enjoy it. And possibly it's dangerous. Not that I'm sorry to miss going to the zoo to have a million laughs staring at animals."

She was conciliatory but determined. "I accept the fact that you're famous. But it doesn't have to be Central Park. Some fathers take their children camping, they make tree houses for them, they play ball with them. Mark would love to have a catch with you right here in our backyard."

"Then somebody will have to teach me how to have a catch. I never played ball. When I was Mark's age I was sitting around greenrooms playing pinochle. And my son will not enjoy me making an ass of myself in front of him. The fun is when Daddy is better than you are. In this family Daddy sings 'Birth of the Blues' and he stars on Broadway and he's as good a father in his way as the guy next door is in his."

"Just because you're a father doesn't mean that you're a *good* father. It takes effort . . ."

"Stop! Time out! I don't need a lecture." I was more out-raged every moment. "What am I, some kind of an ogre? I don't beat my kids, they're not starving in a ghetto someplace. So what if I *can't* walk in the park with them? And know now: I'm *never* going to build a tree house for them. I *hate* outdoorsy and woodsy things. I don't know how to do them. Does that make me Jack the fucking Ripper?"

I ran out of the house and slammed the door behind me. When I returned May was feeding the kids and we didn't talk much, nor did we as we dressed for the evening. Judy Garland was in town to play the Palace and I'd invited her over for Sun-day supper and she brought her daughter, Liza Minnelli.

As the evening went on, Judy started singing and Liza joined her, her voice and confidence blooming. Then Leonard Bern-stein played the piano for Adolph Green, who sang some of the songs he and Betty Comden had written with Lenny for *On the Town*. Jule Styne played and Adolph and Betty sang songs they had written for *Bells Are Ringing*. I performed for them, in-venting some new Charlie Chaplin pieces, trying to do things I didn't do commercially. It was a wonderful show business evening.

I walked over to May, wanting to share it with her. She was with Amy Greene. "Y'know what I was thinking?" I said. "Why don't we do a weekly 'Sunday at Sammy's'?"

"Why don't we talk about that," she said. She didn't like the idea. She didn't like it *a lot!*

When everyone had left, we busied ourselves emptying ash-trays, taking the used glasses to the kitchen. She wasn't in any more of a hurry to talk than I was. But finally we'd run out of stalls, we'd gone upstairs, and we were alone in our room get-ting ready for bed. I said, "May?" She looked at me. Not angry. Sad. "Didn't you enjoy this evening at all?"

She shook her head and her lovely hair swung back and forth and I remembered the first night I had taken her home, to Malibu, with the moonlight shining on it. I could never have imagined we'd ever have a hard moment between us. Yet she was close to tears and I didn't know how to turn them off. Neither hers nor my own, the dry ones that I could feel in my chest, constricting my throat.

"Darling, can't you get a kick out of the people that were here? What it means that they would come to my home?"

"Sammy, I love you but I hate our life." She was startled by the force of her own words. "To be very honest with you, I don't care about a limousine or push-button windows or famous people singing in my living room. I'm sorry"—she began weeping—"but I just can't help that. I understand that it pleases you . . . but I'd rather have spent your night off alone with you. I don't want Judy Garland. I want my marriage, my husband and my children . . . I'm . . . lonely . . ."

I held her in my arms, stroking her hair, wanting her to feel all the love I had for her, not understanding her loneliness but blindly trying to help her across that unhappy wasteland.

We were putting out lights, locking the front and back doors, getting ready to go upstairs, when Sy Marsh called me from the Coast. "Sweetheart! We've hit the jackpot! I have a firm offer from NBC for a full network series, an intimate variety show."

May looked at me with amazement growing to fury. "You haven't had one hour a week for the children with only the show to do. And benefits. And interviews. Now you're taking on a TV series? You might as well live in a hotel between the studio and the theater."

"Darling, I can't give up the prestige of my own network show."

"Sammy, I can't take this lifestyle anymore."

I went over to the bar to fix a drink, as a prop, to give myself time to understand what she was saying. I sat down on the couch beside her and asked, "You don't want this lifestyle?"

"I've told you that. I don't enjoy the rewards of your celebrity. I hate this extravagant way we live. I was happy with our first apartment. I feel like I'm in your way. I think I'd like to take the kids and go back to California until you finish up with the show. I'm sick of pushing them on you. And to be honest, I can't stand to hear myself whining, 'I want to see my husband.' I'd almost rather learn to live without him."

I felt hot and sick and I knew categorically that the last thing in the world I wanted was for May to go away from me with our children. Zoooom! and I saw that I had been risking everything we'd fought so hard for. I had to dig deep for breath. I took her hands in mine. "Darling, don't go. I love you and I love our children. Please stay. I'll cancel the TV series. Screw it. No more press, no more interviews. At least, the absolute minimum. I'll do my show eight times a week, we'll have every day until I go to the theater and all day Sunday. What the fuck, I'll even learn to go on a picnic . . ."

"Whaddya say, Smokey? Listen, is this show *Golden Boy* any fuckin' good? I've got some tickets here for tonight."

"You're in town? Francis, that's great!"

"Now don't get nervous tonight because there's a pro in the audience. After the show we'll go to Jilly's joint. Catch you later, Charley."

I got busy stirring my coffee.

May asked, "What did he say?"

"He's coming to the show tonight."

After a few minutes she said, "Sammy, if Frank wants to go out after the show tonight, I understand we should go with him. He is your friend."

We were at a table for eight in the back of Jilly's, a small bar and restaurant on West 52nd Street, drinking, eating Chinese food. Frank was not married or going with anyone in particular and he had a few girls with him. May was ravishing in her silver dress, seated between two men who couldn't have been very interesting to her, but she was being charming, trying to add something to the conversation. At around two-thirty I told Frank, "Matinee tomorrow," and we said our goodbyes.

In the car home I told May I appreciated the way she'd handled the evening. She said, "Thank *you* for ending it when you did. I know you wanted to stay up all night with Frank."

"No, I didn't." I heard myself say it and wasn't sure of the truth myself. Yes, I *had* wanted to stay up with Frank. But I had also wanted to not want to stay up. What I wanted was to want to go to bed at a normal hour and keep my wife and children happy.

Before putting the light out we looked through the newspapers.

"Do you want to see something beautiful, Sharley Brown?" She handed me Earl Wilson's column in the *Post*, which said, "Night owl Sammy Davis, Jr., is now a domestic animal. Rushes home after the show to be with Beautiful Wife, May Britt, and to kiss their three children good night."

I felt odd, uncomfortable, like it wasn't really about me.

When I got up at noon Tracey, Mark, and Jeff were sitting on the floor watching a Steve McQueen Western. I joined them as Mark hooted, "Wow! Lookit the way he rides. Turns that horse on a dime. Dad, do you know Steve McQueen?"

"Yes, son, you met him at our house when you were a baby. But that particular shot happens to have been done by a stuntman. I was there the day they shot it."

Steve was good on a horse but no better than I was. Maybe not as good.

"Mark, listen, would you like to go horseback riding with me? I'll teach you."

I had my blue jeans and Western boots but I ordered the car for ten o'clock and Mark and I went down to Miller's and we got him fitted out with cute cowboy boots, jeans, a plaid shirt, and I flipped a Western hat onto his head.

We went to a stable on West 67th Street. The riders were dressed as in *The Philadelphia Story*. It wasn't a "stable," it was a "riding academy," and the horses had English saddles. I asked, "Don't you have a horse with a Western rig?"

"No, sir, Mr. Davis. But you'll get used to this after a while. Just hang on to him with your knees."

I didn't want to get used to anything in front of my son. But I couldn't back out. Thank God I hadn't boasted how good I was, planning to let him see for himself. I felt like I was sitting on a rail, holding on to the saddle, which I knew was wrong to do, but the alternative was to fall on my ass. It would be dangerous for me to teach Mark, as I'd told him I would. I asked, "Can we get an instructor for my son?"

By six o'clock that evening my thighs were so stiff I could hardly move my legs except spastically. Me! A dancer, starring on Broadway. I hadn't been spectacular with my son and I'd fucked up with my show.

As I read the newspapers and watched the television news and talk shows, I saw that my image was changing or fading. The domesticated animal image, which was great for Perry Como but not for "Sammy" the saloon singer, the legend of perpetual motion, the swinger, the boozer, and "Wowowoweee-wow, it's a party!" Aside from *Golden Boy* I had to be looking ahead to when I got back to Vegas and Tahoe. One of the reasons for taking a break from clubs was to be missed—not forgotten.

When I got to the theater there was a sign posted on the bulletin board: "Birthday party for Lola. Tonight. Everybody welcome. Love, Hilly."

I was making up when Hilly came by. "Sam? It would mean a lot to the kids if you'd show up tonight." He was looking at me through the mirror and his face was a lot more serious than a birthday party.

"I'll be there, babe."

I called Sy Marsh and asked him to try to revive NBC's interest in me for a series or for anything constructive. "Get me back into the business, baby. And hurry." Then after the show that night I went home and sat downstairs in the living room with May. The kids were asleep, the house was quiet, and I tried to explain it. "Trying to change my lifestyle wasn't a good idea. I used to be an original. Then I stopped being a good

Sammy Davis and I was just ordinary as an 'around the house with the kids' and 'he's taking them to the circus' kind of a father. I got where I am by single-mindedness, by one hundred percent involvement: I ate, talked, breathed, slept, lived show business. Then I started phoning it in. I became a part-time Sammy Davis, Jr. It was insanity. Fortunately, temporary.

"For me to try to be something I'm not, to go with society's image or your image of how a father and a husband should look and act would eventually be a disaster. I can't afford it professionally. Right now I have to work. There's no level road in show business. It tilts up or it tilts down. So I have to grow while the opportunities present themselves.

"I cannot let anything get in the way of 'Sammy Davis, Jr.'—not me, the person—I mean the figure SD, Jr. He is what makes everything happen. I'm not going to get trapped in a false sense of my importance to you and to the children. If Tracey and Mark and Jeff and May have to wait a while till they have hang-out time with me, then that's how it has to be, because 'Sammy Davis, Jr.,' comes before anyone. If what *I* personally want doesn't work for *him*, if I want to play golf but he thinks he should play a benefit, then we play the benefit. He comes first. Period."

On January 7, 1966, I hosted the first *Sammy Davis Jr. Show* on NBC with my guests Elizabeth Taylor and Richard Burton.

I was back in the daily papers. They marveled: "Nobody in history has ever starred in a Broadway musical, taped a TV series, and shot a movie all at the same time." I was hot again. Every move I made turned up the three cherries on the slot machine. The recognition, the career building, the money.

And the excuse not to go home. When I went home I wanted to be so tired, so drained that conversation was impossible. Day by day the chasm between May and me had widened from bickering to silence.

I came home late after the show and a benefit and for the hundredth time we stared at each other in silence.

May was in bed reading. She didn't tell me where she had taken the children that afternoon.

I undressed. I didn't tell her that the rehearsal for the TV show got a standing ovation from the stagehands.

May didn't tell me that Tracey was getting her new teeth.

I didn't tell May that I was doing *Mike Wallace* tomorrow and why not come to the studio.

May didn't tell me that Mark had fallen off his bike and skinned his knee and she'd taken him to the doctor for an antitetanus shot.

We had long ago stopped saying "I love you," but we didn't tell each other *anything* anymore.

From the outside it looked like I was skiing down the Alps without the sticks, and everybody was going, "Look at him . . . he can do it . . . it's miraculous . . ." But inside I was going, "Oh, shit . . . ," waiting to fall, to crash, to have half of my life say goodbye and walk away from me.

I got home so tired one night that I didn't make it upstairs and fell asleep on the couch in the living room. When I woke up, May brought me some juice and coffee.

"Good morning," she said.

"Good morning," I replied.

"The weather's not so good today."

"Yes. But the weatherman said it may clear up."

When you exchange only pleasantries they stop being pleasant.

I think she waited until I was fully awake before she said, "What's the point in this, Sammy? It's only getting worse. We've been through too much together to let ourselves end up disliking each other. I think it's better to walk away from it."

38

The house was emptier than empty, quieter than silent, as though everyone but me had evaporated. May's clothes closet contained only empty hangers. The children's rooms showed no sign that they'd ever been there. Not a toy. Even the wastebaskets were empty. *They really left me. With all my glitter, with all that I could give them, they preferred not to be with me.*

If I'd written a script in which "the wife walks out" I'd have had the "swinger" turn his house into a Playboy mansion, so that when you turned on a faucet out came twenty naked chicks. But I had no desire to celebrate failure. I was lonely for people I hadn't enjoyed when they were there, when I'd had no room for them in my life.

After two years of *Golden Boy* I had nothing more to accomplish on that stage, nothing more to do in New York. I needed to get back into my own world of different shows every night, in different cities, to different people.

May had taken the children to California, to the house she had never liked. And she called regularly to keep me posted.

I asked, "Has the split been tough on the kids?"

"No, they're fine. That you're not here all the time is as natural to them as another child's father who was always around. We got lucky there. With a nine-to-five father he stamps out the door and 'Daddy's gone' and life is different, but this never happened with us. You were always packing and leaving for Vegas or Tahoe, or going to the theater or sleeping because you were exhausted . . ."

I knew that she hadn't meant for it to hurt. On the contrary, she was the mother hen relieved to say that the kids were not suffering. I went upstairs and got into a hot tub. As I was shaving I thought: You can't get them back. You've made a choice, paid a price. But let it not be in vain. Let it not be for nothing that you gave up your family.

That night I did *Golden Boy* for the last time and headed back to Vegas.

I was playing bid whist in the dressing room between shows with John Hopkins. The phone rang. Murphy held his hand over the mouthpiece and whispered, "It's the head of the Civil Rights Commission of Nevada."

"So? What're you whispering about?"

"Maybe you've been revoked and you're not black anymore."

It was Bob Bailey, a man I'd known since before there were any thoughts of civil rights in Las Vegas. He wanted to meet with me and his directors. "Sam, we've been talking with the hotels for years, asking for jobs, but they aren't budging. If they don't make a move in two more weeks, we're going to picket and bring it into national focus. You'll still be playing here then, so we want you to be prepared."

I spoke to Jack Entratter. "You're going to get picketed and it's going to be embarrassing, because I'm going to be on the picket line." He sat forward. "Right, Jack. I'm not going to, quote, be in a hospital recuperating from exhaustion, end quote. I'll be right out front, walking back and forth."

"What should we do?" Jack asked.

"Like I said two years ago, meet them halfway. Hire some bellmen, waiters. You don't have to start with managers. But get some black people being seen working here. And gambling here. Nobody's saying take out an ad in *Ebony* magazine: 'You're Welcome at the Sands.' But if the security guys don't turn purple every time they see a black cat at the door it'll be a step forward. And tell your people to serve them. I mean tomorrow. Not in 'we'll think about it' time, because that'll be too late. Tomorrow."

"The other hotels aren't going to like me, but you've got my word on it."

I looked at him with all the affection you can feel for a man who steps into your fight and says, "They'll have to hit me too." I hesitated, not wanting to push too far, yet it had to be done. "Jack, speaking of the other hotels, what can I do about them?"

"The Hotel Board is having its monthly meeting tomorrow. Come and speak to the guys."

The presidents and owners of the seven Strip hotels met in the boardroom at the Sands. One of the owners smirked: "On what grounds are they going to picket us? They don't work for us. Our own people are happy, well paid. Nobody's on strike. We'll kick their asses into the fuckin' desert. They can't picket shit."

"Sir," I said, "they can and they will picket all the hotels where there are no black people working. It is no longer legally possible to ignore twenty percent of America's citizens when you employ people."

He grunted, "Some fuckin' free country we've got."

They were a handful of powerful men unwilling to accept that a way of life was changing, yet knowing that it was, that history was being made, that an ocean of people was no longer lapping at a fortress wall but that the civil rights movement had gained momentum and, like a tidal wave, it was going to climb right over the wall.

Leaving the meeting, Jack put his arm on my shoulder. "I'm moving on it." In the lobby we saw the only black employee of the Sands Hotel, a bellman. "He's a bright kid," Jack said. "He goes to the front desk this week and we'll start training him. And we've hired ten waiters."

"Jack, over in Westside they've got some pretty classy dealers."

"I'll ask Carl Cohen to go and look at them. Tomorrow."

Weeks later when the NAACP picketed Las Vegas they did not picket the Sands. They did not exempt the Sands because I was playing there but because Jack had moved before the others.

One of the columns wrote, "Is SD, Jr., torching for May Britt? His current dinner date is look-alike Jean Seberg."

Jean was one of the sponsors of the Black Panthers. There was a Hollywood contingent that gave money to the Panthers and she was intensely involved. I didn't start dating her because she looked like May, nor did I think she did other than being very white and blond, but if that's what they wanted to think, I was not sorry to be getting back a little he's-a-bachelor attention, the swinger image which served me.

I went with Jean to a meeting and I saw Ron Karenga there. He was a super-militant, scary, dark glasses, bald head, Fu Manchu mustache, ominous-looking.

The militants in CORE and SNCC and the Panthers as well as the middle-of-the-road groups and leaders—Martin, Jesse Jackson, the NAACP, and the Urban League—were working to arrive at the same place, but they were on parallel lines, and without contact they were wasting effort. They needed a conduit, somebody to make linkage so there could be a cross-action. I told Karenga, "I'd like to meet with you. Talk a bit."

Unsmiling: "If you're sincere, meet me by yourself." He gave me an address on Central Avenue in L.A. just this side of Watts.

I rented an anonymous-looking Chevy and drove it myself, through parts of L.A. where I'd have been afraid to walk if I wasn't known. As I neared the address I began to doubt that

the meeting was a good idea. It was a restaurant with vinyl tables. He was sitting in the back with three of his guys. Oh,
great. But *I* had to come alone. The mothers were sitting there
with do's out to here and beards and black glasses. I'm not talking about shades, I mean *black* glasses.

"Hi, Ron. Guys." Nobody's smiling. Nobody's talking.
Grim. They don't stand up to greet me. They don't invite me to
sit down. "Well . . . guess I'll pull this chair over . . ."

I can't even be sure they're looking at me, because you can't
see an eyeball through those black glasses. These cats were
scaring the life out of me. Meanwhile, I was there and I
couldn't just keep playing their game. "Hey, brothers, you
think I'm scared of you?"

They nodded.

"Well . . . you right *there*." I grinned.

No response. "And you're not our brother."

Karenga said, "Mr. Davis, what is it you want?"

I thought that my presence had been saying, "I'm black too,
let me in, it's cold out there all alone." I wanted to be called
"brother." But their attitude hardened my fears into anger. "A
bit of courtesy would be nice. I did not barge in here. Yes, I
wanted to meet you. But you did agree, you gave me this address. I didn't stumble in here on my way home."

Karenga removed his glasses. "You're entirely right." As he
spoke I heard an educated man. He extended his hand to me.
"If we may, let's start again."

I said, "I just want to help in my way, what you're doing in
your way, once I understand something about how you work."

"What don't you understand?"

"Well, bullshit aside, what's it for? This intimidation. Why
scare everyone to death? What does it get you?"

The man sitting to Karenga's right, a lieutenant, said, "Fear
is a necessary commodity, Mr. Davis. Far too little has happened, and far too little is going to happen until white people
are afraid of black people for a while."

I said, "I understand what you're saying but I worry it

might boomerang. I know a lot of white people who are sincere about integration and equality. I'd hate to see them scared away, to lose their goodwill."

Karenga was shaking his shaved skull. "Job equality, housing equality, educational equality will never come to us from sincerity, because they sincerely don't want to give it to us. It's costly. They don't want to give up their job advantages. Labor didn't make its gains on goodwill. Only the threat of a strike, or violence, or a riot brought management to the table to talk. So we intimidate."

"But why intimidate *me?*" I rubbed my face with my hand. "This don't exactly come off, y'know. I'm not Al Jolson."

"But you ain't black either," the lieutenant said.

I would have laughed but for the tragedy I read into the statement. "I've met some people who disagree with you."

He insisted, "In the vernacular, 'you *is* black, but you don't *be* black.' You married a white woman. You live in a white community. You're publicly associated only with white friends. And you work almost exclusively in white, even Jim Crow towns."

I almost said that it was none of their fucking business how I lived, but as I had gone there to understand them I had to let them understand, me too. I said, "I married the woman I loved. Period. Okay?" They nodded. "I live in the best house that I have the money to buy. I was born in Harlem and I lived in enough second-rate hotels and boardinghouses so that now that I can afford it there ain't no first-class that's first-classy enough for me. Dig?

"As for working places like Las Vegas: nobody in Harlem and Watts has offered me a hundred thousand dollars a week."

Karenga's stone face began to soften, slightly. First at the eyes, then around the mouth. "Well . . . you right *there.*"

We talked for two hours and we made dents in our ignorance of each other. When I'd walked in I'd seen black glasses on blank walls, and they'd seen black skin on a guy who "lived white."

I said, "Jesse's coming into town next week. I'd love to see you guys get together . . ." Obviously Jesse Jackson couldn't be seen with Ron Karenga any more than Shimon Peres and Arafat could meet publicly. "I'd be delighted to give you my home. It's private, all the security you'd want. You guys have to finally get together. You can't be fighting the system and fighting each other . . ."

When they met a few weeks later I had the good feeling that I had done something more tangible than just another benefit, or being seen at a march.

39

There are certain romances that belong in certain cities, in a certain atmosphere, in a certain time. Some kinds of romance don't travel well. You can't take them out of their natural sites and times and transplant them. But where they were born, you hear strings playing and it's sunny.

With Romy it was that way. In Paris we would laugh, we would giggle. There's something about staying up late in Paris, drinking French 75s, being upstairs at the Calvados, coming down to the bar after dinner and the cat's playing the piano late, it was like a movie. There'd be a little mist hanging in the air. We walked to the Champs-Elysées and had the car follow us . . . there was nobody on the streets . . . a little drizzle . . . we walked to the Faubourg St.-Honoré and window-shopped and I felt romantic. I had the impression that it was a moment to hang on to because this was as good as it was ever going to get. In Europe I felt total freedom to be with anyone. Romy and I could go anywhere we wished and nobody raised an eyebrow except to acknowledge that we were two celebrities. There was never any thought of marriage. That was neither her frame of mind nor mine. It was just two people who had met and enjoyed the existence of the other, of being together, at that moment.

I was playing the Olympia in Paris for the first time and I

was the new, hot kid in town. The new kid had been doing these tricks for more than twenty years, they just hadn't seen them over there yet, and for those three weeks I owned Paris. I had met Porfirio Rubirosa through Frank in America. When I got to Paris we used to hang out at a little bar, the New Jimmy, which Régine was just starting.

Rubi was the most elegant man I've ever known. It was easy to understand why the daughter of a chief of state and the heiresses to two major American fortunes had married him. He was charming, erudite, amusing, attractive, and without a doubt the world's best-dressed man. I have always cared about clothes, and I will go to any length to look good. I have spent fortunes on shirts, shoes, suits, hats, jewelry, walking sticks, mink coats, and every possible accoutrement to make sure that even crossing a hotel lobby I look and feel at the top of my profession. But the way Rubirosa dressed made me feel as if I'd fallen off a garbage truck.

I was impressed with the man's knowledge. He could put a reading on anyone. He would trim the fat off everything. People would come in and he'd go, "Bullshit artist." He had unerring instinct. And he knew how to live with nobility and royalty. "Give them the respect they deserve for their rank, then we're all equals."

For no reason I was aware of, in Paris I just wanted to get drunk. Rubi and his buddy Jaime de Mora from Spain were dangerous friends. They'd say, "Have another one," and I'd start in the morning with Rubi before lunch with the salty dog. Jaime would join us and we'd drink all day and night, ending up at the Calvados and be absolutely pissed, but in control— until I stood up. When you stand up whiskey starts finding every opening where a vein is. It's like there are little men inside you and you hear "Hey, there's a spot here, put whiskey in there. Fill that vein. Need more whiskey . . ." "Whiskey coming, whiskey coming . . ."

Sitting at the table, shooting it down, glass after glass, I was being just ruly enough to be company, entertaining. "Okay, everybody want to leave? Well, how 'bout a nightcap at my place across the street? Wonderful! Murphy, Shirley, did you get the check? Wonderful, mahvelous . . ." Then I stand up and it was ". . . bluh . . . bluh . . . bluh . . . Mrphy . . . Mrvey . . . Jerleee . . . Jawwwrgge," and you start to slobber and you go from a sophisticate to a fucking drunkard.

It was raining, five in the morning, and they were taking me back to the George V. Hours ago they'd locked the side door of the Calvados. By 3 a.m. I'd blown off four girls, called them all kinds of names . . . people had been going "shhhhh" in the Calvados, which I "owned" at the time. I'm sitting there ranting, "Mbrh, Shwirtw, lezavunuvr dringggg . . . ?" and not making any sense at all except every other minute out comes a dirty word, clear as crystal, "FUCK" . . . with clarity. "Mrveybby, lezavagdtm . . . MOTHERFUCKER . . . Rubbbbibbbabbe . . ."

They finally got me to the door and Shirley says, "Upstairs. Get upstairs and get into your *bed!*"

I got her into focus. "You don't want me to have any fun, do you?"

"You drank up half of France. Get to your *bed!*"

"No, you don' wan' me to have any fun at all . . ."

Catherine Deneuve and I were seated together at several parties as dinner companions. I liked her, but Rubi said, "No-no-no-no-no-no! Romy. Romy for you." It was not a put-down of Deneuve. He just felt we had a different sense of humor, or any one of a thousand things. Mainly, he adored Romy.

Romy Schneider was a fiery, beautiful lady. Odile and Rubi introduced us. They had a party for me and there she was. Rubi had known we'd have a line of communication. We looked well together. We were both little. Romy only came up to my shoulders but she had such great carriage that you'd think she was five-eleven.

Odile and Rubi had a chic apartment in Paris and a wonderful three-story home outside the city. His memorabilia, his photographs with celebrated people boggled my mind. I knew everybody in the world. But he knew more and better. His and Odile's bedroom was on the second floor. On the third floor he had a gym with a standard-size boxing ring and he'd get into it every day and spar with a professional fighter.

We'd party there and I'd leave at daybreak to go back to the George V, or the four of us would be dining in Paris and then drinking until it was light out and we saw people going to work. As we parted he'd say, "Meet you at eleven o'clock. At the American Bar. . . ." I'd leave a wake-up call and struggle to get myself together and when I got downstairs he was standing at the bar sipping a Ramos gin fizz like he'd gone to bed before the evening news. You never saw a red eye, never puffiness. Impeccably dressed, the brown tweed jacket with the patches on the elbows, gray trousers, paisley shirt, brown suede shoes, argyle socks, and you just wanted to say "Fuck it" and go back to your room, rip off your clothes, and give up. Hanging from the bar to support myself, I implored, "How do you do it?"

He explained reasonably: "Your profession is being an entertainer, mine is being a playboy."

"Have you ever worked, Rubi?" He shrugged. "When would I have time to work?"

As we lunched he said, "There are some nice people you should meet." He mentioned some journalists, some social celebrities, among them Martine and Patrick Guerrand-Hermès and Yves Piaget. "These are good people. Don't waste yourself on shit." And he steered me away from others. I had a lot of people hitting on me. Some countess would say, "Come for the weekend," and Rubi would be in the background shaking his head like "That won't be good for you" or "You don't want to know them." He would never sit down and say, "Now, this is the reason why I said this." That wasn't his style. Sometimes there was a nod in the affirmative. But most of the time it was negative. A sad commentary on people.

The day after I met Romy I asked Rubi, "Who's the best florist in Paris?"

"What are you going to send her?"

"Six dozen roses." He was looking negative. "*Twelve dozen?*"

"No-no-no-no-no-no-no! Just one yellow rose. And have someone bring it in with a bucket of champagne."

I'd been watching all these Europeans kissing women's hands, so at what seemed like the appropriate moment I gave it a shot. Rubi shook his head almost imperceptibly. Later, privately, he explained: "Kissing a lady's hand is done more with the eyes than the lips. If you are being polite to a lady, if, for example, she is somebody's mother, kiss her hand gently and keep your eyes on her hand. However, if she is somebody's ravishing daughter, then you should look her in the eyes as your head lowers to her hand. If she is one with whom you wish to sleep that very evening, then also look her in the eyes as your head comes back up. But never bend more than a little way. Always raise her hand to your lips."

When not being avuncular Rubi was a shit-kicker. He loved to start arguments, get people fighting. "You know what Romy said about you? She doesn't like the grease in your hair. She'd like your hair to be very short."

Romy had a marvelous apartment that was a fifteen-minute drive from the George V. And the way they drive in Paris that's a long way out. I know because I walked it. We had an argument one night and I said, "Oh, yeah? Well, to hell with you." My whiskey told me, "Walk out and slam the door behind you. Show *her!*" One of those suave moves. I walked out into the darkness. She called after me, "Let me ring for a cab."

"No-no-no-no. I'll find my way." And there I was by myself, in the dark on the outskirts of Paris. Never walk out of a place at night in Paris or anywhere without the car waiting. Do it and you're alone. Only Fred Astaire can do that, with a cast of thousands.

We liked the Calvados, and we liked calvados. Toward the end of one evening she said something which made me inform her: "Sometimes you've got no fucking sense of humor."

Lengthy silence. The evening was over. Going downstairs, I decided to kick her. It seemed to me, at that moment, that anybody with no sense of humor required a good kick in the ass. I missed her completely and my body followed my foot and rolled down to the bottom of the stairs. Being totally drunk, I didn't try to protect myself and didn't break anything. I just rolled to the bottom like a basketball. When I got there and the sound of my fall had subsided, I heard her laughing. I stared up at her. She laughed harder, till she was ringing.

Those three weeks with Romy were irreplaceable. I felt like we were living inside a marvelous romantic movie in which I was a duke or a prince and the world was mine. We were together at other times, in other places, but it was never so good. That first, wonderful time was a part of being in Paris, the fun of knowing Rubi, of not being stared at, of briefly being without complications, of being on the rebound and ready to be in love with her in that setting, at that moment.

In London, where I went to play the Palladium, every day was like going into Tiffany's or Cartier's; it was "What's going to happen today that's new and glittery and shiny and bubbly?" and push all the shit behind you, guilt from a failed marriage, three children with a sometime father, being broke, the wearisome fact of being black in a white world—push all that shit behind you, to be handled some other time.

Most afternoons were devoted to styling myself for the act. Onstage I was wearing skintight solid-color jumpsuits with low-slung belts that hit below the waist. Everything was one of a kind. I had the long coats, beaded jackets, bell-bottoms, big puffed sleeves, military braid, beads from Carnaby Street, and the paisley shirts. My Nehrus came from France.

After I got off at the Palladium I hung out with Jimi Hendrix and Mama Cass. Nobody was hitting on Mama Cass, so as a result she was the running buddy, that was her protective covering, to be laughs and fun so you always wanted her in your company. Jimi Hendrix was moody and impressed with himself. He didn't show up except at the smaller gatherings. He'd have his own little group of flower kids around him, sitting in a ring at his feet, and he'd have his guitar and he'd be playing or listening to music, holding court.

Roger Miller had written "England Swings Like a Pendulum Do" and we went to his disco and it was the chicks with the micro-miniskirts and the leather dresses with cutouts at the waist and around the chest. Sundays at lunch we went to Alvaro's on the King's Road, Sibyl's, and it was loose, cats would be smoking shit, but you didn't see anything heavy. Even cocaine was hard to get there at the time. They'd bring in the Jamaica grass and that was supposedly very heavy. I was drinking. I'd take a few pokes of a joint and sit around and talk music.

The sound that was going on in England turned my head around professionally. It was good music, and I got especially hung up on what Blood, Sweat and Tears were doing. It was also the time of Jimmy Webb and "MacArthur Park." As I'm prone to do, I fell headlong into that "England sound," as I had with the "gear," and incorporated it all into my shows: the paisley shirts and beads, the whole Carnaby Street look; "Spinning Wheel," "You Make Me So Very Happy." That was what the sixties looked and sounded like to me.

While I was in London, an American magazine published a cartoon of a portly, elderly man bulging out of a jumpsuit and his matronly wife looking at him critically: ". . . because you're sixty-five, you're a meat packer, and you're *not* Sammy Davis, Jr." I remembered a line that Robert Sylvester had written in the early fifties in the New York *Daily News* when we opened at Bill Miller's Riviera: "God made Sammy as ugly-looking as He could and then hit him in the face with a shovel." Fifteen years go by and suddenly I remember that. I hadn't been aware of hating it at the time, because the important part then was that it was a fantastic review of our act. But I guess it had cut deep for it to stick that long and I wondered if Sylvester had imagined how much those words could hurt. Probably not. Nor could that artist imagine how happy his cartoon was making me—the image which was what I'd have ordered.

I ran into Tom Jones during supper at the Elephant. I was

going to be doing his TV special. We were a good personality combination; we'd do the bumps and grinds together. "I'd like you to sing 'Bojangles,' " he said.

"Mr. Bojangles" was written by Jerry Jeff Walker, who had a hit on it. Neil Diamond had a hit on it, and the Nitty Gritty Dirt Band had a hit on it. At the studio when Tom's manager brought up the subject I said, "I can't do that song. I hate it." I wanted nothing to do with it, with the character. It was the story of a dancer who became a drunk, a bum, and he died in jail. The name "Bojangles" had nothing to do with Bill "Bojangles" Robinson, who never went to jail, was never a drunk, retired rich, and died popular. The song spooked me. I had seen too many performers who'd slid from headlining to playing joints, then toilets, and finally beer halls and passing the hat, reduced to coming backstage to see the star, their pants pressed on a hot electric lightbulb, but with frayed collars and cuffs, and asking, "C'n you lend me some money . . . for grits . . ." Now here comes a song about that kind of a man.

"I don't want to touch that song." No way was I going to be telling people, "Look, here's where I'm going, into the toilet." I walked away from the conversation. "I'm not singing that song."

40

One day while I was playing Washington, D.C., at the Shoreham, I was invited out to Hickory Hill. It was a warm, family-style afternoon, with lunch served on the outdoor terrace, the kids falling out of trees, and a lot of good conversation, but nobody mentioned anything about Robert Kennedy running for President. The whole country was speculating about it but at the Kennedys' home, among friends, nothing.

After a few sets of tennis Bobby had gone into the house to shower. Looking for him, not familiar with the upstairs, I called out to him. A door opened, he stuck his head out and chanted, "Here come de Judge! Here come de Judge!"—a catchphrase I'd been doing on *Laugh-In* with Rowan and Martin.

Bobby had changed clothes and was brushing his hair. I sat on the edge of the bathtub. "What are you going to do, Robert? Are you going to run?"

"I don't know if I can get the nomination."

Disappointed, I said, "Well, if you decide to go for it, you know I'll be out there for you."

One night Bobby and Ethel caught my late show and came backstage. I said, "Let's not go up to the suite, too many people and phones." I loved being with him and with Ethel. They were affectionate to each other, like two comfortable shoes together.

I also enjoyed being with them because Bobby was a marvelous listener.

I said, "I'm sorry to be pushy but I really believe our country needs you. Are you going to run?"

Ethel said, "I wish he'd give you an answer, because he hasn't given me one yet."

"Come on, Robert. We'll all get on your bandwagon."

He half smiled. "Of the group I think you and Peter are the only ones who will. Frank and I still don't talk." Bobby had ordered a ham and cheese sandwich and a beer. He chewed slowly, took a sip of his beer, and as though thinking aloud, said, "It's such a tough race out there . . ."

"But come on, I can cover some bases for you . . ."

He had the habit of rubbing the front of his nose while you talked. He sat there listening to me throw out names I could get to help, rubbing a forefinger up and down the bridge of his nose. "I need some time, a little more time."

As I was checking out on my way to catch a plane to the Coast, Peter called and said, "Bobby's going to run." Then Bobby got on the line and confirmed it and I spoke with Ethel. "Sarge will be in touch with you."

Driving through Washington, passing Pennsylvania Avenue, I felt excited about helping to put another Kennedy, maybe even a better Kennedy, into the White House.

Bobby announced his candidacy a few days later, on March 16, 1968.

Several months earlier I had agreed to do a limited engagement of *Golden Boy* for Hilly in London. We were going to play a month in Chicago to iron out the problems, but we were rehearsing it in New York. On a Thursday which I will always remember to be April 4, 1968, we were onstage, loving the work, doing jokes, when Murphy came up to me. He was crying. "Dr. King . . ."

"Murphy, what is it?"

"They shot him. He's dead." He had meant it as a whisper but others heard it. I rushed to my dressing room and listened to the details being repeated on the radio. The kids in the cast had followed and were listening to it with me. Everybody was paralyzed. Then they started to react. One of the black actors said, "We should kill that motherfucker, we should kill all the white people . . ."

I snapped, "Who are you going to start with, the kids in the show?"

He stared at me, at the others. The black kids were glaring at the white kids. If it can happen with people like this, then what's going to happen with the cats on the street, the brother on the corner in Harlem who's going to blame every white store owner?

I called NBC and got Johnny Carson on the line during his rehearsal. "I've got to come over and say something. New York's gonna blow up."

"You're right. It's happening all over the country."

I don't remember getting into my car, only arriving in it at NBC and going up to the sixth floor, thinking: Don't preach, do it in Martin's name . . . remind them . . . Johnny introduced me, I walked on camera, and the taping resumed. "John, this is one time I'm going to dispense with the jokes and the songs. Ladies and gentlemen, today something tragic happened, a leader, a man who was my friend, was assassinated. The next seventy-two hours could mark the destiny of the next hundred years. I'm going to ask all good-thinking people, all the people that he tried to help, as well as all the people who marched in Selma, in Mississippi . . . if they would be kind enough to remember the man's *dream*, what he believed in, nonviolence. Please. We can't answer his assassination with violence. He had a dream! To destroy that would be the worst tribute we could pay him. So please . . . cool it, please, don't do anything! All my brothers and sisters out there: Don't do it . . . that isn't what the man was about . . ."

Billy Rowe, who'd gone with me to Selma, was waiting for

me and we went to CBS and did the evening news, then ABC. I did the six o'clock news everywhere. As did every black performer people would listen to.

Then I went to Atlanta, to the Kings' house, and paid my respects to Coretta and the children. Martin's father performed the funeral service at the Abyssinian Church. Thousands of people for whom there was no space in the church stood outside and listened to it over loudspeakers.

At the house there was a deep spiritual feeling, also blood-stopping sadness—everyone was aware of what Martin had accomplished and, tragically, but factually, that even his death would be a step forward with all those borderline people who would think: Hold it . . . that's too much. You don't kill such people.

Martin's spirit was alive in that room. Andrew Young and Jesse and I were in a corner. We tried not to get mired in the tragedy we felt. Andrew said, "We have to continue what he stood for." "What're we going to do?" "We'll wait awhile, then all get back together and sit down and see what we have to do, which direction we can go in." "Yes," Jesse said, "they can kill the dreamer but not his dream."

When I got back to New York, Sarge Shriver called. "Bobby said you want to help the campaign. We can meet at the Hotel Plaza, in the bar."

More than ever Robert Kennedy's presidency had urgency to me. Now Bobby was hope. If I were not already committed to a producer, investors, a large cast, and theaters in England and Chicago, I would have taken a few months off from performing and joined the Kennedy campaign full-time. I attended rallies, introducing him as I had done before. One evening we sat together and talked into the night, mostly about how to attract votes, but when we took a break for sandwiches he told me that he was aware of the risk of assassination, that he accepted it because of what he wanted to do for his country. And

I, like everyone around him, was moved by his idealism to the point where I heard the drums, I heard the bugles, I saw the flag flying, and I believed—as I had never before believed in any political person—that marvelous things were coming, that Robert Kennedy was going to lead America into a new age in which all Americans would be free and rich and love each other.

The Illinois and Indiana primaries were coming up and I spent every free hour campaigning for Bobby, often at fund-raising cocktail parties before the show. Essie and Irv Kupcinet gave one for Lake Shore Drive–type people with $500 to pay as entrance fees. I'd get up and say, "You know why you're all here . . . we need your money." It was very easy. They'd paid to get in and expected to give more. It wasn't fighting for your life like we did with civil rights rallies. We'd collect up to $50,000 plus the entrance charge.

Sarge Shriver would give me the list. "This is what you've got to do this week. Can you go to Northwestern on Sunday?" A faculty member would be having a rally or it would be a Students for Bobby Kennedy. Almost every afternoon I campaigned somewhere in Illinois and Indiana. I went out to the universities and talked about Bobby. I drew large crowds because my popularity was high and there was a known association with the Kennedys. The new young black voters were receptive to Bobby; his image with the ethnic groups in general was much stronger than John's had been; he had a deeper emotional key to the black people.

At the University of Chicago one of the students stood up and asked me, "What about the Kennedys' involvement in South Africa?"

Talk about feeling hot and being brought to a dead stop. I said, "I don't know. I don't know what you're talking about."

"Why would you be with the Kennedys when Joseph Kennedy has been and still is involved with the government of South Africa?"

I listened while he did a dissertation with names of companies, dates of investment, and "exploitation of the black labor force." I admitted, "I did not know about that. But in any event that's his father. It has nothing to do with Bobby Kennedy."

"It's all the same money. Isn't it financing his campaign?"

He had me on the ropes. "I'm sorry, I'm talking about the man I know. You want to ask me questions about him? Fine."

Bobby called me that evening. "I understand you had a problem with one of the students this afternoon. Sorry you got roughed up. We should have warned you about that."

"It's true, right?"

"Well, Dad did some things that *now* we aren't too proud of."

The daily papers, reporting the Chicago riots and beatings and arrests, with pictures of kids in physical and emotional agony, made me put down the paper at times to let my heart slow down and catch my breath.

I got Finis Henderson to take me to the black ghetto. As we walked he said, "Not that way. You can't walk there."

"Where can't I walk?"

"Down that street ahead of us. That's the Wall of Respect." He explained that the Panthers, the Keystone Rangers, and other ghetto gangs had established a spot past which nobody who was a part of the establishment could pass. "Don't feel badly, Sam. They wouldn't let Martin Luther King past there. Thought he was too Uncle Tom."

Martin Luther King an Uncle Tom? Talk about prejudice! And myself? I'd paid my dues with three broken noses and a lifetime of insisting on what I believed were my rights. Paid my dues? Hell, I'd learned a Life Membership. I didn't deserve to be an outsider. But I was. I was a member of the black race but not the black community.

I told Finis, "I want to meet with the brothers . . . get to know them, let them get to know me. Not the leaders. I want to meet the kids on the street."

They came into the dressing room after the show. Four of them. Late teens, early twenties. When we were past the amenities I said, "Listen, I want to help. What are you trying to accomplish? Can you use some cash?"

They looked disgusted with me. "No, man. Givin' money don't mean shit. We can *steal* money. Steal the motherfuckin' money. We want your commitment. And we want it on a day-to-day basis."

"You got that. You've always had it. Listen, I marched in *Mississippi* in '66. *Alabama* in '65."

"Don't mean shit today. This is '68."

There was a time when you joined the NAACP and you paid $100 to be a Life Member and that was your commitment to race. But now, suddenly you're standing outside yourself, watching yourself walking along, and you believe you've done good work and you think: I'm a nice cat, and I'm walking down this road . . . and you look down and suddenly there's no road under you. You're hanging in air. Somebody put the road over *there*. And you hear "This is the road now, man. That road over there don't exist anymore." "But that's the way I always went." "No more. Road's over here now."

Finis said, "The Commandos said they'll talk to you." They came to my hotel suite. They walked in angry.

"We don't like you," one of them said instead of hello. "You don't mean shit to us."

I understood that they were testing me. Was I tough? Strong? Or they had to show me how strong they were. I played along with them. "Then fuck you, man. Fuck you in the asshole. If you don't like me, then get the fuck outta my face."

"We don't need no nigguh lives with whitey . . ."

They didn't understand that I was thoroughly included in the hatred felt in Chicago for the blacks. During the show, sometimes I got booed from the audience and in the scene when the white girl refused me, people would applaud. I had four security men, one private and three black Chicago Police Department officers, who were always assigned to me. But these cats didn't know about that, nor did I want them to if I was to give them any sense of support.

Another of them was staring at me, his neck craned forward, peering into my face. I looked at him, giving him the opening he needed. He shrugged. "You don't *look* white."

"Okay," I said, "we can sit here for another hour and you can do numbers on my nose, and I can say 'Fuck you' right back, but then in a few weeks I pack my bags and I'm gone. I'll be in England. That's so far away they don't even know what chitlins is. But you gonna still be right here. Now you can use me while you got me, or you can waste me while you got me."

We started rapping. In reality everything about their lives was a problem. They had no homes, few jobs, and they had a major alienation between them and the white power structure even before the riots had begun. It was the cause of the riots.

"Well, now that we burned down the shit we been livin' in, what we want is for you to go tell 'em t'build first-class apartment buildings for us like they got over on South Shore Drive."

"Wait, wait, wait, hold it," I said. "You ain't never gonna get that. And I ain't gonna *do* that. Them cats on South Shore earned their bread and they saved their bread and that's what you gotta do if you wanta live like that."

"Save money? Shee-uht! We don't even have a Rexall in the neighborhood. How come we can't get a Safeway over there?"

I said, "Because the man ain't gonna come and build a thing for you motherfuckers to burn down again. He ain't just gonna keep buildin' up stuff. And we burnin' it down."

"Well . . . you right there . . ."

"So don't even ask about that stuff. There's certain things we can ask. I'll ask *for* you. But the man ain't stupid. I'll put you together with him . . ."

"We don't wanta meet with the motherfuckers."

"Okay, don't meet with them." I mentioned the name of the publisher of a major black newspaper. "Let me get you with him."

"Shee-uht. Ain't meetin' with no jive-ass motherfucker."

We had all gone from Negroes to blacks but there still wasn't black unity. There was no trust among blacks. I used to say onstage, "For all my brothers and sisters . . . and my cousins . . ." There was a *need* for "brother," for the black handshake, the locked thumbs. It was a search for trust, identity. You had to know: "Yeah, we're all in this boat together."

Bobby won the Indiana primary over Eugene McCarthy. It broke my heart that I couldn't campaign for him in California, my stronghold, but I was going to be in London doing *Golden Boy*.

On the day we were leaving I called to say goodbye and Bobby said, "I'm sorry you can't be with us to the end. If we're lucky enough to win, it won't seem right you not being there."

"That's awfully sweet of you to say. But I'll call you. And Peter'll call me and let me know what's going on."

41

This wild-looking chick in a long white evening dress, high in front, low in back, with ruffles, was at our opening night party in London. She resembled Queen Nefertiti. I grabbed Shirley Rhodes. "Who's that girl?"

"Are you nuts? That's your sister in the play. Altovise Gore."

"Alto doesn't look like *that!*" The part of my sister called for a nondescript girl with a dowdy hairdo who wears an apron-covered housedress because she's always in the kitchen.

Altovise and I flirted but we didn't date. She had her guy in New York and I had a whole lot of London chicks who'd been waiting for me since the last time.

Outside the *Golden Boy* world I had my "upper social group," my pals at the Elephant, and my "lower social group," the rockers—Jimi Hendrix, Mama Cass, the new musical groups, guys from the Stones. They were the wild scene in London and we cooked.

I was still floating under about a bottle of vodka when I felt Murphy nudging me. "Sammy . . . wake up . . . Sammy . . . it's important . . ." I heard him crying. "It was just on television that Bobby Kennedy was shot. In L.A., just after he won the primary . . ."

The phone rang. Murphy handed it to me. "It's Peter."

I was afraid to take it. I didn't want to hear that from someone I had to believe. Peter was almost incoherent. "It's over. It's over, Charley. We'll let you know what we're going to do, but it's over."

He called back within minutes, more pulled together. "Sam. The press will be calling you, they know the relationship. We don't want it known until tomorrow that Bobby is dead. That'll give Ethel time to speak to the kids."

"Of course, Peter. And when you think it's the right moment, tell Ethel that I'm not calling her, 'cause she doesn't need that, but I'm thinking of her. Just remind her that Bobby is with God. Maybe He knew Bobby was too good for this shit down here."

I sat back in bed dreading the television reports, yet unable not to watch them. "He's obviously been seriously injured but we haven't any details yet. The senator had just addressed an assemblage of his campaign workers, acknowledging his California victory, thanking them for their help. He said, 'I think we can end the division in the United States, the violence . . .' and he was shot within five minutes afterward."

I began hanging out mostly with my "lower social group" and got deeply into drinking and partying. I'd smoke some shit and take a hit and always I had a bottomless glass of vodka and Coke, anything to not feel anything. The partying was mostly at my place. These kids would come up and take their clothes off and sit around nude. There was some sex going on, switching partners, group sex, it was there to be had if you wanted it, any kind, any way. It was free-form, and when living got too depressing, hanging out with a group like that got your mind off it, for that moment at least it fogged your brain and you didn't feel so bad. Sex wasn't the point, though. *You didn't want to be alone.* Two or three people would get into bed with you and you'd fall asleep. You had physical companionship, that's what you needed, a quiet, friendly body lying next to you, and you'd sleep.

One morning I was standing on the balcony thinking that I'd gotten my mind off everything, but now the new day had drawn the curtains back and the sadness was still there. I smelled something cooking. I went to the kitchen. Altovise had come up and was there fixing eggs and bacon. "You haven't been eating, so you'd better have a little something . . ."

Altovise attracted me strongly, too strongly. She was too good-looking, too wholesome, fun, easy to be with. Too potentially habit-forming. I hadn't given up my wife and three children to fall into that lifestyle again. Get outta here! I was back and swinging again and there were only three people in this world who counted: Sammy, Davis, and Junior.

We were in the middle of Act Two when I saw a man stand up in mid-theater and come walking down the aisle straight for me. He reached the edge of the stage and then climbed the few steps to get up from the audience. He walked straight toward me on the stage, put his hand in his pocket, and served me with a summons.

In the dressing room Murphy's face crinkled with sympathy. "Sammy, that's embarrassing, in front of your audience, to have a process server climb onto the stage . . ."

"Murph, it happened, it's over, it's past. Forget it. I'll call Harrah's . . . ask 'em to advance me a hundred grand . . . pay off the London shops . . ."

"But maybe it's time to change the spending a little bit, just for your image. We could work out an economy plan . . . I'll take a cut, Sammy. A big one. Anything to help you straighten out."

How can you figure life, or plan it? You need a dresser, someone to pack and unpack and look after your clothes, so you hire a man, the years go by, and he's your best friend, your confidant. He signs my autograph, carries my jewelry and my money. Nobody in the world knows who I want to talk to and what I want and don't want as well as Murphy. Murphy's spent more time with me than with his wife. And he's got six grand-children.

Now he was staring at me, pleading with me to cut his salary and straighten out. I couldn't stand it. I waved my hands in the air and shouted, "I've got no time for this, man, I don't want to know about it! I'll work and I'll pay off everything and fuck it, let's have a party."

42

I played a six-week tour of Europe and took Altovise and four other dynamite chicks from *Golden Boy* with me. Altovise was the mistress of ceremonies, she introduced me, and during my act she'd come on and hand me a drink, light my cigarettes, the girls would dance around me and do jealousy bits over me.

I think that so much emotion had racked my mind and body through the past year that what I wanted was either to get drunk and blur the pain of loss, to simply not feel anything, or to exaggerate life enough so that through the numbness you could feel and enjoy something, almost like sprinkling monosodium glutamate on your emotional system.

In Vegas there were three incredible chicks I was seeing, all featured in different hotel shows. They were with me one night in my place at the Sands. Just the four of us. As dawn was breaking, we were resting, drinking, having a couple of hits, and I was thinking, This is the perfect lifestyle. Not only the physical joy of it but the kick of "He lives with three women." Talk about swinger images. I said, "Y'know what would be wild? You move in here with me and we live together, we run together. We have an exclusive commitment to each other. And we keep it within the confines of us four, absolute fidelity, none of us goes outside of this."

They moved their stuff over to my place by noon the next day. I got them three matching Caddy convertibles and sent out for toys: whips, chains, everything. On our first night "at home" I said, "Hey, why don't you chicks ball and I'll just sit here and watch." You can get off on just the idea of the control you have with that. The off-the-wall physical delight of it was sexually stimulating in the extreme. I felt privileged to be watching those beautiful things going on, but after an hour or so I began waiting for them to pause so I could join them. I waited. And I waited. And I had the distinct impression that they were happy without me.

As I got into bed, by myself, with the three of them still together, I wondered: Have they fallen in love with each other and I'm out?

The next night I stayed away from the suite. When I got home they were each sleeping in their own rooms. I figured that if they weren't together, then maybe I'd been wrong. After a while I slipped out of bed and into one of their rooms.

In the morning, still half asleep, I got "Hey, how come you didn't visit *me* last night?"

It doesn't work because you cannot eliminate the evil of jealousy. Plus, I had a tough enough time committed to one woman, let alone three. That whole segment of my life was an effort to blot out reality, to prove I was a swinger, the life of the party. But the physical part of it, most orgies and things that you go to, I have found, most of it is sad . . . most of the games people play is like taking off the comedy mask and underneath it you see the sad mask.

Only one promise fulfilled itself: when I walked onstage. That was like walking into a friendly home . . . like I could smell the food cooking. The feeling was so precious, so dear that you could wear it. I hated to leave that warmth. But finally, when the applause stopped and the curtain fell and the lights went on, when the people went out to gamble and there were only empty tables with empty glasses, what could I do then? So

I tried not to let them leave. I stretched shows from an hour and ten to an hour and thirty, even forty.

I was playing Harrah's in Lake Tahoe. The house didn't like the long shows, not for the cliché reason of getting the people out to the tables, but because they needed the time to break the room down and turn it around for the next show. When I stayed on too long the next audience was kept waiting outside. But there were nights I couldn't bring myself to break away from all that love.

I'd looked forward to getting back to L.A., where I had a week free, and I'd enjoyed planning parties at the house, being around town, in the hub. But my first day back I felt awful and slept around the clock. When I woke up, Lessie Lee, my cook, made me a steak but I couldn't eat it.

"You wanta aig?" I shook my head. She eyed me bleakly. "Well, if you cain't eat by now, then you better get y'self a doctor."

Gerald Blankfort came over and took some tests. "Your liver enzymes are elevated. Also, I don't like the looks of your throat. Those polyps and your chain-smoking don't have a good future together." For the first time, someone explained to me how vocal cords work: "They rub together and they become callused, they develop nodes, and the hot smoke and nicotine will cause them to stay inflamed. Those nodes can turn into cancer. You have to give up smoking for your throat and drinking for your liver."

"I'm sorry, but this is not a moment in my life to give up smoking. And I'm not too worried about the polyps. I had them in *Golden Boy* and the doctors said the same thing and three months later I was singing better than ever."

"At least cut the drinking."

"Gerry, there is no way I can give up boozing. Not just for the pleasure. It's part of the image. The audience expects it. Take away my drinking jokes and that's seven minutes out of the act. And frankly, I just can't walk on the stage without having something to lean on."

Roman Polanski and his wife, Sharon, gave me a welcome-to-London party. I was there to shoot *One More Time,* a sequel to *Salt and Pepper,* with Peter and with Jerry Lewis directing. I had known Sharon Tate and Roman for a long time. They invited Peter and Jerry and our mutual friends to their flat. Later, after Jerry and the other "straights" had left, we had a little grass, a little coke, booze, fun and giggles.

I called Roman the next day. "Hey, what a ball we had last night. Till when are you guys here?" He said, "Sharon's going back tomorrow. The baby is almost due. I'll join her in a few weeks," and we agreed to get together around the end of the week.

The massacre happened three days later. The killers had tortured Sharon, then hung her upside down and cut the baby out of her womb. The London newspapers were filled with the devastation at her house in L.A., the slaughter of her, Jay Sebring, Abigail Folger, and others I used to run with. Everyone there had at one time or another been into Satanism or, like myself, had dabbled around the edges of it for sexual kicks. Hanging Sharon upside down to torture and kill her was highly ritualistic.

Peter and I were sharing a house on location, and as we read the stories and watched the TV news reports, he said, "We probably would have been there." That was our crowd. I knew that had I been in L.A. and there was a party at Sharon's I'd have been there. But something had saved me. The evil had missed me. But how close I'd come.

Jimi Hendrix died of an overdose in London. I had been with him two days before. It staggered me: while I was over there Sharon and Jay had gotten it here, then I got back here to L.A.

and Jimi died there. Six people I knew in that group had over-
dosed. The fear had always been getting busted by the police.
Now, it seemed, *God* was busting these people.

I knew that I'd been pushing my luck at everything, stretching
the rubber band financially, drugs, debauchery. Ten million dollars after I'd become a star I was deeply in debt. Okay, I'd been
able to call Harrah's and get a hundred-thousand advance and
pay off everybody in London, and I'd called the Sands and gotten
another hundred-thousand advance to pay off everybody in New
York, and more for Beverly Hills, but when was this going to
end? I was almost forty-five years old. I had more clothes than I
had closets, more cars than garage space, more jewelry, more
everything if it could be bought on credit . . . but no money.

Sy Marsh and I opened an office on Sunset Boulevard. I was
playing Boston when he called. "Sammy, did you ever hear of
some people in Chicago called the Commandos? And something called Sammy Davis Jr. Liquors?"

"Sure, babe, why?"

"Well, I got a call a week ago from someone saying, 'Listen,
man, we need money.' "

"Babe, the Commandos are some good cats I met in
Chicago. They needed something to keep them off the streets,
so I helped them to open a liquor store."

"And it's got your name on it?"

"Yeah . . . I think it has."

"Well, I just got another call ten minutes ago, and this 'good
cat' said, 'Listen, motherfucker, you didn't call back, we're
gonna come out and kill you, you white motherfucker.' Sammy,
how much have you given them?"

"I don't know, maybe twenty, thirty thousand."

"Sweetheart, anybody who can lose that kind of money in a
liquor store is a genius. We have to get out of it. Look, this is
the beginning, so cutting away the fat is painful . . ."

I knew he had more bad news. "What's up, babe?"

"Well . . . your plane has to go. It's a major drain."

"But it's a tax write-off . . ."

"It's costing you a quarter of a million a year after taxes."

". . . and my name on it . . . it's a wonderful image . . ."

"It *was!*"

"Okay, you're captain of the business. But it's complicated."

"Why? It's a simple rental against purchase. We're only on the hook for this quarter."

"But there was a letter agreement besides the contract."

"A letter agreement? Where is it?"

"In one of my suitcases, I guess. It says that if we don't buy the plane there's a quarter-million-dollar penalty, which is what they figure it takes to repaint, refurbish, redo the engines . . ."

There was a long silence at the other end, like the start of an ulcer. "Well . . . it still has to go. There's no way to survive it. We'll pay it off somehow . . ." His voice came over stronger. "Listen, sweetheart, hang in, we're making progress."

Staying out of the shops wasn't easy, they were my natural playgrounds, but every time I felt like I needed a new watch I called Sy and he told me the right time.

When I took the act on the road, Altovise and I started dating seriously. Introducing her to a friend, I said, "This is my old lady." She waggled her head in wonderment. "When I was a kid going to professional school, you were the one we all talked about . . . Sammy Davis, Jr. . . . Now you're my guy."

I felt very protective of her. She was full of enthusiasm for life and she was great, great fun; unspoiled, thoroughly natural. She enjoyed my show business friends and they enjoyed her and I admired how in L.A. she'd easily coped with being the out-sider meeting all the lifelong buddies.

I kept thinking how much fun it would be to take this child so steeped in innocence and expose her to my world, the dark side and the light side. I had the feeling that with her I could get myself on the road to a straighter, more productive life. And she would enjoy being a part of my life without resistance to the way I had to live it.

We were on the plane from Los Angeles to Newark en route to the Latin Casino outside of Philadelphia, laughing and giggling, and I said, "Y'know, you're the quintessence of fun." Taking her hand, I said, "I'd love for us to spend the rest of our lives together."

She nodded dreamily, as though she were watching a movie and enjoying the love story, not realizing I was talking about real life.

"Altovise! I'm proposing! Would you like to marry me?"

She sat forward. She smiled like Roman candles. "You mean *us?* Yes. I'd love to be married to you."

"But no children." She was disappointed. "Darling, I've got three great kids I've neglected. I won't do that to any more. I know my limitations and they stop short of being a father."

"Maybe you'll change your mind."

"Know now: I won't. What I'd like for us to do is to be married but remain independent individuals. Married physically, but single mentally. I know that's a contradiction. People are either married or single. Well, I've been both and neither of them is perfect, so I'd like to try something else."

"You want to be married but also fool around?"

"It isn't the physical thing with the broads. What I *don't* want is to say 'I do' and automatically I disappear from the scene and someone asks, 'Whatever happened to Sammy Davis, Jr.?' and they say, 'Oh, he got married, you don't see him around much anymore.' I want to have a great married life with you but I want us to keep out front, in focus. I can't afford to lose that. I want us to have an open marriage. Naturally, neither of us does anything to offend the other. But we'd both have the freedom to have our lifestyles, we can each have our indiscretions, but no major infidelity, nothing to get divorced over. I want the legal thing of it, and I want you to be obligated to me, and me to you, but not too much too suddenly."

I called Carl Barry, the comedian, who lived in Philadelphia, and he arranged the license and we signed the papers, but we didn't have a date set. I didn't want a "wedding" with her parents flying in and my parents flying in and a best man and maid of honor . . . too much commitment to conventional marriage.

One morning, I was supposed to play golf but it was raining. I was drinking coffee and looking out the window. It was a steady, nice, springtime, green-making rain. What I wanted to do most in the world was get married to Altovise. I did the Mike Douglas show that morning and as we left the studio I told her, "Let's do it today. You'd make me proud if you'd become my wife." We were married in the Philadelphia courthouse at 5 p.m. As we left, there was just a bit more than a heavy mist in the air. I took her arm. "Let's walk in the rain." When we got to Rittenhouse Square and we passed Nan Duskin's I bought her a long, black-diamond mink coat and she put it on over her jeans, which were tucked into high boots.

It was exciting to see what happened to her when she slipped on the coat. All that money might smother or dominate another woman, but Altovise wore it like a star.

"You've got talent," I said.

She giggled. "To wear mink?"

"That too. But I meant for being the wife I've always wanted, the wife I need. I don't want a 'gypsy' or 'a nice little housewife' that comes to parties with me once in a while and they say, 'That's Sammy's wife, whatshername,' and she never has an identity. I want you to become a personality in your own right so that when we arrive somewhere it's 'Hey, there's Sammy and Altovise.' "

She swirled the coat around her, then sidled up to me and, opening the coat, closed it around me. Being taller than me, she spoke through the neck opening, like into a funnel. "Aren't you worried I might upstage you?"

I got out of the coat. "Definitely try to upstage me. 'Cause you ain't never going to be able to do it."

43

Mary Benny called. "Jack and I would love to have you and your bride come to dinner on Thursday."

Altovise panicked. "*Jack Benny!* And *Mary Livingstone!*"

"Darling, relax, they're friends."

"*Your* friends, but they don't know *me.*"

"They'll love you because *I* love you, so you open with kings."

"What should I wear?"

"You don't want to blend in like just another wife in a designer dress from Rodeo Drive. Let's keep your own free and youthful style. Be an original. I think you should wear hot pants."

"No, Sammy . . . please, these are older people, they'll think I'm a tramp."

"Not if *I* wear them too. We'll go in matching tuxedo-style hot pants. Trust me. It'll be a giggle."

Sy Devore made them for us and we tried them on together. I looked nice, normal. But she looked like fire alarms going off.

Milton Berle was standing near the front door at the Bennys'. "How does an old Jew like you get such a gorgeous young wife?"

Lucille Ball threw her arms around Altovise. "We're going to be friends, I hope."

I had planned to stay close to her to give her support but Lucy and Polly Bergen took her around the house to show her Jack's small bedroom next to Mary's large one, then brought her into conversation groups, and she was swinging without me; she was laughing, they were all laughing, she'd won everybody over.

In the car I squeezed her hand. "I was proud of you."

She was high on success, rattling on. "Lucy said I should call her and that when you're out of town I should hang out with her and Gary."

"Well, do it. They're wonderful people."

"And Janet Leigh said she wants to propose me for SHARE? Isn't that a charity?"

"Yes, for retarded children. A serious charity. You should join SHARE. Those women are your peers in this town. And you'd be the first black woman ever to be a member."

"Sammy, I'm a gypsy, not a charity woman."

"Don't be scared. Do it."

"How do you know I'm scared?"

"*I'd* be if I were you."

In our suite at the Ambassador she said, "You're going to think I'm so square it's embarrassing but I've *got* to call my father and tell him I met Charlie Bronson and Edward G. Robinson."

I was so pleased that there was no tug-of-war, that my wife was made happy by what I was able to give her. I said, "Darling, enjoy it, keep a little of the stardust. Maintain that naïveté. Keep 'the little girl looking into the candy store.' I'm not saying that everything should be 'Oh, it's a movie star . . . eek!' But I want to always be excited that Mary and Jack Benny invite me to dinner, that I can talk to Fred Astaire. I love that I heard Judy Garland sing with Liza. Savor the moments that are warm and special and giggly. Keep yourself vulnerable to them."

It was fun for me to introduce her to this life. I gave her her first car, a Rolls-Royce with the license plate ALTOVISE. She drove it in a circle around the Ambassador's driveway. She got out and hugged and kissed me, and grabbed my buns. "Y'wanta fool around a little, honey?" and she ran upstairs to tell her mother in New York.

I hadn't anticipated the Daddy Warbucks syndrome, the pleasure derived from being able to give her expensive things. I could never get that with May. If I had put May's name on her license plate it would have embarrassed her. And so would a Rolls. She preferred a station wagon with the kids piled in. May's values were what the world considered better. But Altovise enjoyed and adapted to *my* values.

I loved the image of her shopping on Rodeo or going to lunch at the Bistro Garden, arriving with the right equipment. Granted that status symbols are out of all proportion in Beverly Hills, that it shouldn't be that way—but it *is*, and if she was going to become a part of the Beverly Hills world, then I was delighted that I could provide the right wardrobe and props, and that Alto was tickled to be given them.

I dropped in on our office, a suite of four rooms on Sunset Boulevard in Hollywood. Sy said, "It bugs me that we aren't making any money in the record business. We should get away from Reprise–Warner Bros. and go with the best. I had a talk with Berry Gordy and he was very excited by the idea."

Berry's Motown label was releasing people like the Supremes and the Temptations. He practically owned the top of the charts. We had a press conference to announce that I had signed with Motown, and Berry said, "I believe I can make Sammy Davis the world's biggest recording star." I set aside two weeks for the record sessions and we made two albums. Then they released the first album and it did nothing.

Sy went over to see Berry Gordy. "When are you going to release the next album?"

Berry began hedging. "My men out in the field don't think he's got the Motown sound."

"Of course he hasn't. Sammy sings ballads."

"I'm sorry, but it turns out that it's not the material we're capable of releasing successfully."

In the meanwhile Sy was in touch with Mike Curb, who was the new "hottest record producer in town" and had just been made president of M-G-M Records. Sy confided to him, "We're under contract to Motown but it's the wrong operation for Sammy. If you'd be interested I'll get out of the Motown deal."

"I'm more than interested. I definitely want Sammy Davis."

Sy flew down to Vegas to tell me. I hated the idea. "Mike Curb? That cat's square, white bread."

"What's the difference? The important thing is that when I negotiate the contract I'll make a deal with M-G-M to release our Motown tapes for just a distribution fee. They'll do it 'cause they've got no investment to make back. Which means that instead of a five percent royalty, sweetheart, we'll get sixty percent." He returned to L.A. and called me the next day, gleeful. "Sweetheart, I made the release deal for the tapes, and with the lion's share like we've got, if the album does anything at all we'll make like three million on it. And they're excited about you coming in to record. In fact, Mike's got a single that he did an instrumental on with the Mike Curb Congregation. He said, 'If Sammy would put his voice on it I think it would be great.' He says you've got the youth and exactly the right cuteness about you."

"What's the name of it?"

" 'The Candy Man.' "

"*What?* 'The *Candy* Man'?"

"Something like that. Tony Newley and Leslie Bricusse wrote it for a movie with Disney or something."

"I've heard the song. It's horrible. It's a timmy-two-shoes, it's white bread, cute-ums, there's no romance. Blechhh!"

Sy was getting nervous. "Sweetheart, please—don't make waves. The important thing is that they release your Motown album. You've got to record with Mike Curb's Congregation. You've got to do 'The Candy Man.' "

I hated it but I agreed. When I got back to L.A., Sy went with me to the M-G-M recording session. I looked at the lead sheet for "The Candy Man," forced a smile at everybody, and we did it in one take. I went into the control room to listen to the playback. It was icky cute. I glared at Sy.

Mike Curb said, "Sammy, could you put in a couple of di-ah-do-ah's . . . ?"

"A couple of what?"

"Just some ad-libbing in the middle . . . 'cause I have to bring in the Congregation behind you."

I smiled like sugar, like a candy man, and I went out to the studio and did it again, this time with some di-ah-do-ah's. Then I listened to the playback. Mike Curb was looking delighted. I elbowed Sy and hissed, "This record is going straight into the toilet. Not just around the rim, but into the bowl, and it may just pull my whole career down with it."

"Sweetheart . . . so you invested a little time . . . mainly what we want is for them to release . . ."

"Okay, Sy, we've done it . . . you've had it your way."

44

Altovise came into the bedroom and made signs for me to pick up the phone. "The White House is calling."

It was Bob Brown, one of the founders of the Southern Christian Leadership Conference, who'd worked with Martin Luther King. "I'm coming out," he said. "I need to talk to you." I knew that he'd left his business in North Carolina and was working for President Nixon in Washington.

Altovise and Bob and I sat in the living room. "Sammy, the President has spoken highly of you and he wants your help with some of our programs. *I* want your help. I'd like to see you do some meaningful things, bigger than anything which we as private citizens can do. We have an opportunity to better the lives of many people around this country. We've got Jim Brown with us, and we've got James Brown, we've got good people, but the President wants you. From time to time he asks me, 'How's Sammy doing? Do you think he'd help us with this?' He wants you to be a member of the National Advisory Council on Economic Opportunity."

I was astounded. "Bob, I'm a Democrat. I'm strongly associated with the Kennedys, with Democratic goals."

"Understood, but don't close the door on Nixon. Use his power to accomplish the things you and I believe in. Accept the post on Ec-Op. Later, if you feel he should be reelected, then become a Democrat for Nixon. Or if you don't believe in him, then walk away. But won't it be better to judge him by your own experience firsthand? That's what I did and I say that he feels a commitment to causes you and I believe in. If I'm not right, then why has he got *me* there? The Nixon White House has more black people in high positions than any President has ever had, including JFK."

We saw him to his car. "Think seriously about this, Sammy. I'll be in touch." Alto and I went into the house, to the bar for a nightcap. I said, "I believe Bob Brown. Trouble is, Jim Brown and the others can do it, but if *I* make a move ten guys'll be writing, 'Sammy wants to be Ambassador to Watts.' I'll be an 'opportunist.' Ain't nobody gonna understand me going over to Nixon."

I got Jesse Jackson on the phone and he said, "I'm not a Nixonite, but there's no question that he's carrying on the civil rights programs, he's not scrapping them like he could have." I spoke to others within the civil rights structure, leaders of the NAACP and the Urban League, and the consensus was positive. "If we could get you in there, to have the President's ear . . . we could get some things done."

At my first monthly board meeting we talked about the disenfranchisement of the blacks in America, unemployment among black teenagers, and the drug problem. Proportionately more black people were arrested and harassed over drugs than white people. Even in minor neighborhood disorders it was "We've got no time. Lock 'em up and let the judge straighten 'em out," and suddenly a family man is in jail for three or four years before his trial comes up. We got the Justice Department to look into it.

While I was in town I called Ethel to say hello, to ask about the children. "Mrs. Kennedy isn't in at this moment, but if I can have your number she'll get back to you."

The days and evenings were filled with meetings. Only when I returned a few weeks later did I realize that I hadn't yet spoken to Ethel.

"One moment, please. Who may I say is calling?"

"Sammy Davis, Jr."

She was out. She would get back to me.

But she didn't. I tried once again. Blank wall. Silence.

Nor had Harry Belafonte returned my call as he always had. Nor Sidney Poitier. All of the liberal Democrats, people who had marched for what we all believed in—when I went to work for Nixon they stopped talking to me. Nobody said, "Hey, give me a reason . . ."

During the next six months I was in Washington often. I always went to John's and Bobby's graves. But I didn't call Ethel again. It was an ache. I thought she was wrong, I thought Harry and Sidney were wrong. But I could get sick over it and weep for cherished relationships I'd lost, or I could do what I had to do and say "Fuck it," and kid myself that I meant it.

Before going to my meetings with black businessmen and senators I always started with Bob Brown for a briefing in his office in the Executive Office Building within the White House complex. Bob had four secretaries there, plus three staff people working in the White House. He was not just a conduit on the black situation, he was there on all levels. John Kennedy never had a black man as close to him as Robert Brown was to Richard Nixon.

On the day Mahalia Jackson died I was playing Las Vegas and I got a phone call from Bob. "Sammy, would you go to Mahalia's funeral in an official capacity representing the President?" I told him that it would be a great honor, but I had to be back in Vegas that same evening. "No problem. I'll lay on an Air Force plane to pick you up and bring you back."

As I stood at her grave, watching the coffin being lowered, I was thinking: Mahalia . . . you know all those times we thought: Hell, it ain't never gonna get better . . . Well, sister, who do you think sent me here to pay his respects?

I kept hearing about black kids getting busted in Vietnam for smoking a joint. Of all the GIs over there in the drug rehab hospitals, the majority were black. It was out of kilter. Blacks are a minority. And when I was in San Francisco at Haight-Ashbury there were more white kids than black kids taking LSD and smoking joints. Yet in Vietnam black kids were getting bad discharges for minor abuse, while whites who'd been caught with the same thing were getting off clean. It was causing riots on military bases and on ships. I asked Bob, "Does the President know about this?"

He called me back. "The President asks if you'll go to Vietnam for him, be his eyes and ears and report back to him."

I flew to Washington and Bob and I met with Dr. Jaffe, the head of the President's drug commission, who explained: "The problem lies in the quality of the military in charge there. Vietnam is not a top job, so the assignment does not go to the best people. Like in the embassy jobs: leave London and Paris and the rest of the assignments are bummers. The officers in command there are older men at the ends of their careers. A joint to them is 'dope.' One of them once said to me, 'Those niggers're all dope fiends.' The bigotry is incredible. Chappy James told me, 'There are Army officers in Vietnam who still don't believe black people can fly an airplane.' Their prejudices are damaging these kids' careers and their future lives. If you were to go over there . . ."

"Just give me time to put a show together. While I'm there I'd like to do something for the guys."

Dr. Jaffe said, "I'll send my top people to help you, but it's not going to be pretty for you. The kids are going to think you're a jive-assed motherfucking Uncle Tom coming in . . ."

This was a white man telling me that.

We flew in an Army C-50 with no windows, a heavy transport that usually carried jeeps, like an empty garage, with benches along the sides, no insulation, eating TV dinners on a rough and rainy night: Altovise, the girls who would dance with her,

George and Shirley, my musicians, twenty-five of us. I brought everyone except Murphy. I didn't feel he could handle it.

We landed in the daytime and were put up in a house that was on a level with officers' quarters. Two Vietnamese women, mama-sans, took care of it for us. That evening we met with the officers at a dinner. They served fried chicken.

The next day, arriving at a detoxification center, I saw barbed wire surrounding it and watchtowers with armed guards looking down, like Sing Sing. I walked in and most of the forty or fifty inmates, sixty percent of them black, were sitting in rows glaring at me. I kept my smile going. "Hi, guys."

"Motherfucker, whut you doin' here?"

"I wanta find out why you're in here. How they're treating you. You've gotta fill me in."

"Shit, we don't have t'fill no muh'fuckin' jive-ass in on nothin'. The white man sent you here. He musta told you."

Despite having been warned, it shook me. "No, you've got it wrong, I came over thinking I could do some good."

"Aaagh, bullshit! You here t'use us for a TV special. T'do *yourself* some good." He turned to one of the officers who'd brought me there. "We have t'listen t'this?" Another sneered at me: "Man, what the fuck you know about it? You walk in here with all these motherfuckin' officers, we don't know them, they white. You come in wrong from the git-go."

It was scary, a *mano a mano*, with attitude toward attitude. I wasn't "Sammy," a brother, I was establishment. I'm black and I'm sent there by the white President? Get outta here! They trusted me like they would have trusted Bob Hope if he'd come in talking about drugs.

I put up my hands. "Wait a minute, wait a minute. Just 'cause I don't say, 'Fuck you, motherfuckers,' and because I care, doesn't make me part of the establishment—but incidentally, I *am* part of the establishment, the good part that cares what's happening to you . . ."

"Fuck it, man. Fuck it. Shit. He's bullshitting."

"Okay, but give me a fucking shot at it. If I don't accomplish anything, then you can just go back, or sit here, or whatever you gotta do, and say, 'Look how right we was, he *is* a jive-ass motherfucker.' "

I was wringing wet and beginning to feel that I wasn't going to make it, that this was a loser. I turned to the first guy. "If I'm taping a TV show to take back and get rich on, then where's the fuckin' cameras? In my bad eye? And *you* tell *me* why I'm here at the ass end of the fuckin' world 'steada bein' with ten chicks in Vegas and makin' a hundred grand a week. Like, I'm shrewd, I've got me this snappy jeep to ride 'round in over here 'steada my shitty ol' Rolls-Royce and Caddy convertible . . ." I had their attention and I didn't let go. "Look, man, I've been in the Army. Not as bad as Vietnam is now to you. But it was fucking lousy then for me. I was in the first integrated regiment in the U.S. Army. How'd you like to sleep with twenty-eight rednecks hatin' your ass? You think that ain't payin' your dues?"

It registered. "Hey, man . . . so then what the fuck *are* you doin' here?"

"When I go back and tell Mr. Nixon what it's like here, maybe he'll do something about it . . ."

"And maybe he won't."

"That's no worse than where you are now."

"Okay. Fuckin' right." The rest of them had quieted down. "Whaddya wanna know, bro'?"

I nodded. "Thanks. I want to understand what's going on. Let me communicate it to the top. What can I tell them?"

"You saw the barbed wire? You saw the gun towers? You wanta know why I'm in this *medical facility*? I been here in Nam six months. Killed guys. That's my job. Almost *got* killed. That's my job too. Came in from the fire base. Five bucks to a mama-san, got me a joint and a hit of coke. Urinalysis. Bam. Addict. Get his black ass out on a DD."

Again, once past the hard exterior I heard them crying for help. One of the others asked, "You here to fight drug abuse?"

"I'm here to fight the abuse of *you* . . ." I saw suspicious eyes looking at me, not disbelieving so much as nonbelieving. "I want to hear what's going on, and I can't promise anything except that it will get to the right people. I promise you I will beg them to take the barbed wire down. And the gun towers. Those fuckers are coming down."

I did four big shows on a stage with a full band at Danang and a few others for twelve or fourteen thousand soldiers. Altovise was mistress of ceremonies for those shows. She came out in hot pants. Cats went crazy! I had to fight for my life to get their attention. "Hey! You gotta ease up on my *wife*. That ain't my old lady, that's my wife, *man*. Don't let me come out here and have to cut somebody . . ." And the rapport was building.

THE WHITE HOUSE

April 4, 1972

Dear Sammy,

From the glowing reports which I have received your recent tour of our military bases in Vietnam and Hawaii was an outstanding success. Realizing the many demands on your time I want you to know how much I appreciate your willingness to undertake such an extensive trip. My sentiments are undoubtedly shared by all our servicemen who were privileged to meet you.

Sincerely,
Richard Nixon

Bob's voice boomed with excitement over the telephone. "The Man wants to see you. He wants to have lunch with you. Are you available Thursday? You've got an opportunity. You've got carte blanche to go in there and talk to him, to say anything you want and have the President of the United States listening to you. Use your shot to make long strides forward."

The President put his hand on my shoulder as we walked

into his dining room. "It was a good trip, Sammy. I've heard wonderful reports about it, you've made a lot of friends. And you'll be happy to know that the barbed wire is coming down."

As lunch was served he guided me onto what I was there for. "How can I do some good racially? Where is the help needed? In what form?"

I spoke to him about education. I also asked if he was aware that federal monies were rarely available to black small businessmen as they were to white. At that time no specific proportion of loans had to go to minorities as it does today.

There was a dinner being held in Washington that month by the Negro Republicans. No American President had ever attended their dinner. I asked President Nixon if he would come as a speaker. He said, "I have some close people delegated to attend. I respect the Negro Republicans, I know they influence the black voters . . ." He hesitated. "Incidentally, it *is* okay to say black?"

"Yes, Mr. President, we say black now. Negro and colored are not in use."

He had a notepad and he wrote, "Black is preferred, colored is not," and he asked, "How did that happen?"

I told him about James Brown's song. "It's all changed around, sir. In the old days it was 'If you're white you're right, if you're brown stick aroun', but if you're black you're in back.' When I was growing up, nobody wanted to be called black. Everyone wanted to be called colored. Today colored is an insult to the young kid on the street. He wants to be proud of his blackness."

We returned to the subject of the dinner. "Sir, your presence there would lend great credence to your support of the programs that interest them. *I* know firsthand you're behind them, and I'll gladly do an hour telling them for you, but your appearance, even briefly, would say it better."

As the dinner began there had been no official acceptance or turndown by the President. It was a mixed crowd racially and politically. Every prestigious civil rights leader was present. Among them were the Democrats for Nixon, plus Democrats who were not for Nixon, and important black military, like General Chappy James.

An hour into the evening Bob came over to me, trying to contain his excitement. "The Man's on his way over. You pulled off a coup."

I was on the dais, I'd already performed, when there was a perceptible change in the level of conversation. Suddenly everyone's attention was drawn to one spot, and then here comes the President. The band played "Hail to the Chief," everybody stood and cheered, he shook hands with people as he walked through the room. Coming to me, he stopped, hugged me, and continued to the center of the dais, to the speaker's position.

"Sammy told me I had to be here."

It got a big, warm laugh—especially from me—and then he made a relatively long speech, six or seven minutes, ending, "I would love to stay here, but I've got commitments and I just wanted to come by and let you know . . ." He went out as he'd come in, shaking hands, surrounded by the Secret Service agents.

Jesse looked at me from his seat on the dais and nodded, like "Not bad, old buddy. That was a good move."

M-G-M Records had released my Motown album and "The Candy Man" as a single. "The Candy Man" appeared on the charts at number 56.

Sy got a call from Berry Gordy. "Sy, I see you're with M-G-M and I also see that you're on the charts." Loving it, playing it cool, Sy almost yawned. "Yeah, Berry. First record we release and we're on the charts."

Next week *Billboard* came out: 34 on the charts.

Berry Gordy called Sy. "I see your record's moving up."

Next week: 21 on the charts.

It was incredible, absurd, ridiculous—but a fact. Who can

figure it? Go explain my career! I can name ten songs I recorded that I'd have bet my house would be hits. But: toilet! Now, the one record I resisted, the one record in my life that I *least* expected . . .

It went to number 1.

Berry Gordy called Sy. "I'm just on your phone to admit to you that we blew it."

There are a lot of regional hits, or national hits. Hits in the South, or hits in Australia, or London, but rarely does a record become an international hit. In the middle of the discotheque craze people all over the world were hearing "Who can take the sunrise, put it in a jar? . . . the Candy Man can . . ." People were going, "What's happening with the music business?"

We were in another limo, en route to another airport. I asked Sy, "What about the Motown album?"

"It's a collector's item."

I got the drift. "But there aren't many collectors?"

He groaned like a man who had just lost three million dollars. "Right, sweetheart."

I had also begun singing "Mr. Bojangles" and though I hadn't recorded it I couldn't finish a show without the audience screaming, "Do 'Bojangles' . . ."

We stopped at a light and some kids looked into the car, idly at first, then they saw me and got hysterical. "It's the Candy Man!!!"

As we pulled away I marveled: The two songs that I wanted nothing to do with, the two signature things which everybody associates with me—I backed into them both. Which shows that you can be in this business fifty years and you still don't know anything about it. So go out there and play it by ear, but leave a lot of room for the people to discover something you're doing. Because it's the people who lay it on you.

The 1972 Republican National Convention was scheduled to be held in Miami. Bob Brown called. "The President would like you to be involved. We'd like you to head up a big show at Marine Stadium, where there's going to be a Young Voters for Nixon rally, the new eighteen- to twenty-one-year-old, first-time-out voters. It's scheduled for the night when the President should receive the nomination by acclamation. For your information, normally the President would not make an appearance anywhere until he goes to the floor of the convention and accepts the nomination, but he indicated to me that if you do a show he will appear to speak."

"FOUR MORE YEARS . . . FOUR MORE YEARS . . . FOUR MORE YEARS . . ." The kids were growing hoarse from shouting it . . . the stadium overflowed with young people involved in politics for the first time in their lives. Borne on their enthusiasm, I worked onstage for two hours looking out at thousands of banners and campaign hats and buttons and flags.

I was about to introduce another rock group when a Secret Service agent, holding a walkie-talkie, came over to me. "Sammy, the President is arriving." From the stage I could see a group of bodies moving like a train along the side of the stadium, the President surrounded by an escort of Secret Service, moving quickly through the screaming crowd.

The kids out front were politically tuned in enough to know that it was completely unheard of for him to appear there that evening, so when I announced, "Ladies and gentlemen, Young Voters, the President of the United States," it was pandemonium.

The President did not hurry to quiet the Young Voters, he let them go on screaming, chanting "FOUR MORE YEARS . . . FOUR MORE YEARS . . ." Finally he raised his hands for silence.

"I want to express appreciation to all of the celebrities— that's the word we use for them—for Sammy Davis, Jr., and the marvelous groups that you've been hearing here . . . and I want to ask all of you to realize what it means to them to be here.

"Now, my business is the business of politics. It's a very honored business. I hope lots of you get into it, maybe full-time. But I want you to know that when you're in politics you assume—you have to under our system—that what you're trying to do is get somewhat more than half the vote, and the other man or woman, as the case might be, will get somewhat less than half.

"Now, in show business, which is Sammy Davis, Jr.'s business and the business of others who are here, they are not trying to get half, they're trying to please *everybody*, and so you see when somebody in show business comes and participates in a political rally he or she is doing something that is a very great personal sacrifice and even a personal risk.

"I heard on Monday night one of the commentators question Sammy Davis, Jr., when he was sitting there with Mrs. Nixon in the presidential box, and point out what I had known and what Sammy Davis of course strictly agreed with, that he had been a very enthusiastic supporter of President Kennedy when we ran against each other in 1960 . . . and when the commentator said, 'What is your reaction, Sammy, to the fact that many people who have been your friends and your supporters, perhaps many who think you're great in show business, think maybe that you've turned against them? And that you've done so . . . you've sort of sold out . . . because you were invited to the White House to see the President.'

"Well, let me give you the answer: You aren't going to buy Sammy Davis, Jr., by inviting him to the White House. You buy him by doing something for America."

So touched, so overwhelmed by the realization that my problems were on the President's mind, that he was taking an occasion to try to overcome them for me, I walked up from behind him and put my arms around him, hugged him, and stepped back.

———

That night we had the late news on and Altovise exclaimed, "Hey, look at that . . ." A shot of me hugging the President. "That's my husband up there with the Prez." The morning papers across the country carried the picture on the front pages. Then it was in the newsmagazines and the angry comments started coming in. More than a few people felt that I, a black man, had done a bad thing by hugging the President of the United States. The White House was receiving calls from Republican campaign fund supporters threatening cutoffs. Nobody liked it. The Democrats who had seen me with Bobby and John were angry all along that I had gone to a Republican, and the hug was a catalyst. The black press excoriated me. "Sammy sold us out."

I received a 17 × 20 copy of the photograph, inscribed: "To Sammy Davis, Jr. With grateful appreciation for helping to make the 1972 convention a great success. Richard Nixon." With it was a letter addressed to "Hon. Sammy Davis, Jr."

THE WHITE HOUSE

September 14, 1972

Dear Sammy,

Since the enclosed captured a good deal of the spirit and enthusiasm of the rally and received such wide coverage in the press, I thought you might like to have a copy as a memento. Many thanks to you and Altovise for the great job you both did in helping to make the convention the success it was.

With warmest personal regards,

Sincerely,

Richard Nixon

I was appointed to the board of UNICEF and I went to Europe to do shows in Holland, Germany, Sweden, and England. We spent a few days in Paris and on the plane back to England

I told Sy, "I need a check for $25,000 for Jesse Jackson. I'm flying direct London to Chicago to appear at a fund-raiser for PUSH."

"Sammy, please, you just gave him $25,000 for Operation Breadbasket. Plus you're flying in there to perform."

"Sy, I want to do this."

He despaired. "At least Cartier and Chanel give us charge accounts. How can Jesse expect money you don't have?"

"That's *my* problem. It's not his fault I'm broke."

We stayed overnight in London and were about to leave our suite for the airport when Sy burst in. "Sweetheart, listen, I just got a call from Paris. Chevalier fell out in Deauville and they're desperate for tonight. We could get fifty grand easy for an hour's work. Seventy-five if I squeeze."

"Babe, you know I can't, that I'm scheduled for PUSH. They're expecting me."

Sy appealed to the ceiling, both arms in the air. "I'm going bananas!" He turned to me, softly, reasonably. "Sammy, that's a benefit. Send them the money. Jesse'll understand."

"Babe, if it were just Jesse, he *would* understand. But it's not. It's all them cats on the corner who've been told, 'Sammy's coming.' I can't disappoint the brothers, Sy. That's it!"

Alto and I flew directly to Chicago with George and my rhythm section. Backstage at the stadium I gave Jesse the check. There were about seven thousand people out front.

As I hit center stage smiling, there was a loud booing from the right-hand corner of the stadium. It struck me as with physical force, knocking the wind out of me. It grew louder. I wanted to run off the stage, get away from there, but Jesse's arm was around my shoulder and I heard him reprimanding the audience: "Brothers . . . if it wasn't for people like Sammy Davis you wouldn't be here, we wouldn't have PUSH today. Now, I expected some foolish people were going to react like this because the man hugged the President of the United States. So what? Look at what this gigantic little man has committed himself to over all these years . . ."

The words blurred in my ears as memory of the booing poured in and out of my head. Tears were coming down my face. Jesse tightened his hand on my shoulder. Jesse is very large. My head came up to his chest. He held on to me. I looked at him, wordlessly imploring: *Let go of me. I want to leave.* But he held me there by physical force, wordlessly imploring: *I understand what you're feeling, but stay!*

Then I heard him saying, "I'm going to ask our brother Sammy to sing something, and if anybody doesn't like it, then get up and leave." He didn't understand. I couldn't have spoken, let alone sung. He waited a moment, staring the crowd down. Nobody moved. He turned to me. "I want you to sing 'I've Got to Be Me.' "

I couldn't run, I couldn't stay. I didn't know what to do. The music began and somehow my voice came out and I sang "I've Got to Be Me," and by the end of it they were on their feet and cheering.

But the booing stayed with me.

In Vegas, as we walked through the airport, the skycaps, brothers who'd always waved and shouted, "My man," "Sammy," turned the other way as I went by. There were no black faces in my audience. In recent years I'd been getting a good proportion of black people, but I'd stopped watching that, taking it for granted because I was breaking attendance records—the Nixon people loved me and that was ninety percent of America—but now there were none of my people out there.

Johnny Johnson, the owner of Johnson Publications and publisher of *Ebony* and *Jet*, called me. "I'm sorry about what people are saying, but the brothers on the corner don't know. I say you're with the right man. So what if he's a Republican? You can butter bread with either side of the knife."

But how could I have lost so many friends—white and black—by being with the man who got the most votes of anyone in the history of the White House?

I ran into James Brown, the number one soul brother. He

was also working for Nixon. "Whew," he said, "you're taking a lot of heat. I never got it this way."

Again I saw that another black artist could do something unpopular and it was more or less accepted, but our people put me in a special place. By their definition I had let them down. In their minds there were certain things I could do, certain rules I could break. I married a white woman and I hardly got any heat. But by going with a Republican President I had broken faith with my people.

I had been controversial all my life but at no time did surviving pain make the next time hurt less.

Bob Brown called. "The President said, 'I'd like to arrange for Sammy to entertain at the White House.' "

"I'd be thrilled. I've always wanted to."

"You're joking! I thought that you'd entertained there a number of times."

He was thinking of the Kennedys. "Never."

Bob said, "I need you here in Washington for three days running if possible, to have some meetings, first with me and some others, and then with the President, a private, one-hour breakfast meeting. Just you and the President. And the President would like you to stay at the White House. You and Mrs. Davis, and whomever you need with you."

Richard Nixon showed us to the guest rooms, which were on the same floor as his own quarters. "I wanted the pleasure of having Sammy Davis, Jr., stay at the White House. No black man has slept here since 1914 when Booker T. Washington was a guest of Woodrow Wilson."

". . . Under normal circumstances, ladies and gentlemen, if I'm working in a nightclub or giving a concert I usually build my show. You start off with something amusing and hope that it builds to a climax. I have not had as many hits as people would have you believe. I've only had a couple and I'm going to do one of them to open the show. Under normal circumstances I wait until later, hoping someone will say, 'Isn't he ever going to do it?' but I ain't taking no chances. I'm opening with the heavyweights. Because as we used to say on the corner, this is about as far uptown as I'm ever going to get."

I sang "The Candy Man," "I've Got to Be Me," and I closed with "Mr. Bojangles." The President and Mrs. Nixon were standing, applauding me. Everyone was.

I changed from one dinner suit to another dry one, and went out to the ballroom, to the receiving line, and Altovise and I stood with the Nixons saying good evening to the senators and their wives, the astronauts, to the cabinet members. The President whispered, "When you want me to cut this off, let me know." Then we were seated at a table with the Nixons. I saw Shirley and George on the dance floor, dipping. I was trying to reach them: You're dipping? Nobody dips anymore. Aahhh, go ahead, you're dancing in the White House, do what you want, have some fun. Dip.

The President asked Altovise to dance and I watched my wife dancing with the President. I asked Mrs. Nixon, "May I have the honor?" and then I was dancing with the First Lady.

Senators and their wives came over to our table to say hello. Supreme Court justices, statesmen, the people who ran the country visited to say something nice to me and my wife. The President recalled our first meeting: "When I was a senator from California I went with Pat to the Copacabana, where you were appearing with the Will Mastin Trio, and they informed me at the door that it was sold out, there was no room at all. I asked if it was possible to get word to Mr. Davis that Senator Nixon, a fan of his, would love to be able to see him. You pulled some strings and we sat at your table at the ringside and there was so little room that you performed on top of the piano." At two o'clock the President nudged me. "Whenever you want to leave, don't stand on protocol, we're going to have breakfast together."

When we'd said good night I thought I'd step into the kitchen and say hello to the cooks and the brothers who worked there. I knew very well that Milton Berle did not feel he had to say hello to the Jewish employees everywhere, yet I wanted to take a bow with the brothers. I wanted them to be proud of where I'd gotten. They were having a late snack. I said, "I see you got a Virginia ham over there. Brother, can I have me a little sandwich upstairs? I missed dinner, I couldn't eat before the show." A beautiful tray was sent up.

At 10 a.m. the President and Mrs. Nixon were waiting for us in the President's study. We had a cup of coffee together, then Mrs. Nixon took Altovise to her quarters, where they would have breakfast, and the President and I went into his dining room. Following Bob's advice, I had a list: again, education in the ghettos, black businesses, the Negro College Fund and black colleges in general. They had never had support from any administration, ever.

Bob called me in L.A. "The President talked about you at the prayer breakfast. He came over and shook my hand and told me I'd done a good job. He said how much he enjoyed the show but, more important, how much he enjoyed the breakfast.

"Sammy, you are as close to Nixon, in terms of being able to influence his thoughts, as any black man has ever been to a President. I can't think of any man he holds in higher esteem, white or black. We stood there for about five minutes just talking about you. The Man said, 'Sammy is one of the great living Americans.' He has said that many a time. 'Our friend Sammy, he could make it anywhere. It wouldn't matter what color he was, or what he wanted to do. With his intelligence he could make it at anything, anywhere in the world.' There is almost no limit to what may accrue to black people as a result of this."

It was nice to hear, and I appreciated it, but I couldn't help thinking: As long as God lets me keep my talent. Forget intelligence, forget sophistication, forget the friends I'd made along the way. All I really had was my talent. Without that I wouldn't be welcome at the White House, I wouldn't be able to help anybody, not even myself. If God ever took away my talent I would be a nigger again.

45

Fucking youth freaks. We were in bed watching a rock-'n'-roll show with all these great-looking young kids on roller skates, break-dancing, young skin, young stomachs, young arms, and young legs . . . good music. Young music. I snapped it off.

"Hey! I was enjoying that."

"Sure. My child bride *would*."

She stared at me from her side of the bed.

"Fucking youth freaks. Dumb fucking assholes. Fuck! Fuck!" I turned it back on. How easily the young dancers moved.

Altovise was thinking, biting her upper lip under her lower lip. "Sammy, do you think you're going through the male meno-pause?"

"You must be losing your meno-fucking-mind." But she was right. I hated the sight of fifty. I had this carved-in-granite im-age: the finger-snapping, perpetual motion, tight-pants swinger. But was there anything more depressing than an aging swinger? And how could there be an old Sammy Davis, Jr.? She was holding a copy of *People* magazine with some juvenile on the cover. He'd been in high school yesterday. I fumed. "The whole thing on youth. You pick up a magazine and after thirty you're out of it. Every advertisement. Kids."

She put the magazine out of my sight. "I won't have it around anymore."

I was not going to answer that. Certainly not say thank you. I needed air. "You're in my space. I can't deal with it."

"With what?"

"With anything." I glared at her. "And what are we doing in bed at midnight like a couple of geriatrics?"

"But you said you were tired . . ."

"Fuck tired." I bolted out of bed. "I'm going where there's some action." I called out over my shoulder, "You've got fifteen minutes if you want to join me."

As I shaved I looked in the mirror and saw my father's face on my body. *Black guys don't show their age. Bullshit!* I was shaving two and three times a day because it was coming in gray. I could touch up the hair on my head, but there was nothing you could do with a new growth of beard every few hours. And as much as I hated looking at fifty, I detested the cliché of hating it. I pulled on a pair of tight-fitting chocolate-brown leather pants, a silk shirt, and alligator boots. I stepped out of the house, studied my cars, and chose the Corvette. Altovise came running out behind me.

As we drove down to Sunset, she tried to console me. "Being fifty the way you're fifty is no big deal. Really, it's not old."

"Darling, not for people who wear normal clothes and do normal work. On them it can even look good . . . a little mature, distinguished, but on Sammy Davis, Jr., it's death. I painted myself into a corner with 'Where does he get all the energy?,' the avant-garde clothes, the tight pants, jumpsuits, the whole glitz trip. But do you think a fifty-year-old should be dancing around on a stage in tight pants? Even if the glitz is pretty damned good, isn't it anachronistic? But that's what I am, tight pants and glitz, and I can't suddenly turn into Fred Astaire. They won't buy it from me."

We went to the Comedy Store, a club on Sunset. I felt like some laughs to take my mind off myself. Comics, white and black, who looked like they were wearing their first long pants

were getting up and the first words they said were "Bullshit,
motherfuckers . . ." Without even "Good evening." The lan-
guage, on a stage, made me feel like a hundred. I remembered
Will Mastin telling me not to do impressions of white people
because the audience would think I was making fun of them.
Now here was this black cat calling them motherfuckers and
getting belly laughs.

He put up his hands for quiet. "Motherfuckers . . . let's cool
it with laughs for a sec 'cause there's a gentleman who has done
me the honor of sitting in my audience. I have idolized him
since I was a child when he was already a great star. This magnificent artist is a dinosaur, the last of his kind, his generation,
the end of an era, the golden days of show business. He was
learning our trade in vaudeville—yeah, motherfuckers, vaudeville! You're too young to remember it, by the time you were
born it had died. He's the dean of show business, his name belongs on the Roll of Honor along with Al Jolson . . ."

I stood up. "I'm sorry to interrupt, but my funeral's in half
an hour." The audience applauded and I walked to the stage. I
hugged the asshole who'd done my eulogy and I addressed the
audience. "I want to say something. Our friend here was right
about one thing, I've been in show business for forty-seven
years"—applause—"and it was a very different show business
than you have today. I've always wanted to say something but
I've never had the opportunity which the young performers of
today take for granted. I have had the honor to have played for
royalty and Presidents—and now I thank you for this wonderful opportunity to finally realize my great ambition, which is . . .
to stand on a stage and be able to say 'Bullshit! Bullshit, motherfuckers!' "

We drove over to the Factory. The valet-parking kid looked
too young to have a driver's license. He was gazing at my
Corvette. "Wow, when'd you get it, Mr. D.?"

"I'm Sammy, babe, and it came in this week. I always have
the first one every year."

As we walked into the room I felt a hand rubbing my buns.

I turned around and it was a wild-looking chick. She was a little stoned, enough so she didn't let go of me. She squeezed. "Feelin' *good*, Sammy."

We sat with some kid actors. They were smoking joints and taking hits right there at the table. It was so crowded that nobody could see what anybody else was doing. They offered it around and I took a few hits. I told them, "Come on by the house tomorrow after midnight and see a movie and have something to make you feel good . . ."

I'd seen the bowl in the window of a silver shop in Beverly Hills, a small bowl with a lid. It had probably been made for a man to store his snuff. It was perfect for cocaine. Nothing spectacular, not a bowl bowl, like for winning Wimbledon. It was not even large enough for soup, it was small, it could hold four vials of cocaine, and I'd bought little spoons like you use for salt, and people could dip in. It was an amenity, how to be a proper host today, like you wouldn't have a bar without scotch. Almost any movie you could name at the time had a budget for drugs, ten grand or so a week, below-the-line under "Miscellaneous," to keep the actors going. I filled the bowl and put it next to the mixed nuts.

Everybody was happy, spread around the living room, six or eight of them in the conversation pit, another six or eight on the couch near the windows, and some more at the bar with me. Listening to conversation, I lined up a hit. I don't mean to say I was sniffing up half of Peru, in truth I wasn't a heavy hitter. I was a social drugger. I liked the scene. Even the asinine banter: "What do you propose, for my nose?" But for feeling good I preferred booze, from the taste and effect down to just the pleasure of holding the glass in my hand.

Jack Haley, Jr., was with me. He and Liza Minnelli were lifelong friends of mine and hang-out buddies. I was his best man at their wedding, and Altovise had been the matron of honor. I took my hit and waited for the feeling of well-being to settle onto me. I smiled at Jack. "Nice. But I'm still waiting to get high on this shit. For me, throw all the coke in the ocean, just give me three fingers of vodka." Jack raised his glass in agreement. Yet coke was "today." Booze was Bogey and yester-year and "the older generation." I wished I didn't like it so much.

It was a good evening. I enjoyed sitting behind the bar. I liked the way I looked, the kids all thought my house was fantastic, I was providing good booze, wine, coke, whatever anyone wanted. We showed a new PG movie and then I ran an X-rated and by daylight they had all straggled out. I could have gotten laid five times just with lifestyle groupies. I'd turned thirty-five again.

When Alto and I were in bed she leaned over. "Honey? Sweetie?" I waited. Whenever she called me "Honey? Sweetie?" trouble was on its way. "Listen, we have to remove the mirror from behind the bar or you can't sit there. I mean with people. 'Cause from out front your bald spot shines like the moon."

Dressing for the evening, Alto said, "I love having the projection room, being able to show new movies."

I was thrilled to hear it, to be able to give it to her. I wished I could buy her one piece of jewelry that would cost like four million dollars. The kind that would cost $100,000 just to have a paste copy made of it. The kind of a stone that has a name, like the Hope Diamond. I'd love to give her "the Altovise Emerald." I wished I could say, "Any shopping that you want to do, darling, Neiman-Marcus, Saks, Giorgio, wherever on Rodeo, every time you want to buy something, just go and buy it." I wished I could give her four years like that, let her just go crazy for four years.

While Virgil, my projectionist, was setting up a second film I got up from my pit and went to the bar to remake my drink and I saw a kid filling his coke bottle from my bowl.

I asked Jack Haley. "Did you see that? A druggie bag?"

He was studying my head. "How come you started putting the grease on your hair again? I liked it dry. It looked good."

I leaned toward him. "For your ears only: slicking it down covers the thin spot in back."

He waved away my tonsorial problem. "I saw Frank and Dean over at the Friars last night."

That was strange. Frank always called when he was in town.

Putting out her night-table light, Altovise commented, "Strange about Frank being in town and not calling you."

I snapped, "It's not strange. We're grown men, we're not tied by a cord. Obviously he's busy with other things." I put on my earphones and turned back to the television I was watching. I'd begun using earphones to watch TV so that Alto could sleep, but they served nicely to block out things I didn't want to listen to.

But it *was* strange.

On opening night at Caesars Palace I had only been dancing for three minutes but my legs kept getting heavier, my breathing was visible, I could hardly conceal from the audience that I was puffing and panting. I knew I couldn't get through the full seven or eight minutes that I usually did. From strenuous tap dancing I switched to a soft-shoe. Holding the mike by the cord, I lowered it to the floor close to my feet, and I did some semi-dancing. The audience of fourteen hundred people, fooled by the change of pace, thought they were seeing something extraordinary and they watched as I rested but looked like I was dancing. When I'd caught my breath I ended by going back to the taps on my shoes and beating out: boom diddy boom boom . . . boom boom!—doing a total of four minutes instead of seven. I hated fooling them, but what choice did I have? "Sorry, folks, but I'm getting too old to entertain you." Then get off the stage! But I couldn't afford to do that.

In the dressing room I put five sugars into a cup of coffee and dropped into a chair. Age. Dissipation. Leaning on talent. It was showing. You can't be my kind of an entertainer, at my age, and run yourself stupid partying and boozing and drugging. I used to be able to do it. But I couldn't anymore.

Altovise came backstage with her mother, and my mother, and Shirley Phillips, her mother's close friend. I'd introduced my mother-in-law from the stage. The ladies were all "It was the greatest thing I've ever seen . . ." but Altovise gestured to the makeup room. "Can I talk to you real private?"

"No."

"Well, can I tell you something in your ear?"

I gave her mother the Jack Benny poker face. "I might just let you take her back and age her for another five years."

Alto sat next to me on the couch, cupped my ear with her hands, and whispered, "Was my old man feeling a little down during the dance number? Nobody'd notice it but me, but you didn't have your razzle-dazzle."

"Get outta here." *And don't call me your "old man."* She was looking at me sympathetically. I pushed her away. She laughed and bounced onto her feet. I was beginning to feel our twenty-year difference.

The sugar in my coffee was working. I took a handful of gumdrops to keep the energy level up. "If you ladies will be so kind as to excuse me, I'll be right back." I beckoned to Brian Dellow, my security man, and we went out front to the shopping arcade, the Appian Way, to the fur shop, where I'd noticed luxurious pieces just waiting for a high roller to come in with his girl to celebrate. We returned to the dressing room wheeling a clothing rack. I presented Mrs. Gore with a chinchilla jacket. "Just a little kiss from your son-in-law." I'd bought Mrs. Phillips a fox cape, and my mother a mink jacket.

Altovise was dumbstruck. I turned on her. "Are you waiting to be tossed a fish or do you always sit around with your mouth open?" I looked smugly into her eyes. You wanta talk about razzle-dazzle?

I was in the casino, playing blackjack, not because I felt like gambling but because it was good publicity. People love to say, "Jerry Lewis took over from the dealer," or "My God, I saw Sammy Davis playing with hundred-dollar chips," and it's a reminder that you're there.

I saw Jilly Rizzo. He was watching the action but I had the feeling he'd been waiting for me to see him. I gathered up my chips and we went over to the Garden Room and ordered a drink. I asked, "How's Francis?"

"Sam, you and me been friends a long time and maybe you wanta know that probably why Frank hasn't called is he hears that you're into this coke crap and he says, 'If Sammy's into that, then I don't want to be around him. And I don't want him around me.' "

The one thing I didn't want to hear was that Frank was upset. It winded me. God knows, I could understand it. But I said, "If he wants it that way, then fuck it. I'm not twenty years old anymore, Jilly. It's not like the old days with fingernails in the mouth and 'Oh God, Frank didn't call today!' I'm living my life . . ."

"Sure, Sam. You're doin' business is what counts."

In the dressing room I looked at a framed picture someone had taken of us at the Villa Capri, years before. I hadn't known it was being taken. I'd been sitting on a stool looking down at Frank and the shot of my face caught the love and admiration I always felt for him. Frank sent me a print inscribed: "The same goes for me, Sam. Francis."

That he was disappointed in me was an ache around my heart. Frank had an influence on me that no one else could have had. I'd tried to *be* him, professionally to emulate him, and personally trying to be a swinger, to do the kind of things he did: give me all that, send for this, buy all that, expensive gifts to strangers for a gesture . . . all that stuff is Sinatra. The attitude, the cockiness was Sinatra. Black people weren't cocky in those days. I could never describe what the Capitol Theater date with him meant to me, bringing my grandmother there, his putting his arm around me, telling me, "You should sing . . ." So twenty-five years later to hear he was disappointed in me was a misery. Especially as I knew that as he said it he also said, or would have said, "Keep an eye on him. Don't let him get into any trouble. I'm never going to speak to the little cock-sucker again but don't ever let him get in trouble. And don't *you* call him a little cocksucker."

Why couldn't I call him and say, "Frank, if it means that much to you, then it's history, I'll never touch it again"? But I couldn't let someone else dictate my life.

Playing Caesars was a mistake. The room was too big. I was a hero for filling the place, but it couldn't last, and then it would be "Sammy isn't making it." To fill that room six days a week, two shows a night, with fourteen hundred people, you need a hot record, or a TV series. Or you should have a major divorce. Or be a man just turned into a girl. But a performer like myself should play small rooms. Five hundred seats. Fill that twice a night at $25 per head for two drinks and you're not exactly out of the business. But at Caesars I had to attract fourteen hundred people for every show.

Fortunately I was getting a lot of repeat business. That is key. And the locals. If they come to see you on a Monday or a Tuesday, their night off, and you've been playing that town for years, it's a big compliment. More important, if you *don't* have the local people in your corner, forget it. Out! 'Cause there isn't anybody else going to be there on Monday and Tuesday.

You've also got to have the cabdrivers in your corner, and the guys who drive the hotel limos that pick up the high rollers. These are the first people that most of the Las Vegas visitors speak to, and when they asked, "Who's in town?" I wanted them to hear "Catch Sammy at Caesars, he's swingin'!" So I gave a party for all the cabdrivers in Las Vegas. It started at

3 a.m. I did a show and gave them all the steaks and booze they liked.

Sy called from L.A., distraught. "I can rationalize the cab-drivers. Clever. Good promotion." His voice was vibrating. "But I've got a bill here for sixty thousand from the fur shop at Caesars. It's a mistake, isn't it . . . ?"

I thought: Yes, it was a mistake. But the bill is right.

"Please, Sammy, tell me you didn't buy Altovise another mink coat."

"No, I didn't. I bought one for her mother, my mother, and a friend of her mother."

"Wh . . . wh . . . why?"

"Another magnificent gesture."

"Sammy . . . sweetheart . . . you're almost fifty, which is young if you have money, but it's old if you're broke. I have nightmares that something happens to you, an accident or you get sick and you can't work for a year. What happens to you? Who picks up the mortgage on your house, the bank loans . . ."

Then I would be "Mr. Bojangles," the character in the song, bottoming out. Onstage I began dropping numbers that spooked me, starting with that one. If the audience didn't demand it I didn't sing it. More than ever I feared it. I stopped doing "If I Never Sing Another Song," a Matt Monroe number about a superstar who says that if he never sings another song, it's okay, because he's tasted everything that fame could bring. Well, if you're still on top of the heap, then you can sing that song. But if your voice is getting rough, if you're dragging through performances where you used to fly, if in your mind you're playing the lounges, then don't sing "If I Never Sing Another Song." Dump it before they start thinking: Yeah, he may never sing much again . . .

I was voted "Entertainer of the Year" by my fellow members of the American Guild of Variety Artists, for the fourth consecutive year. The awards ceremony, held at Caesars, was attended by all the main-room stars, the lounge performers and opening acts in town, and many who came in to lend their presence to the awarding of the Georgie, for George M. Cohan, our highest honor for live performance.

In a short speech I disqualified myself from it for the next year, to be gracious, and also perhaps because, knowing the shape I was in, I didn't imagine I could win it a fifth time. For the moment only I knew it—like a beautiful yacht looks fine from outside, but if you're inside, down below, and you can feel the water coming in, you know it's sinking.

To show everybody I was still a superstar I gave a party for the entire city of Las Vegas. I invited every performer from every hotel in town to have steaks and champagne. I stayed for half an hour. It cost me fifty thousand dollars.

Altovise had come back for the awards ceremony and stayed for the last week in Vegas. Elvis was in town and we hung out one night, Elvis, Altovise, me, and his bodyguard. We got into his limousine, my limo followed us, and we hit all the joints, being superstars. Elvis had on a short cape with the high collar, dark glasses, and he had Altovise by the arm and we were running, covering all the lounges, and people were saying, "Look . . . Elvis and Sammy . . ." But what were they seeing? Elvis was troubled and puffy in the face and the contrast was so great from when I had first seen him at the Hilton, when I heard the theme from *2001: A Space Odyssey* and he'd walked out and you heard dong, ta dong, dong dong, dong . . . and he was in shape and he wore the skintight clothes and women were going crazy and men were going, "Yeah . . . he's something!" He'd looked like ice cream and cake then.

And me? I couldn't stand to think about it.

The Harrah's plane picked me up in Vegas and took us to Reno, where I began a four-week run, from which I'd segue into Harrah's Lake Tahoe for another three weeks, without a day off.

Every night, an hour before show time, I called the maître d'
and I heard "We're sold out, Sammy, we'll turn away fifty or
sixty, both shows." But it was frightening. I was a dancer who
couldn't dance anymore, an aging legend of youth and motion.

I did all the off-the-wall things I could think of. I tried to
come alive with the clothes, the jumpsuits, the leather pants, diamond rings on every finger, even his-and-her wigs with Altovise. Brilliant. I spend a lifetime making myself recognizable,
then I put on a wig to look like my wife. Desperation was my
producer. What I was really saying was: "Will somebody help
me, please? I'm losing it . . ."

On Fridays and Saturdays the third show didn't start till
two-thirty in the morning. I played those shows to a thousand
people and didn't get off until five or five-thirty. The sun was always coming up as I went to my suite, relieved, fatigued by
fear. Whereas previously something had lived and breathed between me and the audience, now I couldn't wait for the shows
to be over, to be free of the suspense. As always, I escaped into
debauchery and alcohol to forget that the magic was waning,
that the image was fading and I didn't know how to get young
again.

The party was already under way with all the kids from the
other shows. Room service had set up steam tables with the
Chinese food, and the bartender was taking care of people. Joe
Conforti, a longtime friend who owned the Mustang Ranch,
the biggest whorehouse in Nevada, where prostitution is legal,
always brought over eight or a dozen of the most beautiful, the
wildest girls. I never had to call Joe. He'd always come by to
say hello and bring girls with him. "They're yours, all yours.
The car will wait for them till you're finished." I usually had
my own, but nobody at my parties was ever lonely or in need
of a drink. I was depressed to remember that only ten years earlier I was shooting *Ocean's Eleven* and headlining at the Sands
with Frank and Dean, boozing, partying, staying up all night,
feeling great, and performing at my peak. I wouldn't accept
that I couldn't do it anymore. So I did it harder, later, and we

kept partying till we dropped at nine or nine-thirty in the morning.

I woke up at two o'clock in the afternoon and tried to drag myself out of the booze and after-the-party stupor. My head and my throat ached. Lately my body had been threatening: "If you do that, then I ain't goin' nowhere tomorrow, I ain't gettin' up," and it was finally making good on the threat. I knew I couldn't go on that night. I got Murphy on the phone. "Call Dougie and tell him I've got a touch of flu."

Doug Bushousen, Harrah's number two entertainment manager, knew that the touch of flu was the suiteful of kids and the nonstop partying, but he said, "I'll have to get a substitute for a few days. We can't go dark. I'm going to call the hangar and send the plane to Burbank. I'll tell the pilot that he may be picking somebody up, and he may not. Then I'll get on the phone and start looking. Can you help me with anybody?" I called some friends—Alan King, Don Rickles, Bill Cosby, Liza Minnelli. Liza was available.

As eight o'clock arrived and I was having a drink in my living room instead of being where I should have been, I understood that I was self-destructing. And at the same time I was relieved not to have to face the audience, suffer another test.

On opening night in Tahoe the party started in the dressing room and I carried my glass from the party onto the stage. I was about ten minutes past the opening numbers when a joke didn't get a laugh. The first few rows were just sitting there looking at me. Not a reaction. To a really funny line. I went back to the piano to get a cigarette and whispered to George, "What a stiff crowd! If that didn't turn 'em on, then they've got no switches."

His voice was flat. "They laughed the first time you said it."

Repeating a joke? My God, it was bad enough when I couldn't go on. But to appear on the stage drunk . . . to have them leave there and remember me making drunken mistakes.

That was death. I dug down and started working. I pulled out everything I knew how to do, stuff I hadn't done in years, the quick-draw tricks, the drums, impressions. When the curtain fell I had been on for two hours and I had done a hell of a show.

George walked past me without speaking and went to his dressing room. He was never effusive with praise. When I'd done a great show, as I came off the stage his idea of a compliment was to hit me on my ass and keep walking. But now he ignored me.

I looked into his dressing room. He was taking off his coat. "You don't want to say, 'Nice show, Sam,' or 'Well, you saved that one'?"

He was unsmiling. "You saved it."

Doug and Holmes Hendricksen, Harrah's number one man in entertainment, came in. Doug looked at his watch. I groaned. "You're not really going to do that cliché with me."

"I was trying not to ask 'What the fuck was that all about?' "

"Babe, I started off drunk . . ."

Murphy picked up the ringing telephone. I heard him telling Sy that I was busy, but Sy was insisting.

He sounded out of breath. "Sammy, I need to get with you about the IRS. They insist that we make a commitment and stick to it or they're going to do a thing called 'piercing the veil,' which means going after us personally even though the debt is corporate."

"I don't want to hear about it. Handle it. That's *your* job. I've got the shows to worry about," and I hung up.

I was in Washington for a meeting of the Equal Opportunity board. The Nixons were in San Clemente but the President had said, "Ask Sammy to stay at the White House," like a friend saying, "We're going to be out of town but use the house," and they had sent a presidential car to the airport.

The guards at the gates of the White House saluted and

waved me through. I told the driver, "Wait." I knew the face of one of the guards, a sergeant, around my age. I looked at him, trying to remember, not wanting to be rude. He looked away from my eyes.

"Excuse me, do we know each other?"

"No, sir. Not that I know, sir."

He was lying. He was looking past me instead of at me, trying to show no recognition . . . and then I remembered him, that's how he'd looked through me a lifetime ago, in the Army, Harcourt, the man I'd knocked down and who'd told me, "But you're still a nigger."

He was standing at attention. I saw his name tag, "Harcourt."

"I'm sorry, Sergeant." I told the driver, "You can go now."

This time I was given the Lincoln Room.

At Caesars a lady at ringside smiled and, pointing at my stomach, cooed, "Look at his adorable little pot." I'd been getting that a lot lately and I always smiled back and patted it. But I hated it. It wasn't *me* to have a paunch. I didn't like to see my stomach pushing against my shirt. I stopped eating during the day. Nothing until after the second show. Maybe a cup of soup around five o'clock. My energy level was on the floor. I kept going on coffee with five sugars in it, and vodka with Coke, also for the sugar.

I'd wake up at noon, have coffee, make myself a drink, and I couldn't wait to get back into bed and rest, watching the daytime soap operas from twelve-thirty to four: *Ryan's Hope, One Life to Live, All My Children*, and *General Hospital*. I didn't have the energy for anything else.

Frank and I hadn't spoken in three years except for a few bump-ins with cold hellos.

He was following me into Caesars. A few nights before closing, Altovise came down from L.A. "I saw Barbara Sinatra at the Bistro Garden. She and I are taking you and Frank to dinner when they get here. Just the four of us."

"Alto, this isn't your territory . . ."

"Barbara decided it is. And I agree with her. You two guys love each other; you should talk even if only to call each other dirty names. So if you're going to be stubborn mules, then *somebody* has to have some sense."

They closed the Bacchanal Room for us. Altovise and I had just sat down when Barbara and Frank walked in. He kissed Alto. "Hi ya, Big Al." He looked at me and nodded. The four of us talked about nothing for about thirty seconds. Frank got up, tapped me on the arm, and we went to another booth.

"Sam, I'm so fuckin' disappointed in you, with that shit . . . You deserve better than that. You're the fuckin' greatest talent that ever lived. You going to let this shit destroy you? Give it up. Disassociate yourself from it. Dump it. You're breaking your friends' hearts, Sam. You're a superstar. Establishment. Isn't that sweet enough?" I nodded, feeling emotional that he would make this effort for me. At best it was uncomfortable for him. "Charley, we've never lied to each other."

"No, we haven't."

"Then if you say you're going to give it up, I know you will."

"I'll give it up, Frank."

His mouth and eyes broke into that smile that lights up the world. He said, "And if anybody ever hits you, Charley . . ." He was looking at me, waiting to see if I remembered.

46

Will Mastin lived to be a hundred years old. He died in July 1979. I flew from Lake Tahoe to Los Angeles for the funeral, but I did not go down the night before to see him in the chapel. That dear old showman would not have wanted me to miss a performance.

There was no part of my early life, from childhood until long after I'd become a star, in which I could not see Will's face. Will did not give me my talent, or even understand what to do with it, but he started me on the road and he taught me everything he could, which was a lot. If there had not been a Will Mastin there might not have been a Sammy Davis, Jr.

I woke up feeling stiff, my whole body aching. And angry at myself. Why would anyone sleep on a couch when he's got a king-sized bed in the Star Suite at Harrah's? Bombed was why. Smashed. To not have to look at myself. It had been daylight when the party ended.

I dragged myself to the bar and, ignoring the coffeepot, I pressed away a throb in my forehead and thought of a line in *Another Country*: "Rufus, this shit is got to stop." I sighed. Yeah, Ruf, but not right now. And I poured a vodka and Coke.

I watched the soaps for three and a half hours. Then I still had to get through until eight-thirty in the evening. I would have liked to play golf but I had no energy for it. I didn't want to go shopping and get suicidally creative. And I didn't want to talk to anyone.

Murphy came into the bedroom and told me some friends of mine were coming to the dinner show. I said, "Call 'em back, babe. Tell them to catch the second. The dinner show's too quiet." Hogwash. Lately I hadn't been able to get myself up and cooking until the second, so I kidded myself that the dinner show customers wanted it quiet and easy.

The phone rang. The operator told me the name of the girl who was calling, one of the kids I'd partied with the night before. Kinky. She'd worn a white satin body stocking with the belt made out of handcuffs. "Hi, Sammy, are you ready for some more state-of-the-art sex?" She sounded so young, so energetic, and I felt so old and weary. "Thanks, darling, but I'm going to just hang in here and rest up for my shows."

"You can't do that. We're downstairs. We want to party . . ." And then she hit me with the line from any one of a hundred teenage tits-and-ass movies: "I'm a party animal."

"Darling, call me in a few days," and I hung up.

I'd been guest of honor at a Dean Martin NBC-TV roast and Altovise and I were watching the tape. Phyllis Diller was saying, "Sammy's a man who's come up from the ghetto to become a great star, and he has everything that goes with it, like the mansion he lives in on the best street in Beverly Hills; he wears the best custom-made clothes, expensive jewelry, drives eight foreign cars. Sammy has earned his success. He just hasn't paid for it."

Altovise winced. "The whole country's going to hear we're broke."

"Do you care?"

"Not about the whole country, but our friends, yes."

"Then let's show them it's not true. Let's have a dinner party."

"But it *is* true."

"Darling, it's not *that* true that we can't afford a quiet dinner for twenty-five couples we care about. Nothing spectacular, just simple, nice."

"Do you think so?"

"Of course I do. We're like what Mike Todd meant when he said he was broke but not poor."

We started planning the party. "Lessie Lee can make some of her great legs of lamb . . ." I was rewarded by seeing Altovise get a lift out of it and we started making a list. When the list passed one hundred couples and there were still people we wanted to invite, I said, "Okay, instead of a sit-down dinner we'll give the first party of the 1980s. Call it 'the Decade Party.' Let's invite everybody we like. They won't all be able to come but it will be a nice card. Like 'Happy 1980s.' "

A nice card? They won't be able to come? *Everybody* accepted. They called from London and Paris to say they were going to fly over for it. The Bricusses, the Piagets, the Hermèses, the Rubirosas, ad infinitum. Then we added Infinitum and even *he* was coming!

Watching the news in the breakfast room, I heard Altovise saying goodbye to somebody at the front door. "That was the upholsterer." She poured a cup of coffee, sat down next to me, and showed me a swatch of black leather. "We can't have people over without redoing the bar chairs. They look terrible."

When I came back from lunch at the Daisy, Alto was standing on the back lawn with three men. I went into the breakfast room and waited for them to leave. "Darling, who was that?"

"Construction people the caterers sent."

"Construction?"

"In order to put up the tent which we have to have in case of bad weather, we need to have a platform, but because the lawn slants they have to put it in with steel girders in the ground."

"How much is that going to cost?"

"They're sending an estimate. But they said their crew would have to have the lawn to themselves for three days to install it."

"Darling, as of now, how much do you think we're in for?"

"I don't see how it can cost less than forty or forty-five thousand dollars. Just the two bands, flowers, house polishing, valet parking . . . and of course the four bar chairs, which are five thousand alone, except they really don't count because we have to do them anyway. That leaves the food and drinks . . ."

"Stop." I leaped to my feet. "It was a bad idea. But it's not too late. We'll cancel. I'm calling it off. This show must *not* go on!"

"Honey, you're not serious."

"Serious? It could be terminal. The party's canceled."

"What'll we tell everyone?"

"Tell them that I'm an asshole, tell them that I owe the world, that I have no money, that I'm getting old and I'm losing my talent."

Workmen were on the lawn in the center of the garden finishing a floor mounted on steel girders they'd sunk into the ground. Guys on stepladders were winding flowers around the tent poles. I went into the bar to make a drink and got a look from the floor-polishing crew. I went to the kitchen. Scotty, the captain of our guards, was watching the security TV monitors. "Here comes one of the caterers."

"*One* of the . . ."

Eddie Peterson, our friend and "house manager," looked at the monitor. "It's Rent a Yenta with the turkey, roast beef, the classical food. The second caterer is bringing the soul food at five o'clock." He smiled. "That was a great idea you had, two caterers."

Yeah, back when we were thinking of Lessie Lee cooking for

twenty-five couples and I'd thought it would be a nice touch to have soul food too. Through the window I saw a dozen or more kids in white shirts and maroon pants. Eddie said, "We could only get fifteen valet parkers. For four hundred people we really should have more."

Altovise was in her dressing room posing for me in a gorgeous shocking-pink, sparkling gown. "It's my first Galanos." She blew a kiss at me. "You'd better start dressing."

The cross section of faces was astonishing—directors, producers, the sporting world people, and the superstars, the Old Guard and the new hot kids, obscure white and black actors, the main meat-and-potatoes television people. Loretta Young was at the bar in deep conversation with the Gregory Pecks. Jack Haley, Jr., the world's number one movie buff, grabbed my arm. "My God, Eddie O'Brien! I haven't seen Edmond O'Brien since . . ." Altovise was like a fan at her own party. "Did you see June Haver and Fred MacMurray?"

It was 6 a.m. when everybody had gone home and Alto and I were sitting on our bed. She had tears in her eyes. "Sammy, I'm sorry . . ."

"It wasn't your fault and everybody enjoyed themselves."

"You didn't, and I didn't. And it was my fault. If I hadn't been so stupid about what people think . . ."

"Darling, you were only the shovel. I dug the hole. It was a mistake but it's past. Let's forget about it." But we couldn't. In Hollywood, private parties get reviewed in the trades and the local columns. "The party of the century . . ." "Insiders say the SDJr. blast cost him $100,000." For days the flowers and telegrams kept coming in. Sy came up to the house. "It was a wild party." He was looking at me grimly. "Except the hangover's going to last a year. Thank God you're playing Vegas next week. The bills are all in . . ." I waited. "Seventy-five thousand."

We were silent for a moment, like allowing a poorly chewed hunk of food to work its way uncomfortably down to your stomach.

Sy was staring at me with curiosity. "Sammy, what was the motivation for that?"

"I didn't want people to think I'm broke."

Sy reached me in Tahoe before the first show. "They're going to take away our houses." His voice was tremulous through the phone from Los Angeles. "The lawyers can't hold them off anymore. They're threatening to put a lock on your house, and mine, and then sell them at a public auction if we don't come up with a million four and fast."

When we'd hung up, my chest felt like my heart was trying to break out of it. Nauseated, I put my head below my knees. I lay down on the couch in the dressing room. I had to go on in thirty-five minutes. After a while I got up and sat at the makeup table, staring at the face that stared at me, neither recognizing the other.

When I came off after the show I called the house. Altovise was frightened. "Honey, I didn't want to upset you between shows but a car's been parked across from our entrance all day. Scotty says it has federal government license plates and the driver told him they're from Internal Revenue."

"I'm sorry, darling, there's a problem. I owe them a lot of money and they're talking about putting a lock on our house. Do me a favor. Don't go out. I don't think they'll make a move to take a house if a lady's living in it. At least it would seem to be harder and give us time."

I sat down at the makeup table. I had to go on and do it again. For ten more days before I could get home. I'd had some new clothes planned for the second show. Halfway through I was going to quick-change into hot pants. With the high boots. No man had ever done it. My legs looked good. I liked the Three Musketeers-type shirt, blousy, with the big sleeves. It was comfortable having that fullness to conceal my pot. I did thirty minutes in a tux, then changed into the hot pants. My voice was good, breath control, everything worked.

Holmes and Doug were in the dressing room and I waited for compliments. "Your voice was good . . ." "Yeah, the show ran right on time, on the button . . ."

I said, "Hey, guys, I just did a really swinging show and I'm getting 'Your voice was good . . . show was on the button . . .'?"

There was a dead second or two. Holmes spoke uncomfortably. "Sammy, we're talent buyers, we don't presume to tell great artists what to do on the stage. We just buy what we think is right for our customers."

I could see Doug steeling himself to speak. "What Holmes means is, the show was great . . . *until* the little black Jew came out with his bathing suit on. After that it wasn't very good."

Holmes nodded sorrowfully. "You looked skinny, small, ridiculous."

Later I studied myself in the mirror. I turned away from what I saw. They were right. I had become a clown. It had developed into "What's he going to wear tonight?" Instead of "What songs is he going to sing?" it was "What tricks will he do?"

Sy had flown down. Sitting with me in my suite, he told me, "Apparently when the IRS read about 'the party of the century' it broke the camel's back. They've never been exactly understanding about someone paying twelve hundred dollars for a tuxedo and living on that scale, but the party nailed us." He showed me a résumé of the company's books, specifics on what I had known generally.

I looked up from the figures into the once confident face I had loved for so many years, the man I had always gone to when I was in trouble. "How did we get into this deep a problem, babe? How did we let it go this far?"

He shook his head miserably. "We couldn't pay the bills because we spent the cash."

I appreciated the "we." "You mean *I* spent the cash."

We sat together, suddenly with nothing to say to each other, the Brooklyn kid and the Harlem kid . . . we'd both come so far, but it was short of a win.

"Sam, I'm out of ideas. And I think I'm out of steam. If you'd like me to step down, I will."

"It wasn't your fault, babe. I was unmanageable." I remembered one of our times in Paris. I'd seen a Cartier watch, heavy gold, one of a kind, a prototype, and I'd given it to Sy, engraved: "Till we die. Sam."

Sy stood up. I walked him to the door, then I went with him to the elevator, prolonging the goodbye. Neither one of us reached out to press the button for the elevator. But then the down bell rang, the doors opened. Sy hugged me. "Till we die, sweetheart."

With Sy no longer booking me I signed with the Morris office and told them, "I need money. I'll do industrials, whatever, if the money is right and it doesn't hurt my meat-and-potatoes dates. I'll work seven days a week."

And I prayed that I'd find the strength to do it.

Paying off the government at that rate and putting aside future taxes on those earnings left little money to pay anyone else. Shirley Rhodes, who took Sy's place, got busy on the phone with all of those people with whom we had weekly and monthly bills outstanding. She talked to the butcher, the baker, the candlestick maker, which in this case was my camera store, Sy Devore my tailor, Nat Wise my shirtmaker, the Thunderbird Jewelers in Las Vegas, the Jewelry Factory in Tahoe, the California Jewelers in Beverly Hills, Cartier, Tiffany, Gucci, Dunhill's, the car people, flowers, groceries, laundry and dry cleaning, a one-million-dollar bank loan, everyone. She asked, "Go on hold for us, please? We're going to keep in touch. You'll get a small monthly check. We don't know how long it will take."

She told me, "They all said things like 'Tell Sam not to worry about it. Next year. Or the year after that.'" Then there was a wry look on her face. "You have got to laugh or life will chew you up. The only one to give us a problem is a drugstore over an eighty-nine-dollar bill. All these others are cool in tens of thousands but this druggist was on the phone threatening: 'You owe us eighty-nine dollars. I'm going to sue. I'm going to tell the *National Enquirer*.' "

I had a meeting of the family in the house—Altovise, Lessie Lee, Eddie. I said, "I'm in deep shit. We're broke. We've got to go into complete austerity. *And* we've got to keep it a major secret. Being poor is the one image that this business cannot stand."

We were in the breakfast room and through the window I could see my Rolls-Royce. It had cost $125,000. "Eddie, if we can get over thirty thousand in cash for that car, sell it and we can pay some bills faster." It was gone overnight. I did not sell Alto's cars or touch any of her things.

There were no more powers of attorney, no more signature machine. I signed every check. Never before had I asked where the money was going, not in twenty years in which I'd earned fifty million dollars. I remember a period in which I never asked the price of anything, thinking: It's not chic to ask prices. But what's really not chic is being an asshole.

I was at the Friars Club in the dining room where they have the portraits of me and Frank and Dean and Joey Bishop. A young member came up to me and, glancing at the pictures, then back to me, said, "You're the only one who still looks like yourself."

Didn't he see my stomach? My hair? The face getting hollow? "Thanks, babe. Never more than three packs a day and one bottle of vodka," and I kept walking.

At home I studied myself in the mirror in profile. It wasn't me. It wasn't Sammy Davis, Jr. It was an impersonator who looked five months pregnant. My shirts, always slim and form-fitting, were about to split. I looked terrible. Yet I was down to one small meal a day.

That evening Elizabeth Taylor and Tony Gary and Richard Burton and his wife, Susie, had a quiet dinner with me and Altovise and we wound up sitting around our bar with the champagne flowing and Richard going on magnificently, an endless repertoire, hilariously told, with little asides to Elizabeth like "Darling, you remember when we . . ." and Susie sitting there being very gracious. It was an evening you wanted never to end but I started getting tired. It was only midnight, but I said, "Will you please go home? I'm starting to nod and I don't want to miss anything. Will you please come back another night?"

Elizabeth knew me from the old days when I outlasted everybody. "I don't believe, Samson, that you really said that. You saying good night to us?"

The next night Alto and I went to a party in Malibu. At dinner I whispered to her, "You sit here but I've got to go inside and take a lie-down." When I woke up, Linda Evans was sleeping on one side of me and another gorgeous girl on the other. I looked at these two incredible women: Did I do something rude? Did I hump them? No, they've got their clothes on. Then the girls "woke up" and I understood that they'd come in to do bits with me, that the joke had been: "He'll wake up and not remember what happened."

It was funny. But ominous. What was wrong with me that for two nights in a row I couldn't stay awake with people I enjoyed?

My wardrobe man was at the house and I was showing him what clothes I wanted to take on the road. I gave him the slacks and suits I'd had let out, the new blousy shirts, the stretch-out sweaters I'd bought. I hated having to warn the audiences that they were going to see "my little potbelly" as I took off my coat to do a number. I'd begun doing lines like "I'm a little chunky now . . ." and "Isn't he adorable this way? A little chubs?" I tried to comfort myself by thinking about movie stars, major performers, who had paunches. It still wasn't *me*.

Bill Cosby and I had been friends going back to before *I Spy*, when he was working in the coffeehouses. We did a benefit somewhere, around 1980, we just bounced some lines off each other and the chemistry was right. We played some Harrah's dates and the rapport was positive between us, no upmanship, no "How many laughs is he getting?"

We opened at Caesars. Although sometimes it hurt me in the stomach to hit the big notes, I absorbed the pain. I couldn't dance at all, and had stopped trying. I could do postures, like with "Bojangles," but I was sluggish, stiff, leaden. So I talked a lot, and I got laughs, and I sang as best I could.

I began to feel Bill observing me, watching me. After an early show during our first week he came into my dressing room and pointed at my stomach. "What the fuck is wrong with you?"

I sipped my vodka and Coke and patted my paunch. "Age, babe. I'm not fighting it. Grow old gracefully, they say."

"You're drinking all the time now." It was an accusation. That wonderful, caring face that looked like it had been run over by every kind of trouble and sadness in the world, but still remembered how to smile, was frowning. He said, "Whatever you're doing . . . don't end like this."

My caddy held my drink while I was shooting. After we'd played three holes I told Doug, "I've had it. Bed." He said, "Let's have lunch." I patted my paunch. "Can't, babe. Gets me sluggish before the show." Also, I was too tired to sit at a table. I opened my portable bar and made myself another vodka and Coke for the car ride back to the hotel.

I lay down on my bed but couldn't sleep. I ordered some soup. The vodka had half worn off and I felt like hell. I made myself another and sipped it as I walked to the dressing room.

I put on my makeup but I couldn't get myself together. Even on the worst nights the metamorphosis always set in as the hair got smoothed down and I picked out my clothes . . . but this time I looked at the table and I thought: There's not a fucking piece of makeup here that can save this. Metamorphosis, where are you? I couldn't imagine myself saying, "Good evening, ladies and gentlemen . . ." My feet were swollen, so I was going to go on in slippers. My skin was ashen. My stomach hurt and my jacket was pulling across my body.

I couldn't lift the show off the ground. I was trying with every trick I knew, everything that had ever worked for me, but I just couldn't excite them. As I got near a big note, I knew I wasn't going to make it and so I climbed up under it and a woman called out, "You tried, Sammy. Don't worry about it." But I hadn't tried for it and taken a chance on missing. I'd settled for safe. And I didn't try for the next big note either. My stomach hurt too much. I was functioning at thirty percent. I couldn't sing, my timing was halting. I was embarrassed to be performing like this.

I'd done forty-five minutes when I stopped the music. "Ladies and gentlemen, this has not been a good performance and tonight I'm not capable of making it good, so I ask you to excuse me and accept my hospitality. You are all my guests." When the curtain closed I turned to the band. "God was right. He took Sundays off. He knew. Don't work on Sunday."

By the time I got to the dressing room Murphy had already heard about it. His eyes were blinking. "You picked up the tab for the whole room? For eight hundred people?"

Holmes came in. "Sammy, that wasn't necessary. The show wasn't that bad."

The bill came to $17,000. Within a few days it was in *Time*, *People*, and *Newsweek*. Normally I would have enjoyed seeing stories on my "magnificent gestures" but it only depressed me, reminding me of being inadequate on the stage, impotent in what had always been my kingdom.

I had a week off. I desperately needed a few days of bed rest before opening Reno. Doug called. "Holmes and I were wondering if you could get up here a few days early. There's a TV special, a syndicated show, *The Super Stars and Super Cars*, and it's featuring Bill Harrah's collection of old cars. We were hoping you'd narrate it . . ."

"Babe, count on it." There was no way I would ever turn down Doug and Holmes.

We had some people over the night before I was leaving, but I said good night early and went into my bedroom and lay down on the bed. I fell asleep still dressed. When I awoke, a little groggy, and tried to pull my pants off over my boots, sort of jumping out of the trouser leg, I tripped and fell, banging my ribs against the night table with a ghastly cracking sound.

When I awoke in the middle of the night it felt as if I had a flame against my ribs and I gasped.

"What's wrong?" Altovise jumped awake. I told her and she said, "I'll call Gerry Blankfort."

"Darling, I'll be fine. Just let me get some more sleep."

In the morning she pursued it. "You should have an X ray."

"Alto, the X ray will show I bruised my rib."

I did the TV show in Reno. On the day before opening at Harrah's the pain in my ribs had become unbearable. I had a salad-plate-sized black-and-blue mark and it hurt to breathe deeply. There was no way I could sing. I told Murph, "You'd better get me over to the hospital for some X rays . . . see what's wrong with these ribs. Maybe they can tape 'em or something." As I said it, I had a feeling that it wasn't going to be just a couple of X rays and tape up the ribs, that this time it was serious.

47

The internist at the Warsaw Medical Center in Reno told me, "You have a touch of jaundice, with overt signs of liver damage." He did the thumping thing and I could hear the difference in the sound when he was over my liver. He said, "That's all liquid. I think your liver has backed up on you."

The X rays showed that the ribs were not broken, but he called Gerald Blankfort. "He won't let me do any blood tests but you should know that his stomach is distended, the liver is enlarged. And there are some black marks on the X rays that I don't like. Shadows that reach down low, to the stomach."

Harrah's canceled the engagement and sent me to L.A. on the plane. Gerald was waiting for me when I checked into Cedars Sinai. Within an hour they had taken more X rays, and blood tests, and were giving me antibiotics.

In bed, waiting to hear what was wrong with me, I knew that I'd abused my body past where I could just dry out for a few days and bounce back like new. I wasn't new anymore. I was old and I was rotting away. God must have gotten tired of my bullshit, fed up with picking me up and giving me one more chance and one more chance. Instead He'd let me stay on a downward spiral professionally and physically. He'd let me destroy everything He'd given me, my health, my talent, my ability to perform, until I'd reached the bottom, sick, unfit to climb back up to that marvelous life He'd let me have. Finally I was Bojangles. I wasn't in jail but I was in a hospital decaying. And I'd done it myself. How was it possible to have feared ending this way and at the same time done everything to make it happen? Bill Cosby's voice resounded in my mind. "Don't end like this."

The next day there were more tests but nobody told me anything. Brian and Dino Meminger, my lighting man, set up my suite with a VCR and a lot of my tapes. I hadn't asked for that. How did they know I was going to be here long enough to need my toys?

Shirley canceled all dates for the rest of November and December. "This way you've got no pressure on you to go back until you feel you're ready." She was bullshitting me. How do you cancel big-money dates unless you know something?

My children came by to see me. Covered by a sheet, my potbelly made me look like I was pregnant, while the rest of me was birdlike, and I knew I seemed shrunken, smaller than ever. Tracey and Mark and Jeff smiled at me with fragile, unconvincing cheerfulness, the way you smile at your father who's dying.

I'd fallen asleep and I had the dreamlike feeling of seeing myself looking down at me in the bed, an old man's face, contorted, unhappy. Then a tear dropped out of his eyes and I realized it was my father, that he'd come in while I was asleep. He tried to smile. "You're gonna be fine, Poppa." He'd turned eighty. Lately I'd been doing lines with him like "Hey, Dad, I was just in Vegas and nobody sent you their regards." It broke him up. There isn't that much to laugh about when you're old and out of action and have Parkinson's. When you get old, people placate you but they don't do jokes with you. I was not going to change the relationship we'd always had. When he was vague about something I'd say, "Of course you can't remember things, you're getting so old that all you can remember is the old days . . ." and he loved it. "Yeah, how 'bout that, Poppa? But they're worth rememberin', weren't they?" But now I couldn't think of anything to kid him about. My brain wouldn't work. I couldn't even ad-lib with my father.

Gerald told me, "We'll have to lance your stomach. It has a liquid lining. That's not a middle-aged pot you've got there, it's a reservoir, and we have to get that fluid out of there."

"An operation?"

"Not really. It will be done here in the room. We lance and drain it just like we would if it was a pus sore swollen up."

He brought in a specialist, the nurse gave me a local anesthetic, and they slipped the needle into my stomach. Always frightened to death of needles, now I welcomed anything that might help me. I sat on the edge of the bed, the doctor attached a plastic tube onto the needle, and liquid started dripping out. It filled three and a half quart jars. When the draining was over they took four stitches where the needle had been. The doctor sighed. "Thank God." The liquid was as clear as water. "Had it been cloudy you'd be dying. It would have meant that the liquid was inside your stomach and then it would have been only a matter of time."

It was the first hopeful statement I'd heard in five days. "Then I'm okay?"

"You could be worse," Gerald said. "You can keep your liver in remission by not drinking, but once diseased it's diseased for life. It's not curable like an infection. Part of the liver is destroyed and there's no way of having that piece well again. I want to keep you here another few weeks. We've removed the liquid, and we've consulted as to anything further we should do—transpose veins away from the liver so we have better drainage, or whatever. The consensus is to do no more. Rest. And a strict regimen. No alcohol, no salt."

Altovise brought in a London newspaper. The headline was "SAMMY GIVES UP BOOZE."

My pot, my paunch, was almost all gone. The largest part of the puff had disappeared. It hadn't been middle age at all. No wonder it hadn't responded to dieting. It was all liquid bloat. "There's a period of time necessary for the rest," Gerald explained. "The walls of your stomach have to come back in. We can't tie it in the back, as it were.

"You've been lucky. When alcoholics reach this stage of liver disease, they most often go down, down, down. Further, you're not chemically dependent on alcohol. You haven't had a drink in twelve days, yet you've had no d.t.s, no shakes. All you have is a lifetime habit. You can beat that. But not another drop of alcohol. If you return to drinking you will die quickly. And painfully."

What I learned from sobriety is that alcohol gives you infinite patience for stupidity. In the old days, which was until November 1983, when I got high enough everybody was groovy. I'd have enough booze in me and it would be "Yeah, lemme hear the rest of that." Sober up and your tolerance for nonsense goes right down the drain. You see and hear everything that you'd been able to avoid hearing before.

In a car to the Burbank airport en route to Reno, Murphy started telling me a joke. "These two black cats were in Miami . . ."

"Murph!!! I don't want to hear any jokes."

"I don't know why, Sammy. Why is it you don't like people to tell you jokes?"

"Because, for openers, I know every joke there is. Second, they're usually in bad taste. And third, people like you tell them very badly."

Hey, that was kinda sharp. I realized that I was nervous and wasn't able to hide it behind booze. "Oh, for God's sake, Murphy, tell the fucking joke."

"Well, there were these two black cats in Miami . . ."

The Harrah's stewardess had a Bloody Mary ready to hand me as I walked on. "Thanks, darling. I'm off booze." I gave her a can of strawberry Crush and a large plastic mug that I liked. "Just put these together with a lot of ice."

By the time we were in the air I was looking at Altovise,

waiting for her to say, "That's the worst takeoff we've *ever* made!" But she was looking out the window, calm. Murphy was reading *People* magazine. Brian was absorbed in a newspaper. So was Dino. I looked at the impotent glass of Crush I was holding. It was a revelation how a few ounces of booze had always smoothed the bumps, the air pockets, but when you're straight, everything comes into focus. I'd been on a thousand flights until then and with a double Bloody Mary in my hand everything was cool up there. Now, with only a strawberry Crush, the pilots weren't flying nearly as well as they used to.

At nine-thirty I heard "Thirty minutes, Mr. D." And then it was show time. Leaning against a stool in the wings, I heard all the New Year's Eve sounds, bottles popping, noisemakers, a level of hilarity which tired me. Listening to the overture, I felt too weak to sing those songs.

I said, "Good evening, ladies and gentlemen," accepted their welcome, and then sat on a stool. I did forty-five minutes, all of it sitting down. I sang "Bojangles" from the stool without the physical moves. I didn't feel I could stand on my feet.

Doug said, "It wasn't one of your better shows. But it brought you back."

An hour later I got into bed and stayed there throughout the next day, not sleeping, just giving myself body rest, trying to save it up for the opening.

I used the stool for both shows, and the next night too. Toward the end of the first week I began feeling stronger on my feet, able to function. I missed the booze less, that little drink before I went onstage, but it was depressing to be cheating the audience out of the image they expected. By way of apology I held up my glass of Crush and ridiculed myself. "Look at this for the big swinger."

They applauded. It took me by surprise. Usually you bait them, you know what's going to get a hand, but this was a shock. As I looked out into the lights, the faces I could see were nodding at me, like "Yeah, you stopped boozing. Good on ya."

I went with it. "Frankly, I'm enjoying being straight. It's fun to wake up and know what I did the night before." They applauded. But that time I expected it. Maybe they felt it was time for me to change. Maybe they were changing too. Whatever, it was working for me. They weren't disappointed in me. I said, "I'm pushing sixty. I've played Harrah's for twenty-five years and this year is the first time I've ever come onstage without a drink in me." More applause. "Of course, there's about three years of the twenty-five that I don't remember playing here." The laughter was filled with camaraderie. I said, "Oh? You noticed?" The warmth coming at me was like what you get in your living room with friends. They didn't feel that I had to give them perpetual motion, perpetual youth. It was "Yeah, Sam, we know you from the old days and we dig *you*, not the swinger, not the kid . . ." We were friends growing older together. They wanted what I *am*, not an imitation of what I'd been. In fact, for a fifty-year-old to be playing thirty was dishonest. Maybe that's why gradually I'd been so unhappy with my performances.

Doug was backstage every night, giving moral support. "The shows are better, you're better, you've got more energy. I'm fucking thrilled."

I had been wearing neckties onstage and halfway into my first number I always pulled the tie open. I'd stolen that from Jolson thirty years ago and I suddenly saw it as not only corny but too theatrical, because it was not spontaneous as it was made to look, it was planned. I craved a higher level of ethics. I wanted to walk out pure. Tah-dah. Just a drumroll and the hands outstretched. That's what an entertainer comes from and I wanted that simplicity, that honesty with the audience. I cut out that piece of business. It was the start of a new level of honesty and rapport with the audience. I also stopped coming out with the jewelry on. It had been fun but when it becomes the takeover of what you are, then it's time to back away from it. And for simple showmanship you do not give the people exactly what they are expecting. They were delighted to see me come out clean of all the diamonds. On the other hand, you don't waste a good signature, so toward the close of the show, as I was singing "I've Got to Be Me," I started putting on the rings and it was a giggle because it showed that I was laughing at myself, not a "Hey, look at all this jewelry I've got!" And I'd do a line like "Do you recognize me now?"

I found that I needed solitude for a few hours before the shows. I needed to be alone to prepare. After returning from the edge of the abyss, each show was dear to me. I could no longer make them up as I went along. I owed more to my public and to myself than to walk on and hope for the best. There would be no more "Catch the second show" because I knew the first wouldn't be good enough. I didn't want to say that anymore. Catch any show you want. They all have to be good.

48

The shows were fun again. I told Altovise, "I hate to admit how good I feel." With the surge in my energy level, and maybe the ability to think clearly, I could handle, or adjust to, my age and have fun with the change, settle into it instead of fighting it. I'd do "I've Got You Under My Skin" and get into the bumping and grinding and then "catch myself" and sort of apologize, "That's a little residue from the *old* days," and it got a tremendous laugh because the old customers remembered me that way.

I drank Crush onstage and kidded myself: "I'm glad I gave up boozing. The only bad part is that when I wake up in the morning I know that this is as good as I'm gonna feel all day. Ain't gonna get no better."

I had no doubt that alcohol was poison for me, but I missed that marvelous little buzz. I'm not talking "Let's go get pissed," but that nice little glow, that cocktail that makes the whole system titillate, and you hear little voices: "Hello there, I'm awake, I'm alive. Remember me? I'm your heart." I missed the fun, the camaraderie of "Well, time for a little taste." And I missed a little of the devil-may-care, the scarf-over-the-shoulder.

Oh, did I envy those people who could still have that kick when they wanted it. I wanted to tell my children, "Respect it and you can enjoy it all your life. Abuse it and you'll go the last twenty years or more craving it, but you can't have any, 'cause if you do you'll die."

What I wanted now was solidity, reliability. I only had about two more mistakes left to me. When you're thirty-five and you own a piece of show business and you're doing *Ocean's Eleven*, you come up to bat fifteen times. So you strike out a few times. But when you're pushing sixty you're a designated hitter and every time you're up you'd better do something. I didn't have hit movies, hit records, or a TV series going for me, I had to do it with performance, and with consistency. No more "Wasn't he great tonight?" No. He had to be "great" *every* night, twice a night, and it was not all from being talented and experienced. Much of it was in conditioning, being able to walk out there rested, together. I knew that if I dissipated, ate badly, missed getting the sleep I needed, the audience would feel "Gee, he's sluggish tonight." But if I was in training, if I went out there fresh, lean, at my fighting weight, then it was a bout.

Feeling my oats one night, I told the audience, "I'm going to tell you a story that ain't got no punch line but I think it's amusing." The story was about Fred Astaire and I'd intended it as a lead-in to my Astaire medley. The story is: Fred Astaire's house is across the road from mine, about four houses away, a few hundred yards. One day he was out on his terrace playing his music and I was on mine and I heard this music coming from his direction, great music, Jonah Jones kind of old-fashioned jazz, Billy Butterfield, that kind of thing. I thought: That's Astaire, and I knew he was on his deck listening to it. And I was on my wooden-floored veranda, also listening. When the record ended I stood up and tapped: "boom diddy boom boom . . ." and from across the road I heard him tap back: "boom, boom!"

Well, this long story died like a dog. Nobody even tittered. They just sat there looking at me. The guys in the band started to break up because I'd bombed. I turned to them. "Hey, I told

the people it wasn't so funny . . ." I'd thought it was a wonder-
fully warm story but when the audience just looked at me and
when that broke up the guys in the band, I said, "Okay, it's a
dumb story. I never should have told it. I should have kept it
just for the house. That's what I should have done. I knew it
was going to die. I haven't the faintest idea why I did that. In
fact, I felt myself sinking when I was in the middle of it, I was
thinking: Nothing's going to save this. Do a tap dance, do some
magic, fall down, *something!* . . . Why did I bring this up? I'm
getting all this money, I've got diamonds from thumb to thumb
. . . looking good . . . and I tell a stupid story like that . . ."

By then people were applauding. Yet the fact is that though
it's a cute, charming story, it doesn't belong on the stage. I was
trying to give the audience a little offstage picture, like "This is
something you don't see all the time . . ." and into the toilet it
went. Still, the failure had its value to me. It showed vulnerability: "Hey, not everything he says is slick and good . . . he's like
me, he can fuck up." But being vulnerable is a two-way street:
if they're tuned in enough to sympathize, to catch all the nu-
ances, and to root for you, they're also able to catch even a hint
of phoniness or "routine."

49

"Can you stand some good news?" Shirley asked. "If I tell you that you're solvent, can you live with that, or will you have to go out and spend it?"

"Shirl, I can't go broke anymore. I've been broke too many times and come back."

"Good. Then I can tell you that we're solidly in the black. We've paid off every penny to everybody. Every shop, every club, every bank. And we've got three months' cash on hand." She grinned. "Now do you understand why black is beautiful?"

I'd begun putting the dancing back into the act, gradually, soft shoe, then a little tap and building up to a solid ten-minute chunk. Not in ten years had I done a three-chorus dance. Now I was out there doing it twice a night. People were surprised. "I didn't know he could dance like that." "My God, sure, now I remember, that's how he started." Tap dancing was anachronistic, so it had a nostalgic charm. It was fun doing it, fun having people react to it, so I kept it in, dancing, dancing, dancing . . .

I'd signed to play the role of the Caterpillar in *Alice in Wonderland*, starring Carol Channing. When I showed up for rehearsals with Jillian Lynn, the choreographer, she said, "Why don't you work out a little bit? Warm up."

"Get outta here." I gave her a look and tapped, boom diddy boom boom—boom boom! "Ready."

Tap dancers never warmed up. Our kind of tap isn't a question of getting the whole body in different positions like Fred Astaire and Gene Kelly, who are "ballet tap dancers." Simple tap dancers don't move their bodies much, it's all legs, from the waist down.

"Okay, then," she said, "let's get to work," and we began two weeks of rehearsals, leaping here, leaping over there, jumping up, jumping off things. I hadn't done that kind of "movie dancing" in years and I loved it. In the middle of rehearsing a number I did a turn-around and felt a sharp pain in my hip. Jillian caught it. "What's the matter?" She scolded, "I told you to warm up."

I brushed it off. "The Candy Man is getting old, that's all." After rehearsal I drew myself the hottest tub I could stand and tried to soak away the soreness. What I needed was about four fingers of vodka. But that was out.

On the set the next day it hurt but I kept doing my number. Then, at the finish, a girl had to sit on the Caterpillar's knee. It was more pain than I could stand. My left leg simply failed to support me and I found myself sitting on the floor looking up at Jillian. Alarmed, she said, "You're not *this* old," and she helped me to my feet.

Gerald brought me to Eugene Harris, an orthopedic surgeon. After examination and X rays he said, "Let me show you something," and he put the pictures on a viewer. "That's your hip bone. The dark area is deterioration. Your hip bone is disintegrating."

"From what?" and my mind started churning: All that bad I've done, it's catching up with me. If I hadn't been putting that shit up my nose I'd be all right.

He asked, "How old are you?"

"Fifty-eight, -nine."

"You're suffering from dancer's, or athlete's, degeneration. You've been using your bones and your sockets harder and for more time than they're made to withstand. Since you've laid off alcohol you've got the energy of a twenty-year-old and so you're dancing up a storm and you're paying for it. You're taking a sixty-year-old hip socket and grinding it hard twice a night. Take a piece of wood and do that for ten minutes a night for only a year and see what happens."

"If I slow down the dancing, will it get better?"

"No, the damage is done. But you have a couple of choices. I recommend a hip replacement—that is, a replacement of the total hip joint with a metal or a plastic hip joint."

It ejected me from the chair. I saw myself doddering along the street with a cane. I'm looking at him like I'm Nureyev, like I move and jump, like dancing is my whole life and "What? I'll never do *Swan Lake* again?" But in fact I was a singer doing ten minutes of tap at most and sometimes just two choruses of "I'll Go My Way by Myself . . ." slow, easy. Dancing wasn't my act, it was just a little frosting. But I yelled at the man, "No, no, no! I ain't doing no cuttin'. No way."

He wasn't a snap-your-fingers, shoot-your-cuffs Hollywood guy. Patiently, he said, "You need something done, Sammy."

"What else you got?"

"We could do a reconstruction. We can rebuild that hip bone in there for you, we don't insert anything foreign into your leg, the complications are significantly less, the blood loss is less, but it's only a temporary correction. In its favor, it is not a bridge-burning procedure. Should it fail, then something else can be done. If successful, you'll get a year or a year and a half out of it, maybe two at best. But eventually you'll have to have a hip replacement."

"Let's handle that when we come to it. We'll talk about it. Meanwhile I have a picture to finish."

"I'll give you a muscle relaxant, Motrin. I recommend that you eliminate all dancing. We'll keep an eye on this and hope to defer surgery."

Leaving there, I thought: Surgery? Nobody's ever going to cut into my hip. I'm a song-and-dance man. I didn't mention it to Altovise, or to Murphy or Shirley, or any of the roadies.

Alto and I sat in my office running tapes of *Sammy & Co.*, a talk and performance show I'd hosted in the seventies. I was hoping to learn something from my mistakes, which I was disappointed to see were legion. The reviewers had criticized me for doing phony breakups. It was painful reading it then, but fifteen years later I agreed with them. I saw the trap I'd fallen into. I love to laugh. Not just smile. Laughter. It's healthy. You will humor a joke, a piece of business, with a laugh, a breakup. Humoring a joke is George Burns taking the timing with his cigar before the punch line. But I overshot the road. I watched myself doing phony breakups, laughing too hard at things that weren't that funny, and laughing at things that weren't funny at all. It didn't engender laughter with the audience. People looked at each other. "Why is he laughing?"

I watched myself introducing guests. "My dear friend . . . a great talent . . ." I remembered reading that my introductions were too flowery. It was my vaudeville upbringing of giving another performer all the courtesy possible, verbally "carrying them on," but I belabored it. I'd resented reading it, but they'd been right.

Strange thing, videotape, sitting in a dark room and looking at the ghost of Christmas past. My youth was not attractive to me. I heard and saw myself enraptured by the sound of my voice. I'd thought: What a wonderful thing to hear this articulate young kid on the stage, he's black, and speaks so well. Fine, but I didn't have to go past Olivier.

By way of forgiving myself, I'd had no education, I was self-taught, I respected the value of words, of the resonant voice like Barrymore's. At Ciro's when Jerry Lewis told me, "You talk too English," I'd caught it but not enough. I was in love with the character, the elegance. Unfortunately, I wasn't born sixty years old. I had to work hard, fuck up a lot and consequently learn a lot.

Around December 20 I called Shirley. "Phone them in

Australia and tell them we'll make the tour. I'll open in Sydney January 23. I'll work easy, no fast moves, but I'll sing and talk."

Once committed, I had to understand the performance I would be able to give. I know what I can wring out of an audience. I know I can pull their gut apart. One of my greatest assets is that I'm able to show my vulnerability . . . I can touch them with that. But it's a fine line between drama and cheap theatrics. I love being theatrical. But I didn't want to use cheap theatrics. I didn't want to walk on the stage with a cane in my hand and "Good evening. Let us try and sing some songs for you." Not that the audience wouldn't love it. You talk about a standing ovation? If ever I walked on in Las Vegas with a cane and I just stood there and said, "Good evening, ladies and gentlemen," it would be screams. From the heart. From the soul. Pande-fucking-monium.

But that's Sophie Tucker being wheeled onstage in a hospital bed at the Latin Quarter in New York, with full makeup on: "I just had to come and let my fans know I love you." That's cheap theatrics. And the people loved it: "Who else but Sophie Tucker would have shown up?" "Such a pro!" Get outta here. Cheap theatricality. Of course I could do it, but that doesn't make it right.

Those were the thoughts. I wasn't whimpering, "My career is over." But I had to pull together all of the elements so that when they see the show they go, "Yeah! Go, babe!" Not "Ohhh, poor Sammy, he's out there, and trying . . ."

George called on the afternoon of Christmas Eve. "I hear we're goin' back."

"It's either a go-back or a go-way."

"Then I'd better get onto those arrangements you wanted. How about if I come over tomorrow and we can run through them?" I got a powerful feeling of support from George, who had a house full of family yet was volunteering to work on Christmas.

In the middle of that night, at 3 a.m. on Christmas Day, the telephone rang. Altovise picked it up, then handed it to me. "It's Shirley."

"Yeah, Shirley?"

"He's gone."

I thought she meant that she and George had had an argument and he'd walked out.

She said, "He's gone. He had a heart attack."

The Sydney Hilton advertised it as "Sammy Davis Jnr.'s Return to Show Business." I went downstairs to watch Fip Ricard, our lead trumpet for eighteen years and now my conductor, lead the band through my music. Shirley couldn't take it and left. Not seeing that big bear George, I too had to walk out and go upstairs and cry.

On opening night as I listened to the overture I looked through the curtain. People were standing up in the back and along the sides and I'd been told the room was packed with not only Australian press but English and American. I waited for my musical moment and I pushed myself into the longest walk I'd ever made.

"Good evening, ladies and . . ." I coughed and my voice closed. I tried to speak. Nothing. I whispered to the audience, over the mike, "My voice . . . it's gone." There was nothing else to say, they'd heard it go. I kept whispering, "Can you believe this? Here I've been worrying about my hip and my voice goes!"

I couldn't dance and I couldn't sing. Though I could be amusing, I had no delusions of being Milton Berle. I was helpless. The nightmare had come to pass.

My voice continued to eke out in a whisper, "Let me struggle through a couple of numbers, let's see what happens, see what I can do . . ." The voice came back and went away, came back and went away, like someone was turning my throat on and off.

I had stopped walking onstage with a cigarette in my hand because of a promise I'd made to the Heart Fund, but now I searched the ringside tables for a smoker. "Somebody give me a cigarette, please . . ." and I puffed and relaxed and semi-apologized: "I gave up drinking and drugs. Two out of three ain't *bad*." The voice came back a little, gravelly. "Actually, I went to a hypnotist to stop smoking but it didn't work. He was shining the light in the wrong eye."

I said, "I'd like . . . I'd like to do a show for you people who have paid your money . . ." They laughed sympathetically. I said, "A few years ago I was at Harrah's in Lake Tahoe, Nevada, and I did a show that was not up to my standards and so I picked up the tab for the entire room, and it cost me thousands of dollars, because I didn't want the audience to be disappointed. Now, you can imagine how I feel out here tonight, coming back to Australia, having been away for years, the press, the celebrities, all of you making me feel so at home, I walk onstage, I can't sing, I can't dance, I'm not feeling very funny . . . but I'm not pickin' up this tab! No more magnificent gestures . . . too expensive . . . can't afford that . . ." The laugh started in the back of the room and began to build. "No way," I said. "I'm going to buy you all some champagne . . . but then that's *it*, I ain't pickin' up this whole tab . . ."

Now I'm starting to get laughs, the show business is coming into play. *Yeah, you can work, you can do it . . . just keep dealing honestly with them.* There was a stool near the piano but I was still okay on my feet. I sang "Birth of the Blues" with cracks. I tried "What Kind of Fool Am I?" Ludicrous.

A man at ringside tried to help me. "Sam, do 'Bojangles.' "

I couldn't ignore it because he was right in front of me and his intention was kind. "I'm sorry, I can't do 'Bojangles' for you. My hip is still iffy. 'Bojangles' needs movement to the side and it's too difficult to even attempt. If I tried it you'd see a small Hershey bar stretched out on this stage." They laughed, they were with me. "But give me a rain check and the next time you see me I promise you I'll do it for you, 'cause this mother's gonna heal. I just need a little time." And the people applauded because it was honest. It was theatrical but an honest theatricality.

I did an hour and five with no dancing, no voice at all, and I left the stage with the people cheering. I'd sung horribly, I wasn't that funny, I'd done a poor show. But they knew that I hadn't lost it partying, that it was legitimate, and how hard it was.

The press came out with love letters: "The consummate showman . . ." With the tough Australian press it could have been: "How dare he get on the stage in that condition?" And they would not have been wrong. But they, like the audience, were giving me a pass, it was a Life Achievement award. All of the people who had put me there were saying, "Easy, relax, things'll work out, we'll wait."

I went to see Joan Sutherland's voice teacher, Dr. John Tonkin. He examined my throat and my chest. "You have no polyps, there's no redness down there. There's nothing wrong with your voice physically. You just lost your conductor and lifelong friend, you're tentative about your hip—it's all emotional. When you get the confidence back and when God decides you can sing again, you'll sing again."

I called Fip to bring up the song book and we went over my numbers and took out all the songs which I was not vocally capable of handling, the ones you can't con your way through with a lot of finger snapping. It didn't leave much. I don't have many easy songs.

I struggled through two shows the next night and the next few days singing songs for which I didn't have to sustain a note, like "Bye Bye Blackbird" and "Slow Boat to China," staccato with lots of rhythm. On closing night I still had no voice.

During rehearsal in Adelaide the music was too down-tempo. I called out, "George, will you . . ." I saw Fip staring at me and I heard my own voice. As I went to him I saw the tears in his eyes and I hugged him. "I'm sorry, babe. I'm sorry. You're doing the job. Doing it well."

My voice was better on opening night in Adelaide. By midweek I turned to the band during the show. "Ohhhh, it's coming back." And I started to stretch. Each show I began putting back numbers which I had taken out. By the time I finished Adelaide it was almost normal.

But always there was the awareness that George Rhodes wasn't there. My right hand. My friend. Thirty years. I could feel him there. I could hear his voice humming through the arrangements he had written. I never stopped missing that wall that had always been there, but I was careful to have strength around Shirley, and that helped me. She was doing the same thing. She'd come into the suite, Miss Bubbly, smiling, bouncing, "Good morning, all." I played the grouch: "Here comes Miss Fuckin' Happy Toes. Take a fuckin' hike."

At Melbourne, our last date, on opening night I walked out and sang the first song and I heard the voice that I'd thought I'd never hear again, clear, clean, and I looked at the audience and said, "Ohhh, it's back. Ohhh, it is *back!*" and I wailed. I sang everything I knew, going for the high notes and taking them from above, not crawling up to them in hope, no, I attacked from the sky and I never missed and to me it was like church bells ringing.

50

Altovise and I were weekending with Frank and Barbara at the Springs. Frank and Dean and I—the fun, the jokes, the camaraderie, the comfort of being together prompted me to say, "We've got to do something together again."

They looked at me like "Wonderful. What?"

"Okay, agreed, we've done it in films and nobody's come up with a new idea for us, so we forget a picture. But if we could recapture that excitement we had in Vegas in '60. We're all playing the Bally, there's no conflict . . ."

Frank said, "But there's a lot of people who never get to Vegas. I've been thinking about us doing a tour."

Dean groaned. "Why don't we find a good bar instead?"

"Let me think about it some more," Frank said.

Dean brightened. "The bar?"

Usually ideas which are exciting over a lazy weekend don't look so good the next day. But Frank called me at home on Tuesday. "Smokey, let's do it. It could be exciting. And I think it would be great for Dean. Get him out. For that alone it would be worth doing." He was alluding to the death of Dean's son, Dean Paul, in a plane crash six months earlier.

The way Frank envisioned it we would play 15,000- or 20,000-seat indoor stadiums and large theaters like the Music Hall in New York.

"You think we can draw that much?" Dean asked.

I said, "If they're not going to come and see *us*, then there is no show business."

From the beginning Dean had less enthusiasm for the tour than Frank and I. Losing Dean Paul had shattered him. They had been very close, and Dean Paul was a golden child, a near-professional-level tennis player, likable, a beautiful young man. Dean had continued playing Vegas as therapy, but that was completely different from what our tour would be. In Vegas he has his own audience and there's no travel involved. Being on the road would be stimulating because of the challenge of fresh and different audiences, but physically taxing. Dean certainly didn't need the money, because apart from being wealthy he lives humbly, dresses simply. When he plays Vegas he brings one tuxedo. He hangs it up and that's it. One shirt, one tuxedo. You go into his dressing room and there's nothing there, no makeup, nothing. He wears a pinky ring which Frank gave him and a watch which he himself designed. And that's it! It's a lifestyle not at all like Frank's and mine. I had learned from friends that Dean did not really want to do it, but we were all aware that much of the allure was the return of the Rat Pack and he didn't want to let us down.

Although the news of the tour had long ago leaked out and had appeared in trade papers and columns, it was appropriate to announce it officially. We invited the press to Chasen's at noon. For a smile our plan was to arrive together at that hour in tuxedos and black tie. We met at Frank's house and drove over together.

As we walked in Frank put his hand on my shoulder. "You start it off, Sam." He was still highlighting me, putting me up front. We'd expected a good turnout but the crowd awaiting us was like for a major news event: all wire services, local newspapers, all TV networks and radio, major magazines, and the foreign press. We took our places on a dais and I started it off. "Ladies and gentlemen, we thank you for coming here today . . ."

From behind me I heard Dean's voice. "Is there any way we can call this whole thing off?"

When the laugh quieted I continued. "We want to officially announce that we're going to be 'Together Again,' the first time since Las Vegas in the sixties . . ."

Frank called out, "And definitely the last time."

A reporter asked, "Then this is not the first of an annual event?"

"Look," Frank explained, "Sammy is sixty-two, and he's the kid. I'm seventy-two and Dean is seventy. At our ages the only annual event you hope for is your birthday." He nodded for me to continue.

"We're very pleased to say that American Express is our sponsor and that Home Box Office will be taping one of the performances for emission subsequent to the tour . . ."

I heard Dean asking, "Doesn't he know any regular words?"

Frank explained, "Smokey talks a little English."

"He doesn't *look* English."

"He doesn't look Jewish either! Anyway, what he means is, after we've played all the live dates HBO'll air the tape."

Our chemistry and rapport was still what it had been and the reporters were enjoying it. The success of the Rat Pack or the Clan was due to the camaraderie, the three guys who work together and kid each other and love each other, so it's fun.

The first two rehearsals were held at my house, talk sessions in which we and our producers sat around my bar, went over the general shape of the evening, and ran through some dialogue we'd had written. Our typical jokes: I'd say, "Frank, all kidding aside, we want you to know that we still think of you as the Chairman of the Board." And Dean would say, "Yeah, Frank. You're the chairman and we're bored." Or as Frank finished a song I would be heard over the mike from offstage, "It's wonderful that a man of that age can still sing like that." And Dean would agree: "But let's go out and help him before his oxygen runs out." The best of our humor would happen spontaneously in genuine ad-libs, but until we were onstage, relaxed and cooking, we needed a framework to begin with.

We had a full physical rehearsal with our orchestra at Ren Mar Studios on North Cahuenga in Hollywood. A square-shaped structure had been erected: a duplicate of the stage we'd be performing on in Oakland and most of the other cities. It was an elevated stage, looking like a prizefight ring without the ropes. We needed to rehearse how we'd work and move around under theater-in-the-round conditions. I'd played theaters in the round and Frank had, but not Dean. Only in Chicago and at the Radio City Music Hall would we work with a proscenium.

The stage was carpeted to avoid foot sounds, and had the same microphones, TelePrompTers, everything that we would have everywhere we'd play.

The orchestra brought in from New York was rehearsing under Morty Stevens. I enjoyed watching a fine conductor, seeing the control, watching the music appear to be coming out of his hands, the sounds of different instruments emerging each way he waves or points. I looked over at him, across the studio and through the years to the early fifties, Bill Miller's Riviera, when I'd heard this kid noodling on a clarinet and asked him, "Could you write an arrangement for me of 'Birth of the Blues'?" I'd had no idea that I'd still be singing it that way thirty years later. Now, head of music for CBS, he was conducting forty pieces for Frank, Dean, and me.

Shirley interrupted my reverie. "We've got a problem. That whole big orchestra the contractor hired does not have a single black musician. In 1988! That is *bad*. And we are going to be answering for that all across the country. I can't believe that Frank Sinatra is aware of this."

Frank came in carrying his music in an alligator schoolbag. Dean sat down with us at a table alongside the stage. He looked at Frank accusingly. "Everything I ate last night tasted like your finger. 'Hey, Dean, you should eat this . . .' and he poked his finger in it." " 'Here, eat these string beans, Dean, they're good for you.' " Dean shook his head. "I woke up this morning with your finger in my mouth." He was "on" for the stage managers and the tech crew who were milling around. He felt it his responsibility to be "Dean Martin." As the Clan we were expected to exist together in a constant state of clowning, drinking, and hip banter. In reality, I had my Crush, Dean and Frank had coffee, and we were all deeply concerned about what we were there for.

I said, "Frank, the contractor hired forty white musicians. The only blacks are my lead trumpet, drummer, and bass."

"Shit." He called over the contractor. "What the fuck is this snow-white orchestra? That stinks."

"But, Frank, it's too late to change 'em."

"Bullshit! I want at least thirty percent black musicians. Change 'em."

"That's expensive, Frank. We have to pay three weeks . . ."

"Pay what we have to. Fix it!"

We flew into Oakland on Saturday afternoon before the Sunday performance. To my surprise Frank came with us a day ahead of his schedule. Hundreds of press and fans were there. We had nothing to say to the press until after the performance. Cars pulled up to the sides of our planes and we got away fast. The drive to our hotel took us past the Oakland Coliseum, where the marquee said, "Frank, Dean, Sammy. SOLD OUT." When we arrived at the Hyatt Regency we learned that there had been such an impossible volume of phone calls for each of us that the hotel and our security people had decided to deny that we were there. Anyone trying to reach us would have to know who we travel with and ask for them. The general attention we were getting, the press coverage, and advance ticket sales led us all to feel that we were going to make show business history.

There was a Saturday-night event at the stadium, so our stage, lights, and sound wouldn't be ready until 4 p.m. on Sunday. I woke up around noon. It was a clear, cool day, and I was excited, edgy but confident. I looked through the Sunday papers. Herb Caen's column brought me down a few thousand feet by asking what these old guys were trying to prove and why didn't we stay at home with our pipes and slippers and leave show business to the kids.

We went to the stadium for a sound check at five o'clock. The square stage stood in the center of fifteen thousand unoccupied seats, rising so high around us that the upper levels had giant television screens so the people up there could see the performers' faces. I had never played to that large a crowd in my life except at military bases, never to a paying audience. Ideally, Frank, Dean, and I play small rooms. We're saloon singers. Stadiums are rock-'n'-roll country.

Frank was staring at it too.

Dean asked, "Will someone tell me why we're here?"

I couldn't answer that, and Frank didn't either. We all had our lucrative casino dates in Vegas, Tahoe, Reno, and Atlantic City. Why were we exposing ourselves to ridicule?

I had a light dinner at five-thirty. Dressing to leave for the stadium at a quarter to seven, I watched the evening news, which led off with the presidential primaries, and then: "The Rat Pack is back, Frank Sinatra, Dean Martin, and Sammy Davis, Jr. . . ." and it went on for ten minutes, showing pictures of us together in the sixties, then a live pickup from the stadium, where a girl newscaster described the lines of fans that had been forming, the impossibility of buying a ticket. They were handling a theatrical performance as hard news.

Murphy had gone ahead of me to my dressing room at the Coliseum. The walls were hung with posters of *Ocean's Eleven* and *Robin and the Seven Hoods*, two of the five pictures we had made together in the sixties when the Clan and the Rat Pack were born.

I started doing my makeup. Morty came in dressed in his tux and new black silk shoes. "You're not very excited, are you?" I was looking pointedly at his feet. He blushed. "Who ever sees a conductor's shoes?"

I was strung too high to sit around the dressing room. The hall was jammed with all of our people, lighting men, sound men, musicians, dressers, everyone playing calm, professional, but the atmosphere pulsated with excitement. Beyond where we were standing there was a drone of voices from the stadium.

I looked in on Frank. Dean was sitting on a couch. Frank beckoned and we followed him out, past the people in the hall, to the point at which a curtain concealed the backstage from the stadium. Frank opened the curtain enough for us to look through. All of the seats which at five o'clock had been shining back in our eyes were occupied. He said, "Remember when we did the Summit at the Sands? With all the excitement of packing the place every night?" He looked at Dean. "Remember when you came running back all excited and said, 'The place is packed'?"

Dean had a how-could-I-have-been-so-dumb look on his face. "Of course we packed it. The joint could only seat four hundred people. And we were three big stars."

Frank said, "Tonight we will entertain more people in one show than we did during that entire run in Vegas."

The show was starting. Over the speaker in my dressing room I heard our overture and then Dean's music. I could picture him looking at the audience, laid back, playing the drunk, taking a sip from a glass, then asking his pianist, "How long have I been on?" I heard the sure laugh and him singing, "When it rains it always rains, bourbon from heaven . . ." to the tune of "Pennies from Heaven." When he finished it he asked, "Have I got time for one more?" and he sang, "When you're drinking, you get stinking . . . and the whole world smiles at you . . ."

I had about twenty minutes. I was going to follow Dean and do around thirty-five minutes. Frank would open the second half of the show and then the three of us would work together.

My hands were cold and dry. Unable to sit down and wait, I dressed and walked over to Frank's dressing room. He was in a robe, sitting on the couch, listening to Dean. He'd finished his next-to-last number and there was tremendous screaming and applause and you could tell that those fifteen thousand people were on their feet with excitement.

Frank stood up and as he put his hands on my shoulders I had the feeling that he'd had his arm around my shoulder since 1945 and he'd never taken it off in over forty years, except to push me ahead. I could remember his voice on a dozen occasions, starting when we were a dance act, a flash act to open other people's shows, and he'd had us on the bill with him at the Capitol Theater in New York. "You should sing, Sam. Get yourself a style." . . . "No, Bing does not get third billing. It's me and Dean and Sam on top. Give Bing a box of his own. Sam gets billing over the title." . . . "Go ahead, Smokey, you introduce the next President."

When it was time for me to leave he said, "Give me something that's hard to follow, Charley."

I waited in the wings as Dean closed with "Volare."

I felt grateful for the fact of being there. After all the fears, after all the mistakes, still it wasn't ending for me as "Bojangles," there were no frayed cuffs and collar, I was not a disappointment to the friends, to the events, to the opportunities which had brought me to that moment in which fifteen thousand people were waiting for me. *Lord, thank you. For this, for the friends You've let me have, this wonderful life . . . I still don't know why You want me here, and I'm not asking anymore 'cause I know now You ain't never gonna tell me, but I hope I'm doing it the way You want me to . . .*

I heard them applauding Dean. I felt that old, familiar hunger. For fifty years I'd stood in the wings of theaters and clubs and felt the need to please the people, to stay with them until they loved me. I felt that airiness in my chest that could only be filled by the people who were waiting for me. God had brought me to where I was standing. Now it was up to me. My hands and lips were dry. My mind flashed forward to the walk down the aisle, past the rows of people, then up three stairs to the stage.

I picked up the mike and I was aware of turning, facing the audience on all sides. Banks of blinding light poured down on me from every direction. Morty had begun my opening number, but the people were applauding, so he was vamping till I was ready. For as far as I could see before the lights dissolved every-thing into a platinum infinity, they were standing, applauding, smiling. I felt the clarity of mind that I wanted, the strength in my chest, my legs, my arms. The applause was pumping power into me. The music softened, the people were settling down.

I said, "Good evening, ladies and gentlemen . . ."

EPILOGUE

Sammy had the talent and courage to die as well as he lived.

The tour with Frank Sinatra and Liza Minnelli (originally with Dean Martin) extended through the summer of 1989. Sammy was at a peak. Inexplicably his voice had enlarged and he was singing like a nightingale, hitting high notes with more ease and clarity than he had ever enjoyed in his life. Appearing nightly with Frank and Liza, he recognized that his power on-stage was so great that he was overshadowing even an icon like Frank, and he quietly toned down his performance.

During the latter part of August, Sammy was diagnosed as having cancer of the throat. After all possible tests the consensus was that the tumor had to be surgically removed and that with it would go his voice box. His chances for survival with surgery were estimated at eighty percent, but he would never be able to sing again. With radiation: twenty percent. He elected not to have surgery.

"Listen, fellas, first of all, I don't believe this is the way I'm going out. But if it is, then the world owes me nothing. I've done everything, I've had everything. I've had a better life than I ever thought I would. And if that's the way the cards are dealt, then that's the hand I have to play. But if you take out my voice box you might as well kill me."

News of Sammy's cancer of the throat brought a request that he do a Public Service Announcement denouncing the tobacco companies. "I can't do that. I watched the Surgeon General's Report on television in the sixties, and I continued smoking, enjoying every cigarette for the last thirty years. How can I now say that they're the bad guys?"

After the course of radiation he was told on a Monday that the tumor had disappeared. The British press headlined "SAMMY BEATS THE BIG C." On Thursday the tumor returned.

Chemotherapy was the last hope. It failed. He was told, "Two weeks . . . two months . . ."

Sammy saw few people. Frank, of course, Shirley MacLaine, Dean Martin. He allowed Jane and me to visit him in the hospital. Characteristically, he was sitting up in a chair, wearing silk robe and pajamas, looking majestic. We did not stay long. We had parted from Sammy a thousand times but it was the only time we ever said goodbye.

Sammy left Cedars Sinai Hospital and returned to die on his two acres in Beverly Hills. He told his "family"—his roadies, the men (and Shirley) who had shared in his years of glory—"I don't want any sad faces. I've had every joy and luxury that ever existed. Sixty years of success. If the Man who gave me all that wants to see me, then I'm ready to tell Him thanks.

"Only one thing. I'm not going until I see my grandchild. I *will live* to see my grandchild born." His daughter Tracey was overdue by ten days. She tried everything to induce labor: hikes with May, jumping up and down. Finally she implored her doctor, "My dad could go at any minute. We've got to get this baby out." Sammy's grandson Sam was born by cesarean section on April 20, 1990.

The amazed grandfather sat in a wheelchair in his lush garden, holding his grandson in his arms. Though May and Tracey wanted to take pictures, Sammy would not allow any photographs.

He died two and a half weeks later at age sixty-four.

Reopening and finally closing this forty-year section of my life has given me the experience of reliving those thousands of hours of tears and laughter, mostly the latter, spent with Jane and Sammy as we wrote and prayed for *Yes I Can* and *Why Me?* This work is dedicated to their memory.

Burt Boyar